O'Reilly
AND
Fleming

ViC
Violence in Canada

VIOLENCE UNCHAINED
Media Images

UNNECESSARY ROUGHNESS
Violence in Sports

Cruelty to Animals or
Fit for Consumption?

USE OF FORCE

Terrorism
PROTEST
Genocide

Library and Archives Canada Cataloguing in Publication

O'Reilly, Patricia, and Fleming, Thomas
    Violence in Canada / by Patricia O'Reilly and Thomas Fleming

ISBN 978-1-897160-56-5

A catalogue record for this book will be available from Library and Archives Canada Cataloguing in Publication.

Cover image: *Detail of a North American Totem Pole with People Faces* © AlexAranda, fotolia.com, File: #13337445

Cover and book design by de Sitter Publications

de Sitter Publications
111 Bell Dr
Whitby, ON, L1N 2T1
CANADA

289-987-0656
www.desitterpublications.com
info@desitterpublications.com

Table of Contents

Preface

Patricia O'Reilly
AND
Thomas Fleming

This book is a critical, academic examination of the violence within Canadian society. Violence is one of the overriding and persistent issues in our society. As citizens we are confronted everyday with violence, exposed to images of violence through various forms of media, and charged with dealing with violent behaviour through our systems of laws and social control. Whether we are researchers, students, parents, or politicians, the issues that emerge from our attempts to deal with violence dominate discussions of the conditions that exist in our country. We are concerned with the following kinds of questions:

- ▶ Why do laws concerning animal welfare and abuse appear to be so ineffective? How can laws be drafted to provide more effective protection for animals in our society?
- ▶ How will we deal with cyber-violence at a societal and legal level?
- ▶ Should professional hockey players be subject to criminal charges for assaults that take place during a game?
- ▶ Should violence be legally permitted against terror suspects if lives are in jeopardy?
- ▶ How can we explain and research violence in the Canadian context?

All of these questions are intriguing and socially significant. With some exceptions, humans seek lives that are relatively peaceful and free of violence. There are, of course, individuals who pursue interests in boxing and the martial arts, use of guns for hunting, and other sports or hobbies that contain an element of violence. The popularity of mixed martial arts in Canada and Canadians' choice of television dramas and movies, which often contain violence and extreme violence, demonstrate a level of interest in at least watching violence as a spectator. Extreme forms of violence such as those engaged in by serial killers hold a particular fascination for readers and viewers. Anthony Hopkins and Charlize Theron have both won Best Actor Academy Awards for their portrayals of serial murderers. Slasher movies have enjoyed enormous box office success around the globe. The idea that violence sells is supported by the prevalence of violence in all forms of media, including games, books, movies and television shows.

This book is divided into four sections that will introduce readers to contemporary issues in violence in Canada as well as some of the theories and research methods used to examine various manifestations of violence.

In Section 1, **Thinking About Violence**, Patricia O'Reilly provides a critical analysis of some of the key theories used to explain violence. In Chapter 2, Alicia Tomaszczyk explores the many research methods that have been used to gather information on violence and test theories, including qualitative and quantitative approaches. The chapters included in this section provide a solid foundation for the remainder of the book.

The next section, **Contemporary Issues in Violence**, includes chapters on current and emerging central social issues in Canadian society. The issue of hate and its dissemination in

Canada has been the subject of controversy and new legislation in 2013-4. Cyberbullying has received enormous attention in the media and from the federal government. Hate, in the form of overt racism or bullying over the internet, has considerable implications and has led in some instances to adolescent suicide, and is intolerable in a democratic society. Whether the impact of hate crime is social or cultural exclusion or, in more extreme cases, causes a person to harm themselves or others, hate is revealed in the chapter by Barbara Perry entitled, "Hate in the Peaceable Kingdom." It is an important social problem which has been receiving considerable public and social attention. The harassment of those with disability in the workplace is the subject of the chapter by Susan Barak. As a society, we are increasingly recognizing the violence that can be inflicted by words and everyday discriminatory behaviours. As Barak suggests, people with disabilities are routinely subjected to this kind of violence in the workplace. While the Canadian Bill of Rights has guaranteed certain human rights since its passage in 1960 the politics of the workplace, and the difficulties that disabled people face in securing and keeping good jobs, makes the law a rather blunt and often ineffectual tool. While human rights and labour legislation make harassment of disabled people in the workplace illegal, the remedies available when an infraction of a worker's rights occur do not mean he or she will retain his or her employment. The law guarantees rights, but it does not guarantee that victims will regain full status in their employment; nor does it recompense them for the loss of a lifetime of work.

Chapters 5 and 6 by authors Krista Banasiak and Ken Dowler respectively, explore the role of the media in projecting and propagating images and ideas about violence. The centrality of the media in a society where we are assailed with images, words, and ideas on a 24/7 basis has attracted sustained scholarship over the past several decades, commencing with the seminal work of several Canadian criminologists in the 1980s and early 1990s including Ericson, Baranek, & Chan (1987, 1991); and Fleming (1981). Violence in the media, as we come to understand in these two contributions, has serious ramifications for our society; it desensitizes individuals to violent acts and actors as well as impacting our cultural view of the acceptability of violence as a solution to interpersonal and societal conflicts. Because we live in a society where our direct experience of violence may be limited, the media constitutes a central repository and transfer point for disturbing reports and images about violence in everyday life. Whether the impact of such reports is to be found in increased levels of fear of crime (justified or not), harsher responses to human failings and criminality, or increased acceptance of violent actions, we believe that a critical examination is important for readers.

The final chapter in this section by Lisa Monchalin examines the issue of violence against Aboriginal people in Canada. The mistreatment of Aboriginal people has been documented since at least the 1970s by sociologists, criminologists, and Aboriginal scholars in a wide variety of government reports and academic studies. In Chapter 7, the author provides a unique Aboriginal perspective on this issue, returning voice to Aboriginal people. This chapter provides an important lens through which the dominant culture in Canada can come to view assaults and violence against Aboriginal peoples.

The third section, **Violence in the Home, Family, and Society**, is concerned with violence in the everyday settings in which we live and in the wider context of Canadian society. It is a common mistake to presume that violence is something that happens "somewhere else" in our society rather than in the places we refer to as our homes, or more disturbingly perhaps, in our own family. Monica Pauls and John Winterdyk in their chapter, "Family Violence and Abuse within a Canadian Context" provide an intriguing overview of the extent of family violence and abuse in our nation. Domestic violence assumes many forms, including child abuse and neglect, failure to provide the necessaries of life as required under Canada's laws, assault against spouses, or attacks against the elderly. While the home is often considered a refuge from the tumult of the world, unfortunately for many individuals, it is also a place of attack. In their chapter, "Aboriginal Women and Violence: The Pickton Serial Murders" O'Reilly and Fleming expand our knowledge of violence towards Aboriginal peoples examining the extreme violence of the Robert Pickton murders. Given that more than half of Pickton's victims were Aboriginal women (Fleming and O'Reilly, 2011) and that these murders occurred over several decades, the case raises serious questions about the adequacy of the police's investigative efforts. The findings of an Amnesty International report on this case provided an impetus to explore police services handling of the families of Aboriginal victims and the cases of the missing women. Readers will discover the investigative flaws that permitted Pickton's violence to continue unchecked over a long period of time and the inadequacy of police response to affected families (Amnesty International, 2004).

In their chapter, "Violence Towards Nonhuman Animals" Matsuoka and Sorenson advance a detailed and much overdue account of violence towards non-human animals. Academic scholarship has turned its attention to this important issue since the 1970s and Chapter 10 represents a pioneering contribution in the Canadian context. Whether we are discussing the mistreatment of animals raised for slaughter, neglect or abuse of animals raised as pets in so-called puppy mills, or those used for medical experimentation, this chapter raises questions that deserve further sustained analysis. In the wake of what has been termed speciesism, we, as human beings, are confronted with moral and ethical questions about our society's view of animals Demonstrating that penalties for violence against non-human animals are relatively insignificant, the authors argue that our laws regarding abuse and mistreatment of animals have not been effective. Efforts to curtail the Internet advertisement of puppies and kittens raised in undocumented mills have been largely ineffectual. A recent advertisement in Toronto's subway displays a picture of a pig and a dog, questioning why one is a pet destined for a life of love and care, while another is merely viewed as food. Every day in North America, hundreds of thousands of animals are slaughtered for human consumption, from various species, including cattle, chickens, pigs, rabbits, and horses. This chapter challenges us to raise our consciousness and revisit our view of what is ethical with respect to our treatment of all species of animals.

Ken Dowler's chapter "Unnecessary Roughness; Violence in Sports" is an exciting and thorough analysis of violence in sports. This is a phenomenon that has been receiving sustained media attention recently for several reasons. First, there are the assaults in hockey that have resulted in serious concussions and other issues for players, including sidelining hockey superstar Sidney Crosby. Given the success of a 2013 lawsuit launched by former NFL players in the United States over brain and other injuries with serious, long-term effects, former National Hockey League players have initiated a similar suit against the NHL. The issue of brain injury extends beyond the rink and the football field into other sports, including soccer, rugby, wrestling, boxing, and mixed martial arts events. The use of violence in sports to achieve a victory also raises important issues about the reach of the law into the arenas and sports fields of our nation. It raises the question of when an assault becomes the subject of legal intervention by society. Are deliberate assaults on an individual's head during a sports game protected since they occur in the context of a game, or do they constitute a crime? Does the use of violence in organized professional sports set a bad example for young players, their coaches, and parents? Certainly, the media reports of attacks by coaches and parents on the players in opposing minor league teams causes us to contemplate the impact of the acceptability of violence in professional sports. Indeed, parents and politicians are scrutinizing the issue of violence in sports.

In her chapter, "Criminal Justice Response to Domestic Violence against Women: Feminist Activism and the Canadian State," Jennifer Fraser tackles the complex issue of criminal justice response to domestic violence against women is considered. Domestic violence has only come out of the shadows of the "privacy" of spousal relationships since the mid-1970s when Canadian researchers began to recognize the home as a place of danger. In the wake of the feminist movement, and the swelling of the ranks of women criminologists, research began to take account of the phenomenon of domestic violence (Fleming, 1975). In this chapter, the author critically appraises the limitations of current criminal justice approaches to this important social issue given its widespread implications for the quality of life of its women victims and secondary victims in the home setting. It is clear that feminists have played a key role in moving forward government policy and legal agendas in this area.

In Section 4, our contributors analyze **State Forms of Violence and Control**. We begin with Howard Doughty's chaterr "Canadian Responses to Terrorism: Attitudes and Actions," which focuses on the approaches of the Canadian government to terrorism. We have witnessed a tightening of security in our everyday lives in the wake of 9/11, and amongst the control efforts have been the enactment of laws and the use of new forms of largely unregulated imprisonment to deal with terrorism. State violence is often insidious and unnoticed until individuals become the target of its laws or policies. This chapter critically dissects state responses to domestic and global terrorism by Canada and its implications for freedom and democracy. Chapter 14, "State Violence, Anti-Terrorism, and the Criminalization of Dissent," by Jeff Shantz examines government deployment of anti-terrorism discourse, legislation, and practice in relation to alternative globalization protests and social movement actions. Jeff describes specific pieces of legislation, and threats to liberty contained within, as well as practices of state violence as responses to particular protests, including anti-poverty protests and those against the G8 and G20.

Nicholas Jones and John Winterdyk in their chapter, "Genocide in Canada? The Crimes against Humanity and War Crimes Act" investigate and report on issues involved in the adequacy and reach of legislation and its impact on its intended subjects. Both are important pieces of legislation with far-reaching powers and authority that deserve attention in a reader on violence in Canada.

The final two chapters, "Police Use of Force and the Mentally Ill" by Ron Stansfield and "Forging the Disciplined Global Body: Police Deviance, Lawlessness, and the Toronto G20" by Patricia O'Reilly and Thomas Fleming take as their subject the issues surrounding state control of violence and protest in Canadian society. Increasingly, young people have exercised their right to dissent through Occupy events and the G2O protests in Toronto, for example.The passage of anti-terrorism legislation in Canada has had a chilling effect on public protest and on rights involving freedoms to access information. Individual Canadians who display too much interest in terrorist websites, or pledge monies to organizations deemed to be terrorist-affiliated by Canadian authorities, may be subject to police surveillance, online tracking, interrogation, and interception at border crossings. A cornerstone of democracy is the right to assemble and engage in peaceful protest. It is a right guaranteed under the Canadian Charter of Rights and Freedoms. The policing of the Toronto G20, effected under the reinvigoration and misuse of a decades-old piece of legislation that was intended to protect public works during the Second World War, resulted in the arrest and jailing of over one thousand protestors at a cost of well over a billion dollars. The G20 events virtually shut down Toronto's downtown core to residents and visitors alike and resulted in the arrest of many passersby and peaceful protestors. The police use of aggressive and violent tactics to deal with protest has created a chilly climate for future protests. Despite the call for repeal of the Public Works Protection Act, it is still in force at the time of writing. Chapters 16 and 17 raise important issues concerning the criminalization of dissent within our society and the role of police in protecting, rather than attacking, fundamental rights.

Chapter 16 reviews the law and practice of police interactions with the mentally ill. This is an especially crucial topic given the Yatim case in Toronto and the 2013 Coroner's inquest into the deaths, at the hands of the police, of three other individuals who suffered from mental illness. The chapter addresses the exercise of police powers and their limits and poses controversial questions for readers to consider in the light of these cases.

Finally, as editors we wish to express our gratitude to the authors, many of whom responded to our call for papers and worked under very tight time frames to complete their chapters. We are very grateful to them for their excellent contributions and their unsurpassed collegiality. We would like to thank the copyeditor for this volume, Joanne Muzak, for her valiant efforts in bringing this volume to print. Shivu Ishwaran, who is the publisher of de Sitter Publications, deserves a heartfelt thank you for his hard work and efforts to bring original Canadian research and writing to professors, students, and general readers.

We believe this book is a long-needed resource for those interested in questions of violence in Canadian society. Its collection of materials will provide a valuable resource for those who are interested in the contemporary issues in violence as well as their impact upon Canadians. We trust that the volume has cast a wide net to include a range of topics that have important social, legal, and policy implications for our nation.

References

Amnesty International. (2004). *Stolen sisters: A human rights response to discrimination and violence against Indigenous women in Canada.* Retrieved from http://www.amnesty.org/en/library/asset/AMR20/003/2004/en/cc99816-d57b-11dd-b24

The Canadian Bill of Rights. SC1960, c.44.

Fleming, T. (1975). *Violent domestic assault.* Thesis in partial fulfillment of the M.A. in Criminology. *Centre of Criminology*, Toronto.

Fleming, T. (1981). The bawdy house "boys": Some notes on media, sporadic moral crusades, and selective law enforcement. In *Canadian Criminology Forum*, Toronto: Centre of Criminology.

Fleming, T., & O'Reilly, P. (2011). "Only the silence remains": Aboriginal Women as Victims in the case of the Lower East Side (Pickton) Murders, Investigative Flaws, and the Aftermath of Violence in Vancouver. In D. Newhouse, K. FitzMaurice, T. McGuire-Adams, & D. Jetté

(Eds.), *Well-Being in the Aboriginal community: Fostering Biimaadiziwin* (pp.153-178). Toronto: Thompson.

Ericson, R., Chan, J., & Baranek, P. (1987). *Visualizing deviance: A study of news organizations*. Toronto: University of Toronto Press.

Ericson, R., Chan, J., & Baranek, P. (1991). Representing order: Crime, law and justice in the news media. Toronto: University of Toronto Press.

PART 1
Thinking about Violence

Critiquing Theories of Violence

Learning Objectives

In this chapter you will...

► learn about criminological theories that explain violence

► critically analyze criminological theories

► gain an understanding of violence emerging from subcultures, life circumstances, and decision making within specific lifestyles

► explore the role of the victim in violent crimes

► examine how poverty, economic disadvantage, and our routine activities influence violent crime

Chapter 1

Patricia O'Reilly

Introduction

The chapters contained in this volume are concerned with the myriad forms of violence in Canadian society. While the focus of the contributing authors is upon violence in Canada, violence also has to be viewed through a global lens particularly, for example, in reference to state violence, the "war" on terror, or global efforts at social control (Doughty, 2014; O'Reilly & Fleming, this volume). As will become apparent to readers, violence is pervasive in our everyday lives from face-to-face interactions to violent acts committed either purposefully or as a consequence of state policies and priorities. Violence is not merely confined to the physical act of attack; legally, it is enough to threaten assault (if one has the means of carrying out the threat), to be charged with common assault. There is the violence that flows from harassment, bullying, and hate in written form, on the internet, or spoken at public rallies. Violence leads the news and propels popular entertainment (Dowler, Fleming, & Muzzatti, 2006). On television, laptop, or cellphone, there is a twenty-four hour stream of violent acts that make up the news. Such reportage renders the viewer or listener a secondary victim and raises levels of fear of crime disproportionate to the reality of crime (O'Grady & Leyton, 1992; Silverman & Kennedy, 1993). At a primary level we can be observers of, participants in, or purveyors of violence—from confrontations over minor violations of social norms, to fistfights in bars, to physical combat over traffic incidents (Ross & Antonowicz, 2004). Violence in the home, referred to as domestic violence, represents a major policing and social control issue; it is also one of the most dangerous service calls for police officers (Fleming, 1975).

The resort to physical violence to express anger or, dissatisfaction, resolve conflict, demonstrate physical superiority, or eliminate a perceived threat is a common occurrence in Canadian society. Consider the following statistics on forms of violent crime reported to Canadian police services in 2012. There were 415,000 incidents of violent crime reported to all Canadian police services during this year. To put it another way, this represents more than 100 violent incidents per day. The rate of violent crimes in Canada for 2012 was 1,190 per 100,000 persons (Statistics Canada, 2012). This statistic is not completely accurate because it does not include unreported assaults. This phenomenon is known as the **dark figure of crime,** which refers to all the crimes that are committed but not reported to authorities. Common assault is the third most frequent crime dealt with by the courts, following impaired driving and theft. Major assaults, which include the use of a weapon (level 2) and aggravated assault (level 3), ranks as the sixth most common crime adjudicated at court (Statistic Canada, 2011, 2012). Such reportage renders the viewer or listener as a secondary victim and raises levels of fear of crime disproportionate to the reality of crime.

The aim of this chapter is to provide a critical review of select key theories developed by criminologists to account for violence. The chapter does not deal with theories of state violence or psychological theories concerning violence. However, psychological elements involved in the decision to use crime are discussed as factors. Critical analysis extends the perspective of scholarly constructions of violence to provide an interrogation of the scope and generalizability of these theories and explanations. Viewing theories through a critical lens assists us in determining their theoretical strength.

As we shall discover, no one theory is adequate to account for violent behaviour in society, rather the explanatory value of the theory is often limited to specific forms of violence. Some criminologists and legal scholars use integrated theories (Wolfgang & Ferracuti, 1967), which combine two or more theories to arrive at a more satisfactory theoretical framework (Henry & Milovanovic, 1996, 1999; Cowling, 2011). This theoretical approach is termed **constitutive criminology**. The authors' argument involves a complex blending of many theoretical traditions, including work in philosophy which examines the harm resulting from humans investing energy in harm producing relations of power (Henry & Milovanovic, 1996, p. 7). In constitutive criminology, there are two forms of harm. Harms of reduction are those that emerge from the physical assaults and homicides that occur in our society. Harms of repression prevent human beings from realizing their full potential in life, what Dahrendorf (1979) referred to as "life chances." The theory proposed by these authors directs us to create a new idea of social reality in which violence is produced in the physical realm but also through law and the repressive activities of institutions that limit human potential.

It is important for readers to understand that theories are not fixed and rigid. Rather, they change as new empirical evidence is generated and tested by social scientists to discover the theories' relevance and generalizability. In testing a theory, researchers attempt to learn whether that theory still has explanatory value and determine if cultural changes in society necessitate modifications or additions to the theory so that it retains its usefulness for understanding a form(s) of violence. The rapid transformation of Canadian society in the early twenty-first century including the lightning speed at which technology emerges and the global nature of the human experience, requires a constant re-examination of the adequacy of theories of violence. Cyberbullying, as an example, would not have been a subject of societal concern, legislative efforts, or law enforcement a decade ago. In 2015, cyberbullying is a major public concern, as reflected in media coverage of adolescent suicides and the passage of recent criminal laws related to form of violence in both Canada and abroad.

We now turn our attention to an examination of selected key theories that help us understand the genesis and application of violence in contemporary society.

Subcultures of Violence

One of the central questions that confronted criminologists and legal scholars during the last century is whether the genesis, or origins, of some forms of interpersonal violence reside in a subculture within our society whose norms and values encourage and support violence. Subcultural theory was initially developed by American criminologist Marvin Wolfgang and his Italian colleague, Franco Ferracuti (1967). Their pioneering study took as its subject the examination of various forms of assaultive behaviour, focusing in more detail on the investigation of criminal homicide. More specifically, the authors examined crimes of passion. While television shows and movies focus their storylines in large part upon premeditated murder, it is sobering to understand that the overwhelming majority of murders are classified as cases of manslaughter in Canada, where no planning or deliberation are involved (Boyd, 1988). First degree murder, on the other hand, constitutes only 5 percent of all murders reported to the police. Later, researchers such as Canadian criminologist Neil Boyd (2003) moved our study of homicide towards exploration of the biological roots of violence in males adding a different perspective on the roots of serious violence in society.

For Wolfgang and Ferracuti (1967), premeditated extreme violence, or even the use of force in interpersonal interactions, reflected "basic values that stand apart from the dominant, the central or parent culture [and] is part of a subcultural normative system, and that this system is reflected in the psychological traits of the subculture participants" (p. 92). The authors recognized that there are limitations or factors that must be taken into consideration when applying this theory. First, it required that either the perpetrator or victim uses violence in all situations to resolve issues. However, in both offenders and victims, there is likely to be a history of resorting to violence in a variety of situations. Second, I would suggest that, while violence may emerge predominantly from subcultures of violence, it has difficulties as a theory explaining the violence of individuals who accept and embrace the parent culture. In these cases, both victim and offender typically have a history of violence. This raises a further question: is our parent culture one in which violence is accepted, in more subtle forms, as part of a capitalist society? Individuals in this group choose to use violence for a variety of motivations that often parallel the goals of the dominant culture, such as greed, jealousy, or revenge. If individuals are viewed as either losers or winners in our society, then violent acts may be rationalized as a means to a goal: success, happiness, or power. Third, violence is most prominent in a limited age group. Violence is generally the purview of the young and males. Neither children nor senior citizens represent significant groups of offenders, although rare, such cases may occur, as in the murder of an 85-year-old resident of a nursing home by his 95-year-old roommate. We also understand that children are capable of murder. Canadian criminologists Katharine D. Kelly and Mark Totten (2002), as well as anthropologist Elliott Leyton (2009) have studied children who commit homicide. As well as considering subcultural theory, their work has also examined macro-level factors that may contribute to youth commission of homicide, including poverty, gender, and race (Kelly & Totten, 2002, p. 6). Their analysis also considers the impact of neighbourhoods, families, schools, peers, and the media on youth homicide. Leyton's (2009) study focused upon the dysfunctional families whose children viewed homicide as the sole solution to their intolerable lives. Extreme violence emanated from negligent, over-controlling, or abusive parents who their children viewed as fitting candidates for death. Fourth, Wolfgang and Ferracuti (1967) argue that aggression is a "learned response." They believe that a process of social facilitation and integration transforms the use of violence into a "habit" among the personality characteristics of offenders (p. 191). This idea corresponds well with another theoretical perspective on how behaviour is learned by juvenile delinquents that Gottfredson and Hirschi (1990) developed and called **differential association**. This theory argues, in part, that criminal behaviour is learned in association with others in the context of small groups. Both theories view the intense interactions in small groups and families as central to the development of violent or criminal behaviour.

In contemporary society, two groups are worth considering in terms of subcultures of violence that have emerged in Canada since the late 1980s. The first is the rise of criminal gangs in Canada in both urban and rural areas. Essentially, gangs provide a place to belong and instruct young recruits on the use of violence and intimidation to gain "respect." Well known "outlaw" gangs, including the Hell's Angels motorcycle gang, have frequently used violence to assert their authority over the drug trade and other criminal enterprises in their home "turf." The Hell's Angels are an internationally organized bike gang with chapters located throughout North America and around the world. Second, religious groups that believe in honour killings constitute a unique form of subculture that justifies the murder of women who are believed to have shamed the family. In 2009, Mohammad Shafia, his wife and their son were found guilty of first degree murder in the deaths of his three daughters and his first wife in what was represented as an honour killing. However, thirty-four Imams belonging to the Islamic Supreme Council of Canada later issued a fatwa condemning this practice (*The Globe and Mail*, Feb. 6, 2014).

Instrumental Theory

Felson and Tedeschi (1993a, 1993b, 1994) are highly regarded criminological theorists who developed a unique approach to understanding the genesis and utilization of violence by individuals in society. Their theory is derived from two main sources: rational choice theory (McCarthy, 2002) and the interactionist perspective (Ericson, 1975). Rational choices are made by individuals in their everyday life and involve reflection on the perceived benefits and costs of a particular choice or path of action. Persons who are charged with criminal acts do make rational choices based upon free will, even if in making those choices they are not aware of all of the consequences of their actions. These decisions are often, but not always, made in the course of interaction with others. A bank robbery may be planned, for example, but the heroics of a bank guard are not anticipated so the criminal makes a decision in that specific interaction to shoot the guard. The rational weighing of what course of action to take occurs in a very brief period of time. While the assumption when criminals come before the court is that, if they brought a gun to the bank, they intended to use it. The reality is that, in most cases, the use of the gun is only for the purposes of gaining the compliance of tellers, customers, and security guards. One should be careful not to believe that the word "rational" as used in this theory represents a process of careful consideration. Moreover, we have to consider that when individuals are committing a crime that they are in an aroused state of mind, fearful of being apprehended and facing penalties for their acts. Dietz (1983) argued that rape is often a bi-product of robberies since those involved in the crime reason that there is no significant difference in sentencing if they commit the rape. We should understand that seasoned criminals are well aware of the plea bargaining process and what potential sentences confront them for various crimes.

Felson and Tedeschi (1993a, 1993b) believe that violence emerges in the course of inter-action between the perpetrator and his or her victim. Violence is viewed, in the perpetrator's account, as a means to force the victim to comply with the demands being made or to settle a dispute. Those who use violence are able to weigh the potential success of the interjection of violence to obtain their ends considering those they are interacting with, those who may be an audience, and the potential for violence to be used successfully.

The Seductions of Crime

Katz (1988) developed a theory about the attractiveness of crime and the use of violence. Research by Canadian sociologist Fred Desroches (1995) shows that, contrary to popular belief, bank robbers do not rob banks primarily for the money but rather for the adrenaline rush that flows from the heightened state that is produced by being in a position of power and danger. Katz (1988, p. 8) views crime as having an "experiential creativity" bound up in it. While the violence of killing repulses us, Katz urges us to move beyond our view of crime as "morally unattractive" (p. 8) to fully understand the phenomenon. Murder, for example, emerges out of an interaction wherein the killer feels that the victim has attacked an "eternal human value" most likely demeaning their value as a father, provider, husband, for instance, to such an extent that only the death of the other will restore the murderer's personal worth. For men and women, the attempts by the victim to "disrespect" them soon turn into rage, a more socially acceptable response to a vicious verbal (and or physical) attack. Murder will occur in the home, as we noted in a previous section of the chapter, because the home is a place individuals cannot escape from. Alternatively, for Katz, recreational facilities are also a common place for murder since these are the oasis that people seek as refuge from their everyday lives, problems, troubles and shortcomings. In these latter settings, individuals are less prepared psychologically to confront violence from others, and so may be vulnerable to attack.

Victim Precipitation

One of the central and controversial issues of violent attacks is the role of the victim in precipitating events. This theory examines the behaviour of the victim and is also concerned with issues such as "risky lifestyles," in other words, the world that the victim inhabits that may contribute to their own victimization. Essentially, by placing oneself in deviant or high-risk activities that may involve criminality, one enters a zone in which their normal place within society, and the usual flow of interaction may not be as expected. In such situations, issues of class or social standing may be meaningless and thus precipitate an attack. One example that may underscore this concept of the suspension of the protective social armour produced by class status is the process of entry into correctional facilities for individuals with no previous experience of incarceration. Upon entering this world, the status that they enjoyed outside the institution is largely forfeit, and they must learn a new set of cultural guidelines or risk violent lessons on the norms of the institutional culture.

There are two forms of precipitation: active and passive. In the case of active precipitation, victims' behaviour, whether it involves the use of offensive words or gestures or attitudes that offend those around them, is a cause of the attack launched against them. If we consider this in terms of gang-related behaviour, intrusion on the territory of another urban gang will precipitate a need for the offended gang to exact a violent toll on the offender(s) to re-establish their mastery of a specific physical location in the city. Alcohol and drug use, or a combination of both has been demonstrated by research to be a frequent and recurring issue in manslaughter.

Domestic violence cases provide considerable cause for debate over the issue of victim precipitation. Domestic homicides often involve a victim fighting back against the recurring abuse of a perpetrator. Unfortunately, this can provoke an increased level of violent response, leading to serious injury or death. This is not to suggest that victims are somehow responsible for their own victimization but rather to suggest that responses of victimis can enrage their attackers.

Passive precipitation arises out of the offender's interpretation or view of an action, word, or deed by the victim that the victim did not intend to incite their attacker. Unexpected attacks can be linked to sexual orientation, race, religious belief, style of dress. Teenagers who display themselves on Facebook and subsequently are harassed or stalked are passive victims. Unprovoked violence can also occur in the context of homelessness (Fleming, 1995) where predators view the homeless as easy targets for theft, sexual assault, or violence.

Finally, it should be noted that precipitation should not be confused with blaming the victim. Victim blaming is a common phenomenon that emerges out of ignorance of the victimization experience among other social and cultural factors. Essentially, this approach labels the victim as somehow responsible for his or her own victimization. A classic example of this flawed thinking would be blaming a victim for her own sexual assault based upon the clothes she was wearing or being out at night (Clark &Lewis, 1982).

Routine Activities Theory

Human beings tend to be repetitive in their behaviour, establishing patterns of interaction that are repeated on a daily basis with little modification. Realizing these patterns has been the purview of home burglars and mafia hit men throughout history. When one can establish, for example, the times at which victims are likely to be alone in a home, unguarded, then the task of victimizing them becomes much more attainable for offenders. Cohen and Felson (1979) beleive that there are three components to explain the motivation to commit crime, and, because these crimes may be violent, they hold some interest for those concerned with understanding violence. First, there must be a suitable target for the potential criminal act. Females and the elderly living on their own are especially vulnerable targets. Females who are in certain situations are also at greater risk, at parties or other social occasions (i.e., bars) because they become a suitable target in this theory for violent sexual offenders. Second, there must be the absence of a capable guardian, that is, someone to either protect or act as either a buffer against attack or a witness. Finally, there must be a motivated offender.

Routine activities theory has been used in conjunction with geographical profiling of crimes in order to find solutions to unsolved series of crimes, including arson, sexual assault, and homicide (Rossmo, 2009). By understanding how criminals chose targets, and then further why they are willing to use or escalate the use of violence, requires a consideration of the conditions under which crimes are more likely to occur. Routine activities theory provides a significant link between offender motivation, target selection, and ultimately the conditions under which violence is more likely to be used as a weapon to gain compliance, hurt, or humiliate the victim. In a related theory, Hindelang, Gottfredson, and Garofalo (1978) refer to the principle of homogamy. This is closely related to the concept of risky lifestyles. Fundamentally it posits that a person is more likely to be the victim of violent and other criminal activities if they come into contact on a more frequent basis with groups that contain possible offenders. Thus, sex trade workers (see O'Reilly & Fleming, this volume) are at high risk for being victimized by physical and sexual assaults as well as homicide given their fraternization in a street world of criminals, drug users and dealers, and sexual offenders.

Violence, Poverty and Inequality

There is certainly clear evidence that living in what seem to be hopeless economic circumstances can have a link to violence. First, while it is characterized as a psychiatric disorder, there is arguably a link between explosive violence with a lack of impulse control related to constant frustration in life. Intermittent explosive disorder (IED), characterized by explosive violence which appears unrelated or out of proportion to a stimulus, may provide an explanation for violence used to solve "problems' discovered by Athens (1980, 1992, 1997) in his studies of criminal behaviour resulting in imprisonment. Obviously individuals who are confined to conditions of seemingly unrelenting poverty may be conditioned to react with violence to fulfill their desires on many levels. While not wishing to divorce this condition from its roots in psychology, we would suggest that social conditions must be considered as a contributor to, or factor in, the development of violence in some individuals. Second, there is a need to understand that living in a condition of hopelessness can lead psychologically to maladaptive behaviours. Criminologist Walter Miller (1958) attempted to provide some explanation of this in his theory regarding the primary concerns of the working class. The lower classes focus on fate, autonomy, luck, and street smarts rather than on hard work and education as routes to success. This provides some insight into why there is a tendency in individuals trapped in these circumstances to discount the future. Like Merton's (1968) theory regarding the goals that North American society prescribes for its citizens without the means to legitimately reach those goals, persons who use violence to further their own goals and desires rarely see a better life ahead that is worth sacrificing for in the present.

We often see this form of behaviour associated with gang members in Canadian society and beyond. If young people in your social group do not have good job prospects, have been incarcerated, or have been victims of violence, they may have a greater tendency to be hedonistic. A hedonist approach views the present as most important, a "live for today" attitude in which engaging in various forms of violence to reach the goals pushed by our society, such as the acquisition of wealth, status, and power (Colaguori, 2012), makes sense to the perpetrator. Whether it is obtaining a high-powered car through violent carjacking, mugging someone for his wallet and valuables using a gun or knife, breaking into a house, or using violence to obtain any criminal goal, violence is a shortcut to the things society urges us to consume and celebrate.

The most cited study that confirms this theory is Daly and Wilson's (1988) study of 77 neighbourhoods in Chicago over a period of eight years. They discovered that the murder rate in the poorest areas, where the life expectancy was the shortest (excluding death from homicides), was 156 per 100,000. The murder rate in the wealthiest neighbourhood was 1.3 per 100,000! In an area of low life expectancy of just over 50 years, the use of violence to obtain what one wants often appears as a reasonable choice because, without violence, residents have little chance of ever enjoying luxury items.

Violentization

Lonnie Athens' (1980, 1992, 1997) work on how violent criminals who engaged in aggravated assault, rape, robbery, and homicide viewed their own situations allowed the development of the theory of violentization. Athens' research discovered that the use of violence involves the definition of a situation by the offender as one in which violence should be used. Reflecting the work of other researchers, Athens also found that the concept of a masculine image was tied to violent acts. Many criminals that Athens interviewed adopted the "tough guy" image, perhaps most associated in film with gangsters like Jimmy Cagney and, more contemporarily, Al Pacino (*Scarface*), Robert DeNiro (*Goodfellas*) and Joe Pesci (*Casino*), a self-image that contributed to the use of violence. Athens also discovered that offenders who were supported by a community that approved of violence were more prone to adopt this as an interactive strategy. He also found that offenders engaged in a moral dialogue with a "phantom community" that supported their violent attacks, in other words, finding self-approval for violent solutions from an imagined audience in their mind that supported their choices. The use of violence, for Athens, emerged not spontaneously but through a six-part process where the now violent offender moved from their own victimization to the adoption of violence as a way of reasserting a masculine image and obtaining goals. When they reached this final stage of development, violence was viewed as the solution to problems and issues, and is engaged in with the slightest provocation, or in many cases, no discernable provocation whatsoever (Rhodes, 1999). Serial killer and organized crime hit man, Richard Kuklinski (nicknamed "The Iceman"), who was responsible for the deaths of dozens of people, described his movement from victim to aggressor as a teenager; he recalls a moment of epiphany in his development that mirrors Athens stages of development:

> One day I just decided I've had enough of this picking … and I went upstairs and I took a bar which the clothes used to hang on in the closet, and I went back downstairs and there were like six young men still figuring they were going to mess with my head. We went to war. To their surprise I was no longer taking the beating I was giving it. (Ginsberg, 1992. The Iceman Interviews)

Kuklinski's motto in life, which reflected his use of violence both to support a certain standard of living and his view of others is encapsulated in his statement, "If you hurt somebody they'll leave you alone, good guys do finish last."

Conclusions

In this chapter, some of the leading criminological theories concerning violence have been critically analyzed. I have not dealt with theories of state violence, leaving that discussion to Part 4 of the book. Further, feminist theories, which are central to contemporary theorizing about violence are explored in depth in Part 3 in the contexts of violent domestic assault, family violence and murderous attacks against sex trade workers.There are many theories which have emerged from psychology and biology which are dealt with to some extent in other contributions to this volume. The theories explored here provide a roadmap for explanatory efforts to account for the genesis and use of violence in interactions between individuals in Canada. No theory, as I have indicated, provides a fully satisfactory explanation of violent behaviour because the complexity of human interaction is extremely resistant to single theories. The value of combining insights from contending theoretical perspectives can provide explanations that are more generalizable and more fully satisfactory as researchers, policymakers, and the general public attempt to understand violence. I began this chapter by suggesting that violence is pervasive in Canadian society. By continuing research efforts, social scientists and other researchers in related disciplines will move us closer to practices and policies that are more effective in both stemming violent behaviour in Canada and addressing its root causes. Readers are encouraged to engage in critical thinking about each of the theories presented and consider the weaknesses and strengths of each, as well as the possibility that multiple theories may be combined to provide more satisfactory explanations of violence in our society.

Keywords

Constitutive criminology, dark figure of crime, differential association, homogamy, instrumental theory, routine activities theory, subculture, violentization

Review Questions

1. What role do subcultures play in generating and legitimizing violent crime?
2. What role can theories play in helping society to reduce violent crime?
3. Given the number and rate of violent assaults that occur in Canada every day, can you suggest criminal justice or other policies to deal with this problem?
4. Which of the theories in this chapter gives the most satisfactory explanation of the reasons why individuals commit violent crime?
5. Because violence is a significant feature in the media and sports, would dealing with the issues surrounding violence in these areas have a positive effect on the use of violence in Canadian society?

References

Athens, L. (1980). *Violent criminal acts and actors: A symbolic interactionist study.* London: Routledge, Kegan & Paul.

Athens, L. (1992). *The creation of dangerous violent criminals.* Chicago: University of Illinois Press.

Athens, L. (1997). *Violent criminal acts and actors revisited.* Chicago: University of Illinois Press.

Boyd, N. (1988). *The last dance: Murder in Canada.* Toronto: Prentice Hall.

Boyd, N. (2002). *The beast within: Why men are violent.* Vancouver: Greystone.

Clark, L., & Lewis, D. (1982). *Rape: The price of coercive sexuality.* Toronto: Women's Press.

Cohen, L. E., & Felson, M. (1979). Social change and crime rates: a routine activity approach. *American Sociological Review, 44,* 588-608.

Colaguori, C. (2012). *Agon culture*. Toronto: de Sitter Publications.

Cowling, M. (2011). Postmodern policies? The erratic interventions of constitutive criminology. *Internet Journal of Criminology,* Nov. 9, 1-17.

Dahrendorf, R. (1979). *Life chances: Approaches to social and political theory.* London: Weidenfeld and Nicolson.

Daly, M., & Wilson, M. (1988). *Homicide*. New York: Aldine DeGruyter.

Desroches, F. (1995). *Force and fear: Robbery in Canada*. Toronto: Canadian Scholar's Press.

Dietz, M.L. (1983). *Murder for profit*. Chicago: Nelson Hall.

Dowler, K., Fleming, T., & Muzzatti, S. (2006). Constructing crime: Media, crime and popular culture. *Canadian Journal of Criminology and Criminal Justice, 48*(6), 837-850.

Ericson, R. V. (1975). Criminal reactions: The labelling perspective. West Mead: Saxon House.

Ericson, R. V., Baranek, P., & Chan, J. (1987). *Visualizing deviance: A study of news organizations*. Toronto: University of Toronto.

Ericson, R. V., Baranek, P., & Chan, J. (1991). *Representing order: Crime, law and justice in the news media*. Toronto: University of Toronto Press.

Felson, R. B., & Tedeschi, J. T. (1993a). Aggression and volence: Social interactionist perspectives. Washington, DC: American Psychological Association.

Felson, R. B., & Tedeschi, J. T. (1993b). A social interactionist approach to violence: Cross-cultural applications. *Violence and Victims, 8,* 295-310.

Fleming, T. (1975). *Violent domestic assault*. Toronto: Centre of Criminology.

Fleming, T. (1995). *Down and out in Canada: Homeless Canadians*. Toronto: Canadian Scholar's Press.

Ginsberg, A. (1992). *The Iceman Interviews*. USA: Home Box Office.

Gottfredson, M., & Hirschi, T. (1990). *A general theory of crime*. Stanford, CA: Stanford University Press.

Henry, S., & Milovanovic, D. (1996). *Constitutive criminology: Beyond postmodernism*. Thousand Oaks, CA: Sage Publications.

Henry, S., & Milovanovic, D. (1999). *Constitutive criminology at work: Applications to crime and justice*. Albany, NY: SUNY Press.

Hindelang, M., Gottfredson, M.R., & Garofalo, J. (1978). *Victims of personal crime : An empirical foundation for a theory of personal victimization*. Cambridge, M.A.: Ballinger.

Katz, S. (1988). *Seductions of crime: Moral and sensual attractions in doing evil*. New York: Basic Books.

Kelly, K., & Totten, M. (2002). *When children kill: A social psychological study of youth homicide*. Toronto: Broaview.

Leyton, E. (2009). *Sole survivor: Children who murder their families*. London: John Blake.

McCarthy, B. (2002). New economics of sociological criminology. *Annual Review of Sociology, 28,* 417-442.

Merton, R. K. (1968). *Social theory and social structure*. San Francisco: Free Press.

Miller, W. (1958). Lower class culture as a generating milieu of gang delinquency. *Journal of Social Issues, 14*(3), 5-20.

O'Grady, W., & Leyton, E. (1992). *Crime and public anxiety: A Canadian case*. Institute of Social and Economic Research. St. John's: Memorial University.

Rhodes, R. (1999). *Why they kill*. New York: Vintage.

Ross, R. R., & Antonowicz, D. (2004). *Antisocial drivers: Prosocial driver training for prevention and rehabilitation.* Springfield, IL: Charles Thomas.

Rossmo, K. (2009). *Criminal investigative failures.* Boca Raton, FL: CRC Press.

Silverman, R., & Kennedy, L. (1993). *Deadly deeds: Murder in Canada.* Toronto: Nelson.

Statistics Canada. (2011). Centre for Justice Statistics. *Integrated Criminal Court survey 2010/11.* Retrieved from http://www.statcan.gc.cawww.statcan.gc.ca

Statistics Canada. (2012). *Police reported criminal statistics in Canada, 2012.* Retrieved from http://www.statcan.gc.ca

Tedeschi, R. T., & Felson, R. B. (1994). *Violence, aggression and coercive action.* Washington, DC: American Psychological Association.

The Globe and Mail. (2012). Honour killings `un-Islamic,' fatwa declares in wake of Shafia trial. Retrieved from http://www.statcan.gc.cawww.theglobeandmail.com/news/national/honour-killings-un-islamic-fatwa-declares-in-wake-og-shafia-trial/article 5437101

Wolfgang, M, & Ferracuti, F. (1967). The *subculture of violence: Toward an integrated theory in criminology.* London: Tavistoc.

Methods for Researching Violence

Chapter 2

Learning Objectives

In this chapter you will...

► learn basic definitions used in social research methods

► explore what strategies of social inquiry social researchers use to explain and understand violence

► distinguish between qualitative and quantitative methods and describe their advantages and disadvantages for researching violence

► develop an understanding of the different parts of the research process such as the research design, data collection, data analysis, and the dissemination of information

► gain an understanding of the ethical challenges social researchers encounter when studying sensitive topics and vulnerable populations

Alicia C. Tomaszczyk

Introduction

Explaining Violence

Social researchers have attempted to explain violence in social interactions and more broadly as social phenomena in the context of society in general. The study of violence encompasses many different research topics, each one with its own set of methodological challenges to overcome. Researchers in the field of theoretical violence have been debating the definition of violence since the 1970s. The practice of studying violence involves thinking critically about the contentious issues of how violence can and should be defined and how social scientists engage in applying and measuring these definitions (Kolbo, Blakely, & Engleman, 1996, p. 281; Dutton & Kropp, 2000, p.178). Social researchers who desire to collect personal information about people's experiences with violence have raised various methodological questions. Recently, social researchers have attempted to address a number of central questions, including:

1. How violence can be measured?
2. What is the best way to collect information about people's experiences with violence?
3. What do we know about the information we have collected?
4. Does the information have a bias?

5.How do we address the bias?
6.How can we study sensitive topics ethically?

Since the beginning of the twentieth century, criminologists, sociologists, historians, and psychologists have created new methods to adapt to our changing understandings of violence and the myriad ways of viewing and conceptualizing violence. Evaluating the methods violence researchers use is crucial for providing decision makers with evidence on which to base and construct policies that might reduce violence (Lee & Stanko, 2003, p. 2). Methodological approaches to studying violence often involve diverse research populations and may use surveys or interviews to collect data. One reason for the emphasis on survey research over more qualitative face-to-face interviews is people's occasional reluctance to share their experiences of violence with a researcher. Special care needs to be taken when dealing with sensitive topics, and social researchers have to be sensitive to the ways in which research participants are affected by the ways we document violence. Asking participants to recall traumatic memories may lead to further emotional harm for the participant (Lee & Stanko, 2003, p. 2). In some research settings, social researchers also have to think about self-endangerment when studying violent populations such as gangs or aggressive offenders.

Historical Methods

In the past, sociologists have researched violence using methods such as **documentary analysis** and **secondary data analysis**. Documentary analysis refers to an "examination of documents for the study of the social and/or historical world" (Lee & Stanko, 2003, p. 53). A document is a "physically embodied text where the containment of the text is the primary purpose of the physical medium" (as cited by Lee & Stanko, 2003, p. 53). Emile Durkheim's famous study of suicide (1897) is an example of a documentary analysis that explored suicide rates among Protestants and Catholics using government records and secondary data. Secondary data is data that has already been collected. Although other methods have been developed and are used by sociologists today, documentary analysis and secondary analysis remain important but are less popular techniques for sociologists compared to the survey or interview method (Girard, 2009; McConnell et al., 2011).

Girard (2009) examined transcripts of public debates on domestic violence legislation in Ontario, Canada to understand how men's rights advocates construct the problem of domestic violence. She analyzed the public hearings from Ontario's Bill 117, An Act to Better Protect Victims of Domestic Violence and found that men's rights activists collectively construct the problem of domestic violence by disqualifying women's experiences. Girard's exploration of the public debates revealed that men's rights activists used counter feminist constructions of domestic violence to further an anti-feminist agenda.

Criminologists often use statistical results based on aggregate data to examine violence in interpersonal relationships (Orsagh, 1979). For example, McConnell et al. (2011) used the Canadian *Incidence Study of Reported Child Abuse and Neglect (CIS-2003)* core data to examine the factors that influence child maltreatment investigation outcomes for children of parents with cognitive impairments. The CIS-2003 core data includes process and outcome data on maltreatment investigations of children of parents with cognitive impairments. Pritchard and Butler (2003) examined child homicide rates in the United States and other major Western countries between the years 1974 and 1999. Using the World Health Organization's standardized mortality data and the General Population Rates for Homicide, the authors analyzed ratios of change for children's homicide.

Another type of documentary analysis is **content analysis.** This refers to a "research method that uses a set of procedures to make valid inferences from text" (Weber, 2004, p. 117). Barker and Human (2009) used newspapers from the LexisNexis database. The authors classified the criminal activity of four motorcycle gangs: the Hell's Angels' motorcycle club (MC), the Outlaws MC, the Bandidos MC, and Pagans MC. Similarly, Dowler and colleagues conducted content analyses of crime in the media to understand how crime is portrayed to the public (Dowler, 2004; Welsh, Fleming, & Dowler, 2011). Dowler (2004) examined 400 episodes of American and Canadian local news coverage employing quantitative and qualitative methods. Dowler coded the data for occurrences of criminal acts, criminals, victims, and criminal justice agents as well as the underlying meaning of news images and dialogue. The content analysis revealed similarities between American and Canadian local crime news. Moreover, this research helped to explain how local news content is influenced by owners of news media and advertisers, whose main objective is to increase media consumption.

Historically, documents, accounts, and other records were the objects of study for sociologists to understand violence. Questionnaires and interviews were not in popular use for studying society; nor were the social sciences as a discipline institutionalized. Data about the everyday activities of individuals in society were scarce, aside from observational studies such as those conducted by nineteenth-century social critic Henry Mayhew or early-twenty-first-century French historian Louis Chevalier. In his work *London Labour and the London Poor: A Cyclopeida of the Condition and Earnings of Those That Will Work, Those That Cannot Work, And Those That Will Not Work* (1851), Henry Mayhew conducted ethnographic interviews with criminals such as prostitutes, thieves, and beggars (1965). Mayhew describes the everyday lives of the working and non-working poor in the mid-nineteenth century to create a set of facts on crime, such as the geographical location of crime and the occurrences of criminal activity (1969). Similarly, Louis Chevalier employed a survey to study the everyday lives of urban working class Parisians in the nineteenth century in his work *Labouring Classes and Dangerous Classes [1958]* (1973). Chevalier focused his analysis on the relationship between urbanization and crime in an attempt to explain how crime is a systemic issue. According to Chevalier, criminal activities arose as a result of the failure of the economic system to adjust to a growing population. For example, Chevalier notes the wide spread occurrences of prostitution during the rise of the industrial era.

With the exception of the British Empire and other empires of the colonial era, which collected information about the population through a **census,** there were few public records about the majority of humanity. Prison, mental hospital, poorhouse, and workhouse records were meticulously recorded in England, for example. Records were often dispersed in parish churches or local council headquarters in Great Britain. This meant that social researchers would have to first discover that the record exists, acquire permission to access the records, and then travel to the location where the records were kept. Despite the invention of the Internet in the 1970s and subsequent rise of the information age in the 1990s, many records are restricted to social researchers, and, as in the past, we can be denied access to the information. In Canada, Canadian citizens have the right to access information in federal government records under the Access to Information Act (1985) and the Privacy Act (1985) (Statistics Canada, 2011). The Privacy Act ensures citizens the "right to access personal information held by the government and protection of the information against unauthorized use and disclosure" (Statistics Canada, 2009).

Documents can be used to generate both quantitative and qualitative data. This allows the researcher to conduct an extensive analysis of patterns of violence and analyze descriptions, interpretations, and meanings of violence (Lee & Stanko, 2003, p. 54). Researchers may evaluate their data extracted from documents according to four criteria: authenticity, representativeness, credibility, and meaning (Scott [1990] as cited by Lee & Stanko, 2003, p. 54).

Quantitative and Qualitative Perspectives on Violence

Quantitative and **qualitative approaches** to studying violence present different frameworks for examining objective and subjective experience. However, both approaches can emphasize the creation of inter-subjective, credible knowledge, and the study of subjective experiences (Murphy & O'Leary, 1994, p. 215). Critics charge that the richness of human experience and contextual dimensions are often lost in objective ratings systems of quantitative research. In addition, the quantitative method often obscures the role of values in research. Qualitative research attempts to address this loss of information by clarifying or extending objective results from scales and by making values explicit (Murphy & O'Leary, 1994, pp. 216-219). According to Strauss and Corbin (1990, p. 17), qualitative research "produces findings not arrived at by statistical procedures or other means of quantification" (as cited by Murphy & O'Leary, 1994, p.209). Murphy and O'Leary (1994) describe the qualitative approach as having an emphasis on naturalism, **inductive reasoning**, holism, qualitative data, personal contact, unique case orientation, context sensitivity, and design flexibility (p. 210). Nonetheless, qualitative research often utilizes a small number of participants to collect subjective views and judgments. This means that researchers have to find ways to combine different subjective perspectives by acknowledging competing theoretical perspectives and interests. To assess the reliability of qualitative data, researchers often use **inter-coder reliability** to check for consistency in among interviewers' coding decisions. By combining qualitative and quantitative approaches, social researchers can expose peoples' subjective experiences and the social context while evaluating the accuracy of claims using **deductive reasoning** to get a detailed understanding of interpersonal violence (Murphy & O'Leary, 1994, p. 219).

Strategies for Explaining Violence

Quantitative Research

Measuring violence

Social scientists have developed standard ways of measuring the impact of violence on the population (Lee & Stanko, 2003, p. 2). Experimental studies have been used by violence researchers to develop standard units of measurement to systematically observe the different dimensions of constructions of violence. Violence researchers have developed measurements of psychological and physical conflict in romantic relationships, including dating, being married, and cohabiting. For example, Straus et al. (1996) describe a Conflict Tactics Scale (CTS), which is a measure of two facets of relationship violence. CTS measures the extent to which partners in a romantic relationship engage in psychological and physical attacks on each other. CTS also measures romantic partners' use of reasoning or negotiation to cope with conflicts. In these studies, violence researchers revise the scale to enhance the validity and reliability of the measure by rewording items to increase their clarity and specificity. Critics of the CTS argue that this measure overlooks the context and subjective meanings associated with family violence (McCarroll et al., 2000). McCarroll et al. (2000) conducted a study of 31,801 active duty army men and women using the CTS. They found that aggressive respondents were more likely to omit items on the scale compared to less aggressive individuals who omit none. Findings from these studies suggest that the CTS is perhaps not the most reliable measure, since some groups of individuals respond differently to the questionnaire items in a systematic way.

Experiments have also been used by social scientists to assess the practical application of interviewing techniques. A study by Drapeau, de Roten, and Körner (2004) examined the relationship patterns of child molesters. The authors used a Core Conflictual Relationship Theme (CCRT) method which involves conducting non-directive, **semi-structured interviews** with child abusers and outpatients (p. 267). In the interview, the participant is asked to explain what had brought him or her to therapy (p. 267). The participant is then given a series of relationship episodes, which are brief summaries or vignettes of interactions the subject had with another person. Interviewers rate the participant's relationship episodes using three criteria: the wishes, needs, motivations, or intentions of the participant; the response of the other to the participant; and the response of the participant to other (p. 267). In a follow up study, Drapeau (2006) compared interactions involving child abusers and his/her therapist with those involving child abusers and his/her parent using the CCRT (n = 20). Drapeau found high **inter-rater reliability** for child abusers' relationship patterns, which demonstrates high stability for the CCRT measure.

Social researchers studying violence often use **self-report** measures to assess the participants' mental state and personality (Walsh, MacMillan, & Jamieson, 2003; Thackeray et al., 2007; Walsh et al., 2007). A self-report involves taking an inventory of a participant's symptoms, behaviours, and personality by having him or her fill out a **questionnaire**. Self-reports are utilized by researchers in various quantitative studies such as experiments, **interviews, and surveys**. Hilton, Harris, and Rice (2003) examined the accuracy of self-report measures. High school students' self-reports for verbal, physical, and sexual aggressive were compared to students' responses to a **scenario-based self-report questionnaire**. They found low agreement between the two measures. Their findings suggest self-report measures should be interpreted with caution and further investigation into their validity is required.

Experiments

Social researchers sometimes use **experiments** to study and to test the effectiveness of **intervention programs** aimed at mitigating violence in interpersonal relationships. An experiment involves taking two or more matched groups and then treating one group but not the other. Both groups are measured before and after treatment, and then the researcher compares the changes in the treated and untreated groups (Pawson & Tilley, 2004, p. 54). One of the benefits of conducting an experiment over a survey is that it has high explanatory power; that is, it can effectively explain the results using specific theories. Experiments can also be better at explaining sensitive topics in violence, such as abuse and memories of abuse in family and romantic relationships (Erickson & Drenovsky, 1990).

Eyssel and Bohner's (2011) study used an experimental design to examine the conditions that facilitate the biasing effects of the rape myth acceptance (RMA) on judgments of blame in rape cases for 330 participants. Two experiments involved **participants** reading short **vignettes** that depicted a rape case. Vignettes are used in violence research to help researchers discover the conditions under which a person might or might not commit violent or deviant acts (Schwartz, 2000, p. 830). In experiment one, Eyssel and Bohner varied the amount of case-irrelevant information about the defendant and plaintiff. They found a **positive relationship** between RMA scores and the amount of irrelevant information. Participants who held high RMA were less likely to blame the defendant when they had read more irrelevant information. In experiment two, participants were **randomly assigned** to two groups. One group was made to believe that they had been subliminally exposed to additional case information. The other group constituted the **control group**. Participants in the **experimental group,** who were primed to believe they were "entitled to judge," were more likely to be biased by their RMA compared to the control group. In a Canadian study, Cummings, Pepler, and Moore (1999) looked at family aggression patterns and behavioural problems of children aged 6 to 12 who were recruited from shelters for battered women. The shelter children were compared with children from non-violent families, including two-parent families, single-mother-headed households, and homeless families. Shelter girls who had been exposed to recent inter-parental wife abuse showed more internalizing and externalizing behavioural problems than boys and girls in two-parent or single-parent homes.

Experiments using visual prompts. Social researchers interested in investigating people's perceptions of violence can use an experimental design that exposes participants to a visual **stimulus,** such as video recordings or computer games, in order to measure participants' evaluations or reactions to the visual material. For example, Erickson and Drenovsky (1990) examined the reactions of 45 men and 68 women using an experimental computer game that depicted an abusive relationship. In the scenario, participants were led to believe that they were playing a game with another student. The participants were instructed that the objective of the game was to match his or her number with a computer's choice and the choice of his or her partner as well. The computer chose either number one or number two. Points were assigned in denominations of 50 if both the participant and his/her partner matched the computer's choice, 25 if only one of them matched the computer, and zero if neither of them matched the computer. To create an abuse-like situation for the participant, each participant was also informed that his/her partner had access to a special button that controlled the participant's loss of points with simultaneous gain in points for his or her partner (pp. 240-241). The researchers measured participants' tendencies to leave relationships using four conditions of severity and frequency of abuse. Erickson and Drenovsky found the frequency of abuse influenced women's decisions to leave an abusive relationship while men's decisions were affected by the severity of abuse. An experiment by Witte and Kendra (2010) examined whether women's history of physical intimate partner violence influenced their ability to detect danger in physically violent dating situations. One hundred and eighty-two women viewed a video depicting psychologically and physically aggressive encounters between heterosexual dating partners and were asked to make repeated judgments about the interaction. They found that participants who were victims of intimate partner violence were less likely to recognize the danger in the video vignette compared to non-victims.

Experiments involving memory recall of traumatic events and abuse. Violence researchers have also looked at autobiographical memory recall for memories directly associated with abuse in psychiatric and non-psychiatric populations. In a non-psychiatric sample of students, Stokes, Dritschel, and Bekerian (2008) prompted participants to recall past traumatic memories using the Children's Autobiographical Memory Inventory (CAMI) and the Autobiographical Memory Task (AMT). They found students who had suffered childhood sexual abuse reported significantly lower semantic recall compared to the control groups. In another study involving memory recall, Futa et al. (2003) assessed coping mechanisms women use to deal with stressful childhood memories and stressful events (n=196). Women selected to be in the study either had no history of abuse, had a history of abuse, had experienced physical abuse history, or had experienced both sexual and physical abuse. Women with an abuse history reported significantly poorer adult adjustment than did non-abused women and different coping strategies were predictive of adjustment for abused and non-abused women.

Sampling and recruitment. A statistical practice used by quantitative researchers is sampling. A sampling technique allows the researcher to select a subset of individuals from within a population and then make inferences about the population based on knowledge acquired about the sample (Hedges, 2004, pp. 63-64). In violence research, social researchers utilize probability samples to collect information for a representative sample of the population. For quantitative researchers interested in studying **hidden populations**, people who engage in deviant or concealed activities and are hard to locate, conducting a **probability sample** may seem like an impossible task. Nevertheless, skillful researchers have developed techniques for sampling hidden populations. For example, Bouchard and Tremblay (2005) used the **capture-recapture method** to estimate the size of a hidden population of active offenders. The capture-recapture method allows quantitative researchers to derive the odds of arrest by estimating the incidence of crime events. The underlying assumption of this statistical technique is that the odds of arrest are derived by defining a population of individuals involved in a particular line of activity and who have the same characteristics as those offenders but have not been arrested. This sampling technique is used to provide an indication of the likelihood that the pool of motivated offenders participating in a given criminal activity will be arrested for a related offense (Bouchard and Tremblay, 2005, pp. 735-736). Probability samples can also be used to select members from a population of interest for recruiting people for face-to-face interviews. For example, Schafer, Caetano, and Clark (2002) assessed agreement about intimate partner violence in a sample of couples in the United States. They used a **multi-stage probability sampling** to select couples, and then **face-to-face interviews** were conducted with the couples in their homes.

Violence researchers who use survey and interview modes of data collection also use **non-probability** sampling to select individuals to be included in the study (Rothman, Exner, and Baughman, 2011). An example of a non-probability sampling strategy is Targeted Neighborhood Sampling. For the Targeted Neighborhood Sampling technique, the researcher uses police reports of family fight calls to target particular areas within a city for recruitment. Christopher et al. (2008) compared the Targeted Neighborhood Sampling technique to the **conven-**

ience sample method and found the method can be used to more effectively recruit a community sample of couples who have experienced intimate partner violence (p. 99).

Surveys

Mail, telephone, and face-to-face. Violence researchers often rely extensively on survey data to understand deviant segments of the population for topics such as bullying in school, intimate partner abuse, and the effects of media on fear of crime (Chiricos, Eschholz, & Gertz, 1997). Survey research is a type of quantitative research that systematically collects information from a sample of individuals by asking the same questions, then recording and analyzing their answers. Quantitative surveys provide sociologists with information that can be categorized or coded for statistical purposes (Murphy & O'Leary, 1994, p. 216). The different modes of surveys are: telephone, face-to-face, mail or self-administered, and online. Self-administered questionnaires can be used to measure individuals' attitudes, behaviours, and beliefs. For example, Eisler and Schissel (2004) administered questionnaires to 2,600 school-aged children in Saskatchewan, Canada to understand the relationship between poverty and victimization. For the survey, students were asked to respond to a 12-page questionnaire inquiring about their attitudes and practices regarding their feelings of victimization and their encounters with the justice system (pp. 361-362).

An advantage of telephone surveys is that they save time and can reduce the cost of conducting interviews compared to face-to-face, which increases the overall efficiency of the data collection process. Another advantage of the **telephone survey** is that it can be as effective as face-to-face interviews for sensitive topics (Reddy et al., 2006). Meyer (2010) investigated intimate partner violence focusing on the well-being of victims and their children using telephone interview data from the government of Australia's *International Violence Against Women Survey 2002-2003*. Studies often use a combination of face-to-face or telephone interviews in addition to a mail survey to collect information about participants. Walsh, MacMillan, and Jameison (2002) examined the relationship between a history of parental psychiatric disorders and history of child abuse. Using a representative sample of 8,548 respondents from the Ontario Mental Health Supplement, a report produced annually by the province, the authors used face-to-face **structured interviews** to explore participants' parental psychiatric history, and then participants were asked to complete a child maltreatment self-report to measure the severity of childhood physical and sexual abuse. Quantitative researchers can also use semi-structured interviews to collect information about individuals. For example, Stanley et al. (2006) explored male same-sex intimate violence in a sample of 69 gay and bisexual men. Participants were selected from a community at random using the random-digit-dialing technique. Telephone semi-structured interviews were used to explore the intimate relationships between gay and bisexual men.

Research using online surveys to study interpersonal violence is relatively new, and few researchers have utilized **online surveys** despite their advantages, such as low cost for administration and speedy data collection compared to other survey modes. An example of a study using an online survey examined the issue of cyber bullying in a sample of adolescent Internet users. Patchin and Hinduja (2006) found that cyber bullying poses strain on adolescents and may be related to school problems and delinquent behaviours offline. In another study, Chaulk and Jones (2011) examined **Online Obsessive Relational Intrusion** and its relationship to online social networking sites. The authors conducted a quantitative study using **frequency analysis** of students' behaviours on Facebook. They found that online social networking sites function as facilitators for Online Obsessive Relational Intrusion. Researchers' wariness of online surveys is well-founded at this point in technological development. Web surveys generally have lower response rates compared to other survey modes; there are often software and Internet provider incompatibility issues; and maintaining a web survey requires specific knowledge of Internet survey software.

Secondary analysis of survey data. Collecting survey data can be a time-consuming and difficult process because of problems associated with obtaining funding, creating interview schedules, piloting the survey, briefing interviewers, sorting out **coding** problems, devising categories for open-ended questions, and inputting coded data into a computer database (Dale, Arber, & Procter, 2004, p. 136). For these reasons, social researchers may conduct a secondary analysis of survey data (Wormith & Ruhl, 1987). For example, Avakame (1999) used data from the American National Crime Victimization Survey (1992-1994) about rape to test the **hypothesis** that females in the labour force increase their rape victimization "by frustrating resentful males into using violence as an ultimate resource in subjugating females" (p.942). However, results showed that in a nationally representative sample, unemployed women are more likely to be raped than employed women and that poor, older, and unmarried white, suburban females are most likely to be at risk for rape victimization. Similarly, Chartier, Walker, and Naimark (2010) employed data from the Ontario Health Survey, a population health survey, to study the effects of adverse childhood experiences on adult health and health care utilization. They found a cumulative effect of adverse childhood experiences on adult health problems. According to Chartier, Walker, and Naimark the risk of poor adult health increases with the number of reported adverse childhood experiences.

Survey research can also be used to track the development of changes in individuals by examining the characteristics of people at multiple points in time, also called a **longitudinal survey design** (Letourneau, Fedick, & Willms, 2007). For example, in a longitudinal survey of children exposed to domestic violence, the Canadian National Longitudinal Survey of Children and Youth, Letourneau, Fedick, and Willms (2007) explored the relationship between exposure to family violence and parenting behaviours over time. They found mothers of children exposed to domestic violence compensate for exposure to violence in their parenting interactions with their children. In a three-wave dataset of Canadians, Pagani et al. (2010) investigated the link between mothers' reported trajectories of family dysfunction and indirect aggression in children. Similarly, Temcheff et al. (2008) used data from the Concordia Longitudinal Risk Project, a survey of people from inner-city schools in Montreal who were recruited as children in the 1970s. The authors studied the link between aggressive behavioural styles in childhood and the risk of committing violence toward children and spouses later on in life.

Survey research is a widely accepted practice for most social scientists but this method is not void of pitfalls. According to Lindhorst and Tajima (2008), survey research has failed to address the contextual factors impacting intimate partner violence. As you read above, early measures constructed by violence research, such as the CTS, are limited to simple counts of behaviours. Social researchers looking at the contextual factors that shape behaviours argue that we need to consider the cultural and historical context to understand the meaning of the situational context of people's lived experiences involving violence. In an attempt to bridge this gap, researchers have pointed out that quantitative studies need to be designed more effectively by taking care to work through conceptualizations and operationalizations of variables, so that participants' experiences are contextualized (Amaya-Jackson et al., 2000; Lindhorst & Tajima, 2008).

Qualitative Research

Grounded theory. Qualitative research has grown in popularity for violence researchers since the 1980s. Qualitative research explores information in the form of words, pictures, sounds, and other visual material. Some qualitative researchers use a **grounded theory approach** to construct a theory and discover the dominant social and structural processes that account for variations in behaviour in a particular situation (Giesbrecht and Sevcik, 2000). In this approach, the research questions emerge from a concurrent exploration of data analysis and data collection. A grounded theory approach is usually useful when there is little information about the area of study under examination. For example, Wuest and Merritt-Gray (2008) interviewed a sample of women whose relationships had become non-violent (n=27). The authors used a **constant comparison method analysis** of grounded theory to generate similarities and differences in emerging theory.

Semi-structure and in-depth interviews. A common strategy for collecting qualitative data is the semi-structured or in-depth interview. Violence researchers conduct interviews to provide a more thorough and detailed assessment of participants' experiences compared to structured interviews (Wolfer, 1999). For example, Merali (2009) conducted semi-structured interviews with English-proficient and non-English-proficient South Asian brides who entered Canada after recent immigration policy changes. Merali examined brides' understandings of sponsorship and their experiences with martial resettlement. An interesting study by Hathaway and Atkinson (2003) reviewed interviews with tattoo artists and drug reform advocates and developed tactics aimed at eliciting informants with multiple interpretive standpoints. Hathaway and Atkinson findings suggest that a "good cop, bad cop" approach may help researchers to build a stronger rapport with their respondents. The researchers found that using a confrontational approach in interviews is suitable when the interviewer shares an intimate familiarity with the informant to the research topic (p. 179). Another study, which examined the practical application of interviewing techniques in violence research, compared using one-time and repeated interviews to understand women's experiences with chronic community violence (Wolfer, 1999). Wolfer found that in-depth interviewing about traumatic events may underestimate the level of women's experience with chronic community violence. Wolfer suggests that repeated weekly interviews provide a more comprehensive assessment of women's experiences with chronic community violence than in-depth interviews (p. 1070).

Another method used in interviews is the **Timeline Followback Spousal Violence** (TLFB-SV) technique. The Timeline Followback Spousal Violence is an event history calendar method used to assess the daily patterns and frequency of spousal violence. Using a sample of 104 men entering a spousal violence treatment program, along with their female partners, Fals-Stewart, Birchler, and Kelley (2003) tested the Timeline Followback Spousal Violence technique. Interviews were conducted with participants and their partners pre-treatment, post-treatment, and quarterly thereafter for one year. During interviews, participants were asked to identify days of male-to-female and female-to-male physical aggression that occurred between them. The TLFB-SV subscales had **temporal stability** and **concurrent** and

discriminate validity. In a more recent study, Lam, Fals-Stewart, and Kelley (2009) evaluated the psychometric properties of the Timeline Followback interview method for children's exposure to partner violence. Participants were men entering batterer's treatment. Participants were interviewed with their female partners and their custodial child. The scale had temporal stability and strong evidence of concurrent, discriminate, and **criterion** validity.

Focus groups. Focus groups in violence researcher are often used to pilot survey instruments or structured interview questions (Lavoie, Robitaille, & Hébert, 2000). A focus group is a type of group interview in which an interviewer or moderator asks questions to a group, and answers are given in an open-ended discussion among group members. Furthermore, the focus group has the unique advantage in that it can collect a combination of observations of social interactions between participants and the context of participants' interactions with the researcher. Lavoie, Robitaille, and Hébert (2000) examined aggression in teen dating relationships using discussion groups with 24 Canadian teens aged 14 to 19. The focus group provided the researchers with a means for an in-depth investigation of teen aggression and explored new areas for discussion. In some research situations, group interviews may be more effective for gathering data about violence, especially with young males who tend to divulge little information about their experiences (Lavoie, Robitaille and Hébert, 2000, p. 9).

Participant observation and ethnography. Qualitative researchers can also collect data through **participant observation** and **ethnographies**. Participant observation refers to observations carried out by the researcher when the researcher is playing an established participant role in the scene being studied (Atkinson & Hammersley, 1994, p. 248). Whereas ethnography is a form of research that explores the nature of a particular social phenomena, uses unstructured data, investigates a small number of cases, and analyzes data using the explicit interpretations of the meaning and functions of human actions (Atkinson & Hammersley, 1994 p. 248). For example, Colburn (1985) examined the symbolic dimensions of illegal assaults among ice hockey players in games in Toronto and Indianapolis. Colburn took field notes to describe the social context of violent incidents on the ice and conducted interviews with 160 amateurs and professional players in organized hockey. Colburn also gathered **direct observation** of interpersonal assaults and had informal conversations with players about those assault incidents. Participant observation- and ethnography-based studies often employ non-probability sampling methods such as **snowball sampling** to select participants to be interviewed. Another example of a participant observation study by Baron and Hartnagel (1998) examined the influence of sub-cultural, economic, and victimization factors on violent behaviour of homeless male street youths (n=200). Sample selection involved immersing researchers in particular geographical areas and then approaching respondents and screening their eligibility using selection criteria. Additional contacts were initiated by youths who were informed about the researcher's presence or through introductions from previously interviewed subjects (p. 174). Other researchers using participant observation and ethnography have utilized **participatory action research** and **institutional ethnography** to study formal systems from the standpoint of women who have experienced abuse. Institutional ethnography is a method developed by Dorothy Smith that enables the researcher to study the social organization of knowledge and experience (Varcoe & Irwin, 2004, p. 82). Institutional ethnography involves interviewing individuals or conducting focus groups with groups of individuals to gain an in-depth understanding of interpersonal violence from the standpoint the individual.

Qualitative research projects that investigate violence often use multiple methods such as **in-depth interviews**, participant observation, and focus groups to provide detailed descriptions of the everyday experiences of individuals (Varcoe & Irwin, 2004; Jones, 2008).

Phenomenology and discourse analysis. Both quantitative and qualitative researchers use semi-structured interviews to explore perspectives and the meanings of certain experiences, but the data are interpreted in different ways. Quantitative research relies on the grouping of information into categories to demonstrate a pattern; whereas interpretive research attempts to understand people's **phenomenological** experiences and what their experiences mean to them. Few studies have examined violence using a phenomenological methodology, even though it can be used by the researchers to understand a research topic through the participants' own choice of words. The phenomenological method enables the researcher to explore the contextual and cultural aspects of their participants' experiences with interpersonal violence (Shim & Hwang, 2005). Shim and Hwang (2005) examined how arrest policies influence domestic violence in minority communities. The authors used a sample of Korean American social workers who provided services to Korean domestic violence victims. Using a phenomenological method and semi-structured interviews, the researchers explored participants' perceptions about their clients' experiences of arrests in domestic violence situations. The researchers identified themes and then grouped the themes together into four main categories. Descriptions of each theme for each category were refined and elaborated though multiple re-readings of the transcribed interviews. Another approach to a phenomenological investigation of violence uses the **Phenomenological-Hermeneutic method,** which can be employed to analyze life stories of interpersonal violence. The Phenomenological-Hermeneutic method makes the assumption that a life story is not constructed at random. According to Kacen (2011), a life story can reflect the narrator's normalizing strategy to deal with past and future events. The objective of this method is to determine how "the strategy at the foundation of the story serves the storyteller's goals from his or her perspective" (Kacen, 2011, p. 33). The interviewer's aim is to avoid asking the participant questions that may affect the way he or she tells the story. Interviews are then transcribed and analyzed using the **Hermeneutic Case Reconstruction method**. The Hermeneutic Case Reconstruction method is a three-stage method based on "abduction logic"; it consists of locating the facts in the text, raising hypotheses and seeking empirical confirmation in the text, and forming theoretical generalizations (Kacen, 2011, p. 33). Other researchers interested in the life stories of victims of interpersonal violence have also employed **discourse analysis**, an analysis of texts that focuses on how knowledge and meaning are created through the use of language (Banks, 2001; Crocker, 2005).

Mixed methods research. An emerging method for studying violence is the mixed method approach. Mixed methods research combines qualitative and quantitative approaches in order to understand a social problem from multiple perspectives. A mixed method approach allows the researcher to conduct an empirical investigation based on information about the context, demonstrating continuity in observations and increased complexity of the analysis (Lee & Stanko, 2003, p. 3). For example, Fuentes (2008) utilized **life-history interviews** and structured interviews to examine the relationship between women's experiences with abuse and their risk of contracting sexually transmitted infections (STIs). The life-history interviews helped Fuentes to identify the specific risk factors such as depression, substance abuse, and age of first sex, associated with abused women's risk of infection. The structured interviews revealed that abused women were at a higher risk of contracting STIs compared to women who did not experience abuse. The mixed method approach enabled Fuentes to explain the link between abused women and the risk for STIs.

Intervention Studies

Results from experiments, surveys, interviews, and text-based analyses have helped violence researchers to produce evidence for policymakers that informs prospective frameworks for prevention programs. Prevention programs enable the government and non-government organizations to intervene in violent relationships or situations of violence to help prevent further occurrences. Social researchers also use intervention studies whereby the researcher assigns the prevention treatment to one group of participants and compares the outcome with a control group to determine the effectiveness of a treatment or program (Looman, Abracen, & Nicholaichuk, 2000). For example, Marsch, Bickel, and Badger (2006) evaluated a program, called the HeadOn: Substance Abuse Prevention for Grades 6-8 to help prevent drug abuse by educating students about drugs. Marsch, Bickel, and Badger found that students who were in the program were more accurate in their objective knowledge about drug abuse prevention compared to students in a life skills group. A study by Scott (2004) examined the factors influencing attrition in batterer treatment programs. Participants were 345 men who enrolled in a batterer treatment program over the course of one year, 61.4% of whom dropped out of treatment. Counselor ratings of the stage of change, which are processes of change that guide the individual through a series of stages, significantly predicted treatment completion after controlling for demographics, contextual, and personality variables.

Intervention studies use a variety of measures, including self-reports. Romano and De Luca (2006) evaluated the effectiveness of a treatment program for males who experienced sexual abuse in childhood (n=5). Participants were issued a treatment manual that required them to record on daily basis feelings of self-blame, anger, and anxiety using a series of **self-report ratings**. Romano and De Luca found that the treatment manual decreased feelings of self-blame and anger in participants.

Intervention studies often focus on improving technique for assessing the data quality of participants' memories of abuse. Since the mid-1990s, social researchers have developed a **life-events calendar method** to serve as an extension of traditional self-report **surveys** (Sutton, 2010, p. 1038). The life-events calendar method enables interviewers to collect participants' summaries of events that occurred within a designated period of time. Interviewers and interviewees work in cooperation to chart when various events occurred in the interviewees' lives (Sutton, 2010, p. 1038). The life-events calendar method facilitates participant recall more effectively compared to traditional self-report surveys. In a review of the literature evaluating the life-events calendar method, Sutton (2010) found that participants with unstable lives and cognitive difficulties respond favourably to the life-events calendar because of its interactive mode of administration and its use of mental and visual cues. Sutton also points out the life-events calendar method offers the researcher a cheap and potentially more practical solution for analyzing retrospective longitudinal data compared to traditional **panel designs**.

Ethical Considerations in Violence Research

Violence is a sensitive topic, especially for people who have experienced it firsthand. It is imperative that social researchers take into consideration the ethical implications for studying sensitive topics that may threaten participants' well-being by asking intrusive questions or revealing information that is stigmatizing or incriminating (Lee & Stanko, 2003, p. 3). Shaver (2005) examined the methodological and ethical challenges for research projects with sex workers and other **marginalized** populations. Shaver points out three issues with studying marginalized populations. First, Shaver argues that the size and boundaries of the population are unknown, which makes it hard for researchers to get a representative sample. Second, membership in hidden populations can often involve individuals engaging in stigmatized or illegal behavior and this poses ethical issues for the researcher regarding participants' **privacy** and **confidentiality** of their information. Third, the researchers must play a legitimizing role by grounding the study design in strategic comparisons that reveal the heterogeneity within marginalized populations (Shaver, 2005, p. 314). Shaver's guidelines for ethical, non-exploitive methodologies involve developing techniques to access local networks and increase the representativeness of the sample, while adopting participant-centered and harm-reduction guidelines that serve to protect the participant. Another important issue related to researching vulnerable populations is that researchers may have trouble establishing a strong rapport with respondents who are perhaps afraid of divulging incriminating information. Gazit and Maoz-Shai (2010) examined contradictory research strategies, *studying up* and *studying across* using two field studies on the Israeli-Palestinian conflict. The authors argue that when researchers and their participants have similar ethno-national affiliation and military experiences, "the dichotomous relations between them breakdown and give way to a dense web of expectations" (p. 275). Schwartz (2000) argues that researcher ethics are particularly difficult and important in this field of study not only for the potential emotional trauma to the participants but also the potential for actual re-victimization.

Current Research Directions

In Canada, social researchers have examined various types of violence, such as domestic abuse, bullying, trauma, deviant behaviour, victimization, and aggression in sports. There is also a body of research that focuses on evaluating the effectiveness of intervention programs. Social researchers use a variety of strategies to explain and understand violence in Canadian society. Experiments, surveys, structured interviews, and secondary data analyses are the methodological tools quantitative researchers utilize to explain violence. The qualitative approach strives to understand people's experiences with violence. Qualitative researchers use methods such as focus groups, participant observation, in-depth interviews, ethnography, and textual analyses. A researcher's choice of strategy will depend on the topic and the nature of the specific research questions being investigated. Even though social researchers usually stick to one strategy – qualitative or quantitative – when conducting research, violence research often employs mixed method approaches to obtain a more comprehensive understanding of violence.

Researching violence has its difficulties; participants can be hard to access and unwilling to divulge personal information that could embarrass them, threaten their safety, or incriminate them. For studying a sensitive topic like violence, social researchers need to develop research designs that help them gain access to participants, promote building a strong rapport between the participant and the researcher, and ensure data is collected in an ethical manner. Improving current research designs would help social researchers to better understand how and why violence occurs. Quantitative researchers should focus on ameliorating measures of violence to capture its multidimensional nature. Qualitative researchers need to continue exploring the contextual aspects of an individual's experience to understand the different meanings Canadians have of violence. It is imperative that social researchers continue to find ways to improve their methods for collecting, analyzing, and disseminating data so that policymakers will be able to make more informed decisions on social problems relating to violence.

Questions for Review

1. How would you define violence and how would you measure it?
2. What is the distinction between qualitative and quantitative methods? Which method do you prefer? Why?
3. What are some ethical issues researchers should consider when studying violence?
4. What is the significance of violence research for social policy?
5. Which research strategy would be most suitable for studying why bystanders of school yard bullying are often unwilling to intervene?

References

Amaya-Jackson, L., Socolar, R. R. S., Hunter, W., Runyan, D. K., & Colindres, R. (2000). Directly questioning children and adolescents about maltreatment: A review of survey measures used. *Journal of Interpersonal Violence, 15*(7), 725-759.

Atkinson, P., & Hammersley, M. (1994). Ethnography and participant observation. In N. K. Denzin & Y. S. Lincoln (Eds.), *Handbook of qualitative research* (pp. 248-261). Thousand Oaks, CA: Sage Publications.

Avakame, E. R. (1999). Females' labor force participation and rape: An empirical test of the backlash hypothesis. *Violence Against Women, 5*(8), 926-949.

Banks, C. (2001). Women, justice, and custom: The discourse of "good custom" and "bad custom" in Papua New Guinea and Canada. *International Journal of Comparative Sociology, 42*(1-2), 101-122.

Barker, T., & Human, K. M. (2009). Crimes of the big four motorcycle gangs. *Journal of Criminal Justice, 37*(2), 174-179.

Baron, S. W., & Hartnagel, T. F. (1998). Street youth and criminal violence. *Journal of Research in Crime and Delinquency, 35*(2), 166-192.

Bouchard, M., & Tremblay, P. (2005) Risks of arrest across drug markets: A capture-recapture analysis of "hidden" dealer and user populations. *Journal of Drug Issues, 35*(4), 733-754.

Chartier, M. J., Walker, J. R., & Naimark, B. (2010). Separate and cumulative effects of adverse childhood experiences in predicting adult health and health care utilization. *Child Abuse and Neglect, 34*(6), 454-464.

Chaulk, K., & Jones, T. (2011). Online obsessive relational intrusion: Further concerns about Facebook. *Journal of Family Violence, 26*(4), 245-254.

Chevalier, L. (1973). *Laboring classes and dangerous classes in Paris during the first half of the nineteenth century.* (F. Jellinek, Trans.). New York: H. Fertig.

Chiricos, T., Eschholz, S., & Gertz, M. (1997). Crime, news and fear of crime: Toward an identification of audience effects. *Social Problems, 44*(3), 342-357.

Christopher, F. S., Pflieger, J. C., Canary, D. J., Guerrero, L. K., & Holtzworth-Muroe, A. (2008). Targeted neigborhood sampling: A new approach for recruiting abusive couples. *Journal of Family Violence, 23*(2), 89-100.

Colburn K., Jr. (1985). Honor, ritual and violence in ice hockey. *Canadian Journal of Sociology, 10*(2), 153-170.

Crocker, D. (2005). Regulating intimacy Judicial discourse in case of wife assault (1970 to 2000). *Violence Against Women, 11*(2), 197-226.

Cummings, J. G., Pepler, D. J., & Moore, T. E. (1999). Behavior problems in children exposed to wife abuse: Gender differences. *Journal of Family Violence, 14*(2), 133-156.

Dale, A., Arber, S., & Procter, M. (2004). A sociological perspective on secondary analysis. In C. Seale (Ed.), *Social research methods a reader* (pp. 136-140). New York: Routledge Taylor and Francis.

Drapeau, M. (2006). Repetition or reparation? An exploratory study of the relationship schemas of child molesters in treatment. *Journal of Interpersonal Violence, 21*(9), 1224-1233.

Drapeau, M., de Roten, Y., & Körner, A. C. (2004). An exploratory study of child molesters' relationship patterns using the core conflictual relationship theme method. *Journal of Interpersonal Violence, 19*(2), 264-275.

Dowler, K. 2004. Comparing American and Canadian local television crime stories: A content analysis. *Canadian Journal of Criminology and Criminal Justice, 46*(5), 573-576.

Dutton, D. G., & Kropp, P. R. (2000). A review of domestic violence risk instruments. *Trauma, Violence and Abuse, 1*(2), 171-181.

Eisler, L., & Schissel, B. (2004). Privatization and vulnerability to victimization for Canadian youth: The context of gender, race, and geography. *Youth Violence and Juvenile Justice, 2*(4), 359-373.

Erickson, R. J., & Drenovsky, C. K. (1990). The decision to leave an abusive relationship: The testing of an alternative methodological approach. *Journal of Family Violence, 5*(3), 237-246.

Eyssel, F., & Bohner, G. (2011). Schema effects of rape myth acceptance on judgments of guilt and blame in rape cases: The role of perceived entitlement to judge. *Journal of Interpersonal Violence, 26*(8), 1579-1605.

Fals-Stewart, W., Birchler, G., R., & Kelley, M., L. (2003). The timeline followback spousal violence interview to assess physical aggression between intimate partners: Reliability and validity. *Journal of Family Violence, 18*(3), 131-142.

Fuentes, C. M. M. (2008). Pathways from interpersonal violence to sexually transmitted infections: A mixed-method study of diverse women. *Journal of Women's Health, 17*(10), 1591-1603.

Futa, K. T., Nash, C. L., Hansen, D. J., & Garbin, C. P. (2003). Adult survivors of childhood abuse: An analysis of coping mechanisms used for stressful childhood memories and current stressors. *Journal of Family Violence, 18*(4):227-239.

Gazit, N., & Moaz-Shai, Y. (2010). Studying-up and studying-across: At-home research of governmental violence organizations. *Qualitative Sociology, 33*(3), 275-295.

Giesbrecht, N., & Sevcik, I. (2000). The process of recovery and rebuilding among abused women in the conservative evangelical subculture. *Journal of Family Violence, 15*(3), 229-248.

Girard, A. L. (2009). Backlash or equality? The influence of men's and women's rights discourses on domestic violence legislation in Ontario. *Violence Against Women, 15*(1), 5-23.

Hathaway, A. D., & Atkinson, M. (2003). Active interview tactics in research on public deviants: Exploring the two-cop personas. *Field Methods, 15*(2), 161-185.

Hedges, B. (2004). Sampling. In C. Seale (Ed.), *Social research methods a reader* (pp. 63-72). New York: Routledge Taylor and Francis.

Hilton, N. Z., Harris, G. T., & Rice, M. E. (2003). Correspondence between self-report measures of interpersonal aggression. *Journal of Interpersonal Violence, 18*(3), 223-239.

Jones, L. (2008). The distinctive characteristics and needs of domestic violence victims in a Native American community. *Journal of Family Violence, 23*(2), 113-118.

Kacen, L. (2011). The "Extended Self" and "It" in the dynamics of violent relationships: Learning from personal life stories on social conflicts. *Journal of Family Violence, 26*(1), 31-40.

Kolbo, J. R., Blakely, E. H., & Engleman, D. (1996). Children who witness domestic violence: A review of empirical literature. *Journal of Interpersonal Violence, 11*(2), 281-293.

Lam, W. K. K., Fals-Stewart, W., & Kelley, M. (2009). The timeline followback interview to assess children's exposure to partner violence: reliability and validity. *Journal of Family Violence, 24*(2), 133-143.

Lavoie, F., Robitaille, L., & Hébert, M. (2000). Teen dating relationships and aggression An exploratory study. *Violence Against Women, 6*(1), 6-36.

Lee, R. M., & Stanko, E. A. (2003). *Researching violence: Essays on methodology and measurement.* New York: Routledge Taylor and Francis.

Letourneau, N. L., Fedick, C. B., & Willms, J. D. (2007). Mothering and domestic violence: A longitudinal analysis. *Journal of Family Violence, 22*(8), 649-659.

Lindhorst, T., & Tajima, E. (2008). Reconceptualizing and operationalizing context in survey research on intimate partner violence. *Journal of Interpersonal Violence, 23*(3), 362-388.

Looman, J., Abracen, J., & Nicholaichuk, T. P. (2000). Recidivism among treated sexual offenders and matched controls Data from the regional treatment centre (Ontario). *Journal of Interpersonal Violence, 15*(3), 279-290.

Marsch, L. A., Bickel, W. K., & Badger, G. J. (2006). Applying computer technology to substance abuse prevention science: Results of a preliminary examination. *Journal of Child and Adolescent Substance Abuse, 16*(2), 69-94.

Mayhew, H. (1965). Selections from London labour and the London poor (Chosen with an introduction by John Lewis Bradley). London: Oxford University Press.

Mayhew, H. (1969). London's underworld; Being selections from "Those That Will Not Work," The fourth volume of "London Labour and the London Poor." (P. Quennell (Ed.). London: Spring Books.

McCarroll, J. E., Thayer, L. E., Ursano, R. J., Newby, J. H., Norwood, A. E., & Fullerton, C. S. (2000). Are respondents who omit conflict tactics scale items more violent than those who omit none?: A methodological note. *Journal of Interpersonal Violence, 15*(8), 872-881.

McConnell, D., Feldman, M., Aunos, M., & Prasad, N. (2011). Child maltreatment investigations involving parents with cognitive impairments in Canada. *Child Maltreatment, 16*(1), 21-32.

Merali, N. (2009). Experiences of South Asian brides entering Canada after recent change to family sponsorship policies. *Violence Against Women, 15*(3), 321-339.

Meyer, S. (2010). Seeking help to protect the children?: The influence of children on women's decisions to seek help when experiencing intimate partner violence. *Journal of Family Violence, 25*(8), 713-725.

Murphy, C. M., & O'Leary, K. D. (1994). Research paradigms, values, and spouse abuse. *Journal of Interpersonal Violence, 9*(2), 207-223.

Orsagh, T. (1979). Empirical criminology: Interpreting results derived from aggregate data. *Journal of Research in Crime and Delinquency, 16*(2), 294-306.

Pagani, L. S., Japel, C., Vaillancourt, T., & Tremblay, R. E. (2010). Links between middle-childhood trajectories of family dysfunction and indirect aggression. *Journal of Interpersonal Violence, 25*(12), 2175-2198.

Patchin, J. W., & Hinduja, S. (2006). Bullies move beyond the school yard: A preliminary look at cyberbullying. *Youth Violence and Juvenile Justice, 4*(2), 148-169.

Pawson, R., & Tilley, N. (2004). Go forth and experiment. In C. Seale (Ed.), *Social research methods a reader* (pp. 54-62). New York: Routledge Taylor and Francis.

Pritchard, C., & Butler, A. (2003). A comparative study of children and adult homicide rates in the USA and the major western countries 1974-1999: Grounds for concern? *Journal of Family Violence,18*(6), 341-350.

Reddy, M. K., Fleming, M. T., Howells, N. L., Rabenhorst, M. M., Casselman, R., & Rosenbaum, A. (2006). Effects of method on participants and disclosure rates in research on sensitive topics. *Violence and Victims, 21*(4), 499-506.

Romano, E., & De Luca, R. V. (2006). Evaluation of a treatment program for sexually abused adult males. *Journal of Family Violence, 21*(1), 75-88.

Rothman, E. F., Exner, D., & Baughman, A. L. (2011). The prevalence of sexual assault against people who identify as gay, lesbian, or bisexual in the United States: A systematic review. *Trauma, Violence and Abuse, 12*(2), 55-66.

Schafer, J., Caetano, R., & Clark, C. L. (2002). Agreement about violence in U.S. couples. *Journal of Interpersonal Violence, 17*(4), 457-470.

Schwartz, M. D. (2000). Methodological issues in the use of survey data for measuring and characterizing violence against women. *Violence Against Women, 6*(8), 815-838.

Scott, K. L. (2004). Stage of change as a predictor of attrition among men in a batterer treatment program. *Journal of Family Violence, 19*(1), 37-47.

Shaver, F. M. (2005). Sex work research methodological and ethical challenges. *Journal of Interpersonal Violence, 20*(3), 296-319.

Shim, W. S., & Hwang, M. J. (2005). Implications of an arrest in domestic violence cases: Learning from Korean social workers' experiences in the U.S. *Journal of Family Violence, 20*(5), 313-328.

Stanko, E. A. (2003). *The meanings of violence.* New York: Routledge Taylor and Francis Group.

Stanley, J. L., Bartholomew, K., Taylor, T., Oram, D., & Landolt, M. (2006). Intimate violence in male same-sex relationships. *Journal of Family Violence, 21*(1), 31-41.

Statistics Canada. (2009). Access to Information and Privacy. Retrieved from http://www.tbs-sct.gc.ca/atip-aiprp/index-eng.asp

Statistics Canada. (2011). Access to Information Act (R.S.C., 1985, c. A-1). Retrieved from http://laws-lois.justice.gc.ca/eng/acts/A-1/

Straus, M. A., Hamby, S. L., Boney-McCoy, S., & Sugarman, D. (1996). The revised conflict tactics scale (CTS2) Development and Preliminary Psychometric Data. *Journal of Family Issues, 17*(3), 283-316.

Stokes, D. J., Dritschel, B. H., & Bekerian, D. A. (2008). Semantic and episodic autobiographical memory recall for memories not directly associated with childhood sexual abuse. *Journal of Family Violence, 23*(6), 429-435.

Sutton, J. E. (2010). A review of the life-events calendar method for criminological research. *Journal of Criminal Justice, 38*(5), 1038-1044.

Temcheff, C. E., Serbin, L. S., Martin-Storey, A., Stack, D. M., Hodgins, S., Ledingham, J., & Schwartzman, A. E. (2008). Continuity and pathways from aggression in childhood to family violence in adulthood: A 30-year longitudinal study. *Journal of Family Violence, 23*(4), 231-242.

Thackeray, J., Stelzner, S., Downs, S. M., & Miller, C. (2007). Screening for intimate partner violence: The impact of screener and screening environment on victim comfort. *Journal of Interpersonal Violence, 22*(6), 659-670.

Varcoe, C., & Irwin, L. G. (2004). "If I killed you, I'd get the kids": Women's survival and protection work with child custody and access in the context of women abuse. *Qualitative Sociology, 27*(1), 77-99.

Walsh, C. A., Jamieson, E., MacMillan, H., & Boyle, M. (2007). Child abuse and chronic pain in a community survey of women. *Journal of Interpersonal Violence, 22*(12), 1536-1554.

Walsh, C., MacMillan, H., & Jamieson, E. (2002). The relationship between parental psychiatric disorder and child physical and sexual abuse: Findings from the Ontario health supplement. *Child Abuse & Neglect, 26*(1), 11-22.

Walsh, C., MacMillan, H. L., & Jamieson, E. (2003). The relationship between parental substance abuse and child maltreatment: Findings from the Ontario Health Supplement. *Child Abuse and Neglect, 27*(12), 1409-1425.

Weber, R. P. (2004). Content analysis. In C. Seale (Ed.), *Social research methods: A reader* (pp. 117-124). New York: Routledge Taylor and Francis.

Welsh, A., Fleming, T., & Dowler, K. (2011). Constructing crime and justice on film: Meaning and message in cinema. *Contemporary Justice Review, 14*(4), 457-476.

Witte, T. H., & Kendra, R. (2010). Risk recognition and intimate partner violence. *Journal of Interpersonal Violence, 25* (12), 2199-2216.

Wolfer, T. A. (1999). "It happens all the time": Overcoming the limits of memory and method for chronic community violence experience. *Journal of Interpersonal Violence, 14*(10), 1070-1094.

Wormith, J. S., & Ruhl, M. (1987). Preventive detention in Canada. *Journal of Interpersonal Violence, 1*(4), 399-430.

Wuest, J., & Merritt-Gray, M. (2008). A theoretical understanding of abusive intimate partner relationships that become non-violent: Shifting the pattern of abusive control. *Journal of Family Violence, 23*(4), 281-293.

Recommended Readings

Castelli, E. A., & Jakobsen, J. R. (2004). *Interventions activists and academics respond to violence*. New York: Palgrave Macmillan.

Lee, R. M., & Stanko, E. A. (2003). *Researching violence:Essays on methodology and measurement*. New York: Routledge Taylor and Francis.

Schinkel, W. (2010). *Aspects of violence: A critical theory*. New York: Palgrave Macmillan.

Stanko, E. A. (2003). *The meanings of violence*. New York: Routledge Taylor and Francis Group.

Wallace, B. C., & Carter, R. T. (2003). *Understanding and dealing with violence: A multicultural approach*. Thousand Oaks, CA: Sage Publications.

Glossary

Attrition: occurs when participants drop out of the study overtime, reducing the size of the sample.

Capture-recapture: a method that uses sampling to infer the size of a population.

Census: a systematic enumeration of a population.

Coding: a data analysis procedure that involves organizing data into categories through a process of assigning labels to segments of data.

Concurrent validity: a type of validity that measures the degree of agreement between a measure and an established measure or existing criterion to observe if one predicts the other.

Confidentiality: an ethical principle that requires social researchers to keep participants' personal information private.

Constant comparison method analysis: a systematic analytic process in the grounded theory method that involves repeatedly comparing observations to new evidence over the length of the research process.

Content analysis: a method of analysis that is used for studying documents, texts, and other forms of human communications. The method involves organizing segments of data into categories using the process of **coding**. The content analysis can be employed to conduct quantitative and qualitative research.

Control group: the group of participants in an experimental study that does not receive the stimulus or treatment.

Convenience sample: non-probability sampling procedures that involves selecting participants haphazardly (based on availability).

Criterion validity: a type of validity that measures the degree of agreement between a measure and some external criterion.

Deductive reasoning: a mode of logic in which specific **hypotheses** are derived from general principles.

Direct observation: a procedure in data collection that involves making observations on a social phenomenon while immersed in the social setting.

Discourse analysis: a method of analysis of forms of human communication that focuses on how language is used to create reality.

Discriminate validity: a type of validity that measures the degree to which two unrelated measures are unrelated.

Documentary analysis: an approach to analyzing documents that focuses on how the intentions and motivations of the creator influence the production of the document within a historical context.

Ethnography: an approach to studying social life in which the researcher immerses himself or herself in the social setting to record observations over an extended period of time.

Experiment: a research design for testing a relationship between variables in a controlled setting by ruling out alternative explanations.

Experimental group: the group of participants in an experimental study that receives the stimulus or treatment.

Face-to-face interview: a mode of interviewing in which the researcher conducts the interview in the immediate physical presence of the interviewee.

Focus group: a method of qualitative interviewing where groups of people are assembled to discuss an issue. The discussion is facilitated by a moderator.

Frequency analysis: a type of descriptive statistic that counts the number of instances an attribute of a variable is observed in a sample.

Grounded theory: an inductive approach to studying social life that generates theories from an analysis of themes.

Hermeneutic case reconstruction: a qualitative method that systematically analyzes biographical self-presentations.

Hidden population: a segment of the population that is difficult to access.

Hypothesis: a testable statement.

In-depth interview: a mode of qualitative interviewing where the interviewer asks the interviewee open-ended questions and then records the answers.

Inductive reasoning: a mode of logic in which general principles are derived from specific observations.

Institutional ethnography: a technique in ethnographic research for studying social life that allows researchers to explore the institutional social relations that structure everyday life.

Intercoder/rater reliability: a measure of the degree of agreement on the coding of items.

Intervention studies: a type of research where researchers systematically evaluate the effectiveness of a program.

Interview: a procedure in data collection where an interviewer asks an interviewee questions and then records the answers.

Life-events calendar: a method for collecting data retrospectively from participants. Participants record their autobiographical memories by marking time on a calendar. This method facilitates participants' recall of information and events.

Life-history interview: a type of interview where the interviewer asks the interviewee to describe or tell the narrative of his or her life.

Longitudinal survey: a research design where data is collected on participants over a period of time.

Marginalized population: a segment of the population that is excluded from the rest of society making them difficult to access.

Mixed methods: a research design that employs both quantitative and qualitative approaches.

Multistage probability sampling: a probability sampling design where sets of cases are selected within clusters and then units are sampled from within those clusters.

Non-probability sampling: a process of selecting cases to be part of a sample not at random.

Online Obsessive Relational Intrusion: unwanted and repeated intrusions of an individual's privacy over the Internet by another individual in pursuit of a relationship.

Online survey: a survey mode where the interviewee completes a questionnaire on a webpage and then the data is relayed back to the researcher over the Internet.

Operational definition: a procedural definition of a concept. Operationalization is the process of specifying the operations of a concept to measure a variable.

Panel design: a type of longitudinal study where data is collected by the same group of people over time.

Participant observation: a systematic method for studying social life that involves direct observation.

Participant: someone who is the subject of research.

Participatory action research: an approach to studying social life in which the researcher works collaboratively with the participants and serves as a resource for them.

Phenomenology: a method of inquiry that assumes social reality is constructed through interaction. Phenomenologists draw on experiential data to understand the intentionality and structure of human consciousness.

Phenomenological-hermeneutic method: a mode of interpretation that assumes that a life story is not constructed at random but reflects the narrator's normalizing strategy to deal with past and future events

Positive relationship: a correlation between continuous variables when one variable increase as the other increases.

Privacy: an ethical principle that requires social researchers to not reveal participants' personal information.

Probability sampling: a process of selecting cases to be part of a sample at random.

Qualitative approach: a method of inquiry that relies on non-numerical interpretations of data. Qualitative methods aim to discover the underlying meaning of text and images and other non-numeric data.

Quantitative approach: a method of inquiry that relies on numerical interpretations of data. Quantitative methods aim to describe and explain social phenomenon through numerical representation of observations.

Questionnaire: the instrument in survey research that is used to gather information about a respondent. Questionnaires contain a list of questions that respondents answer.

Randomly assigned: an experimental technique where each participant has an equal and known chance of being selected.

Reliability: criteria for evaluating the quality of measurement based on the degree of its consistency.

Scenario-based self-report questionnaire: a technique used in survey research that employs vignettes to describe a set of problems to the participant. The participant answers questions based on the vignette without interference from the researcher.

Secondary data analysis: a method for studying social life that examines documents and preexisting statistics that were collected by other researchers.

Self-report: a procedure in data collection where the participant records their own answers to a set of questions.

Self-report rating: a procedure in data collection where the participant rates a set of items and then records their answers.

Semi-structured interview: a type of interview where the interviewer asks interviewees a set of general questions. In semi-structured interviews, interviewers have the flexibility to change the order and wording of questions and ask respondents follow-up questions.

Snowball sampling: a type of non-probability sampling that involves selecting participants and then asking those participants to identify other potential participants.

Stimulus: the variable that is being manipulated in an experiment.

Structured interview: a type of interview where the interviewer asks interviewees questions in the same order and using the same wording.

Survey: a research design that involves a researcher asking a respondent a series of questions on a topic or issue using questionnaires or structured interviews.

Telephone survey: a type of survey where the interviewer collects information from a respondent over the phone and records the data.

Temporal stability: a type of reliability that measures the degree to which a measure is consistent over time.

Timeline Followback Spousal Violence: a type of interview that involves participants recording their experiences of abuse by marking time on a calendar. This method facilitates participants' recall of information and events.

Validity: criteria for evaluating the quality of measurement based on the degree of its accuracy.

Vignettes: a technique in which participants are presented with a series of hypothetical scenarios; then participants are asked how they would respond if confronted with that scenario.

PART 2

Contemporary Issues in Violence

Hate in the Peaceable Kingdom

Chapter 3

Barbara Perry

Learning Objectives

In this chapter you will...

▶ distinguish between legal and sociological definitions of hate crime

▶ recognize and understand the limitations of hate crime data

▶ gain an understanding of the impact that hate crime has on individuals, communities, and social values

Introduction

Hate crime is a vital area of inquiry for Canadian scholars. Such violence represents a direct threat to the basic principles of Canadian multiculturalism in that it has the potential to present significant obstacles to the ability or willingness of affected com.nunities to engage in civic culture. Consequently, hate crime violates our commitment to human dignity and equity. Given the centrality of multiculturalism policy in Canada, these broader implications of hate crime have been surprisingly neglected. From approximately 2010 to the time of writing this paper, I have developed and maintained a website clearinghouse of Canadian research on hate crime. The search for relevant materials has revealed a serious dearth of literature. A review of what is available offers up little more than a handful of academic papers (e.g., McKenna, 1994; Schaffer, 1996), a significant number of government reports (see, e.g., Roberts, 1995; Janhevich, 2001; McDonald & Hogue, 2007), and dozens of anti-violence/anti-hate websites (e.g., B'Nai Brith; and National Anti-Racism Council). For example, Julian Roberts (1995) produced a much cited review in 1995, but it was largely restricted to an analysis of available statistics and an assessment of data collection methods and practices. Janhevich's (2001) Centre for Justice Statistics has a similarly narrow focus. A 1994 Department of Justice report entitled *Hate-Motivated Violence* is devoted exclusively to legislative measures (Gilmour, 1994). McDonald and Hogue's (2007) more recent study is much more detailed but acknowledges that there is still a dire lack of Canadian data or scholarship on hate crime.

This is not to imply that Canada is free of the stain of hate. Like most other Western nations, Canada has had its share of bias-motivated violence – hate crime – throughout history. From the periodic assaults on First Nations communities to the riotous attacks on Chinese labourers in the 1880s, to the spate of anti-Semitic violence in Montreal and Toronto in the 2010s this country has proven itself to be less inclusive than its international image would suggest. Indeed, the presence of such violence gives lie to the "myth of multiculturalism" that is so deeply embedded in our national psyche. As the Right Honourable Beverley McLachlin (2003) stated in her LaFontaine-Baldwin address, "In Canada, we vaunt our multicultural society, yet still racism, anti-Semitism and religious intolerance lurk in our dark corners." This chapter offers an overview of relevant definitions, data, and justice responses to hate crime followed by an assessment of the myriad layers of impact associated with this particular form of violence.

Defining and Measuring Hate Crime

Typically, legal definitions of *hate crime* have followed the lead of the model legislation as set out by the Anti-Defamation League, which states that "A person commits a Bias-Motivated Crime if, by reason of the actual or perceived race, color, religion, national origin, sexual orientation or gender of another individual or group of individuals, he violates Section _____ of the Penal code (insert code provisions for criminal trespass, criminal mischief, harassment, menacing, intimidation, assault, battery and or other appropriate statutorily proscribed criminal conduct)." This is very much like the language used in the Canadian sentencing enhancement provision (S718.2a): "a sentence should be increased or reduced to account for any relevant aggravating or mitigating circumstances relating to the offence or the offender, and, without limiting the generality of the foregoing, (i) evidence that the offence was motivated by bias, prejudice or hate based on race, national or ethnic origin, language, colour, religion, sex, age, mental or physical disability, sexual orientation, or any other similar factor."

However, such legalistic definitions say nothing about the power relations endemic to the act. Consequently, Perry (2001) has developed the following definition of hate crime, which has come to be widely cited in the sociological literature:

> It involves acts of violence and intimidation, usually directed toward already stigmatized and marginalized groups. As such, it is a mechanism of power, intended to reaffirm the precarious hierarchies that characterize a given social order. It attempts to recreate simultaneously the threatened (real or imagined) hegemony of the perpetrator's group and the "appropriate" subordinate identity of the victim's group. (Perry, 2001, p. 10)

What is especially useful about this definition is that it recognizes that hate crime is a structural rather than an individual response to difference. Moreover, by emphasizing both violence and intimidation, it allows us to consider the continuum of behaviors that might constitute hate crime. According to the legal definitions, hate crime involves an underlying violation of criminal law or some other statute. From a sociological perspective, this is not very satisfying. It neglects legal forms of violence – what might be called *hate incidents* – that nonetheless cause harm to the victim and his or her community. The literature on violence against women, for example, has long argued for a broader understanding of what constitutes violence and indeed crime. Thus, it is important to keep in mind that the violence to which we refer runs the continuum from verbal harassment to extreme acts such as assault, arson, and murder. Clearly, not all incidents that fall within this definition will be "crimes" from a legal perspective. Yet they do constitute serious social harms regardless of their legal standing. By their very frequency and ubiquity, some of the most minor types of victimization – name calling, verbal harassment, and so on – can have the most damaging effects.

The available data sources on hate crime in Canada are limited. The annual General Social Survey (GSS) and the Ethnic Diversity Survey each include some rather weak questions on hate crime. And, as noted above, there have been a number of Justice Canada and Statistics Canada reports that attempt to measure hate crime. For example, through its Juristat reports, Statistics Canada has published annual hate crime reports since 2004. The 2013 report documents just over 1,300 hate crimes in 2011, 3.9 per 100,000 (Allen & Boyce, 2013). The most frequent victims were black people (21%), gay and lesbian people (18%), and Jewish people (15%). While the majority of offences were non-violent, offences motivated by sexual orientation were, in contrast, violent in two-thirds of the reported cases.

In 2005, the Ontario Attorney General and Minister of Community Safety and Correctional Services established the Hate Crimes Community Working Group (HCCWG) to explore and advise on the dynamics of hate crime in Ontario. In 2006, they released a comprehensive report of their findings. The report reflected the voices of the communities most dramatically affected by hate crime. Specifically, the HCCWG identified seven communities that appear to be especially vulnerable to hate crime: Aboriginal peoples; African Canadians; Asians; people of Jewish faith; people of Muslim faith; lesbian, gay, bisexual, and transgender people; and South Asians. Participants in the public hearings, focus groups, and other similar venues consistently stressed the pervasiveness of bias and hate crimes in their collective lives. For many, such incidents were so common as to have been "normalized" as a standard part of life.

Both the official and unofficial data must be considered carefully. Crime, generally, is underreported, and hate crime is even more problematic in this respect. It is useful, then, to turn to a consideration of the role of the different layers of the criminal justice system as a means of making sense of the dearth of reporting and information available to us.

Criminal Justice Responses to Hate Crime

The criminal justice response to hate crime has been varied and broad, ranging from legislation to specialized police hate crime units, to anti-violence projects, to the array of services known as victim-witness services, and both individual and, more recently, community victim impact statements. Within these contexts, the task of the criminal justice system is not only to mitigate the negative effects of hate crime for individual victims but the communities to which they belong.

In contrast to the breadth of US legislative initiatives, Canada has relatively few statutory tools with which to confront hate crime. In 1970, amendments to the Criminal Code recognized as criminal offences promotion of genocide (S.318), public incitement of hatred likely to lead to breach of the peace (S.319.1), and wilful promotion of hatred (S.319.2) when directed against specified "identifiable groups." In 2001, a bias-motivated mischief provision was added (S.430.4.1). Somewhat distinct from these provisions is S.718.2, which is a sentence enhancement statute. It is at this latter context that community impact noted below becomes an important consideration, since it may be one of the factors that mitigates a sentence.

Exacerbating the legislative limitations, very few cases have made their way to the courts. This is captured in McDonald and Hogue's (2007) recent Justice Canada document, *An Exploration of Needs of Victims of Hate Crime*, in which they report the infrequency of prosecutions under the relevant provisions:

From 1994/5 to 2003/2004 there have been a total of twelve prosecutions and six convictions under s.318 of the Criminal Code (advocating genocide) ... Under s.319 (incitement to hatred), from 1994/95 to 2003/2004 there have been a total of 93 prosecutions and 32 convictions. ... No charges have been recorded under s. 430.4.1 (mischief relating to religious property) in this same time period. A review of published case law indicates that between 1996 and 2006 at least 23 cases have applied hate as an aggravating factor in sentencing (hate as an aggravating factor in sentencing (s.719.2(a)(i)). (McDonald & Hogue, 2007, p. 16)

The explanation for the rarity of hate crime prosecutions arises from constraints in two key areas: prosecutorial decision making, and police decision making. Prosecutors face a difficult tension in balancing "hatred" against free speech protections. More concretely, as US scholarship has begun to demonstrate, prosecutors find it exceedingly difficult to "prove" motive (Bell, 2002).

Additionally, prosecutors are, of course, reliant on police decision making. Unfortunately, there is ample evidence to suggest that police are hesitant to identify or investigate hate crimes (Bell, 2002, 2009; Nolan, Bennett, & Goldenberg, 2009; Parker, 2009). Bell (2009) identifies an array of structural limitations on police recording of hate crime:

Different levels of organizational procedure exist around hate crimes. In order to be reported, hate crimes must be recognized, counted, and eventually reported. There are vast differences between police departments whether, the degree to which, and in what way officers are trained. Training specifically focused on hate crime factors often leads to increased hate crime reporting. Other institutional factors which increase hate crime reporting include the level of supervision in crime investigations and whether there is departmental policy regarding hate crimes. (p.35)

Additionally, police indirectly play a role in the very first decision point, that is, in whether the victim decides to report the incident. In addition to the limitations imposed by law enforcement agencies are those presented by trends in public underreporting. In fact, some argue that hate crimes are even more dramatically underreported than other Uniform Crime Report offences (Berrill, 1992; Weiss, 1993). Typical reasons for failing to report include fear of retaliation, the sense that nothing could be done, or the sense that the incident was not serious enough to bother police with. Moreover, victims may well fear secondary victimization at the hands of law enforcement officials or perceive that police will not take their victimization seriously.

Given the assumption that "hate crimes hurt more" (e.g., Iganski, 2001, Perry & Alvi, 2011), the failure of police to fully address hate crime is problematic. It may have the effect of further exacerbating the anxiety created by the initial incident. It is important, then, to document the wide-ranging impacts so that police, prosecutors, and judges will understand that it is not just individuals whose needs must be considered but also those of their immediate and extended communities.

The Impacts of Hate Crime

Hate crimes are very different in their effects, as compared to their non-bias-motivated counterparts. Specifically, British scholar Paul Iganski (2001, p. 629) contends that there are five distinct types of harm associated with hate crime:

- ▶ harm to the initial victim;
- ▶ harm to the victim's group;
- ▶ harm to the victim's group (outside the neighbourhood);
- ▶ harm to other targeted communities; and
- ▶ harm to societal norms and values.

Individual Impacts

Research suggests that first and foremost among the impacts on the individual is the physical harm: bias motivated crimes are often characterized by extreme brutality (Levin & McDevitt, 1992). Violent personal crimes motivated by bias are more likely to involve extraordinary levels of violence. Additionally, the empirical findings in studies of the emotional, psychological, and behavioural impact of hate crime are beginning to establish a solid pattern of more severe effect on bias crime victims, as compared to non-bias victims (see, e.g., Herek, Cogan, & Gillis, 2002; McDevitt et al., 2001). Among these impacts:

- ▶ Victims of bias crimes have been attacked for being different, for being misunderstood, and for being hated. Because the basis for their attack is their identity, they may suffer a deep personal crisis.
- ▶ When a bias crime is committed against a member of a minority group, the victim frequently perceives the offender as representative of the dominant culture in society who may frequently stereotype the victim's culture.
- ▶ If their membership in a target group is readily visible, victims of bias crimes may feel particularly vulnerable to a repeat attack. This heightened sense of vulnerability may result in the feeling of hopelessness.
- ▶ Victims may become afraid to associate with other members of the group that has been targeted, or may fear seeking needed services, believing that these actions increase their vulnerability.
- ▶ As a result of the victimization, bias crime victims may respond by more strongly identifying with their group – or conversely, by attempting to disassociate themselves or deny a significant aspect of their identity.

Community Impacts

Beyond these immediate individual effects, however, hate crimes are also "message crimes" that emit a distinct warning to all members of the victim's community: step out of line, cross invisible boundaries, and you too could be lying on the ground, beaten and bloodied (Iganski, 2001). Consequently, the individual fear noted above can be accompanied by the collective fear of the victim's cultural group, possibly even of other minority groups likely to be victims. Weinstein (1992) refers to this as an *in terrorem* effect: intimidation of the group by the victimization of one or a few members of that group (see also Perry & Alvi, 2011).

Hate crimes promote fear and insecurity among minority communities, whether the crimes are based on skin colour, race, religion, ethnic origin, or sexual orientation. Without question, awareness of the potential for hate crime enhances the sense of vulnerability and fearfulness of affected communities. This, after all, is the intent of hate crime – to intimidate and instill fear in the whole of the targeted community, not just the immediate victim. Interestingly, when asked to define hate crime, many participants in my study of community impacts explicitly acknowledged the nature of these "message crimes":

> Hate crimes occur because people have learned to dislike difference. They occur because people want to feel superior to and have power over others. They are probably more likely to be committed by groups of young people who are looking to act out. They are meant to scare everyone, not just the victim. (Asian female)

For many, the message is received loud and clear; they do feel themselves to be equally vulnerable to victimization, and, thus, they are fearful. Upon reading a scenario describing a hypothetical hate crime, an Asian male observed, "I feel for Jim – his safety and well-being. I also think that could've been anyone else leaving that meeting and that we all are vulnerable."

The cumulative impact of hate crime and its *in terrorem* effects can be to reinforce the sense of inferiority or of oppression experienced by affected communities. Indeed, my argument has long been that the intent of hate crime is to reassert the subordination of victims and their communities. In *In the Name of Hate*, I contended that, through bias-motivated violence, perpetrators attempt to reaffirm their dominant identity, their access to resources and privilege, while at the same time limit the opportunities of the victims to express their own needs (Perry, 2001). The performance of hate violence, then, confirms the "natural" relations of superiority/inferiority. It is a form of interpersonal and intercultural expression that signifies boundaries. And, significantly, the boundary is "capable of organizing personal interactions in sometimes lethal ways" (Cornell & Hartmann, 1998, p. 185).

In this context, too, members of vulnerable communities can read the intended message. More significantly, the effect is, in fact, to render them more uncertain about their place in society. It does leave them feeling somehow "less worthy" than the presumptive offender. This is explicit in the following comment by a lesbian in one of my focus groups:

> Whether they were directly or indirectly made towards me, in my opinion, these were hate crimes as they left me feeling lesser than the other person, as they were directed attacks on my self-esteem and confidence. (Lesbian)

This response is relatively common among immediate victims of hate crime. The fact that it is also a sentiment that emerges among vicarious victims speaks to the power of such violence to intimidate and silence whole communities.

Faced with the normativity of fear-inducing violence, members of vulnerable communities learn to negotiate their safety (Mason, 2009). They adopt an array of strategies for managing their vulnerability, often through changes in behavioural patterns. Across studies, participants expressed the necessity to alter their performance of identity in accordance with what they recognized as the socially established rules for "doing difference." They reported changing routine activities, habits, and ways of being in the world: "Even if you ran to escape they still chased after you. I then knew to travel/move in packs with friends. Never walk alone, bring reinforcements/witnesses and cell phone." In this way, people of colour, gay men and lesbians, and others deemed inferior are kept "in their place." Violence reinforces the boundaries – social and geographical – across which they are not meant to step.

Two communities appear to be especially prone to this identity management. Members of LGBTQ communities frequently referred to the effects of fear on their decisions to reveal their sexual orientation to others. A gay male states it succinctly: "I have tried to look 'less gay.'" A lesbian shares similar sentiments: "I constantly challenge homophobic/heterosexist comments or ideals. I sometimes dress more feminine than I'd like, just to break down stereotypes. I'm often perceived as being 'straight' because of this." Both comments reflect the extent to which the fear of crime results in a careful crafting of one's identity so that they are less visible and thus less vulnerable. These statements vividly demonstrate how many LGBTQ participants modify their behavior and alter the way they express themselves to conceal their sexual orientation and thus decrease the possibility of victimization.

Likewise, in the current context of heightened Islamophobia, many Muslims are challenged by the risk of violence. This is particularly true for those who are "visibly" Muslim by virtue of their dress or appearance. This means that Muslim women who are covered have become especially vulnerable to Islamophobic violence. Consequently, managing their own safety – and thus their identities – has become crucial for Muslim women. Significantly, recognizing the visibility represented by the hijab, many women have come to question their choice to be covered. One young Muslim woman provides her assessment of the impacts:

> It makes women more reluctant to wear the hijab or to stand out in that sense. Because they're afraid of what might happen to them if they were to become a visible Muslim and if they were to wear the hijab. So I see a lot of people say, "the reason I don't wear is because I'm afraid. I'm afraid of what people might think. I'm afraid of what people might do. So I keep it to myself."

In this respect, the potential for anti-Muslim violence serves its intended purpose of enforcing appropriate public performances at the very least. Sadly, the risk of victimization often means that victimized communities are forced to prioritize their safety over their expression of identity.

Social Impacts

Hate crime throws into question not only the victim's and the community's identity but also our national commitment to tolerance and inclusion. The persistence of hate crime is a challenge to democratic ideals. It reveals the fissures that characterize its host societies, laying bare the bigotry that is endemic within each. In short, the persistence – and in fact periodic flurries – of hate crime gives lie to the Canadian canon of multiculturalism. The shock and incomprehension expressed by participants in a recent study are also symptomatic of a loss of innocence with respect to Canadian values, for the shock was consistently a reflection of shattered illusions. Illustrative comments like the following have been common across the studies that I have conducted:

> This is a crime. I feel very sad for Jim, but also I feel a sadness for the state of a community where people feel it is appropriate to harass someone because of their orientation (gay male).

> The hurt is strong as in Canada we are supposed to live in society without fear of attack.

Such sentiments highlight the fragility of the mantra of multiculturalism. The underlying ethos is not necessarily the daily reality for vulnerable communities who both experience and fear violence motivated by ideals in direct contrast to those embedded in the national mantra. The messages of inclusion, participation, and engagement are matched by their mirror images in the acts of violence inspired by racism, heterosexism, and other related -isms. It should be noted that in this Canada is not unique. Writing of the Australian paradox, Chris Cunneen (1997) highlights the irony wherein "a liberal democracy, with its commitment to anti-discrimination, simultaneously functions within an institutional framework which can be described as having pervasive racism" (p. 138). The cultural, social, and political mood in Western nations like Canada and Australia uneasily supports both a disabling and enabling environment for hate.

Reason for Optimism: The Mobilizing Effects of Hate Crime

In some cases, hate crime has been a catalyst for positive change. That is, patterns of persistent violence, or highly publicized cases – like the 1998 Matthew Shepard or James Byrd cases in the United States – often have the unintended effect of mobilizing victim communities and their allies. We saw some evidence of this in Ontario in response to the alleged incidents of hate crime against Asian anglers north of Toronto. Indeed, community outcry resulted in the establishment of an inquiry into those events (Ontario Human Rights Commission, 2007, 2008).

The objects of hate violence can and do develop constructive alternatives to the prejudice and violence that confronts them. One First Nations male indicated that hate can be unlearned: "I think it is learned. It is learned partly in our educational system, it is learned in the home and is learned through the media culture. I would suggest that the only good news is that hate can be unlearned." As this suggests, the bigotry that underlies hate crime can be confronted in productive ways.

Whether individually or collectively, there is value in challenging hate crime and the biases that inform it. There were participants who were relatively optimistic about the potential for change and who suggested progressive strategies for harnessing the energy of vibrant communities to counteract both the potential for and the impact of hate crime. For example, one respondent remarked, "This story makes me want to help educate people so that future generations will be more accepting and less afraid. Education is the key to eliminating irrational fears." Indeed, earlier, we noted that respondents claimed to have changed their patterns of behaviour in order to avoid victimization, as did the following Muslim woman:

I had never really worn the hijab before, but for a short period of time, right after 9/11 I started wearing it as like, a sign of defiance, you know? And I like also knew that because it wasn't my style and I wasn't going to keep it on for too long but it was definitely a time when I felt like being more visibly Muslim was necessary for me to deal with the ... all the anti-Muslim sentiments and hate that was going around like in my school and but I remember ... and it wasn't ever directed as me and I wasn't really challenged after that. I just wanted to feel defiance. (Female, Toronto)

One constructive behavioural shift noted by many was that they felt inspired to react at an individual and/or collective level:

In an attempt to promote gay rights and tolerance I donate money to Egale, join protests, have written in local newspapers, questioned charitable/social agencies with regards to their policies and resources for dealing with LGBT community clients. In the scenario above I would help to ensure factual media coverage of the event to shed light on the issue of homophobia/gay bashing – perhaps work with a neighbourhood community group to deal with the issue. (Gay male)

It is these sorts of reactions to the normativity of violence that will ultimately present the greatest defence. To use the moment of victimization to confront and challenge oppression speaks volumes. In particular, it says to the perpetrator that affected communities refuse to "stay in their place" and will instead fight for a reconstructed definition of what that place is. Moreover, such resistance also sends a powerful message of strength and solidarity to the communities themselves.

Keywords

Hate crime, violence, policing, impacts, counter-mobilization

Review Questions

1. What is the difference between legal and sociological definitions of hate crime?
2. List the limitations of hate crime data?
3. How does hate crime impact individuals, communities, and social values?

References

Allen, M., & Boyce, J. (2013). Police-reported hate crime in Canada, 2011. *Juristat*. Ottawa: Statistics Canada. Catalogue no. 85-002-X.

Bell, J. (2002). *Policing hatred*. New York: New York University Press.

Bell, J. (2009). Policing and surveillance. In F. Lawrence (Ed.), *Responding to hate crime* (pp. 31-50). New York: Praeger.

Berrill, K. (1992). Anti-gay violence and victimization in the United States: An overview. In G. Herek and K. Berrill (Eds.), *Hate crimes: Confronting violence against lesbians and gay men* (pp. 19-45). Newbury Park, CA: Sage.

Cornell, S., & Hartmann, D. (1998). *Ethnicity and race: Making identities in a changing world.* Thousand Oaks, CA: Pine Forge Press.

Cunneen, C. (1997). Hysteria and hate: The vilification of Aboriginal and Torres Strait Islander people. In C. Cunneen, D. Fraser, & S. Tomsen (Eds.), *Faces of hate: Hate crime in Australia* (pp. 137-161). Leichhardt, NSW: Hawkins Press.

Gilmour, G. (1994). *Hate-motivated violence.* Ottawa: Department of Justice Canada.

Hate Crimes Community Working Group. (2006). *Addressing hate crime in Ontario.* Toronto: Attorney General and Minister of Community Safety and Correctional Services.

Herek, G., Cogan, J., & Gillis, J. R. (2002). Victim experiences in hate crimes based on sexual orientation. *Journal of Social Issues, 58*(2), 319-339.

Iganski, P. (2001). Hate crimes hurt more. *American Behavior Scientist, 45*(4), 627-638.

Janhevich, D. (2001). *Hate crime in Canada: An overview of issues and data sources.* Ottawa: Statistics Canada.

Levin, J., & McDevitt, J. (1992). *Hate crimes: The rising tide of bigotry and bloodshed.* New York: Plenum.

Lim, H. A. (2009). Beyond the immediate victim: Understanding hate crimes as message crimes. In P. Iganski (Ed.), *Hate Crimes: The consequences of hate crime* (pp. 107-122). Westport, CT: Praeger.

Mason, G. (2009). Body maps: Envisaging homophobia, violence, and safety. In P. Iganski (Ed.), *Hate Crimes: The consequences of hate crime* (pp. 49-72). Westport, CT: Praeger.

McDevitt, J., Balboni, J. Garcia, L., & Gu, J. (2001). Consequences for victims: A comparison of bias- and non-bias motivated assaults. *American Behavioral Scientist, 45*(4), 697-711.

McDonald, S., & Hogue, A. (2007). *An exploration of the needs of victims of hate crime.* Ottawa: Department of Justice.

McKenna, I. (1994). Canada's hate propaganda laws – A critique. *Ottawa Law Review, 26,* 159-183.

McLachlin, B. (2003). *The civilization of difference.* LaFontaine-Baldwin Address. Toronto: The Institute for Canadian Citizenship.

Noelle, M. (2002). The ripple of effect of the Matthew Shepard murder: Impact on the assumptive worlds of members of the targeted group. *American Behavioral Scientist, 46*(1), 27-50.

Noelle, M. (2009). The psychological and social effects of anti-bisexual, anti-gay, and anti-lesbian violence and harassment. In P. Iganski (Ed.), *Hate Crimes: The consequences of hate crime* (pp. 73-106). Westport, CT: Praeger.

Nolan, J., Bennett, S., & Goldenberg, P. (2009). Hate crime investigations. In F. M. Lawrence (Ed.), *Hate Crimes: Responding to hate crimes* (Vol. 5) (pp. 71-88). Westport, CT: Praeger.

Ontario Human Rights Commission. (2007). *Fishing without fear: Report on the inquiry into assaults on Asian Canadian anglers.* Toronto: Ontario Human Rights Commission.

Ontario Human Rights Commission. (2008). *Preliminary findings: Inquiry Into assault on Asian Canadian anglers.* Toronto: Ontario Human Rights Commission.

Parker, R. (2009). Police training. In F. M. Lawrence (Ed.), *Hate crimes: Responding to hate crimes* (Vol. 5) (pp. 51-70). Westport, CT: Praeger.

Perry, B. (2001). *In the name of hate.* New York: Routledge.

Perry, B., & Alvi, S. (2011). "We are all vulnerable": The *in terrorem* effects of hate crime. *International Review of Victimology, 18*(1): 57-72.

Roberts, J. (1995). Disproportionate harm: Hate crime in Canada. Ottawa: Department of Justice.

Schaffer, M. (1996). Criminal responses to hate-motivated violence: Is Bill C-41 tough enough? *McGill Law Journal, 41,* 199-250.

Weinstein, J. (1992). First amendment challenges to hate crime legislation: Where's the speech? *Criminal Justice Ethics, 11*(2), 6-20.

Weiss, J. (1993). Ethnoviolence's impact upon and response of victims and the community. In R. Kelly (Ed.), *Bias Crime* (pp. 174-185). Chicago: Office of International Criminal Justice.

Suggested Readings

Allen, M., & Boyce, J. (2013). Police-reported hate crime in Canada, 2011. *Juristat.* Ottawa: Statistics Canada. Catalogue no. 85-002-X.

Hate Crimes Community Working Group. 2006. *Addressing hate crime in Ontario.* Toronto: Attorney General and Minister of Community Safety and Correctional Services.

Perry, B. (Ed.). (2009). *Hate crime.* 5 Vol. Westport, CT: Praeger.

Disability Harassment: Disabling Violence in the Ontario Workplace

Chapter 4

S.B. Barak

Learning Objectives

In this chapter you will...

► recognize the concept of harassment as on the continuum of violence

► learn about critical perspectives of employment issues and health

► define and understand key issues related to disability harassment in the workplace

► identify key legislation pertinent to harassment in the Canadian workplace

► gain an understanding of the ramifications of disability harassment on individuals and organizations

---

Introduction

This chapter looks at harassment as a significant form of violence in the workplace and specifically covers issues related to disability discrimination, human rights, and employment law, including the duty to accommodate, since these often work in lockstep in the course of a disabled person's work-related experience (Malhotra, 2006). Given that in our society most people want to work, and that most will experience disability at some point in their lives either firsthand or vicariously through someone close to them, issues of disability and the workplace are of broad concern (Schriner, 2001; Simon, 2013). As Holzbauer and Berven (1996) eloquently declared, "Now is the time for experience, counselling practice, research, and public policy to come together to understand the problem of disability harassment, find ways to combat its occurrence, and identify strategies to assist individuals who must deal with its effects" (p. 482). As we examine developments since that call to action, it is evident that there has been movement towards this end. Let us review this issue to learn more about it and how we can continue to make strides towards a more accessible and inclusive workplace in Ontario and Canada.

Shakespeare (2006) observed that, "Perhaps disabled scholars often emphasize the dimension of disability which they most directly experience" (p. 4). Having not only witnessed the pain of numerous victims of workplace disability harassment in Ontario, as a counsellor, caseworker, and coworker, but having endured the lived experience of harassment after sustaining a workplace injury, my observations confirm the rapidly growing body of research that decries the phenomenon of disability harassment as epidemic (Namie, 2003, 2007; Shannon, 2004). Although there are potential pitfalls in research with a personal connection, in the case of critical disability studies, a case can also be made in support of the rallying cry, "Nothing about us without us" (Charleton, 1998).

Terminology remains an active topic of debate within the field. Despite the undoubtedly good intention of the people-first language found in Ontario legislation (OHRC, 2007), I have become more accustomed to the term *disabled people* (vs. *people with disabilities*) in alignment with the social model perspective of disablement (Barnes & Mercer, 2010, 1990).

Overview: Mapping the World of Workplace Harassment

Internationally, people are increasingly recognizing and responding to the rampant problem of violence at work and emphasizing that violence can no "longer be accepted as a normal part of any job" (Chappell & Di Martino, 2006, p. 296). Hilgert (2009) charges that workers' health and safety "constitute a major human rights crisis" and that "work-related injury and illness indicate a staggering global problem" (p. 43). Although the literature on harassment in the employment context is growing along with the burgeoning number of incidents reported, a gap still exists regarding disability harassment, which reflects what Saxton (2009) notes as a "disturbing evidence of tolerance in our society for certain kinds of violence directed at people with disabilities" (p. 4). The International Labour Organization (ILO) refers only specifically to the grounds of sexual and racial harassment in the workplace (Rogers & Chappell, 2003), echoing the evolution of legal advances that developed first on those axes to later influence disability activism. Other works on human rights have also neglected disability issues (Devine, Hansen, & Wilde, 1999; O'Byrne, 2003), which is a reflection of the marginalization of disabled people, especially in the wider world of work.

What is Disability Harassment?

Harassment exists on a "toxic continuum" that ranges "from incivility to violence" (Ghosh, Jacobs, & Reio, 2011, p. 3; Hollomotz, 2013). It is recognized as a pervasive problem in relation to the regular mistreatment of disabled people in particular (Saxton, 2009; Sobsey, 1994). Stigma and its attendant effects of othering have been present as long as recorded history, and since ancient times disabled people have been portrayed as animalistic and disentitled (Fawcett, 2008; Stiker, 1999). This stigmatization is often at the root of the discrimination that spawns violence and harassment against those who do not readily fit the labour market's image of the "ideal worker" (Foster & Wass, 2012, p. 705).

Disability harassment is a neglected issue in disability law. The term *disability harassment* first appeared in the professional literature only in 1993 (Holzbauer & Berven, 1996, p. 479). While the phrase disability harassment may be relatively new, the experience of violence generally and harassment specifically has been a long-standing problem for disabled people in a wide range of organizational settings (Ravaud & Stiker, 2001). On the legal front, since the early 2000s, disability harassment cases pertaining to primary and secondary education settings have been somewhat successful, but, overall, for the "the abled-disabled" in the work world, the picture has been far bleaker (Garland-Thomson, 1997). While the acceptance of disabled people's right to an education has been more readily accepted in society and the courts, it appears that the recognition of disabled people's right to work for an income has lagged (Weber, 2007). Employment is an important social determinant of health. That is, employment affects one's health and well-being and ability to participate as a productive member of society (Mikkonen & Raphael, 2010).

The Canadian Human Rights Act and provincial human rights legislation prohibit discrimination on protected identifiable grounds, including disability. According to the Ontarians with Disabilities Act (ODA) (2001), *disability* means:

(a) any physical disability, infirmity, malformation or disfigurement that is caused by bodily injury, birth defect or illness
(b) a condition of mental impairment or developmental disability
(c) learning disability or dysfunction in one or more of the processes involved in understanding or using symbols or spoken language
(d) mental disorder
(e) injury or disability for which benefits were claimed or received under the insurance plan established under the Workplace Safety and Insurance Act (WSIA), 1997. (OHRC, 2008b, pp. 64-65)

Harassment and Intimidation at Work

McMahon and Shaw (2005) describe disability intimidation as equivalent to harassment but belonging more distinctly to the workplace domain. Disability intimidation includes "bothering, tormenting, troubling, ridiculing or coercing a person because of a disability" (McMahon and Shaw, 2005, p. 139). These issues may manifest in harsher performance standards, stricter surveillance or disciplining, undesirable work assignments, toleration of unwelcome verbal abuse, comments, or threats. The Canadian Centre for Occupational Health and Safety (CCOHS, 2007) subsumes intimidation under its definition of harassment: "any behaviour that demeans, embarrasses, humiliates, annoys, alarms or verbally abuses a person and that is known or would be expected to be unwelcome. This includes words, gestures, intimidation, bullying or other inappropriate activities (p. 2).

Bullying and Mobbing

The CCOHS (2007) elaborates on bullying and mobbing in the workplace as forms of mistreatment that negatively impact the credibility or personal well-being of an employee, often carried out by a person in authority whose actions may "humiliate, demoralize or otherwise undermine" (p. 90) the targeted individual. Mobbing is similar; however, the offensive behaviours are carried out by a group. Often including patterns of behaviour that may be subtle, these behaviours serve to "exclude, punish, and otherwise humiliate the intended victim" (p. 90). Comments in the line of constructive feedback that are meant to assist an employee would not usually be considered a form of harassment. Warning signs of crossing the line include unwelcome communication in any format (verbal, written, gestures) or actions detrimental to the target, such as starting rumours about him or her, criticizing him, isolating or excluding her, and taking credit for or sabotaging his or her work (p. 91).

Often the bully may have authority over the victim in the hierarchy of the organization (Yamada, 2000), although it must be acknowledged that mobbing can flow laterally and upward as well as downward. Actions characteristic of bullying management may include intentionally setting unrealistic goals, ignoring or blocking requests, deliberately changing work guidelines or areas of responsibility, and unwarranted punitive behaviour (CCOHS, p. 92).

Stigma and Disability Harassment

Chan et al. (2005) sought to anatomize what animates workplace disability discrimination, comparing their findings to the available literature on attribution theory, which looks at common perceptions of various types of what they term impairments. There were more cases of perceived discrimination against people with conditions that also bear more stigma such as mental illness and HIV/AIDS than against conditions such as cancer or cardiovascular disease. When disabilities are functional but not visible, there is an assumption of normality that breeds a suspicion of malingering when productivity varies disappointingly from expectation (Garland-Thomson, 1997). Although disclosure is necessary in order to obtain accommodations for medical reasons, stereotypes may bear stigma, and this divulgence, consequently, can create more issues than solutions (Hall, 2008; MacPherson, 2006).

There appears to be a shift internationally towards recognizing the social model of disability (simply put, the idea that society creates barriers that disable a person with impairments, and it is these barriers that should be eliminated) as opposed to the long-reigning medical model, which focuses on rehabilitating the individual to fit the prevailing conception and structures of the normate. This broad turn was signaled by the UN Convention on the Rights of Persons with Disabilities (CRPD), which has been in force since May 2008. It consciously omits the use of the word *special*, indicating the real understanding that disabled people may require accommodation but their needs are the same as all people have. The CRPD also extends the right to work to all forms of employment, including sheltered workshops, which may not have previously been covered by employment legislation (Bruyère & Murray, 2009, p. 218; Harpur, 2012).

Paradoxical Harassment: Bullying Competence and Disability

Research shows that those targeted are often highly regarded, principled, competent at their jobs, and typically cooperative by nature. Yamada (2000) explains that bullies are usually of higher status within an organization and that targets are usually nice people, vulnerable, and "the bold, best, and brightest" (p. 482). In other words, the harassment, which is meant to force the targets out by making the working environment intolerable, is in part provoked by the fact that the targets do nothing to merit dismissal. Paradoxically, researchers have long recognized that competent, independent disabled people tend to engender a reaction of intolerance by normates more than those who appear more vulnerable and conforming to charity-based stereotypes (Katz, 1981). Fine and Asch (1988) further enumerate studies that indicate that non-disabled people appear to feel more unease in dealing with a disabled person who manages his or her work competently than one who fills the previsioned handicapped role and needs help. Disabled people who defy the role of grateful subservient and pursue self-actualization beyond others' expected conceptions may find their efforts at advancement stymied, often by subtle means. This is consonant with the striking number of related Canadian legal cases rising out of elite university and academic settings (Chouinard, 1995; *Memorial University v. Matthews*, 1994). Typically, the employer may use the idea of bona fide occupational requirements or proffer the rationalization of operational needs to deflect charges of discrimination in declining employee requests for training or enhanced opportunities within the organization, vacation time, and leaves of absence.

Intersecting Identities

Although employers and employees alike often tout the value of diversity, they often fail to acknowledge that growing diversity also brings the potential for conflict and bullying, especially when appropriate conflict management strategies are not in place (OECD, 2009; Wilson, 1996; Yamada, 2000). It is widely emphasized that teaching tolerance and consciously creating respectful environments where the dignity of all is fostered will promote a positive outcome in allaying the possibility of harassment occurring or being tolerated (Wilson, 1996). It is worth noting that in seeking to develop equal relationships between those of the dominant normate (Garland-Thomson, 1997) and others such as disabled people, the idea of people meeting as equals is critical. By definition, a superior in an organizational hierarchy has an unequal advantage in terms of power and prestige, hence the propensity for bullies to be bosses (Weber, 2007; Yamada, 2000).

Harassment may be an outgrowth of discrimination, albeit not an inevitable one. Discrimination may be considered built-in by definition if it is in fact disability-based, which parallels gender (whether male, female, or otherwise) harassment. Simi Linton (1998) points out that society tends to ascribe similar characteristics to women and people with disabilities: dependency, emotionality, passivity, lack of mature judgment. In fact, women and girls are reported to be the largest group in the global disability population, and their abuse "is a problem of epidemic proportions" (Blanck, Adya, & Reina, 2007, p. 95). Disabled women are most often unemployed, and when they do work, they are often "doubly disadvantaged" (OHRC, 2001, p. 18) and experience unequal conditions (Schriner, 2001), from hiring to training to promotion. Furthermore, disability organizations report that disabled women are often subject to harassment at work (Blanck, Adya, & Reina, 2007; Carr, Huntley, & MacQuarrie, 2004; England, 2002; O'Hara, 2004). Compounding and confounding the issue of which identifier triggers harassment when a person can be identified under more than one protected ground, Lennard Davis (2002) describes the pervasiveness of the assumption that violence against a member of a racial minority with a disability is because of race, when the violence could have been disability-motivated.

Malhotra (2006) reported that the labour market participation rate had actually worsened for disabled people in Canada from 1991 to 1996, based on census data, with disabled Aboriginal people faring far worse than other disabled men and women. Overall, disabled Aboriginal people were only half as likely as non-disabled people to be employed and to sustain full-time employment. Similarly, this statistic bears out in the fact that disabled people are doubly more likely to live in poverty than those who are non-disabled. Although discrimination against various nationalities and ethnicities may wax and wane with subsequent waves of immigration, disabled people have historically been vulnerable to scapegoating and exclusion across many cultures, time, and geographical locations (Ravaud & Stiker, 2001; Stiker, 1999).

Vulnerable Populations

Workplace harassment may become an entrenched pattern for those disabled people with a history of abuse, who may stay too long in dysfunctional situations and have a higher tolerance and even normalized expectation of violence (Flannery, 2004; Sobsey, 1994). They may be reluctant to leave what they may yet regard as a relatively stable position and have to face another uncertain job search. Having learned early to deny their own thoughts, feelings, and perceptions, and that addressing or protesting violence may only yield more violence, long-victimized individuals may display what has been characterized as learned helplessness and be ineffective at self-advocacy or even accessing and trusting potential allies. When subjected to ongoing harassment one may lose the capacity to cope effectively over time; there is a synergism between stress and the aggravation of other disabilities, each in turn exacerbating the other in a truly vicious cycle. Iwasaki and Mactavish (2005) confirm "greater perceived abuse risk or vulnerability among women with disabilities" (p. 204) and assert that employment-related stress, including harassment, specifically contributes to elevated physical and psychological fatigue, intensifying hardships in accomplishing daily living activities.

The Impact of Trauma

Harassment often causes serious trauma, including low morale, stress, anxiety, and inability to work, and therefore warrants the clear support of the law in terms of enforcement and enhancement of maximum legal remedies (Cantin, 2000). The trauma of harassment often results in further disablement in the form of medical conditions from high blood pressure to digestive problems to depression or PTSD (Cantin, 2000; Yamada, 2000). It is well documented that the effects of harassment may even drive a victim to suicide (Cantin, 2000; Vega & Comer, 2005; Yamada, 2000), and it is noteworthy that "less direct kinds of harassment are at least as harmful if not more so than serious types of direct harassment due to the frequency and insidiousness of indirect harassment behaviour" (Holzbauer & Bergen, 1996, p. 481). Harassment, in particular by a supervisor, has also been linked to an employee's self-medication to alleviate anxiety and/or depression resulting from the feelings of powerlessness and lack of control over his or her life that this abuse induced (Richman et al. 1997). According to some researchers, harassment is a more "devastating problem for employees than all other work-related stresses put together" (Thomas, 2005, p. 286). Harassment is a cause of cognitive impairment that makes an individual unable to focus on his or her job and therefore lowers his or her levels of performance. In other words, harassment as a phenomenon itself may create disability where there was none before.

Considering the Toll

Despite attention to the notion that "social justice in the workplace is at least as much about the quality of social relationships as it is about statistical effects" (England, 2003, p. 429), disabled people have experienced the least progress of any other group covered by the Employment Equity Act. Of the four designated groups covered by the act (women, people with disabilities, Aboriginal peoples, and visible minorities), people perceived to have mental health issues are often the most stigmatized and fare the worst (p. 430). This is a crucial notion in relation to legal ramifications because pursuing justice in court or other formal settings may subject the victim to a hostile cross-examination that may biologically re-traumatize them, although sometimes survivors undertake this process idealistically in the belief that it may help others (Herman, 1997). Public costs and private gains must be carefully measured; some consider the pursuit of justice might come at too high a price (Matsakis, 1996). Considering the toll that harassment has already taken on a victim, and the frequency of resulting depression with its attendant potential for suicide, legal remedies must not be taken lightly, and it would be good practice to ascertain that appropriate additional supports are accessible for a plaintiff. Bearing in mind that disabled people are disproportionately at lower income levels globally, including in all Canadian provinces, they would also likely be at a disadvantage by not being able to retain private legal counsel in the event that this would be required.

Regardless of venue, and despite rules against reprisal, people may fear the repercussions of pursuing their rights in a legal forum on their long-term employability. Many feel that the blame-the-victim mentality may result in their being tainted and impact their ability to obtain references and present well on their résumé and in subsequent interviews in a future job search, should their work environment be so poisoned that there is no going back. While it is understandable that people choose not to pursue legal means to fight harassment due to the toll it may extract, as a matter of principle, to give up and go away as the harassment intended could be said to be the wrong thing in that it enables abuse to continue not only unimpeded but perhaps empowered. Still, if the ultimate goal for an individual is rewarding employment, a person may choose to forego the battle, fearing it may cost too dearly in relation to their long-term career prospects (Weber, 2007).

A Business Perspective for Employers

Those who promote the hiring of disabled people argue that, in light of projected labour shortages, this group represents an overlooked but valuable pool of potential workers. Disabled people often make competent and reliable workers and the cost of accommodations and benefits is rarely significant (Fernandez, 2005). When discussing harassment, business often suggests that bullying has a negative impact on productivity due to increasing absenteeism and turnover and may lead to a violent workplace incident. There seems to be an emphasis on addressing bullying not so much because it is morally wrong and harmful to the victim but because the victim might be dangerously provoked and create a safety issue for others (Smith, 2000). It is no secret that there is a cynical suspicion that enhanced legislation against harassment may spur spurious complaints from individuals who are simply seeking time off with pay and that compliance with legislation is motivated by the impetus to reduce potential liability. Thus, businesses approach the issue of harassment from a risk management perspective to avoid the quandaries of legal claims, in particular for wrongful termination both by victims as well as by those fired for committing harassing behaviour (Gonzalez, 2008). Organizations are well-advised to recognize that harassment is absolutely unacceptable through education, training, and mass communications (Kirewskie, 2002).

Workplace Roles and Responsibilities: A Closer Look at Accommodation

An accommodation is an adjustment provided so that a disabled person is not disadvantaged. An employer is generally required to provide accommodation to the point of undue hardship (Malhotra, 2003). A central principle of accommodation is that of dignity and respect, yet it is not uncommon that a request for accommodation may trigger a cascade of events that engender and escalate disability harassment. Such a request by definition entails disclosure and, in the case of disability, may render an employee vulnerable, particularly in instances where the disability is "invisible," such as in the case of a mental or learning disability, chronic illness, or addiction. Employers may fear that granting accommodations in such cases may trigger a flood of requests from other employees or create resentment by others who view these arrangements as unfairly privileging their co-workers. In fact, this kind of accommodation – that which might benefit many people in general – is least likely to be freely granted (Roberts, 2003). Confidentiality becomes an issue as situations are discussed in a variety of venues, and conflicts may ensue in a less than cooperative climate, not uncommonly in these tough times where it is a given that people are under pressure to deliver. In a scenario where a job modification results in redistribution of tasks to another employee and therefore increases that person's workload, this burden could conceivably make for strained relations over time. Roberts (2003) recounts one abhorrent story of a case where instead of installing an automatic door, a company relegated door-opening duty for a disabled person to different employees on a rotating basis. Appallingly, one "door lady" demanded: "If you want the door opened, bark like a dog" (p. 149).

According to the OHRC (n.d.b), employers, unions, and disabled people all share responsibility for working together in a collaborative process to ensure that the accommodation process will be effectively and appropriately accomplished. Theoretically, everyone involved should cooperatively share information and actively seek solutions, again without reprisals. However, making this happen is not always straightforward, friendly, and timely (Hilborn, 2007; Uppal, 2005). The person requesting accommodation on the basis of disability will need to disclose certain information that will likely involve providing medical documentation. The *Keays* case (*Honda v. Keays*, 2008) illustrates that the manner in which medical documentation is obtained may descend into harassment, and cooperative discussions may feel more like a pretence to gather information for the employer's rather the employee's benefit. That harassment often attends the process of accommodation speaks to the issues that materialize when policy must be put into practice (Rayside & Valentine, 2007). Furthermore, while these testimonials are usually required for accommodation, the price of this support is the necessity of adopting the sick role and becoming a patient again, in the realm of the medical model, rather than a citizen with full rights and participation (McColl, Boyce, & Shortt, 2006).

Intimidation and harassment are reportedly rife in conjunction with reporting a workplace injury or illness, and there are many cases of terminations or disciplining of workers who complain (Hilgert, 2009). Perhaps it is to be accepted that business itself is by nature at odds with prioritizing workers' health and safety as a necessary obstacle to profit. Therefore, international human rights law, including the Universal Declaration of Human Rights and the International Covenant on Economic, Social and Cultural Rights, holds governments responsible for the protection of working conditions that are fair, safe and healthy (Hilgert, 2009).

The Legal Arena

Since the heart of the issue of disability harassment is that it is a human rights issue rooted in discrimination detrimental to health, welfare, and well-being, the mainspring of related current legislation is undoubtedly influenced by the renowned United Nations Declaration of Human Rights, born out of the ashes of the ultimate atrocities and crimes against humanity of the Second World War, including the deliberate experimentation on and extermination of disabled people (Friedlander, 2001). Bickenbach (2001) argues that broad visions need to be framed so that their means of implementation are also delineated and that there will be a subsequent follow up and accounting of outcomes. Therefore, we see that international law must be filtered down to national and provincial legal arena. Harassment complaints are frequent in Canada in relation to human rights statutes and frequently involve serious workplace discipline that may have as much impact on an employee as a criminal conviction (Adell, 1993). However, the fact that the problem of harassment is so rampant may ironically work against a plaintiff in court. Unfortunately, judges have used the argument that a negative situation is common in order to mitigate its perception as of a grievous nature (Waterstone & Stein, 2008).

Canadian Legislation

In 2004, Quebec was the first Canadian province to specifically include psychological harassment as workplace violence when it passed a law mandating employers to take reasonable action to prevent and stop it for all workers, irrespective of protected grounds. Saskatchewan amended its Occupational Health and Safety Act (OHSA) to explicitly expand the definition of harassment to encompass psychological harassment as well as physical violence in 2007. In Ontario, Bill 168, the Ontario Health and Safety Amendment Act (Violence and Harassment in the Workplace) went into force in 2010 and made applicable to all workers protections that up until then were explicitly related to enumerated grounds. British Columbia has followed with three 2013 WorkSafeBC policies designed to prevent or minimize bullying and harassment. Seminal disability studies scholar and activist, Zola, wrote extensively on disability as ubiquitous. His "vision was of social policy that can successfully benefit all human beings, given the full range of human variation" (Bickenbach, 2001, p. 580). This kind of expansion of rights protections in Canadian legislation to cover all workers is an example of the manifestation of his conception.

Discrimination on protected grounds is prohibited in Canada under the Charter of Rights and Freedoms and the Canadian Human Rights Act. The Ontario Human Rights Commission (OHRC) suggests that many barriers that disabled people face are due to the attitudes of other people and declares that it is essential to dismantle this social aspect of disability. The Ontario Human Rights Code protects the equal rights of disabled people in areas related to employment, including membership in trades or vocational associations, among other areas of life. It is important that in Ontario people are protected from disability discrimination even if only by virtue of perception or association and that the OHRC has worked actively to disseminate relevant information widely and accessibly, in clear language (OHRC, n.d.a, n.d.b). Part and parcel of the right to equal treatment is the right to freedom from harassment in the workplace, which is made explicit in the Ontario Human Rights Code (OHRC, 2007, p. 163). Also spelled out is the right of individuals to claim and enforce their rights under other applicable legislation, such as the Ontarians with Disabilities Act, 2001 and Accessibility for Ontarians with Disabilities Act, 2005 (OHRC, 2007, 2008a), without reprisals, as well as the right to refuse to infringe on another's rights under these Acts. This could come into play, for instance, if a supervisor or other worker is directed by their management superior to deal with another employee in a way that might itself comprise a violation of the Act. Both Acts specify that in the event that "an accessibility standard or any other regulation conflicts with a provision of any other Act or regulation, the provision that provides the highest level of accessibility for persons with disabilities with respect to ... employment ... shall prevail" (OHRC, 2007, p.

697). The Canada Labour Code provides similar protections for industries that fall under federal, rather than provincial jurisdiction, such as the charter banks, postal service, inter-provincial and international transportation, and broadcasting (Snyder, 2007).

Note that the Workplace Insurance and Safety Act, 1997 provides for loss of earnings, health care, and labour market re-entry benefits in approved claims for people with work-related injuries and disabilities, and that it is possible to file claims for psychological damage due to harassment. This route would preclude the pursuit of other related legal claims for damages due to the no-fault set up of the administrator, the Workplace Safety and Insurance Board (WSIB).

Addressing Gaps: Some Cautions

As discussed, a safe and just workplace is meant to be a human right. Having laws in place shapes the visions that our society will pursue. Laws that enhance the protections of the rights of those protected on certain enumerated grounds tend to be later extended to other groups. Bearing in mind the primacy of universal rights and social justice, it is important that advocates do not fall into the trap of pitting differentiated groups of disabled people against one another. Some writers in the field have suggested that our energy should lie in advocating for the least well-off who are not engaged in a workplace at all, perhaps fearing that complaints will result in keeping more people on the outside from ever entering the workforce in any capacity (Malho-tra, 2006). If dignity is at the essence of claiming our human rights, then it may be argued that disabled people must claim them as full participants in society or risk falling into old paternalistic object-of-pity stereotypes. Yet, in court cases, typically the respondent appeals any decision for the plaintiff, reinforcing the situation that those prepared to fight are in for a lengthy battle that could conceivably prolong the damaging effects of the injuries sustained.

What Will Help? In Pursuit of Solutions

One of the reasons that accommodation is so crucial is that it facilitates disabled people's partic-ipation in the workforce, and over time, integration may in and of itself help change attitudes, as diverse people interact together regularly on an equal basis. More wage subsidy programs could make possible the entry or re-entry of more disabled people into the workplace. England (2003) cites Waddington and Diller's observation that the civil rights model contests the idea that social exclusion is an unavoidable consequence of disability. With the goal of reforming mainstream social institutions to be inclusive rather than ghettoizing disabled people on a paral-lel track, prejudices will attenuate, and the need to resort to legal intervention may decline (p. 436). Studies confirm that formalized, comprehensive equity programs are effective in closing gaps between designated groups and other employees relative to organizations without them (p. 437). Pre-employment and assertiveness training for disabled people has been suggested (L'Institut Roeher Institute, 1995), and this may be advised but we must make sure that a vulner-able person is not made to feel responsible for being victimized. Also, it has been found that confronting harassment directly often does precipitate vituperative retribution and some actually advise against this often recommended step (LeVan & Martin, 2007, p. 156).

Most people who have health insurance benefits obtain it through their employers or social welfare benefits. If a person has a disability that affects stamina and cannot work full time, they may not qualify for employment health benefits but may make too much money to maintain welfare health benefits. This may discourage working for pay and consequently contribute to the marginalization of disabled people. Therefore, more generous alternative government-supported health benefit arrangements could be beneficial.

Similarly, the media could help by disseminating and normalizing the presence of a range of diversely abled people across a spectrum of roles and arenas. Public service announcements and support from politicians and community leaders and educators all have a vital role to play in helping to shape a future where human rights is not merely a lofty declaration but a lived reality. Care must be taken in the area of ethical advocacy; too often in the past, disabled people have had their own organizations and groups usurped or coopted by the mainstream to become an industry of non-disabled people benefiting from disabled people (Russell, 1998).

A sea change may occur as more people recognize that the inclusion of disabled people benefits non-disabled colleagues as well (Waterstone & Stein, 2008), through the creation of a more flexible, compassionate working environment that is often linked to greater productivity and loyalty and reduced absenteeism. Although in an ideal world everyone would do and be good for goodness' sake, sometimes in reality it is more important that people do the right thing, even if for less than noble motivations, than not take right action. Eventually, these new values and behaviours take on a life of their own and, over the course of a generation, become a truly integrated norm rather than an exception, as we have seen in the strides forward with the civil rights and feminist movements.

Areas for Further Action and Research

Freire has stated that "knowledge requires praxis to be genuine" (qtd. in McRuer, 2006, p. 236), but it is easier to take a theoretical position on principle without having to live the aftermath. Support must therefore be clearly implemented from the top down in organizations. The law is an arena formed and dominated by the powerful; those in power often tend to identify with those others also in power. As proponents of the social model would point out, leaders – that is, people with power – make a conscious decision to act in a way that leads others to impose stigma on the person with the disability; it is not the disability that causes the stigma. Therefore, champions must come from on top as well as the grassroots for a movement to progress optimally; the importance of leadership walking the talk and modelling ethical behaviour cannot be overstated for its influence over the rest of an organization (Wiley, 1998). Despite the business case for the inclusion of people with a range of disabilities as part of the fabric of a diverse Canadian workforce, stigma still pervades most organizations, which makes it harder for disabled people to enter and remain attached to the labour force. Thus, legal remedies remain a most powerful force towards disabling prejudice (Waterstone & Stein, 2008). And in Canada, progressive legislation appears to be attentively retuned as more prominent successes for plaintiffs increasingly amass at a pace concurrent with each strengthened piece of legislation, although research will be required to follow this trend. It will also be interesting to see if other provinces update their own workplace violence and harassment policies. An updated and closer look at the interplay of intersectionalities, discrimination, violence, and harassment would also be a welcome addition to the literature, and an examination of disability harassment among women at work might be another area for further investigation (Mizrahi, 2004).

Conclusion

At the heart of this topic and much of our critical discourse is the centrality of values to perspective and how these values influence everything from everyday actions to policies and procedures to legislation and its enactment. Changing legislation means that its impact needs to be reassessed on a regular basis; updates bring a concomitant need to re-conceptualize progress in the specific arena of employment-related disability harassment. As with accommodation, policies and strategies that are helpful with disabled people are transferable and generalizable throughout the workforce, and it will be interesting to see if new provincial legislation against violence and harassment in the workplace affects harassment related to disability or other protected grounds, just as "by protecting and respecting the dignity of others our own dignity is enhanced" (Allen, Crasnow, & Beale, 2007, p. v).

Despite the limitations of the formal law as a route to social change, the law plays a vital part in the vanguard towards the elimination of disability discrimination and harassment in the world of work. Legal change may propel changes in behaviour due to fears of liability, but over time attitudes will also change as more disabled people enter the public sphere and participate there as equals. It is my hope that this exploration may serve as a meaningful step towards consolidating knowledge as a prelude to ongoing advocacy in the area of human rights and social justice for disabled people in the workplace. Let us capitalize on the momentum of recent legislation against workplace violence and harassment to achieve tangible gains in actualizing the vision of respect for all in a fair and inclusive workplace environment in concert with our Canadian Charter, with dignity as its lodestar (Shannon, 2007).

Keywords

Disability, harassment, accommodation, social model of disability, social determinants of health

Review Questions

1. Why is it important to recognize harassment as a form of violence?
2. Discuss the longstanding phenomenon that disabled people have been targets of discrimination, violence, and harassment.
3. In a 2010 speech to the Ontario Bar Association, M. David Lepofsky remarked that "persons with disabilities [are] the weirdest minority of all. This is because we are the minority of everyone — we are the minority of everyone because everyone either has a disability, or gets one if they live long enough" (p. 1). Discuss your ideas about intersecting identities and the longstanding issue of stigmatization of disabled people in light of the assertion that we must all be negatively affected by this issue.
4. What is a social determinant of health and how significant is [safe] employment as a factor?
5. The Accessibility for Ontarians with Disabilities Act requires that the province be fully accessible in terms of goods and services, facilities, and employment by the year 2025. What are barriers to fully accessible employment and how do they tie in to the issue of disability discrimination and harassment?

Author Acknowledgement

Ideas presented in this chapter have been developed from my unpublished paper, "Of Tort and Trauma: The Vital Nature of Legal Remedies to Address and Redress Disability Harassment in the Workplace," presented in 2010 at the National University of Ireland at Galway, the Osgoode Hall Graduate Law Student Association, Toronto, and the York Institute for Health Research, Toronto, and at Liverpool Hope University, UK, in 2011, and from my poster "'Bark Like a Dog': Disability Harassment in the Workplace," presented in 2013 at the UCLA Disability Symposium and the Critical Disability Studies Student Association Conference at York University, Toronto.

References

Adell, B. (1993). Workplace disciplinary rules and procedures in Canada. *International Labour Review, 132*(5-6), 583-603.

Allen, R., Crasnow, R., & Beale, A. (2007). *Employment law and human rights* (2nd ed.). New York: Oxford University Press.

Barnes, C., & Mercer, G. (2010). *Exploring disability: A sociological introduction* (2nd ed.). Cambridge: Polity Press.

Bickenbach, J. E. (2001). Disability, human rights, law, and policy. In G. L. Albrecht, K. D. Seelman, & M. Bury (Eds.), *Handbook of disability studies* (pp. 565-584). Thousand Oaks, CA: Sage.

Blanck, P., Adya, M., & Reina, M. V. (2007). Defying double discrimination. *Georgetown Journal of International Affairs, (8)*1, 95-104.

Bruyère, S. M., & Murray, B. (2009). The human rights of workers with disabilities. In J. A. Gross & L. Compa (Eds.), *Human rights in labor and employment relations: International and domestic perspectives* (pp. 213-234). Champaign, IL: Labor and Employment Relations Association.

Canadian Centre for Occupational Health and Safety (CCOHS). (2007). *Violence in the workplace: Prevention guide* (3rd ed.). Hamilton, ON: CCOHS.

Cantin, J.-M. (2000). *Abuse of authority in the workplace: A form of harassment.* Scarborough, ON: Carswell.

Carr, J., Huntley, A., & MacQuarrie, B. (2004). *Workplace harassment and violence report.* London, ON: University of Western Ontario, Centre for Research and Education on Violence against Women and Children.

Chan, F., McMahon, B. T., Cheing, G., Rosenthal, D. A., & Bezyak, J. (2005). Drivers of workplace discrimination against people with disabilities: The utility of Attribution Theory. *Work: A Journal of Prevention, Assessment and Rehabilitation, 25*(1), 77-88.

Chappell, D., & Di Martino, V. (2006). *Violence at work* (3rd ed.). Geneva: International Labour Office.

Charleton, J. I. (1998). *Nothing about us without us: Disability oppression and empowerment.* Berkeley: University of California Press.

Chouinard, V. (1995). Like Alice through the looking glass: Accommodation in Academia. *Resources for Feminist Research, 24*(3/4).

Davis, L. (2002). *Bending over backwards: Disability, dismodernism, and other difficult positions.* New York: New York University Press.

Devine, C., Hansen, C. R., & Wilde, R. (1999). *Human rights: The essential reference.* Phoenix, AZ: Oryx Press.

England, K. (2002). Social policy at work? Equality and equity in women's paid employment in Canada. *GeoJournal, (56)*4, 283-294.

England, K. (2003). Disabilities, gender and employment: Social exclusion, employment equity and Canadian banking. *Canadian Geographer, (47)*4, 429-450.

Fawcett, B. (2008). Disability and violence. In B. Fawcett & F. Waugh (Eds.), *Addressing violence, abuse and oppression: Debates and challenges* (pp. 155-162). New York: Routledge.

Fernandez, S. (2005). *Disabilities in the workplace.* American Management Association/ Human Resources Institute.

Fine, M., & Asch, A. (1988). Disability beyond stigma: Social interaction, discrimination, and activism. *Journal of Social Issues, 44*(3), 6-14.

Flannery, R. B. Jr. (2004). *Post-traumatic stress disorder: The victim's guide to healing and recovery* (2nd ed.). Ellicott City, MD: Chevron.

Foster, D., & Wass, V. (2012). Disability in the labour market: An exploration of concepts of the ideal worker and organisational fit that disadvantage employees with impairments. *Sociology, (47)*4, 705-721.

Friedlander, H. (2001). The exclusion and murder of the disabled. In R. Gellately & N. Stoltzfus (Eds.), *Social outsiders in Nazi Germany* (pp. 145-164). Princeton, NJ: Princeton University Press.

Garland-Thomson, R. (1997). *Extraordinary bodies: Figuring physical disability in American culture and literature.* New York: Columbia University Press.

Ghosh, R., Jacobs, J. L., & Reio, T. G. (2011). The toxic continuum from incivility to violence: What can HRD do? *Advances in Developing Human Resources, 13*(1), 3-9.

Gonzalez, G. (2008, January 21). Ontario law targets on-the-job harassment. *Business Insurance.* Retrieved from http://www.businessinsurance.com/cgi-bin/printStory.pl?article_id= 23905

Hall, B. (2008, August 28). Ontario divisional court upholds rights of employees with mental illness. Retrieved from http://www.ohrc.on.ca/en/resources/news/lanecom

Harpur, P. (2012). Embracing the new disability rights paradigm: The importance of the Convention on the Rights of Persons with Disabilities. *Disability & Society, (27)*1, 1-14.

Herman, J. L. (1997). *Trauma and recovery.* New York: Basic Books.

Hilborn, T. (2007). The duty to accommodate: All parties have a responsibility to ensure successful accommodation. *Education Law Journal, (17)*1, 161-167.

Hilgert, J. (2009). A new frontier for industrial relations: Workplace health and safety as a human right. In J. A. Gross & L. Compa (Eds.), *Human rights in labor and employment relations: International and domestic perspectives* (pp. 43-72). Champaign, IL: Labor and Employment Relations Association.

Hollomotz, A. (2013). Disability, oppression and violence: towards a sociological explanation. *Sociology, (47)*3, 477-493.

Holzbauer, J. J., & Berven, N. L. (1996). Disability harassment: A new term for a longstanding problem. *Journal of Counseling and Development, (74)*5, 478-483.

Honda v. Keays. [2008] S.C.J. No. 40, 2008 SCC 39, [2008] 2 S.C.R. 263, [2008] 2 R.C.S. 362, [2008] CLLC para. 230-25, EYB 2008-135085, J.E. 2008-1354, 166 A.C.W.S. (3d)

685, 66 C.C.E.L. (3d) 159, 2008 Carswell, Ont. 3743, 376 N.R. 196, 294 D.L.R. (4th) 577, 239 O.A.C. 299, 92 O.R. (3d) 479, File No.: 31739. Supreme Court of Canada. Retrieved from LexisNexis Quicklaw database.

Iwasaki, Y., & Mactavish, J. B. (2005). Ubiquitous yet unique: Perspectives of people with disabilities on stress. *Rehabilitation Counseling Bulletin, (48)*4, 194-208.

Katz, I. (1981). *Stigma: A social psychological analysis.* Hillsdale, NJ: Lawrence Erlbaum Associates.

Kirewskie, C. (2002). Review of *Abuse of authority in the workplace: A form of harassment, McGill Law Journal, 47,* 469-472. Retrieved from LexisNexis Quicklaw database.

LeVan, H., & Martin, W. M. (2007). Bullying in the U.S. workplace: Normative and process-oriented ethical approaches. *Journal of Business Ethics, 83,* 147-165.

L'Institut Roeher Institute. (1995). *Harm's way: The many faces of violence and abuse against persons with disabilities.* North York, ON: L'Institut Roeher Institute.

Linton, S. (1998). *Claiming disability: Knowledge and identity.* New York: New York University Press.

MacPherson, D. L. (2006). Damage quantification in tort and pre-existing conditions: Arguments for a re-conceptualization. In D. Pothier & R. Devlin (Eds.), *Critical disability theory: Essays in philosophy, politics, policy, and law* (pp. 248-266). Vancouver: University of British Columbia Press.

Malhotra, R. A. (2003). The duty to accommodate unionized workers with disabilities in Canada and the United States. *Journal of Law & Equality, 2*(1), 92-155.

Malhotra, R. A. (2006). Justice as fairness in accommodating workers with disabilities and critical theory: The limitations of a Rawlsian framework for empowering people with disabilities in Canada. In D. Pothier & R. Devlin (Eds.), *Critical disability theory: Essays in philosophy, politics, policy, and law* (pp. 70-86). Vancouver: University of British Columbia Press.

Matsakis, A. (1996). *I can't get over it: A handbook for trauma survivors* (2nd ed.). Oakland, CA: New Harbinger Publications.

McColl, M. A., James, A., Boyce, W., & Shortt, S. (2006). Disability policy making: Evaluating the evidence base. In D. Pothier & R. Devlin (Eds.), *Critical disability theory: Essays in philosophy, politics, policy, and law* (pp. 25-46). Vancouver: University of British Columbia Press.

McMahon, B. T., & Shaw, L. R. (2005). Workplace discrimination and disability. *Journal of Vocational Rehabilitation, 23*(3), 137-143.

McRuer, R. (2006). *Crip theory: Cultural signs of queerness and disability.* New York: New York University Press.

Memorial University of Newfoundland v. Matthews. [1994] N.J. No.446, 1991 St. J. No.4108, Newfoundland Supreme Court – Trial Division. Retrieved from LexisNexis Quicklaw database.

Mikkonen, J., & Raphael, D. (2010). *Social determinants of health: The Canadian facts.* Toronto: York University School of Health Policy and Management. Retrieved from http://www.thecanadianfacts.org/

Mizrahi, R. (2004, May). Hostility to the presence of women: Why women undermine each other in the workplace and the consequences for Title VII. *Yale Law Journal, 113*(7), 1579-1621.

Namie, G. (2003). Workplace bullying: Escalating incivility. *Ivey Business Journal, 68*(2), 1-6.

Namie, G. (2007). The challenge of workplace bullying. *Employment Relations Today, 34*(2), 43-51.

O'Byrne, D. J. (2003). *Human rights: An introduction.* Toronto: Pearson.

O'Hara, B. (2004). Twice penalized: Employment discrimination against women with disabilities. *Journal of Disability Policy Studies, (15)*1, 27-34.

Oliver, M. (1990). *The politics of disablement: A sociological approach.* New York: St. Martin's Press.

Ontario Human Rights Commission. (2001). *An intersectional approach to discrimination: Addressing multiple grounds in human rights complaints.* Toronto: Author. Retrieved from http://www.ohrc.on.ca/english/consultation/intersectionality-discussion-paper.pdf

Ontario Human Rights Commission. (2007). *Ontario labour & employment legislation 2007-2008: An unofficial publisher's consolidation.* Aurora, ON: Canada Law Book.

Ontario Human Rights Commission. (2008a). *Human rights at work* (3rd ed.). Toronto: Carswell Thomson.

Ontario Human Rights Commission. (2008b). *Human rights policy in Ontario* (4th ed.). Toronto: Carswell Thomson.

Ontario Human Rights Commission. (N.d.a). Disability - Workplace Roles and Responsibilities: Fact Sheet. Retrieved from http://www.ohrc.on.ca/en/resources/factsheets/workplace

Ontario Human Rights Commission. (N.d.b). What is disability? Fact sheet. Retrieved from http://www.ohrc.on.ca/en/resources/factsheets/disability1

Ontiveros, M. L. (2009). Employment discrimination. In J. A. Gross & L. Compa (Eds.), *Human rights in labor and employment relations: International and domestic perspectives* (pp. 195-212). Champaign, IL: Labor and Employment Relations Association.

Organisation for Economic Co-operation and Development (OECD), Directorate for Employment, Labour and Social Affairs. (2009, April). *Sickness, disability and work: Keeping on track in the economic downturn.* Retrieved from http://www.oecd.org/dataoecd/42/15/42630589.pdf

Pothier, D., & Devlin, R. (Eds.). (2006). *Critical disability theory: Essays in philosophy, politics, policy, and law.* Vancouver: University of British Columbia Press.

Ravaud, J.-F., & Stiker, H.-J. (2001). Inclusion/exclusion: An analysis of historical and cultural meanings. In G. L. Albrecht, K. D. Seelman, & M. Bury (Eds.). *Handbook of Disability Studies* (pp. 490-514). Thousand Oaks, CA: Sage.

Rayside, D., & Valentine, F. (2007). Broadening the labour movement's disability agenda. In G. Hunt & D. Rayside (Eds.). *Equity, diversity, and Canadian labour* (pp. 156-181). Toronto: University of Toronto Press.

Richman, J. A., Rospenda, M., Nawyn, S. J., & Flaherty, J. A. (1997). Workplace harassment and the self-medication of distress: A conceptual model and case illustrations. *Contemporary Drug Problems, (24)*1, 179-200.

Roberts, P. (2003). Disability oppression in the contemporary U.S. capitalist workplace. *Science & Society, (67)*2, 136-159.

Robichaud v. Canada (Treasury Board)/The Queen [1987] 2 S.C.R. 84. In Cantin (2000), *Abuse of authority in the workplace: A form of harassment* (pp. 22-23). Scarborough, ON: Carswell.

Rogers, K. A., & Chappell, D. (2003). *Preventing and responding to violence at work*. Geneva: International Labour Office.

Roulstone, A., & Mason-Bish, H. (Eds.). (2013). *Disability, hate crime and violence*. New York: Routledge.

Russell, M. (1998). *Beyond ramps: Disability at the end of the social contract*. Monroe, ME: Common Courage Press.

Saxton, M. (Ed). (2009). *Sticks and stones: Disabled people's stories of abuse, defiance and resilience*. Oakland, CA: World Institute on Disability.

Schriner, K. (2001). A disability studies perspective on employment issues and policies for disabled people: An international view. In G. L. Albrecht, K. D. Seelman, & M. Bury (Eds.). *Handbook of Disability Studies* (pp. 642-662). Thousand Oaks, CA: Sage.

Shakespeare, T. (2006). *Disability rights and wrongs*. London: Routledge.

Shannon, D. W. (2007) *Six degrees of dignity: Disability in an age of freedom*. Carp, ON: Creative Bound.

Shannon, H. S. (2004). Workplace incivility and other work factors: Effects on psychological distress and health. In WSIB Research Secretariat. (2009, July 8). *Solutions for workplace change: Findings of completed projects* (p. 142). Retrieved from http://www.wsib.on. ca/wsib/wsibsite.nsf/LookupFiles/DownloadableFileFundedProjectResults/$File/Research Results.pdf

Simon, C. C. (2013, November 1). Disability studies: A new normal. *New York Times*. Retrieved from http://www.nytimes.com/2013/11/03/education/edlife/disability-studies-a-new-normal.html

Smith, G. (2000). *Work rage: Identify the problems, implement the solutions*. Toronto: Harper-Business.

Snyder, R. M. (2007). *The 2008 annotated Canada Labour Code*. Toronto: Thomson Carswell.

Sobsey, D. (1994). *Violence and abuse in the lives of people with disabilities: The end of silent acceptance?* Baltimore, MD: Paul H. Brookes.

Stiker, Henri-Jacques. (1999). *A history of disability*. Ann Arbor: University of Michigan Press.

Thomas, M. (2005). Bullying among support staff in a higher education institution. *Health Education, 105*(4), 273-288.

Uppal, S. (2005). Disability, workplace characteristics and job satisfaction. *International Journal of Manpower, 26*(4), 336-349.

Vega, G., & Comer, D. R. (2005). Sticks and stones may break your bones, but words can break your spirit: Bullying in the workplace. *Journal of Business Ethics, 58*, 101-109.

Waterstone, W. E., & Stein, M. A. (2008). Disabling prejudice. *Northwestern University Law Review, 102*(3), 1351-1378.

Weber, M. C. (2007). *Disability harassment*. New York: New York University Press.

Wiley, C. (1998). Reexamining perceived ethics issues and ethics roles among employment managers. *Journal of Business Ethics, 17*(2), 147-161.

Wilson, T. (1996). *Diversity at work: The business case for equity*. New York: John Wiley.

Yamada, D. C. (2000). The phenomenon of "workplace bullying" and the need for status-blind hostile work environment protection. *Georgetown Law Journal, 88*(3), 475-536.

Violence in the Media and its Social Consequences

Krista Banasiak

Learning Objectives

In this chapter you will...

► explore the similarities and differences between entertainment and news media

► learn about the socially constructed nature of representations of violence in the media

► identify the organizations and individuals involved in the social construction process and understand the factors that influence their decisions

► learn about the social consequences associated with the (mis)representation of violence in the media critically analyze, question, and discuss violent media content

Introduction

In June 2010, the City of Toronto was transformed into something that resembled a military fortress: a large security gate, 3.5 kilometers long and three meters tall, was built around some of the city's most prestigious buildings; police patrolled the streets by the dozens; and individuals were stopped at random for "searches." In total, the *Globe and Mail* (Clark, 2010) reported that $675 million were spent on security and security-related services. Indeed, during the G20 summit, one would have hardly recognized Toronto to be the vibrant, bustling, cultural and business capital of Canada. The public was told that these extreme measures were designed ensure the safety of citizens, tourists and protesters, and to protect those involved with these monumental events, such as visiting dignitaries and state officials. Throughout the summit, the media made it appear as though that money was well spent. Media coverage constructed a narrative that included images of police cars on fire, protesters rioting in the streets, and individuals dressed in black (part of the "Black Bloc") vandalizing the streets of Toronto. Images of acts of violence pervaded the popular media. Readers of print media and television and Internet news viewers were left with the impression that such stringent security measures were necessary.

Yet stories emerged from a new and growing body of sources that countered these media accounts of the events at the G20 summit. "Citizen journalists" struck back to ensure the full story of what took place during those two weeks was told (Greer & McLaughlin, 2010). Protesters on the ground and spectators alike used their iPhones, cameras, and other forms of digital media to document instances of what they considered to be unprovoked police brutality, of peaceful protests needlessly disrupted by security forces, and of searches of "individuals of a suspicious nature" that appeared unfounded. These videos, photos, and stories were uploaded to popular social networking sites, such as Facebook and YouTube. While they did not receive the same attention as reports from organized media, these citizen journalists made a significant impact in the telling of the story of what took place during the summit. Their reports also can be argued to have made a substantial contribution to the opening of investigations into police brutality, human rights violations, and the misuse of laws that continue today, some four years following the G20 (Marin, 2010; McMurtry, 2011; Morden, 2012; O'Reilly & Fleming, this volume).

So, what does this demonstrate to us as scholars of violence and media? Simply put, it shows us that, due to time and resource limitations, the media cannot always portray all sides of a given argument or event. When representing or reporting, they must be selective in what they choose to portray, and their selection process is heavily influenced by a number of factors, including advertising revenue, audience interest, corporate control of news media. This same process takes place in the production of popular entertainment shows (Dowler, Fleming & Muzzatti, 2006).

Creating Violent Content

Crime and violence are central to both news media and entertainment media such as films, true-crime books, and television shows. Violence is now engrained as one of our most popular forms of entertainment. Violence is one of the central pillars of public entertainment in news programs, reality crime shows such as *Cops*, *To Serve and Protect*, or *The First 48*, and crime and forensics shows such as *CSI*, *Criminal Minds*, and *Law & Order*. This chapter will investigate violence in the media, examining both entertainment and news programming. As these are more similar than different, they can be discussed in tandem.

Let us first consider the different forms of television programming in which violence is portrayed. Generally, entertainment media refers to programming that is fictional and produced creatively to entertain an audience. News media is commonly understood to be a more objective account of world events, although this has been disputed by authors who suggest that news programming is biased (Herman & Chomsky, 2002; Lundman, 2003; Wilcox, 2005). These two forms of media appear to have entirely different objectives; however, news and entertainment media are heavily entwined. Although there are often disclaimers at the outset of television shows that distinguish facts or events drawn from actual cases and those portions of the presentation that are fictional in nature, crime shows frequently depend on popular news events as their storylines. Entertainment shows, both fictional and those categorized as "reality television," also boast "realistic" portrayals of crime and justice, yet the programming is highly stylized and edited to attract audience interest (Carmody, 1998).

The making of the news involves a intensely creative process as well. For example, the media has been shown to create and report entirely new forms of violence such as "freeway violence" (a more intense form of "road rage") or "wilding" (a phenomenon in which a group of youths band together to go on a rampage and attack individuals at random) (Best, 1999; Welch, Price, & Yankee, 2004). Furthermore, selecting news stories for coverage is subjective as everyday millions of events transpire all over the world but only a few are reported. Media agents must take into account sources, advertising revenue, and perceived audience interest when deciding which stories to select for reporting. The making of news is a process of human decision making about what will actually comprise the final product shown to the public (Cohen & Young, 1973; McCormick, 2010; Tuchman, 1976; Zelizer, 2005). Crimes that fit a news trend will be selectively reported, which creates the impression that public risk is heightened and causes fear amongst the public that far in exceeds any real danger (Best, 1999; Chiricos, Eschholz, & Gertz, 1997; McCormick, 2010).

Cultivation theory was developed to explain this phenomenon. Proponents of this theory argue that exposure to violent media will affect audience members' attitudes toward the world (Gerbner et al. 2002). Research points to a "cultivation" of fear wherein observers begin to see the world as a dangerous place, and may lose their trust in others. Such scholars argue that those who watch more television are more fearful of the world than those who watch less, as viewing hours upon hours of violent programming may lead audience members to develop a distorted view of the actual amount of crime being committed. Furthermore, the theory predicts that those who consume more hours of violent programming will believe they are more likely to be a victim of violent crimes themselves than the statistics reveal. In the end, the audience's level of fear is disproportionate to the actual risk of violence they face.

Overestimating the threat of violence impacts individuals' sense of safety and may cause people to unnecessarily alter their behaviours. People experiencing heightened senses of fear may refrain from staying out late, avoid certain locations that are perceived as unsafe, install home alarms or join self-defence classes, with the intent of protecting themselves against a less-than-likely violent encounter (Garofalo, 1981a; McCormick, 2010).

Let's consider an example of how this creative process plays out. Most of us think of crime waves as something occurring "on the street" – that a particular type of crime is on the rise that poses a threat to our safety. Yet, as Sacco (2005, p. 8) notes, crime waves are more complex than this common understanding implies. For Sacco, crime waves are social problems that involve an increasing social awareness of a particular crime. Claims-makers, such as politicians, the police, journalists, and the media, influence this process by directing the public's attention to a specific crime or violent act. Thus, a crime wave may take place regardless of whether or not the reported incidences of that crime have increased.

In 1976, New Yorkers expressed a vast public concern about what seemed to be a rise in youth violence against senior citizens. While police records did show an increase in crimes against the older citizens, this increase was true for crime in general; it was not that the elderly were singled out as a target so much as that crime was rising generally. Furthermore, when it came to the most serious crimes, such as homicide, police statistics showed a decrease of 19% in the number of elderly citizens murdered (Fishman, 1978, p. 532). If official statistics showed a significant drop in such crimes, what precipitated the fears of a crime wave against the elderly?

In his classic work on the topic, Fishman (1978) outlines the process through which news workers *create* crime waves. To help reporters and editors navigate through the large volumes of crime and other available news that arrives daily, they turn often to law enforcement as sources of information. Editors "help" by organizing the news into a theme: "a unifying concept [that] presents a specific news event, or a number of such events, in terms of some broader concept" (Fishman, 1978, p. 534). To illustrate, the story of an 82-year-old woman may be reported as "the latest instance of the continuing trend in crimes against the elderly," instead of as an anomaly (p. 534). The police in turn respond by supplying journalists with stories that fit the theme. Eventually, many news stations join in reporting on the topic, creating an environment saturated with stories about crimes against the elderly. Combined newscasts from different media groups leads to the impression that crime against senior citizens is on the rise, when in reality, it is simply the effect of journalistic processes.

A more recent example of a media-constructed crime wave is the public concern in the 1990s over school violence. While a small number of school shootings did take place, the Columbine shooting being the most notorious, the media presented these incidents as a pattern (Kupchik & Bracy, 2009). From 1990 to 2001, the US experienced a steep decrease in the amount of violent youth crime committed. Youths committed only 13% of all violent crime during the second half of the 1990s, yet the American public estimated that youths under the age of 18 committed 50% of all violent crimes (Glassner, 2004). News groups presented school shootings as trends as opposed to rare cases, resulting in a disproportionate amount of public fear. While the number of deaths reported in American schools dropped to a record low in the 1996-97 school year, fear of violence in schools remained high. The media played an active part in constructing this fear by reporting any incident where a child was caught with a gun or made a death threat in school. Furthermore, when the news media referenced the anniversaries of prominent examples, such as the Columbine school shooting, and the potential for such tragedies to reoccur, school violence appeared ubiquitous to the public and the fear of youth violence was kept alive (Glassner, 2004; Kupchik & Bracy, 2009). Therefore, in late 1997, when a handful of school shootings did take place, the public was primed and ready to see this as proof of the trend of continuing violence in schools (Glassner, 1999, p. xv). A similar process underlies the production of moral panics (Cohen, 2002).

Key to the process of news production is classifying stories as newsworthy, or not. Generally, newsworthy events are stories that deviate from our "normal" expectations. They are unusual or strange, stories that involve elite people, stories that are part of an existing "theme" (such as crime against the elderly or youth violence) and those that are shocking, sensationalistic, and dramatic (Hall et al. 1978, p. 53). Therefore, newsmakers rely heavily on stories with severe violence: violent stories entail many of the aforementioned characteristics of "newsworthiness." Here, the old journalistic mantra rings true: if it bleeds, it leads!

Furthermore, news is presented in a dramatic fashion in order to capture the attention of the audience (Doyle, 2006). It can sometimes look more like an entertainment show than news. Dramatic music, video footage of family members in tears, and shots of police and yellow "caution" tape all appeal more to our emotions than to our intellects, creating the entertainment value of the news. What's more, the extent to which audience members distinguish between the news and entertainment shows when making daily decisions about their lives is unclear. The two reinforce each other, and it is their dual impact that is said to exert influence upon the audience (Doyle, 2006). It is next to impossible to tease out the separate effects of news and entertainment programs on audience opinions, worldviews, and behaviours. All things considered, Surette (1998 p. 17) says it may be more appropriate to entitle both forms of programming "infotainment" – a term that denotes the way in which the lines between entertainment and news have been blurred and, hence, so too have the lines between reality and fiction. Therefore, for this analysis, joining these two kinds of media together is sensible. I will use the term "violence in the media" to refer to both journalistic and entertainment portrayals of violence.

Misrepresentation: Violence in the Media vs. Official Crime Statistics

Research has shown that the violence portrayed in the media differs significantly from official crime statistics (Garofalo, 1981b; McCormick, 2010; Perlmutter, 2000). Returning to our example of the G20, many peaceful protests took place where social activists holding sit-ins, walking the streets with signs and chanting, passing out flyers outline their concerns and other forms of awareness-raising activities. Yet, news coverage of the protests at the summit left an entirely different impression. The news did not focus on people singing peace hymns or groups offering "free hugs." Considered by newsmakers to be less newsworthy than activists engaging in criminal activities, these groups were largely ignored. The news inaccurately portrayed the events of those two weeks, making downtown Toronto appear more dangerous than was actually the case.

Examining other forms of crime, the same trend holds true: violent crime is overrepresented while nonviolent crime receives little coverage. As Sacco (2005, p. 84) notes, the major databases used by crime researchers all clearly demonstrate that property crimes, for example, are more prevalent than violent crimes, yet this is not reflected in media portrayals of crime. One study found that in the United States, while murder accounted for only 0.2% of all crime known to police, it was the subject of 26.2% of crime news. Alternatively, nonviolent crime accounted for 47% of crime known to police and made up only 4% of crime news stories (Surette, 1998, p. 68). Research comparing articles from England's most popular newspapers echoed such findings with large discrepancies found between actual occurrences of offences in official statistics and representations of crime in the news (Naylor, 2001).

Of particular interest is the representation of female victims of crime in news media. Of the victims reported in England's most popular newspapers, 55.1% are female, whereas in criminal statistics, women account for only 38.6% of victims of homicide (Naylor, 2001). When violence against women is reported, stories of "stranger violence" (the attack of a woman by someone unknown to her) receive the heaviest coverage. This is out of sync with the reported occurrence of violence against women, most of which occurs in the home or through intimate partner violence (DeKeseredy & Hinch, 1991). These stories of stranger violence are overreported because they make good news: they are shocking, entail negative and graphic consequences, and involve complex detective work that makes for great "stories." The unfortunate consequence is to confirm women's beliefs that the outside world is unsafe while inferring that the private sphere is safe – the exact opposite of what official reports show to be true. And while acts of random violence against arbitrarily chosen women do occur, the media's focus upon them influences public opinion and can have an important impact upon the allocation of funding towards more police night patrol, street lighting and rape alarms, and away from other prevalent social concerns (Naylor, 2001).

Sexual offences and acts of extreme violence such as murder receive the most coverage in both news and entertainment media. The media tends to personify such acts, addressing their individual circumstances while ignoring their broader social contexts (Graber, 1980; Sacco, 2005). In the media, violent offences are attributed to the personal problems of the individuals who commit them, such as the perpetrator's family circumstances, relationship issues, or other problems reported as unique to his or her situation. We see the same phenomenon when looking at crime shows: the stories often revolve around a disturbed perpetrator that is presented as heartless. Episodes of *Law & Order* follow this formula: a deranged, inherently evil individual commits a heinous act, and it is up to the special investigations unit to solve the crime and punish the wrong-doer for his (it is usually his) transgressions via the omnipotent, omnipresent, and worshipped criminal justice system.

Reinforcing Damaging Stereotypes: Violence, Race and Gender

What is missing from these shows and many news reports are discussions surrounding the underlying political, social, and economic issues that contribute to violence. These omissions serve individuals in positions of power in that audiences are encouraged to blame violent behaviour on those who commit it, instead of encouraging the audience to question or attempt to change the larger social structure. Similarly, the media tends to feature a large number of solved crimes: fictional shows are designed to "resolve" the crime, and the news emphasizes resolutions as well. Reporting stories in this manner emphasizes the success of police as crime fighters (Doyle, 2006), legitimizing their role and power.

A consistent finding among researchers is that the media represents individuals in a way that devalues minorities and idealizes the white middle-class demographic (Bjornstrom et al. 2010; Klein & Naccarato, 2003; Welch, Price, & Yankee, 2004). These two groups are presented and represented unevenly by the media. Content analysis clearly demonstrates that systematic inequalities persist in representations of violence among and between races. Studies in both the United States and Canada have shown that victims from minority groups receive less coverage, are less likely to appear on the front pages of newspapers, and are more likely to be on the back pages or to not appear in the paper at all (Gilchrist, 2010; Lundman, 2003; Wortley, 2002). The time spent discussing crime victims in television news is also skewed with white victims having more time devoted to them than members of minority groups. In the United States, black and Hispanic groups continue to be oppressed by media. The same has been found in Canada: stories of black female crime victims tend to be placed on back pages or ignored completely (Wortley, 2002).

Still, in Canada, the most highly disenfranchised groups are Aboriginal. A comparative study of how popular Canadian newspapers depicted white and Aboriginal females who were either missing or murdered revealed that Aboriginal victims had three and a half times less coverage than white victims. White victims were more likely to appear on the front page than Aboriginal victims, whose articles were often hidden amongst advertisements. This lack of coverage is intimately related to the subordinate social, cultural, and political position of Aboriginal peoples in Canada (Gilchrist, 2010).

The previous findings contribute to a hierarchy of victimhood. The media distinguishes between "good" and "bad" victims; "good" victims are those that are judged to be innocent and in need of saving, and "bad" victims are those seen as unworthy or past the point of redemption (Jiwani, 2008). This binary is related to race, class, and gender. White, middle-class women have traditionally occupied the highest position on the list of "good" victims, with white men and then racialized individuals of both genders following thereafter. The tone of the report also differs depending on the race of the victim: reports of white victims are more sympathetic and tend to characterize the situation as "tragic." Gilchrist (2010) found that white victims are associated with adjectives that describe beauty, boldness, and commitment (e.g., "devout," "so beautiful," "imaginative," "promising," and "vibrant"). On the other hand, such adjectives are rarely used to describe victims that are members of a visible minority group.

Media portrayals minimize violence against minority group members and privilege stories of white victimization, yet Caucasians are actually the least likely group to be victimized by violent crime. The media provides an inaccurate picture of vulnerability to violent crime (Bjornstrom et al., 2010). The representation of minority groups is not proportionate to their actual experience of violence, and as we shall see below, this has real-life consequences.

While minority groups are underrepresented as victims of violence, they are overrepresented as perpetrators (Bjornstrom et al., 2010; Buckler & Travis, 2005; Wortley, 2002). When compared to police statistics and self-reports of crimes committed, researchers find that white individuals commit more acts of crime than do other racial categories (except homicide) (Wortley, 2002). Yet a large number of these crimes go unreported by the news. Consequently, it appears as though individuals of African descent account for more of the violent crime than can be verified by police statistics, although this is difficult to prove concretely as crime statistics in Canada cannot, by law, be collected by race.

The media also attributes blame differently to perpetrators dependent on their race. When writing about Caucasian perpetrators, media personnel construct a narrative of individual blame for the act: the perpetrator is reported as defective and thus solely carries the burden of guilt. However, when the perpetrator is a member of a visible minority group, and especially when the perpetrator is black, the media places blame on the shoulders of the black community, demonizing the group by speaking of "black gangs" or "a breed of young killers" (Wilcox, 2005, p. 525). The attribution of blame to an entire racial group contributes to the development of what we in sociology refer to as the "ecological fallacy." This term describes the way in which we sometimes attribute to individuals characteristics that have been said to describe a group. It is the false belief that an individual embodies all attributes associated with the group of which he or she is a member. In this situation, it can have negative consequences as individuals of African descent may be unfairly judged based on popular media perceptions as opposed to by their personal character.

Masculinity has generally been associated with violence, aggression, and dominance, but there exists here a distinction between racial groups as well: the media normalizes white male violence, representing it as part of "being a man." Alternatively, black male violence is often described as "exceptional" and "vicious," a more extreme kind of violence than is expected by the norms of masculinity. Black male violence is characterized as worse, more extreme, and more outrageous than that carried out by white males. All of this together normalizes violence in the black community and leads to an image of black people, and black working-class males in particular, as dangerous and volatile (Wilcox, 2005).

By overrepresenting males and minority group members as perpetrators, the media reinforces racial and gender stereotypes and/or promotes hostility towards such groups (Barlow, Barlow, & Chiricos, 1995; Dixon, Azocar, & Casas, 2003). Caucasians overestimate the likelihood that they will be victimized by a member of a minority group: statistics show that white individuals are actually three times more likely to be victimized by another white person than a person of a visible minority group (Klein & Naccarato, 2003). This fear, however, is not surprising when we consider the media's treatment of minorities discussed above. The inaccurate representations shape public opinion of certain groups, leading to differential treatment and misguided policy outcomes. On that note, let us now turn to the ways in which media representations influence the public.

Effects of Violent Content on the Audience and Public Policy

Distorted representations of crime and violence have real-life social consequences. Most people get their information about the world through news. Very few individuals have actual lived experience with violence. In fact, 95% of respondents to a survey conducted for the Canadian Sentencing Commission stated that their knowledge about crime in Canada came primarily from the mass media (Tanner, 1996, p. 8). Research shows that the public's estimate of the level of crime and violence in the world to be imprecise. When asked to rank the prevalence of certain types of crimes, the public's ordering more closely resembles the presentation of crime in the media than that found in official statistics (Sheley & Ashkins, 1981). As previously mentioned, this results in the cultivation of fear among the public that is disproportionate to the amount of risk individuals face in reality.

News personnel rely heavily on public officials, such as police and politicians, as sources (Sacco, 2005, 19). Both groups benefit from the public's elevated fear of crime and violence since citizens turn to them for protection. Politicians willingly promote "tough on crime" policies because they are uncontroversial and unlikely to alienate voters – almost everyone can agree that they would like safer streets. Instead of proposing policies that would address the underlying causes of crime and violence, such as poverty, inequality, and institutionalized racism, politicians propose laws that pander to the public's fear, such as mandatory minimum sentences and hiring more police. These measures have not in the past led to a decrease in crime rates; however, they have been shown to garner more votes for the politicians who propose them (Sacco, 2005, p. 150).

Studies carried out in the United States show that those who consume violent media are likely to agree to forceful solutions to social and political issues such as being "tough on crime," capital punishment, initiatives such as the war on drugs, military interventions, and the right to possess arms (Eyal et al., 2006; Holbert, Shaw & Kwak, 2004; Shanahan, 1998). Public support for the death penalty has been increasing since the 1970s, as has support for the "three strikes" laws implemented in the United States since the 1990s. This is true despite the fact that actual rates of violent crime have been declining since the beginning of this period. Support for military spending has also increased, especially since 9/11, and there has been a rise in militia group membership since the 1980s. Alongside these trends we have seen increasing violence in television, films, and video games (Eyal et al., 2006). Recalling the tenets of cultivation theory, this is not surprising. If the consumption of media affects people's beliefs about human nature in a negative way, then political attitudes and opinions will also be implicated. Believing that the world is a threatening place and that one is personally at risk for violence may lead individuals to endorse more aggressive solutions to political and social problems, particularly for self-protection. There is strong evidence that this is the case, especially considering the fact that the association between violent TV consumption and "aggressive political opinions" persist even when we control for other influential factors such as familial upbringing, religious beliefs, and personal experience with crime (Eyal et al., 2006, p. 418).

The American government's tendency to "declare war" on various social problems (e.g., drugs, poverty, crime, inflation) is a concrete manifestation of this trend. The preoccupation with violence translates into a metaphor that seeks to diminish complex social problems. Instead of viewing them as issues that must be tackled with sensitivity on a number of different fronts, they become problems to be eradicated. As Best (1999) notes, "the melodrama of war, its insistence that social problems can be understood as a straightforward struggle between good and evil, constrains discussion of alternative policies" (p.156). This metaphor leads to the expectation that the problem will disappear quickly, and this is rarely the case. Changing systemic problems that are engrained in society happens over a long period of time, and improvements are generally modest at best.

Why then, if we know that there are real-life consequences to these media portrayals, do such representations continue to perforate the media we consume on a daily basis? Like a corporation, the media is a profit-driven driven business. Decisions for programming are made based upon potential for financial gain, and this gain comes mainly from advertising revenue. Besides the creative product of the news or entertainment programming, the media produces an audience. The programming on television is an "attention-getting" mechanism that attracts an audience, transforming it into a commodity to be sold to advertisers (Smythe, 2001). We, the audience, become a packaged product defined by our demographics (gender, age, socioeconomic status, racial/ethnic identification, etc.), and companies pay for the right to advertise to us. The larger the audience media content attracts, and the more desirable theirs attributes (groups, such as the upper-class being most desirable due to their large amount of disposable income), the more a network can charge advertisers for the privilege of this audience's attention, and, hence, the more profit the network will pull-in. As was discussed earlier, some stories are considered more appealing than others in terms of garnering a large audience. These stories are those that are unusual, shocking, or exciting. For this reason, crime and violence are prioritized while many highly problematic social issues (health care, poverty, immigration, etc.) receive little coverage. The media interprets such stories as "dull" and likely to receive low ratings and produce less revenue than other more sensationalistic stories.

Moreover, Western media is owned and operated largely by powerful, wealthy individuals who benefit from the capitalist social system. Therefore, they have a stake in reporting stories in ways that perpetuate the status quo, thus preserving the advantages afforded by their position in the power structure (Herman & Chomsky, 2002; Sacco, 2005, p. 91). Returning again to the coverage of the G20 protests in Toronto, one could argue that the official news stories portrayed the protests as violent and in need of control in order to legitimate the power of the state and leave the current power structure intact. The violent representation of activists overshadows critique of the social hierarchy and its resultant system of oppression, domination, and class inequalities, and leaves little space available to question these broader social concerns (Hussey & LeClerc, 2011, p. 298).

Conclusion

In sum, this chapter leads us to reconsider the way we think of violence in the media. It troubles the general public's common idea that the news media portrays objective accounts of reality. Media representations of crime and violence are socially constructed through a dynamic, interactive process between groups with a stake in media output. The media, a profit-driven industry owned and operated largely by the wealthy, features violent stories that are dramatic, shocking, and sensationalist that attract large audiences and results in higher advertising revenue. Non-violent crimes are glossed-over or neglected all together since they lack the ability to interest audiences in large numbers. Moreover, more coverage is given to crimes perpetrated by minority group members.

This media equation misrepresents the amount of violent crime actually taking place on the streets and leads to serious social consequences. The overrepresentation of crime increases public fear to levels that are disproportionate to the actual risk of encountering violence, and harmful negative stereotypes of groups such as the Aboriginal, Hispanics, and individuals of African or Caribbean descent are perpetuated. Politicians capitalize on the public's fear by introducing tough on crime policies that attract worried voters who seek protection from the perceived threat of violence, even though such measures have not been shown to deter offenders or decrease crime rates.

Therefore, the media's representation of violence and its social consequences are the product of a complex construction process based on the relations between interested social groups. As consumers of the media, we must challenge ourselves to think critically about its content. What we see on TV, read in the newspaper, or click through on the Internet should not be taken as the capital T Truth. Instead, we must understand that there are multiple ways of representing crime and violence and challenge ourselves to ask questions such as: who benefits from representing violence in this manner? Whose story is being told? Whose voices are neglected? What is the social consequence of framing violence in this manner? How might we conceptualize the violence differently? Taking an active role in analyzing what we consume enables us to occupy our own place in the media construction process as conscious participants capable of evaluating and shaping the world around us.

Keywords

Violence, media, news, representation, crime

Review Quetions

1. How does the structure of the influence the violent content in both the news and entertainment programming?
2. Describe the news creation process and how it contributes to the overrepresentation of violence and crime.
3. List 3-5 racial and gender stereotypes found in violent media content.
4. What are the social consequences of media (mis)representations of violence?

References

Barlow, D. E., Barlow, M. E., & Chiricos, G. E. (1995). Economic conditions and ideologies of crime in the media: A content analysis of crime news. *Crime and Delinquency, 41,* 3-19.

Best , J. (1999). *Random violence: How we talk about new crimes and new victims.* Los Angeles: University of California Press.

Bjornstrom, E., Kaurman, R. L., Peterson, R. D., & Slater, M. D. (2010). Race and ethnic representations of lawbreakers and victims in crime news: A national study of television coverage. *Social Problems, 57*(2), 269-293.

Buckler, K., & Travis, L. (2005). Assessing the newsworthiness of homicide events: An analysis of coverage in the Houston Chronicle. *Journal of Criminal Justice and Popular Culture, 12*(1), 1-25.

Carmody, D. (1998). Mixed messages: Images of domestic violence on "reality" television. In D. Carmody (Ed), *Entertaining crime* (pp. 159-174). New York: Aldine de Gruyter.

Chiricos, T., Eschholz, S., & Gertz, M. (1997). Crime, news and fear of crime: Toward an identification of audience effects. *Social Problems, 44* (3), 342-357.

Clark, C. (2010, November 7). $675-Million Spent on G20 Security. *Globe and Mail.* Retrieved from http://www.theglobeandmail.com/news/politics/675-million-spent-on-g20-security/article1787599/

Cohen, S. (2002). *Folk devils and moral panics: The creation of the mods and rockers.* London: Routledge.

Cohen, S., & Young, J. (Eds.). 1973. *The manufacture of news: A reader.* Beverley Hills, CA: Sage Publications.

Davis, J. & Frazier, B. (Writers), & Foerster, A. (Director). (2010, January 13). The uncanny valley [*Criminal Minds*]. In M. Gordon (Producer). Studio City, CA: CBS Television Studios.

DeKeseredy, W. S., & Hinch, R. (1991). *Woman abuse: Sociological perspectives.* Toronto: Thompson Educational Publishing.

Dixon, T., Azocar, C., & Casas, M. (2003). Race and crime on network news. *Journal of Broadcasting and Electronic Media, 47*, 495-520.

Dowler, K., Fleming, T., & Muzzatti, S. L. (2006) Constructing crime: Media, crime and popular culture. *Canadian Journal of Criminology and Criminal Justice, 48*(6), 837-865.

Doyle, A. (2006). How not to think about crime in the media. *Canadian Journal of Criminology and Criminal Justice, 48*(6), 867-885.

Eyal, K., Metzger, M. J., Lingsweiler, R. W., Mahood, C., & Yao, M. Z. (2006). Aggressive political opinions and exposure to violent media. *Mass Communication and Society, 9*(4), 399-428.

Fishman, M. (1978). Crime waves as ideology. *Social Problems, 25*(5), 531-543.

Garofalo, J. (1981a). The fear of crime: Causes and consequences. *The Journal of Criminal Law and Criminology, 72*(2), 839-857.

Garofalo, J. (1981b). Crime and the mass media: A selective review of research. *Journal of Research in Crime and Delinquency, 18*, 319-350.

Gerbner, G., Gross, L., Morgan, M., Signorielli, N., & Shanahan, J. (2002). Growing up with television: Cultivation processes. In J. Bryant & D. Zillmann (Eds.), *Media effects: Advances in theory and research* (pp. 43-68). Mahwah, NJ: Lawrence Erlbaum Associates.

Gilchrist, K. (2010). "Newsworthy" victims? *Feminist Media Studies, 10*(4), 373-390.

Glassner, B. 1999. *The culture of fear: Why Americans are afraid of the wrong things.* New York: Basic Books.

Glassner, B. 2004. Narrative techniques of fear mongering. *Social Research, 71*(4), 819-826.

Greer, C., & McLaughlin, E. (2010). We predict a riot?: Public order policing, new media environments and the rise of the citizen journalist. *British Journal of Criminology, 50*(6), 1041-1059.

Graber, D. (1980). *Crime news and the public.* New York: Praeger.

Hall, S., Critcher, C., Jefferson, T., Clarke, J. N., & Roberts, B. (1978). *Policing the crisis: Mugging, the state, and law and order.* Basingstoke, UK: Macmillan.

Hamilton, J. T. (1998). *Channeling violence: The economic market for violent television programming.* Princeton, NJ: Princeton University Press.

Herman, E.S., & Chomsky, N. (2002). *Manufacturing consent: The political economy of the mass media.* Toronto: Random House of Canada Ltd.

Holbert, R. L., Shah, D., & Kwak, N. (2004). Fear, authority, and justice: Crime-related TV viewing and endorsements of capital punishment and gun ownership. *Journalism & Mass Communication Quarterly, 81*, 343-363.

Hussey, I. & LeClerc, P. (2011). "The big smoke" screen: Toronto's G20 protests, police brutality, and the unaccountability of public officials. *Socialist Studies, 7*(1-2), 282-302.

Jiwani, Y. (2008). *Discourses of denial: Mediations on race, gender, and violence.* Vancouver: University of British Columbia Press.

Klein, R. D., & Naccarato, S. (2003). Broadcast news portrayal of minorities: Accuracy in reporting. *American Behavioural Scientist, 46*(12), 1611-1616.

Kupchik, A. & Bracy, N. (2009). The news media on school crime and violence: Constructing dangerousness and fueling fear. *Youth Violence and Juvenile Justice, 7*(2), 136-155.

Lundman, R. J. (2003). The newsworthiness and selection bias in news about murder: comparative and relative effects of novelty and race and gender typifications on newspaper coverage of homicide. *Sociological Forum, 18*(3), 357-386.

Marin, A. (2010, December). *Caught in the act: Investigation into the Ministry of Community Safety and Correctional Services' conduct in relation to Ontario Regulation 233/1 – under the Public Works Protection Act.* Retrieved from http://www.ombudsman.on.ca/Ombudsman/files/58/581252d9-1809-4291-831b-88e9adb480c5.pdf

McCormick, C. (2010). *Constructing danger: Emotions and mis/representations of crime in the news.* Black Point, NS: Fernwood Publishing.

McMurtry, R. R. (2011, April). *Report of the review of the Public Works Protection Act.* Retrieved from http://www.mcscs.jus.gov.on.ca/stellent/groups/public/@mcscs/@www/@com/documents/webasset/ec088595.pdf

Morden, J. W. (2012, June). *Independent civilian review into matters relating to the G20 summit.* Retrieved from http://www.tpsb.ca/g20/ICRG20Mordenreport.pdf

Naylor, B. (2001). Reporting violence in the British print media: Gendered stories. *The Howard Journal, 40*(2), 180-194.

Perlmutter, D. (2000). *Policing the media: Street cops and public perceptions of law enforcement.* Thousand Oaks, CA: Sage.

Sacco, V. (2005). *When crime waves.* Thousand Oaks, CA: Sage Publications.

Shanahan, J. (1998). Television and authoritarianism: Exploring the concept of mainstreaming. *Political Communication, 15*, 483-495.

Sheley, J. & Ashkins, C. D. (1981). Crime, crime news, and crime views. *The Public Opinion Quarterly, 45*(4), 492-506.

Smith, S. L., Lachlan, K. & Tamborini, R. (2003). Popular video games: Quantifying the presentation of violence and its context. *Journal of Broadcasting and Electronic Media, 47*, 58-76.

Smythe, D. (2001). On the audience commodity and its work. In M. G. Durham & D. M. Kellner (Eds.), *Media and cultural studies: Key works* (pp. 230-256). Malden, MA: Blackwell Publishers Inc.

Surette, R. (1998). *Media, crime, and criminal justice: Images and realities.* Belmont, CA: Wadsworth Publishing Company.

Tanner, J. (1996). *Teenage troubles: Youth and deviance in Canada.* Scarborough, ON: Nelson Canada.

Tuchman, G. (1976). Telling stories. *Journal of Communication, 26,* 93-97.

Welch, M., Price, E., & Yankee, N. (2004). Youth violence and race in the media: The emergence of "wilding" as an invention of the press. *Race, Gender & Class, 11*(2), 36-58.

Wilcox, P. (2005). Beauty and the beast: Gendered and raced discourse in the news. *Social and Legal Studies, 14*(4), 515-532.

Wortley, S. (2002). Misrepresentation or reality? The depiction of race and crime in the Toronto print media. In B. Schissel & C. Brooks (Eds.), *Marginality and condemnation: An introduction to critical criminology* (pp. 55-82). Halifax, NS: Fernwood.

Zelizer, B. (2005). Journalism through the camera's eye. In A. Stuart (Ed.), *Journalism: Critical Issues* (pp. 167-176). New York: Open University Press.

Violence Unchained: Media Images, Behaviour, and Attitudes

Kenneth Dowler

Chapter 6

Learning Objectives

In this chapter you will...

▶ learn about the portrayal of violence in film and television, video games and news media

▶ explore the relationship between media violence and aggression

▶ gain an understanding of the relationship between media consumption and fear of crime

▶ examine media effect theories

▶ develop and understanding of moral panics and their relationship with violence within the media

Introduction

Within society, "real" violence is generally abhorred, condemned, and punished. Yet, within the media, it is celebrated and glorified. In fact, images of violence permeate all forms of media, including films, television, print and broadcast news, video games and the Internet. Quite simply, exposure to violent images and stories (fictional and non-fictional) are both widespread and graphically displayed. For example, it is estimated that the average child will be exposed to at least 16,000 murders and over 200,000 other acts of violence before they reach the age of eighteen (Osofsky, 1999; Bushman & Anderson, 2009). Moreover, critics argue that media violence is more graphic and sadistic, which may lead to reduced empathy towards victims of real violence (Daly & Perez, 2009). Paradoxically, despite the noticeable increase in violent imagery, "actual" violence within society has been on the decline (Ferguson, 2013). As such, the purpose of this chapter is twofold: first, to discuss the portrayal or depiction of violence within various media formats; and second, to examine the impact of media violence on viewer or audience attitudes and behaviours.

Graphic, Explicit, and Disturbing: Depictions of Violence in the Media

The film *The Prisoner* (2013) features a copious amount of violence and that violence is both graphic and disturbing. In the film, the protagonist ruthlessly tortures a young man whom he mistakenly believes abducted his daughter and her friend. The line between morality, justice, and truth becomes invariable blurred, as the audience desires justice but also struggles to cope with the extreme violence and torture meted out by the protagonist. Within contemporary film, the notion of justice is rooted in retribution and punishment. In a study of portrayals of crime and justice on film, Welsh, Fleming, and Dowler (2011) find that violent crime is constructed as an invasion of evil into the domestic sphere by predatory criminals, in which retribution is the ultimate response. Criminals are constructed as predatory others, which is in stark contrast to victims, who are idealized as affluent and/or middle-class. Quite simply, violence is committed by deviant predatory outsiders who are portrayed as "psychotic super criminals" (Surette, 2007). In these films the protagonist relies heavily on themes of revenge and vigilantism. In essence, the justice system is viewed as ineffective, and the only recourse for violent crime is retributive violence on the part of victims and/or criminal justice agents.

Films and Television

In his analysis of the history of film violence, Kendrick (2009) argues that "people have been shooting and stabbing and slaughtering each onscreen since the movies began, and the only difference between then and now is that filmmakers have adopted and made conventional increasingly graphic means of depicting these violent behaviours" (p. 14). According to Kendrick (2009), the fundamental shift occurred in the 1960s, when explicit cinematic violence moved from the "seedy" grindhouse B-movies into the respectable mainstream. He argues this first started in Europe and Japan (especially samurai films), then into American films, largely due to the popularity of Alfred Hitchcock's Psycho (1960) and Birds (1963). Kendrick (2009) further discusses how the representation of violence is connected to societal mores and values, which change over time. Simply put, not only is violent images a useful marketing tool, it represents broader cultural and societal shifts in attitudes toward representations of violence.

In television and film, fictional acts of violence can create a sense of excitement amongst some viewers. There is little doubt that violence within both television and film has increased substantially over time. Since the 1950s, violence in televised programs has been studied with content analysis. Content analysis is a scientific method in which a social science researcher systematically codes the number of violence incidents that appear within the medium analyzed. For example, an analysis of ten American television stations in one day featured 1,846 acts of aggression, with 175 scenes of death; 389 programs featured grievous bodily harm, 362 depicted shootings, and 673 showed fights, beatings, and serious threats (Robinson, 2011).

From 1998 to 1999, the Center for Media and Public Affairs examined over 100 movies, 283 television episodes, and 189 music videos (Robinson, 2011). Their report identified over 8,350 scenes of violence, with over half (4,204) being serious forms of violence, including murder, rape, kidnapping, and assault. Highlights of the report include:

▶ Popular television series averaged six violent scenes per episode, at rate of 18 per hour;
▶ The top 50 Hollywood movies averaged 46 scenes of violence – 29 were life threatening – at a rate of 15 per hour.
▶ Twenty-five made-for-television movies averaged five violent scenes per movie, at a rate of seven per hour.

- Twenty-five made-for-cable television movies averaged 15 violent scenes per movie, at a rate of nine per hour.
- MTV music videos averaged four violent scenes, at a rate of 15 per hour.

Rates of violence in film and television have actually increased since about 2000. The highly popular movie, *SAW* (2004), spawned numerous sequels, and numerous producers/directors copied the extremely graphic formula. Quentin Tarentino's *Django Unchained* (2012) was a commercial success despite criticisms for its overt violence. Even the highly popular series *Harry Potter* and *Twilight* feature many acts of violence. Interestingly, studies have found that the explicitness of violent and sexual content significantly increased following the rating system's initiation in 1968. In fact, the rating system has allowed for even more violent content in PG-13 films (Nalkur, Jamieson, & Romer, 2010). Moreover, a recent study found that the top-grossing Hollywood films of 2012 depicted more gun violence in films rated PG-13 than R-rated films (Bushman et al. 2013). Overall, scenes of violence, in Hollywood biggest blockbusters have more than doubled since 1950 (Bleakley, Jamieson, & Romer, 2012).

Video Games

The first video games surfaced in the 1970s. Although the games were quite rudimentary, there were campaigns to limit or ban their consumption by children. For instance, a campaign was launched against the eight-bit arcade game *Death Race* (based on the movie of the same name), which featured indistinct car-shaped "blobs" that would run over stick figures, turning them into tombstones. However, it was not until the 1990s that violent games became a prominent feature within the gamer's world. In the late 1980s and 1990s, the clear market leader, Nintendo had game standards such as "no excessive blood and violence" and "no sex" (Kent, 2001, p. 465). Yet the benefits of violence and gore became apparent when rivals Nintendo and Sega created versions of *Mortal Kombat*. *Mortal Kombat* pushed the limits of violence to new levels with torso-ripping "fatality" moves. Interestingly, the Sega version, which featured more blood and gore, outsold the Nintendo version three to one, which lead to Nintendo's decline as market leader. Some insiders came to the conclusion that violence sells, and games began to feature more and more graphic violence. Interestingly, the lesser-known *Night Trap* featured a male protagonist who protected a houseful of scantily clad women from vampires. *Night Trap* caused such a commotion that US Senator Joe Lieberman proposed video game regulations. In an attempt to appease congress, *Night Trap* was pulled from the shelves and the video game industry founded the Entertainment Software Rating Board, a self-monitoring panel that instituted a tiered rating system to track sexual and violent content (Kent, 2001).

Today, there are literally hundreds of shooter games, in which the sole purpose is to maim and kill a computer or online opponent. These games have become increasingly realistic and graphic. The *Call of Duty* and the *Grand Theft Auto* series are top sellers and are increasingly played by younger children (Anderson & Warburton, 2012). The *Grand Theft Auto* series allows gamers to speed, crash, run over and kill innocent bystanders and police officers, and even have sex with prostitutes. Similarly, the *Call of Duty* series has been criticized as glorifying war and being overtly graphic in terms of violence (Jansz, 2005). As discussed later in the chapter, critics of the games argue that children exposed to these violent games are more likely to be aggressive and lack empathy for real-life victims of crime. However, a direct relationship between video game violence and actual violence has not been conclusively established (Ferguson, 2013).

The News Media

The news media includes both print (newspapers, magazines), broadcast (local, national, and cable news) and online media (all formats). Like the entertainment media, the news media features a vast amount of violent content. Research clearly shows that violent crime is over-represented within all news media formats. In fact, many researchers argue that violent crimes are considered more "newsworthy," which is why they are prominently featured within various news media formats (Chermak, 1994, 1995; Dowler, 2004a). However, the portrayal of violence within news media varies considerable from the entertainment media. For the most part, entertainment media is fictional, as well as celebrated and glorified. The news media presents real incidents of violence, with real victim and real consequences. As such, many scholars argue that the violence in the news media can also be more upsetting and scary than what is seen in films, television shows, or video games (Dowler, 2003). Nonetheless, there are some similarities between news media and entertainment media. Studies show that news media ignore the causes of violent crime, over-emphasis and over-report violent crimes, and portray violent crime in a very sensationalistic manner (Chermak, 1994, 1995; Dowler 2004a, 2006).

Lack of Crime Causation

It is rare for news reports to examine the causes of violence, the motive for a particular crime, or the effectiveness of the criminal justice system (Graber, 1980). Chermak (1994) finds that causes of crime are mentioned in approximately 2% of all crime stories, while motives for specific crimes are presented only 20% of the time. Crime reporting is often criticized for ignoring the relationship between violence and broad social conditions. Humphries (1981) suggests that while news reports associate criminal violence with youth, maleness, and minority membership, they ignore the historical view of how labour markets and related institutions shape employment opportunities and the size and composition of the pool of people to arrest. Humphries (1981) argues that portraying violence as perpetrated mainly by pathological individuals precludes alternative explanations. Crime portrayals are almost exclusively based on individual characteristics rather than social conditions and the causes of crime are rooted in individual failings rather than social explanations. Deviant or violent behaviour is viewed as an individual choice while social, economic, or structural explanations are ignored and deemed irrelevant. For example, a news report about a single mother accused or convicted of child abuse may describe her as "disturbed" and ignore issues that may have contributed to the abuse such as poverty or lack of adequate daycare or social services (Gorelick, 1989, p. 423). In essence, the news media fails to consider other factors that may be related to the issue of violence. Most crime news is episodic, describing crime events as if they are isolated form larger social, historical, environmental contexts. The lack of explanations for crime and violence complicates the problem of exaggerated frequency in news stories by leaving the impression that violence is inevitable.

When "experts" are used, their general statements reflect societal outrage or condemnation of the perpetrator of violence. Welch, Fenwick, and Roberts (1998) conducted a content analysis of expert quotes in newspaper feature articles on crime. Experts were divided into state managers, which included politicians, criminal justice officials and practitioners, and intellectuals, including professors and non-academic researchers. Welch and colleagues (1998) finds that state managers are significantly more ideological (in both crime causation and crime control) insofar as they neglect the connection between social conditions and crime. While intellectuals are more often to cite societal factors as the cause of crime, their messages are more likely to be obscured by the sensationalistic coverage of the crime. Overall, research concludes that the causes of violence are rarely examined and experts employ ideological rhetoric to explain violence.

Overemphasis on Violent Crime

Neglecting alternative observations, the media depiction of crime greatly overemphasizes individualized acts of violence. The more serious the crime, the greater the chance it will appear as a news story (Dowler, 2004a; Surette, 2007). For example, Graber (1980, p. 39) finds that non-violent crimes make up 47% of crimes known to the police, compared to only 4% reported in news stories. Sheley and Ashkins (1981) find that violent crime make up 20% of the offences but account for 87% of the media reports. Similarly, in a study of three major television networks over a 12-year period, Randall, Lee-Simmons, and Hagner (1988) report that violent crime is disproportionally featured relative to property crime. A Canadian study on newspapers reveals a similar relationship. Doob (1985) finds that 55% of crimes reported are violent, while less than 6% of Canadian crimes are violent in nature. Similarly, research in Great Britain finds that newspapers over-reported crimes against persons and underreported theft and burglary in proportion to their incidence in official crime statistics (Ditton and Duffy, 1983; Smith, 1984; Mawby & Brown, 1984). Chermak (1994) compared print and broadcast media over five American cities. He finds that seriousness is an important variable, influencing decisions about selection and production of news. Serious personal offences such as murder, rape, and robbery are significantly more likely to be presented. Finally, in study comparing US and Canadian markets, Dowler (2004a) found that homicide was overrepresented within the local broadcast news. Even small markets, with very few local homicides had similar numbers of homicides presented on their local newscasts. Essentially, local newscasts would either extensively cover a local homicide or include coverage of a homicide outside of the local market to fill a quota of violent stories. In sum, overemphasis or overreporting of violent crime is consistent and well-established in the literature. Nonetheless, research on media representations of violent crime is dated and requires updated studies to determine if there have been changes in the presentation of violence.

Sensationalistic Coverage of Crime

Basically, crimes of violence are over-represented because they are considered more sensationalistic than property crimes. Jerin and Fields (1994, p. 200) report, "the major factor in crimes being reported by the media is not the crime itself, but the circumstances surrounding the crime, the public nature of the offender or victim, or the humorous nature of the incident." For example, a number of studies show that presentation of a story depends on whether the incident is peculiar, extraordinary, and dramatic (Chermak, 1994).

Another element of sensationalism is what Ericson et al. (1987) call "personalization." This is when a crime becomes newsworthy because of the identity or plight of the persons involved, for instance, when the victim or offender is someone famous such as a mayor, celebrity, professional athlete, or even a relative of someone famous (Chermak, 1994). Moreover, Dowler (2004b) found that newsworthiness was often based on minority status. Minority victims received less coverage and that coverage was less sympathetic than non-minority victims. Further, the media tends to reinforce stereotypes that associate minority status with criminality and violence (Dowler, 2004b; Dowler, Fleming, & Muzzatti, 2006).

The Impact of Media Violence and Viewer Attitudes and Behaviour

There is little debate that violence within the media has increased and that violence has become more graphic. However, the impact of violence in the media on aggressive behaviour and/or attitudes is less certain.

Media Consumption and Aggression

Children and young adults are exposed to and watch all forms of media, including television, film, Internet, and video games. It is estimated that children (ages 2 to 18) consume an average of 38 to 45 hours per week of television, film, Internet, and video games (Anderson & Bushman, 2001). More recent research (Bushman & Anderson, 2009) found:

▶ On average, two- to five-year-olds spend 32 hours a week in front of the TV (including watching television, DVDs, DVR, and videos, and using a game console);

▶ On average, six- to eleven-year-olds spend 28 hours a week in front of the TV;

▶ Approximately 71% of eight- to eighteen-year-olds have a TV in their bedroom; and

▶ In 53% of households of seventh to twelves graders, there are no rules about TV watching.

Estimates suggest that an average child will see 200,000 violent acts and 16,000 murders on TV by the age of 18 (Osofsky, 1999). In fact, two-thirds of all programming contains some form of violence (Bushman & Anderson, 2009). As a result, there are literally thousands of academic studies that have attempted to determine a link between exposure to violent media and violent behaviour. This link also is termed *criminogenic media*, which "refers to media content that is hypothesized as a direct cause of crime" (Surette, 2007, p. 66). Although, the relationship is very complex, the general public has supported the idea that media violence is criminogenic. For instance, public opinion polls show that respondents consistently report that the media is partially responsible for crime and violence in society. Two out of three Americans believe that television violence is an important cause of crime, whilst one out of four believes the movies, television, and the Internet are a primary cause for gun violence (Surette, 2007).

Won't Somebody Please Think of the Children?

Some researchers argue that exposure to violent images have detrimental effects on children. There are a number of empirical studies that reveal that children who are exposed to violent images in the media have an increased probability of aggression, are desensitized to violence, experience nightmares, fear being harmed, and lack empathy for others (Anderson & Bushman, 2002; Bushman & Huesmann, 2001; Frost, Wortham, & Reifel, 2001; Huesmann et al.

2003; Johnson et al. 2002). They vociferously claim that the relationship between media violence and aggression is clear and indisputable. They even argue that the link between media violence and aggression is as strong as the link between smoking and health problems (Ferguson, 2013). They go as far to claim the scientific debate about whether exposure to media violence causes increases in aggressive behaviour is over and should have been over 30 years ago (Anderson, Gentile, & Buckley, 2007).

Granted, the research evidence reveals a strong link between media violence and aggression. In a meta-analysis, Anderson and Bushman (2002) examined all the major research methodologies, including experiments, cross-sectional correlational studies, longitudinal studies, intervention studies, and meta-analyses. In each methodology, they found media violence was significantly associated with aggression or violence. Nonetheless, the association between media violence and aggressive behaviour is riddled with theoretical and methodological problems.

First, the issue of causation is a central problem with the supposed relationship. The direction of the relationship between media violence and aggression is unclear. For example, it may be that children that are aggressive are more likely to enjoy watching more violence than other children. Quite simply, we cannot assume that watching violence causes aggression or violent behaviour. Longitudinal studies attempt to solve the problem of causality. Longitudinal studies will follow participants/respondents over time to determine if media violence causes an increase in aggression. Although, longitudinal studies may reveal that the media consumption occurred prior to the aggressive or violent behaviour. The violence or aggressive behaviour may not actually be the sole result of consuming violent media; there may be intervening factors or variables that confound the relationship.

As such, the second problem is the relationship between media violence and aggression may be the result of intervening factors or spurious variables (Huesmann et al., 2003). The complex relationship between media violence and aggression merits an examination of multiple variables. In fact, research has consistently shown that media effects are either limited or weakly associated with aggression or violence (Ferguson, 2013). Some researchers argue that media effects are intertwined with other factors such as personality, family violence, and parenting. For example, some research shows that media effects are stronger for children who experience negative life events, such as family violence or poor parenting (Ferguson, 2013; Surette, 2007). In essence, violent media is not the sole cause or the most important cause of violent or aggressive behaviour. There is undoubtedly an association between violent media and social aggression, but its strength and pattern is not known at this time (Surette, 2007).

Third, although a link between media violence and social aggression exists, the measurement of aggression is both inconsistent and unsound. Many studies involve children in laboratory experiments. However, these studies may only be studying short-term imitation and not long-term changes in aggressive behaviour. Moreover, social aggression can include rude behaviour, and one can be aggressive without actually being violent and/or breaking the law. Therefore, some researchers contend that the link between media violence and criminal behaviour needs separate investigation (Surette, 2007; Ferguson, 2013).

Overall, the relationship between criminal behaviour and media violence is very difficult to study. Experiments are almost impossible to conduct and most of the evidence is based on anecdotal stories rather than empirical research. Empirical research on a society-wide media criminogenic effect involves aggregate data and is likely to be small and influenced by other criminogenic factors (Surette, 2007). As a result, there have been very few empirical studies on the criminogenic effects of the media. Hennigan et al. (1982) examined crime rates prior to and after the introduction of television in the 1950s. Although she found no relationship with violent crime, she did find an increase in property crimes, at least initially. She surmised that viewers who were poorer and less educated may have felt resentment or frustration by watching the predominantly middle class be portrayed on television. Thus, some viewers may have turned to crime as a way of acquiring desired goods. Granted, the media can influence consumer wants and desires, as is evident by large spending on advertisements, but the relationship between media consumption and criminal rates is largely speculative and not based on research evidence (Surette, 2007).

There is, however, a substantial amount of anecdotal evidence that the media can influence individual criminal behaviour. So-called copycat crime occurs when an individual is inspired by a prior, media-publicized crime and incorporates major elements of the crime into his or her criminal behaviour. The awareness of copycat crimes is not a new phenomenon. In fact, concerns around copycat effects led to censorship of Hollywood films. In 1929, the Payne Foundation examined the social impact of films, which eventually led to the Hays Commission. The Hays Commission, in turn, was established to scrutinize the content of Hollywood films. The film industry created a code to regulate film content. Films were forbidden "to teach methods of crime, inspire potential criminals with a desire for imitation, or make criminals seem heroic and justified" (Surette, 2007, p. 70).

Notwithstanding early concerns, specific knowledge about copycat crimes is limited. Researchers rely on anecdotal evidence, which for the most part is very compelling. There are numerous real-life cases in which criminal participants mimic previous, high profile incidents. Nonetheless, research shows that copycat criminals have criminal histories and have the propensity to commit criminal actions. Thus, the media may not cause the criminal or violent behaviour but serve a more pragmatic purpose, teaching or inspiring individuals to commit future criminal or violent activity (Surette, 2007).

Media Consumption and Fear of Crime

Overall, the relationship between media consumption and fear of crime is unclear, as the findings are mixed (Surette, 2007). Early researchers argue that heavy media consumers develop a "mean world view" or view that is typified by "mistrust, cynicism, alienation, and perceptions of higher than levels of threat of crime in society" (Surette, 1990, p. 8). Gerbner et al. (1980) found that respondents that viewed a large amount of television were more likely to feel a greater threat from crime, take more precautions against crime, and believe crime is more widespread than statistics show. Other early studies confirm a direct and strong relationship between television viewing and fear of crime (Barille, 1984; Bryant, Carveth, & Brown, 1981; Hawkins & Pingree, 1981; Morgan, 1983; Williams, Zabrack, & Joy, 1982; Weaver & Wakshlag, 1986). More recent studies reveal that viewing local television news is related to increased fear of and concern about crime (Romer, Jamieson, & Aday, 2003; Eschholz, Chiricos, & Gertz, 2003). Conversely, a review of the research by Eschholz (1997), updated by Ditton et al. (2004, p. 598) found that the majority (73%) of studies showed no or little relationship between newspaper and television consumption and fear of crime.

Nevertheless, Winkel and Vrij (1990) proposed the similarity hypothesis, which advocated that the degree that the viewer or reader "identified with the victim to the degree to which one's neighborhood is seen to bear resemblance to the described locale, and to the extent to which the described form of crime is similar to the form of crime one fears" (p. 263). Simply stated, the audience identifies with the victim, crime, and/or danger.

A review of the research found that the relationship between media presentations and crime was dependent on characteristics of the message and the audience (Heath & Gilbert, 1996). Presentation of large amounts of local crime news resulted in higher fear among respondents, (Brillon, 1987; Sheley & Ashkins, 1981), while the presentation of increased amounts of non-local crime news had the opposite effect by making the local viewers feel safe in contrast to other areas (Liska & Baccaglini, 1990). Moreover, Chiricos, Padgett, and Gertz (2000) found that local and national new consumption was linked to fear of crime. The effect of local news on fear of crime, however, was stronger for respondents who resided high crime areas and those who had a victimization experience.

According to audience effects, fear of victimization will depend on the characteristics of the audience member viewing the crime story. Some studies revealed that residents in high-crime urban areas who watched high levels of television were more likely to report being afraid of crime (Doob & MacDonald, 1979; Gerbner et al., 1980). Additionally, direct victimization was another factor, and research has found that media sources were more significant when direct experience was lacking (Gunter, 1987; Liska & Baccaglini, 1990; Skogan & Maxfield, 1981). For instance, research has found that media impact was strongest for females, whites, and the elderly, segments of the population least likely to be victimized (Liska & Baccaglini, 1990). Similarly, Chiricos, Eschholz and Gertz (1997) found that the frequency of watching television news and listening to the news on the radio was significantly related to fear. They found that television news consumption was significantly related to fear only for white females between the ages of 30 and 44. Correspondingly, an early study found that viewing crime on television had a greater effect for women and whites, who had low victim risk compared to males and non-whites (Gerbner et al., 1980).

Although, the link between news consumption was unclear, there was evidence that viewing crime dramas or shows might increase levels of fear among viewers (Rubin, Perse, & Taylor, 1988; Hawkins & Pingree, 1981). Chiricos Eschholz and Gertz, (1997) found that fear of crime is related to watching violent television shows. While Dowler (2003) found that crime show viewing was positively related to fear of crime. Similarly, Eschholz, Chiricos, and Gertz (2003) found that fear of crime increased with the viewing of crime dramas, crime reality and crime tabloid programs.

Experimental studies involving children revealed that heavy viewing distorted children's perception of violence in society and increased fear (Dominick, 1990). In a study of Australian school children, for example, Pingree and Hawkins (1981) found that children who were heavy viewers of American crime programs held the most negative views. This supports the idea of "mean world syndrome," which suggests that heavy viewers of television are more likely to believe the world is a scary place because of high levels of violence and disorder. Similarly, an experimental study of college students found that heavy viewers of action adventure programs were more fearful than light viewers (Dominick, 1990).

Media Effect Theories

George Gerbner and associates (1980) proposed cultivation theory, which espoused the notion that television viewing has a long-term effects that are small, gradual, and indirect but cumulative and significant. Cultivation theorists emphasize the effects of television viewing on attitudes rather than behaviours of the audience. Heavy viewers "cultivate" attitudes or preconceptions that are consistent with the world of television programs rather than the "real world." Proponents of the cultivation hypothesize argue that heavy viewers develop a mean worldview in which they presuppose that the violence and misery that they observe on television equates to the real world. Heavy viewers also come to believe in the "law and order" approach to justice, which reinforces the mantra of harsh penalties and tough laws. In terms of attitudes about crime, cultivation theorists argue that, as opposed to light viewers, heavy viewers believe that crime is more serious, and these heavy viewers experience more anxiety or distress about crime.

Supporters of the cultivation hypothesis contend that resonance increased cultivation. Resonance is when the audience members identify more closely with depictions of characters or persons that resemble or are similar to their own characteristics or social location. That is, race, age, class, and gender of the characters on television might impact viewers in different ways, depending on the viewer's own social characteristics or location. Media consumers construct meanings according to their social location, which in turn inform and activate meaning for them. Thus, social location research analyzed the relationship between the subject's life circumstances, demographic characteristics, and media presentations (Fiske, 1986).

Four categories of social location research have been identified: the vulnerability thesis; the substitution thesis; the resonance thesis; and the affinity thesis. Research studies have concluded that the vulnerability thesis, which stated that women and elderly populations were generally more likely to feel at risk than younger males, had not been well supported (Skogan & Maxfield, 1981). Conversely, there was some support for the substitution thesis, which suggested that people such as high-income elderly women who have not been exposed to criminal situations, might, after watching the news or crime shows, substitute the reality of their lives with the idea that they will be future victims of criminal behaviour (Gunter, 1987). Other studies have found substantially significant findings that supported the resonance theory that male viewers from low-income backgrounds exposed to criminal situations would have greater feelings of resonance with people involved in arrests on television than other people (Doob & MacDonald, 1979, Gerbner et al., 1980; Chiricos, Padgett, & Gertz, 2000). Finally, the affinity thesis had been supported by evidence that individuals that viewed a preponderance of characters with similar demographic characteristics, who were victimized on television, subsequently would be more likely to fear being victims of criminal behaviour themselves (Escholz, Chiricos, & Gertz, 1997).

Moral Panics

A discussion about moral panics is merited to fully understand the impact of violence in the media on public attitudes. A moral panic refers to any event or occurrence that triggers alarming, sensational, and copious media coverage. Not only do these media "stories" heighten public awareness of an issue, they also may be reinforced by reactive laws and public policy.

These stories may exaggerate a "social problem" and/or create fear, anxiety, and anger over a perceived threat to social order that is either misdirected or overstated.

In his discussion of moral panics, Jock Young introduces the concept of deviance amplification, when sensational media coverage of deviant behaviours unintentionally increases rather than confines outward deviance. Young (1971) also comments on how media coverage can construct and distort a moral panic:

> The media, then – in a sense – can create social problems, they can present them dramatically and overwhelmingly, and, most important, they can do it suddenly. The media can very quickly and effectively fan public indignation and engineer what one might call "a moral panic" about a certain type of deviancy. (p. 37)

Originally published in 1972, Stanley Cohen's *Folk Devils and Moral Panics: The Creation of the Mods and Rockers* (2002) provided the definition of moral panics that future researchers would most often cite. Similar to Young, Cohen examines differing social reactions to deviance and their roles in constructing both deviant and condoned behaviours. The concept of moral panic has been applied to many social phenomena and has also entered into public consciousness (Jewkes, 2010). First published in 1994, Erich Goode and Nachman Ben-Yehuda's *Moral Panics: The Social Construction of Deviance* (2010) includes a comprehensive analysis of the typical characteristics of many moral panics. Goode and Ben-Yehuda's (2009, p. 37-43) itemization of five key attributes of moral panics can be summarized as follows:

1. Concern – There must be a measurable increase in the level of anxiety arising from the belief that a group's behaviours pose a significant threat to society, a response seen by those who experience it as a rational response to a definite social danger.

2. Hostility – The source of the alleged social danger must be viewed with resentment as an easily identifiable group independently responsible for the danger its behaviours pose to society.

3. Consensus – Considerable agreement that a threat to society exists need not be achieved throughout society, but must be achieved within a segment of the public large or powerful enough to neutralize opposition to its preferred definitions or policies.

4. Disproportionality – The amount of public concern over a perceived social threat must be out of proportion to the measurable or evident level of danger posed.

5. Volatility – Moral panics tend to arise suddenly and dissolve quickly, sometimes leaving behind lasting social changes.

Some scholars argue that the linkage between violence in the media is overstated as a cause of "real violence" and actually resembles a moral panic. (Ferguson, 2013). For instance, Ferguson (2013) claims that "concerns have come and gone that media such as comic books, jazz, rock, rap, role-playing games, and books, as well as television and movies, would lead to waves of rebelliousness, violence and moral degradation. New media such as video games and the Internet inevitably stoke the flames of fear with waves of advocates and politicians expressing concern over the fate of supposedly vulnerable children and teens" (p. 37). As such, it is important that the notion of moral panics be included in discussions regarding the relationship between media consumption and violent or aggressive behaviour.

Conclusion

There is little doubt that media images of violence have increased and have become visibly more graphic and disturbing. Violent imagery permeates all forms of media, and some scholars argue that these images contribute to violent behaviour amongst youth. Yet the relationship between media consumption and actual violent behaviour is far from certain and will likely never be fully answered. In fact, there are so many factors that are related to actual violence that it would be impossible to suggest a causal link between watching violence and actually committing violence. Furthermore, the relationship between media consumption and fear of crime is also uncertain. There is some research that suggests that heavy viewers of violence may be more fearful of crime but other factors tend to mitigate this relationship. In the end, one might argue that an increase in violent media will not necessary lead to greater levels of violence or fear within society. However, one thing is certain: politicians and other pundits will use media violence as a scapegoat to explain violence within society rather than investigate more concrete reasons for violence, such as lack of gun control, mental health awareness, and social inequities.

Keywords

Media violence, film & television, video games, news media, aggression, fear of crime, cultivation theory, moral panics.

Review Questions

1. Compare and contrast the portrayal of violence in film and television, video games, and the news media.
2. The news media tends to ignore the causes of violent crime, overemphasizes violent crime, and portray violent crime as sensationalistic. Please discuss.
3. Please discuss the complex relationship between media exposure and aggressive behaviour amongst children.
4. Describe the theoretical and methodological problems in examining the relationship between media violence and aggressive behaviour.
5. Please describe cultivation theory and how it impacts attitudes toward crime.
6. What is a moral panic? Please provide examples to help explain.

References

Anderson, C. A., & Bushman, B. J. (2001). Effects of violent video games on aggressive behaviour, aggressive cognition, aggressive affect, physiological arousal, and prosocial behaviour: A meta-analytic review of the scientific literature. *Psychological Science, 12*(5), 353-359.

Anderson, C. A., & Bushman, B. J. (2002). The effects of media violence on society. *Science, 295*(5564), 2377-2379.

Anderson, C. A., Gentile, D. A., & Buckley, K. E. (2007). *Violent video game effects on children and adolescents.* New York: Oxford University Press.

Anderson, C.A., & Warburton, W.A. (2012) The impact of violent video games: An overview. In W. Warburton & D. Braunstein (Eds.), *Growing up fast and furious: Reviewing the impacts of violence and sexualized media on children* (pp. 56-84). Annandale, NSW, Australia: The Federation Press.

Barille, L. (1984). Television and attitudes about crime: Do heavy views distort criminality and support retributive justice? In R. Surette (Ed.), *Justice and the media: Issues and research* (pp. 141-158). Springfield, IL: Charles C. Thomas.

Bleakley, A., Jamieson, P. E., & Romer, D. (2012). Trends of sexual and violent content by gender in top-grossing US films, 1950-2006. *Journal of Adolescent Health, 51*(1), 73-79.

Brillon, Y. (1987) *Victimization and fear among the elderly.* Toronto: Butterworths.

Bryant, J., Carveth, R.A., & Brown, D. (1981). Television viewing and anxiety: An experimental examination. *Journal of Communication, 31,* 106-119.

Bushman, B. J., & Anderson, C. A. (2009). Comfortably numb: Desensitizing effects of violent media on helping others. *Psychological Science, 20*(3), 273-277.

Bushman, B. J., & Huesmann, L. R. (2001). Effects of televised violence on aggression. In D. Singer & J. Singer (Eds.), *Handbook of children and the media* (pp. 223-254). Thousand Oaks, CA: Sage.

Bushman, B. J., Jamieson, P. E., Weitz, I., & Romer, D. (2013). Gun violence trends in movies. *Pediatrics, 132*(6), 1014-1018.

Chermak, S. M. (1994). Body count news: How crime is presented in the news media. *Justice Quarterly, 11*(4), 561-582.

Chermak, S. M. (1995). *Victims in the news: Crime and the American news media.* Boulder, CO: Westview Press.

Chiricos, T., Eschholz, S., & Gertz, M. (1997). Crime, news and fear of crime: Toward an identification of audience effects. *Social Problems, 44,* 342-357.

Chiricos, T., Padgett, K., & M. Gertz. (2000). Fear, TV news, and the reality of crime *Criminology, 38*(3), 755-785.

Cohen, S. (2002). *Folk devils and moral panics: The creation of the mods and the rockers.* New York, NY: Routledge.

Daly, L. A., & Perez, L. M. (2009). Exposure to media violence and other correlates of aggressive behaviour in preschool children. *Early Childhood Research and Practice 11*(2), 1-13.

Davis, K. (Producer), & Villeneuve, D. (Director). (2013). Prisoners [Motion Picture]. United States: Alcon Entertainment.

Ditton, J., & Duffy, J. (1983). Bias in the newspaper reporting of crime news. *British Journal of Criminology, 23,* 159-165.

Ditton, J., Chadee, D., Farrall, S., Gilchrist, E., & Bannister, J. (2004). From imitation to intimidation: note on the curious and changing relationship between the media, crime and fear of crime. *British Journal of Criminology, 44,* 595-610.

Dominick, J. R. (1990). *The dynamics of mass communication.* New York: McGraw-Hill.

Doob, A. N. (1985). The many realities of crime. In A.N. Doob & E.L Greenspan (Eds), *Perspectives in Criminal Law: Essays in Honour of John LL. J. Edwards*, pp. 61-80. Toronto: Canada Law Book.

Doob, A., & MacDonald, G. (1979).Television viewing and fear of victimization: Is the relationship causal? *Journal of Personality and Social Psychology, 37,* 170-179.

Dowler, K. (2003). Media consumption and public attitudes toward crime and justice: The relationship between fear of crime, punitive attitudes, and perceived police effectiveness. *Journal of Criminal Justice and Popular Culture, 10*(2), 109-126.

Dowler, K. (2004a). Comparing American and Canadian local television crime stories: A content analysis. *Canadian Journal of Criminology and Criminal Justice/La Revue canadienne de criminologie et de justice pénale, 46*(5), 573-596.

Dowler, K. (2004b). Dual realities? Criminality, victimization, and the presentation of race on local television news. *Journal of Crime and Justice, 27*(2), 79-99.

Dowler, K., Fleming, T., & Muzzatti, S. L. (2006). Constructing crime: Media, crime, and popular culture. *Canadian Journal of Criminology and Criminal Justice/La Revue canadienne de criminologie et de justice pénale, 48*(6), 837-850.

Ericson, R. V., Baranek and Chan, J.B. (1987) *Visualizing: Deviance: A Study of News Organization*. Toronto: University of Toronto Press/Milton Keynes: Open University Press.

Ericson, R. V., Baranek, P. M., & Chan, J. B. (1991). *Representing order: Crime, law, and justice in the news media.* Milton Keynes, UK: Open University Press.

Eschholz, S. (1997). The media and fear of crime: A survey of the research. *Journal of Law and Public Policy, 9*(1), 37-59.

Eschholz, S., Chiricos, T., & Gertz, M. (2003). Television and fear of crime: Program types, audience traits and the mediating effect of perceived neighborhood racial composition. *Social Problems, 50*(3), 395-415.

Ferguson, C. J. (2013). *Adolescents, crime, and the media: A critical analysis.* New York, NY: Springer.

Fiske, J. (1986). Television: Polysemy and popularity. *Critical Studies in Mass Communication, 3*(4), 391-408.

Frost, J. L., Wortham, S., & Reifel, S. (2001). Play and development. Upper Saddle River, NJ: Prentice Hall.

Gerbner, G., Gross, L., Morgan, M., & Signorielli, N. (1980). The mainstreaming of America: Violence profile No. 11. *Journal of Communications, 30,* 10-29.

Goode, E., & Ben-Yehuda, N. (2009). *Moral panics: The social construction of deviance* (2nd ed.). Maldon, MA: Wiley-Blackwell.

Gorelick, S. M. (1989). "Join our war": The construction of ideology in a newspaper crime-fighting campaign. *Crime and Delinquency, 35*(3), 421-436.

Graber, D. A. (1980). *Crime news and the public.* New York: Praeger.

Gunter, B. (1987). *Television and fear of crime.* London: John Libbey.

Hawkins, R., & Pingree, S. (1981). Uniform messages and habitual viewing: Unnecessary assumptions in social reality effects. *Human Communication Research, 7*(4), 291-301.

Heath, L., & Gilbert, K. (1996). Mass media and fear of crime. *American Behavioural Scientist, 39,* 379-386.

Hennigan, K. M., Del Rosario, M. L., Heath, L., Cook, T. D., Wharton, J. D., & Calder, B. J. (1982). Impact of the introduction of television on crime in the United States: Empirical findings and theoretical implications. *Journal of Personality and Social Psychology, 42*(3), 461-467.

Huesmann, L. R., Moise-Titus, J., Podolski, C. L., & Eron, L. D. (2003). Longitudinal relations between children's exposure to TV violence and their aggressive and violent behaviour in young adulthood: 1977-1992. *Developmental Psychology, 39*(2), 201-21.

Humphries, D. (1981). Serious crime, news coverage, and ideology: A content analysis of crime coverage in a metropolitan paper. *Crime and Delinquency, 27*(2), 191-205.

Jansz, J. (2005). The emotional appeal of violent video games for adolescent males. *Communication Theory, 15*(3), 219-241.

Jerin, R. A., & Fields, C. B. (1994). Murder and mayhem in USA Today: A quantitative analysis of the national reporting of states' news. In G. Barak (Ed.) *Media, Process, and the Social Construction of Crime: Studies in Newsmaking Criminology,* 187-202. New York, NY: Garland Publishing Inc.

Jewkes, Y. (2010). *Media and crime* (2nd ed.). Thousand Oaks, CA: Sage.

Johnson, J. G., Cohen, P., Smailes, E. M., Kasen, S., & Brook, J. S. (2002). Television viewing and aggressive behaviour during adolescence and adulthood. *Science, 295*(5564), 2468-2471.

Kendrick, J. (2009). *Film violence: History, ideology, genre.* London, UK: Wallflower Press.

Kent, S. L. (2001). *The ultimate history of video games: From Pong to Pokemon – The story behind the craze that touched our lives and changed the world.* Rocklin, CA: Prima Communications.

Liska, A., & Baccaglini, W. (1990). Feeling safe by comparison: Crime in the newspapers. *Social Problems, 37,* 360-374.

Mawby, R. I., & Brown, J. (1984). Newspaper images of the victim: A British study. *Victimology, 9,* 92-94.

Morgan, M (1983). Symbolic victimization and real-world fear. *Human Communication Research, 9*(2), 146-157.

Nalkur, P. G., Jamieson, P. E., & Romer, D. (2010). The effectiveness of the motion picture association of America's rating system in screening explicit violence and sex in top-ranked movies from 1950 to 2006. *Journal of Adolescent Health, 47*(5), 440-447.

Osofsky, J. D. (1999). The impact of violence on children. *Future of children, 9*(3), 33-49.

Pingree, S., & Hawkins, R. (1981). U.S. programs on Australian television: The cultivation effect. *Journal of Communication, 31,* 97-105.

Randall, D. M., Lee-Simmons, L., & Hagner, P. R. (1988). Common versus elite crime coverage in network news. *Social Science Quarterly, 69*(4), 910-929.

Rideout, V. J., Foehr, U. G., & Roberts, D. F. (2010). *Generation M2: Media in the Lives of 8 to 18 year olds.* Mento Park, CA: Kaiser Family Foundation.

Robinson, M. B. (2011). *Media coverage of crime and criminal justice.* Durham, NC: Carolina Academic Press.

Romer, D. Jamieson, K., & Aday, S. (2003). Television news and the cultivation of fear of crime. *Journal of Communication, 53*(1), 88-104.

Rubin, A., Perse, E., & Taylor, D. (1988). A methodological examination of cultivation. *Communication Research, 15,* 107-134.

Sheley, J. F., & Ashkins, C. D. (1981). Crime, crime news, and crime views. *Public Opinion Quarterly, 45*(4), 492-506.

Skogan, W., & Maxfield, M. (1981). *Coping with crime.* Beverly Hills, CA: Sage Publications.

Smith, S. J. (1984). Crime in the news. *British Journal of Criminology, 24*(3), 289-295.

Surette, R. (1990). *The media and criminal justice policy: Recent research and social effects.* Springfield , IL: Charles C. Thomas.

Surette, R. (2007). *Media, crime and criminal justice: Images and realities* (2nd ed.). Belmont, CA: Wadsworth.

Weaver, J., & Wakshlag, J. (1986). Perceived vulnerability to crime, criminal experience and television viewing. *Journal of Broadcasting and Electronic Media, 30,* 141-158.

Welch, M., Fenwick, M., & Roberts, M. (1998). State managers, intellectuals, and the media: A content analysis of ideology in experts' quotes in feature newspaper articles on crime. *Justice Quarterly, 15*(2), 219-241.

Welsh, A., Fleming, T., & Dowler, K. (2011). Constructing crime and justice on film: Meaning and message in cinema. *Contemporary Justice Review, 14*(4), 457-476.

Williams, T., Zabrack, M., & Joy, L. (1982). The portrayal of aggression on North American television. *Journal of Applied Social Psychology, 12,* 360-380.

Winkel, F., & Vrij, A. (1990). Fear of crime and mass media crime reports: Testing similarity hypotheses. *International Review of Victimology, 1*(3), 251-266.

Young, J. (1971). The role of the police as amplifiers of deviancy, negotiators of reality and translators of fantasy. In A. Editor (Ed.), *Images of Deviance* (pp. 27-61). Harmondsworth, UK: Penguin.

Understanding Violence and Affecting Aboriginal People through an Aboriginal Lens

Learning Objectives

In this chapter you will...

► describe and understand elements of Aboriginal circular thinking vs. Westernized linear thinking

► identify impacts of genocidal policies and residential schools

► recognize the effects of intergenerational trauma on Aboriginal people

► outline risk factors related to violence affecting Aboriginal people

► describe reasons why Aboriginal people suffer from various risk factors related to violence

Chapter 7

Lisa Monchalin

Introduction: Overrepresentation in Violence

Compared to non-Aboriginal Canadians, Aboriginal people are three times more likely to experience a violent victimization, which includes sexual assault, robbery, and physical assaults (Brzozowski, Taylor-Butts, & Johnson, 2006; Perreault, 2011). These violent victimization rates are highest for Aboriginal females, with the rate of violence three and a half times greater when compared to non-Aboriginal females (Brzozowski, Taylor-Butts, & Johnson, 2006, p. 5). This data is derived from the General Social Survey on Victimization conducted by Statistics Canada. It collects data by surveying a representative sample of Canadians living in the ten provinces.

Data also revealed that, in 2009, Aboriginal peoples were found to be almost twice as likely as non-Aboriginal peoples to be physically or sexually assaulted by their partner or spouse and were more likely than non-Aboriginal people to report multiple victimizations (Perreault, 2011, p. 10). Those victims of spousal violence were also twice as likely as non-Aboriginal victims to be injured as a result of violence, and they feared for their lives. The most severe forms of violence, including being hit with an object, strangled, beaten, threatened or assaulted with a firearm or knife, or forced to engage in an unwanted sexual act, were reported by Aboriginal victims at a rate that was double than of non-Aboriginal victims (Perreault, 2011, p. 10).

Reports of those who experienced non-spousal violence, which constitutes sexual assaults, robberies, and assaults committed by anyone other than the victim's partner, were reported at a rate twice that of non-Aboriginal peoples. For example, 5% of non-Aboriginal people reported experiencing non-spousal violence, while 12% of Aboriginal people reported non-spousal violence in 2009 (Perreault, 2011, p. 10).

Statistics Canada also reported that 13% of all Aboriginal women aged 15 years or older, living in the provinces, had been violently victimized during 2009 (Brennan, 2011). This is close to 67,000 Aboriginal women who were violently victimized in only one year alone. Of those women who reported being victimized, more than a third experienced victimization on two or more occasions (Brennan, 2011, p. 7). Overall, Aboriginal women and girls are considerably more likely to die as a result of violence, as compared to other Canadian women and girls (Human Rights Watch, 2013, p. 25). Amnesty International (2004, p. 23) reveals that Aboriginal women in Canada, aged 25 to 44, are five times more likely than non-Aboriginal women in the same age group to die of violence.

In 2010, the Native Women's Association of Canada's Sisters in Spirit Initiative estimated that 582 Aboriginal women in Canada had gone missing and/or been murdered since 1980 (Native Women's Association of Canada, 2010, p. 18). They believe there are still many more to document, as 582 was the last number to which their nationally acclaimed database gathered before the federal government, under Prime Minister Stephen Harper, cut the organization's funding. Pearce (2013) documented cases of missing and murdered women in Canada between the span of 1946 to 2013, identifying 824 missing and murdered Aboriginal women. The Royal Canadian Mounted Police (2014) documented 1,181 cases of missing and murdered Aboriginal women between 1980 and 2012, identifying 1,017 who have been murdered and 164 who are still missing.

Between 1997 and 2000, the rate of homicide committed against Aboriginal women was 5.4 per 100,000, compared to the rate for non-Aboriginal women of 0.8 per 100,000 – a rate that is nearly seven times higher for Aboriginal women versus non-Aboriginal women (O'Donnell & Wallace, 2011, p. 43). For Aboriginal men it is even worse. The rate of homicide committed against Aboriginal men was 12.2 per 100,000, verses non-Aboriginal men whose rate was 1.8 per 100,000 (Brzozowski, Taylor-Butts, & Johnson 2006, p. 7). Aboriginal peoples are also overrepresented as persons accused of homicide. The rate of those accused of homicide was ten times higher for Aboriginal peoples. Non-Aboriginal peoples represented 1.1 accused persons per 100,000 and Aboriginal people represented 11.2 accused persons per 100,000 (Brzozowski, Taylor-Butts, & Johnson 2006, p. 7).

Aboriginal people are also more likely to be incarcerated more often than non-Aboriginal people (Hylton, 2002, p. 19). Despite comprising only 4.3% of Canada's total population in 2011, Aboriginal adults 18 years and older accounted for 17% of adults admitted to remand, 18% admitted to provincial and territorial custody, 18% admitted to federal custody, 16% admitted to probation, and 19% admitted to a conditional sentence in 2007/08 (Statistics Canada, 2013; Perreault, 2009, p. 9). Furthermore, federally incarcerated Aboriginal offenders are more likely to have committed violent offences, as compared to non-Aboriginal federally incarcerated offenders (Trevethan, Moore, & Rastin, 2002).

The majority of Aboriginal peoples in Canada live in an urban area. According to Statistics Canada 2006 Census, 54% of Aboriginal people lived in an urban centre, which is an increase from 50% in 1996. For those that do live on reserves, rates of violent crime on-reserve have been reported as higher than anywhere else in the country (Totten, 2009, p. 138; Brzozowski, Taylor-Butts, & Johnson, 2006, p. 10). More specifically, compared to the rest of Canada, rates for violent crime on reserves is six times higher for homicides, seven times higher for sexual assaults, and eight times higher for assaults (Brzozowski, Taylor-Butts, & Johnson, 2006, p. 10). The only violent crime that is not more frequent on-reserve as compared to the rest of Canada is robbery. The rate of robberies committed off-reserve is almost two times higher than on-reserve (Brzozowski, Taylor-Butts, & Johnson, 2006, p. 10).

Almost half of all adult charges laid on-reserve in 2004 were for violent crimes. This was followed by other Criminal Code violations (41%) and property crimes (10%) (Brzozowski, Taylor-Butts, & Johnson, 2006, p. 10). In contrast, the largest proportion of adult charges laid against crimes committed off-reserves were for other Criminal Code incidents (40%) followed by property offences (32%) and violent crimes (28%) (Brzozowski, Taylor-Butts, & Johnson, 2006, p. 10).

Rates of youth crime on-reserve are higher than the rest of Canada, most notably for homicide, where young offenders were accused of committing homicides at a rate 11 times higher than youth in the rest of Canada (National Crime Prevention Centre, 2012, p. 9). However, youth both on and off reserves are the least likely (in comparison to adults) to be accused of a violent crime, which is consistent with research that indicates that youth are less likely to commit violent crimes in general as compared to adults (National Crime Prevention Centre, 2012). At the same time, however, Totten (2009) reveals that there is an epidemic of Aboriginal youth gang violence in some parts of Canada. He explains that young Aboriginal gang members are committing suicide and killing each other at rates that surpass any other group in Canada. He further notes, that about 22% of known gang members in Canada are Aboriginal, and there exists between 800 and 1,000 active Aboriginal gang members in the prairie provinces (Totten, 2009, p. 136). Gangs include the Indian Posse, Manitoba Warriors, and Native Syndicate. Many times, violence begins right with initiation into the gang. For males, initiation might mean having to survive a beating (Totten, 2009, p. 137). For many females, they might be "gang-banged" as part of their initiation into gangs (Totten, 2009, p. 139).

All of this violence affecting Aboriginal peoples is not traditional. This is not to say that traditional Aboriginal societies never experienced violence. However, when violence occurred it was not accepted or tolerated. It was not until societies were interrupted by the colonizing West that traditional governance structures and cultures were disrupted, thus leading to increases in violence affecting our peoples. Various traditional societies would all have their own means to deal with crime, but it is safe assumption to say that violence was not part of our cultures.

Dominant discourses surrounding the overrepresentation of Aboriginal peoples as victims and offenders of violence are still unfortunately predicated on the idea that Aboriginal peoples need to somehow change to fit the current system (Monture-Angus, 1998, p. 362). Rather than continuing to approach issues of Aboriginal overrepresentation from such a viewpoint, which is amenable to "us and them" or "our and their" binaries, it is more productive to attempt to understand these issues from a broader Aboriginal perspective.

This chapter begins by providing an overview of the explanations for Aboriginal people's high contact with the justice system, both as victims and offenders of crime and violence as revealed from the current literature. Once this literature has been reviewed, these explanations are explored using an Aboriginal ideological lens in an attempt to better understand these high rates of crime and violence. We conclude by outlining the next steps forward toward change.

Doctrines of Conquest and Discovery

Forty years before Europeans even reached the Americas, a collection of theological and legal rulings had been established that gave Europeans the right to dominate any non-Christian peoples and take over any unclaimed land (Venne, 1997, pp. 185-186). The documented rulings explained that Europeans had "the right to attack, conquer and subjugate Saracens, pagans, and other enemies of Christ wherever they were to be found," and "recognize title over any lands and possessions" (Rodriguez, 1997, p. 469). These rulings, known as "The Doctrine of Discovery," were international legal norms that have framed many oppressive, racist policies and actions throughout history (Venne, 1998).

When the European explorers arrived in the Americas they were following an engrained tradition of conquest and discovery, and they believed they had a right to conquer and control anyone who might pose as a threat to European civilization and Christian norms and goals (Venne, 1998, pp. 2-3). Aboriginal people immediately became objects of international legal doctrine and colonial subjects in their own land as the Europeans advanced their goals (Berkhofer, 1978, p. 115). The doctrine of discovery became the justification for many colonization efforts, efforts that were based on dehumanizing conceptions, given that they described Aboriginal peoples as "infidels," "beasts," and "savages," among other shameful depictions (Berkhofer, 1978, pp. 9-23). The doctrines of discovery influenced understanding of Aboriginal peoples since first contact and are still engrained in many policies throughout North America today.

Genocidal Polices and Residential Schools

When Europeans began to arrive in larger numbers they not only took Aboriginal people's lands and defined them as lesser beings, they also considered them obstacles to their creation of a Euro-Canadian civilization (Rice & Snyder, 2008, p. 49). For example, although various peace and friendship treaties were agreed to between Aboriginal and European settler nations, settler governments did not uphold the agreements. Various policies, acts, regulations, and laws were created to impose a system of European governance on Aboriginal people. Soon Aboriginal people began to be displaced from their land and pushed onto "Indian Reserves" to accommodate European people (new Canadians) and their interests. In 1876, the Government of Canada passed the Indian Act. Although it has been amended throughout the years, it still remains very similar to its original 1800s paternalistic form. This act has imposed government structures on Aboriginal communities. It gave the federal government total control of Aboriginal landholding patterns, economic and resource development, even control over Aboriginal people's ability to practise culture and traditions. Up until 1951, Aboriginal people could be arrested if they were caught practising traditional dances or ceremonies, and any ceremonial items would be confiscated (Backhouse, 1999, p. 53).

This act still authorizes the federal government to administer and regulate First Nation communities and lands. It imposes a political structure different from traditional political structures. The act continues to use the notion of "Indian Status," which defines who is legally an "Indian" and who is not, based on a system of registration. This current system of registration has its roots in a racist, archaic blood quantum concept. Such a concept was based on who used to be legally deemed as having enough Aboriginal blood to be Aboriginal.

Another policy, which is no longer enforced today but still has a lasting legacy, is the Canadian government's implementation of Indian residential schools, which was in effect in Canada from 1831 to 1996. These schools were managed by Christian churches and financially supported by the Canadian federal government (Cote & Schissel, 2002, p. 177). In 1931, the schools reached their peak, with over 80 schools in operation throughout Canada (Fournier & Crey, 2006, p. 143).

Initially, it was voluntary for Aboriginal students to attend residential schools. Some families sent their children because they were being inundated by colonizers who made them feel that this might be the best way forward for their children. However, there were still many families who did not want to send their children to these schools. Thus, in 1920 the federal government made it mandatory for all Aboriginal children to attend residential schools (Kelly, 2008, p. 23). Parents who refused to send their children to these schools were threatened with fines or imprisonment (Furniss, 1995, p. 108).

Up until the 1960s, Aboriginal people could not vote and were not even considered Canadian citizens (Kelly, 2008, p. 24; Furniss, 1995, p. 108). Therefore, they had no voice or repercussion against authorities who would take their children and put them in these schools (Furniss, 1995, p. 108). Authorities took children by force from families and put them in residential schools where they were forced to stay for about ten months of every year (Kirmayer et al., 2007, p. 68). During their stay they were denied communication with their families, so not to be influenced by their traditional culture. Many schools were far distances from students' homes to assure that they could not travel back and have access to family or any of their traditional practices.

Although these schools claimed to provide good quality education for Aboriginal children, it has since been discovered that this was only a small piece of their purpose. Rather, their true intended purpose was to solve what the Canadian government called their "Indian Problem" (Chrisjohn & Young, 2006, p. 61). In these schools, children were subjected to forced assimilation into Euro-Canadian culture. Many were falsely taught that their culture was the way of the devil and were threatened with the fear of going to hell if they continued to practise anything related to their traditional culture. Instead, they had to learn and practise Christian religions. Students were forced to learn English and/or French and were not allowed to speak their traditional languages. Most other "educational" activities were centered on industrial education, aimed at preparing students for life in the "lower fringes of the dominant society" (Kirmayer et al., 2007, p. 66; Dickason, 2002, p. 315).

Immediately upon attending the schools, children would be assigned a number and their traditional names were replaced by an English or French name (Fournier & Crey, 2006, p. 148). They had their traditional long hair or braids cut or shaved off and their traditional clothing confiscated and replaced by standard issue uniforms (Kelly, 2008, p. 24; Fournier & Crey, 1997, p. 57; Fournier & Crey, 2006, p. 148). Many of the children suffered abuses, including emotional, physical, and sexual abuses, with sexual abuse actually found to have reached epidemic levels (Milloy, 1999, p. 298; Kelly, 2008, p. 24; Cote & Schissel, 2002, p. 177; Chansonneuve, 2007, p. 11; Corrado & Cohen, 2003, p. 41; Grant, 1996, pp. 225-231). In fact, in 1990, the special advisor to the minister of national health and welfare on child sexual abuse declared that "closer scrutiny of past treatment of Native children at Indian residential schools would show 100% of children at some schools were sexually abused" (Milloy 1999, p. 298).

Furthermore, the Truth Commission on Genocide in Canada (2001) report revealed that Christian churches and the federal government were actually involved in the murder of over

50,000 Aboriginal children who had attended these residential schools (as cited by Smith, 2005, p. 40). The long list of horrific offences committed by the church and their officials include "murder by beating, poisoning, hanging, starvation, strangulation, and medical experimentation" (Smith, 2005, p. 40). For example, if a child spoke their Aboriginal language, torture, such as "public whippings," "lashes," and/or forcible confinement for days, was used as punishment (Smith, 2005, p. 40; Fournier & Crey, 1997, p. 59). Needles were stuck through children's tongues, often left for extended periods of time (Chrisjohn & Young, 2006, p. 49).

Some children were also beaten into unconsciousness and to the point of serious permanent or semi-permanent injuries, such as broken limbs, fractured skulls, shattered eardrums (Chrisjohn & Young, 2006, p. 49). In reference to Rupert's Land Industrial School near Selkirk, Manitoba, Fournier and Crey (2006) explain,

Young girls of eight or nine still bore bruises on their bodies several weeks after being strapped, they said. During an investigation, the Anglican principle admitted he fed the children rancid butter and crept into the dormitories at night to kiss the little girls, but he was reprimanded, not removed. (p. 148)

Some children in the residential schools were used in pedophile rings that were organized by the clergy, police, and business and government officials (Truth Commission on Genocide, 2001, as cited by Smith, 2005, p. 40). There were forced abortions in female children who had been impregnated by men in authority (Chrisjohn & Young, 2006, p. 49). Children were also involuntarily sterilized, and former students revealed that some of the schools had unmarked graveyards where murdered babies were buried – babies that had been born to Aboriginal girls who were raped by the priests and other church officials (Smith, 2005, p. 40; Chansonneuve, 2007, p. 11).

Through the implementation and operation of the residential schools, Canadian governments, major Canadian churches, and Canadian citizens all played a major part in the commission of genocide upon Aboriginal people (Chrisjohn & Young, 2006, p. 77). Although all may have not played a firsthand role in these schools, many were obsequious with their existence, thus complicit in their operations. Genocide is the systematic and deliberate annihilation and elimination of a racial, political, or cultural group. Although policies did not directly state that the intention was to murder Aboriginal children, many Aboriginal children did die. Some of which whom were murdered (Chrisjohn & Young, 2006, p. 60-61). Yet to commit an act of genocide does not require direct killing of people; it is about the destruction and eradication of a people or group of people (Chrisjohn & Young, 2006, p. 60). These schools were in place to completely eradicate Aboriginal people in Canada, be it through forced sickness, "accidental" killing, assimilation, and/or cultural destruction. The intent of the Canadian government in these activities was made very clear in numerous documents and public statements. For example, in 1920 and in reference to Bill 14, which was an amendment to the Indian Act to allow the federal government to enfranchise (remove someone's Indian Status) anyone they saw fit, there was also a reinstatement of the government's right to impel attendance at residential schools:

I want to get rid of the Indian problem. I do not think as a matter of fact, that this country ought to continuously protect a class of people who are able to stand alone. That is my whole point. Our objective is to continue until there is no Indian question, and no Indian department and that is the whole object of this Bill (Duncan Campbell Scott qtd. in Chrisjohn and Young 2006, 61).

Intergenerational Legacies

Even though many of the policies that were enacted throughout the 1800s and 1900s are no longer in place, their legacy still influences Canada's relationship with Aboriginal peoples, a relationship that can be described as "controlling, disempowering and exploitative" (Rice & Snyder, 2008, p. 50). Many abuses experienced in the residential schools have since leaked back into communities; so even after the schools were closed, the effects echoed through the lives of following generations (Gagné 1998). As Sellers (2013, p. xv) explains, for many Aboriginal people, their childhoods – which are their most vulnerable and impressionable years – were spent as residential schools; thus, mental, emotional, and spiritual growth was extremely interrupted as a result of the horrible treatment they experienced. Many inter- and intragenerational effects have been identified, including loss of culture, language, traditional values, and family bonding, as well as a decrease in life skills, parenting skills, self-respect, and, for some, respect for others (Jacobs & Williams, 2008, p. 126).

These accumulated effects are now linked to addiction, prostitution, homelessness, suicide, family violence, and post-traumatic stress disorder, among other issues (Chanson-neuve, 2005, pp. 43-48, pp. 50-53; Wesley-Esquimaux & Smolewski, 2004; Gagné, 1998; Jacobs & Williams, 2008, p. 126; Cote & Schissel, 2002; Corrado & Cohen, 2003; Söchting et al., 2007). Furthermore, many of these legacies to which the literature attests are the same or related factors that research identifies as related to crime and violence. Common factors related to crime and violence includes family abuse, lack of parental supervision, academic failure, unemployment, high mobility, substance abuse, delinquent friends, extreme poverty and poor living conditions, and living in crowded conditions, just to name a few (Hawkins et al., 1992; Sampson & Laub, 1993; Brzozowski, Taylor-Butts, & Johnson, 2006; World Health Organization, 2010). Some of these factors have been identified through various research studies that examine crime affecting Aboriginal people. For example, La Prairie (1994) inter-viewed 621 inner city Aboriginal people in Canada who were considered vulnerable to crime, victimization, and the criminal justice response; that research found that people were poor, had substance abuse problems, had low education levels, and had experienced child violence and other forms of family violence (La Prairie 1992, 1994, 2002). Seventy-five percent of people interviewed reported experiencing violence in their families (La Prairie, 1994, p. 406). Being a victim of family violence as a child was found to lead to increased alcohol problems for youth; eighty-three percent of people who reported drinking "all the time" also reported having been victims of family violence as a child (La Prairie, 1994, p. 418). Child exposure to family violence was also found to increase associations with the criminal justice system in later juvenile or adult life (La Prairie, 1994, p. 421).

Research recounting experiences of six Aboriginal gang members in Winnipeg also iden-tified similar related factors; it revealed that addictions and drug abuse, violence, and family disintegration were very common among Aboriginal gang members and, in fact, were described as normal "everyday" events which these men grew up with (Comack et al., 2009, pp. 1-5).

These intergenerational legacies serve as explanations for the increased experience and rates of violence among Aboriginal people. Colonialism, assimilationist governmental policies, and residential school experiences, and their interrelated historical traumas, carry on into the following generations. Exposure to traumatic factors such as physical, sexual, mental, and emotional abuse, lingers within communities and families, triggering subsequent generations to experience parallel traumas. In some cases, it might cause the next generation to turn to coping mechanisms, such as alcohol or drug abuse to ease emotional pain associated with such traumas (Maté, 2012). It is not an absolute that exposure to traumatic factors will cause next generations to mirror abuse or violence, or to be impacted by it in some way, however, the likelihood significantly increases if exposed to such trauma as compared to those who never experienced such trauma. As Maté (2012) explains, people's lives become shaped by their upbringing and environment, and it has a direct link in shaping their future behaviour. Consequently, as Maté (2012) contends, those brought up with violence and abuse have a predisposition to acting out in violent and angry ways, and in many cases will turn to substance abuse to cope. According to Atkinson (2002), traumatic symptoms, such as turning to alcohol to cope or acting out violently, are natural human responses to disasters or tragedies (p. 52). Thus, these traumatic symptoms are "the natural and predictable reactions of normal people … to abnormal experiences" (Atkinson, 2002, p. 52).

Aboriginal Worldview

This chapter now seeks to build on these explanations by framing it within a broader Aboriginal ideological lens. The explanations for Aboriginal overrepresentation that these studies provide are indeed useful and do provide a productive foundation upon which to examine Aboriginal people's experiences of violence. However, these explanations alone do not move us towards solutions, given that focus largely remains on individuals and communities rather than addressing the broader social structures and dominant discourses, which are rooted in, and upheld by colonialism.

This Aboriginal lens is not one that should be assumed to be a worldview of all Aboriginal people, as there is a large diversity of Aboriginal cultures across Canada, with numerous uniquely distinct Aboriginal cultural groups, which all have different and sometimes overlapping cultural traditions. Furthermore, according to Dickson-Gilmore and La Prairie (2005), at least 70% of the modern Aboriginal population now live a complex urban lifestyle, with many contemporary Aboriginal people having limited contact with or awareness of their traditional heritage or culture. Thus, it should in no way be assumed that the "Aboriginal worldview" or "Aboriginal lens" being referred to here is a worldview held by all Aboriginal people. Instead, the worldview used here reflects my mixed heritage as a combination of Algonquin, Métis, Huron, and Scottish, and it is influenced by my own teachings, experiences, and research.

Thus, according to some, we currently live in a world where the dominant epistemes, or methods of knowing, are derived from the European Enlightenment, which tend to centre on scientific method, reason, and, generally, a more linear mode of thinking (Newhouse, 2004, p. 139; Sioui, 2008). In contrast with these ways of perceiving and knowing the world, some traditional Aboriginal thought embraces circular thinking. The circle is seen as a symbolic representation of life's creative process itself, and such a conceptualization of experience, by its very nature, prompts a sacred relationship between all things in the universe; this structure of relationships includes all of humanity and understands all of humanity as being a family (Sioui, 2008, p. 104). Furthermore, Aboriginal cosmologies and epistemologies understand phenomena in circular cycles, conceptualizing all things as coming from Mother Earth, and returning to Mother Earth, including all people, plants, animals, and so on. Linear thought, on the other hand, has been described as "the incapacity to see and feel the sacred relation that exists between all beings in the universe" (Sioui, 2008, p. 83). According to Fixico (2009, p. 67) those with a linear mind thinks about all things related to themselves, with themselves being at the centre. These Westernized methods of knowing are what currently dominate Canadian knowledge systems.

Mother Earth, the Land, and Father Sky, the Cosmos

Absolon and Willett (2004, p. 8) explain that Aboriginal culture is comprised of histories that have been passed down through generations via oral traditions such as storytelling, ceremonial songs and teachings as well as rituals and sharing. Histories such as these are usually sought out through contact with Aboriginal Elders. Elders are looked upon for advice, healing, counsel, and inspiration of the past and present. They have become the historians of their nations and philosophers and teachers of their traditions (Couture, 1998, p. 36).

Much Aboriginal knowledge and tradition has been explained as being rooted in a relationship with Mother Earth, the land, and Father Sky, the cosmos (Couture, 1998, p. 37). As Helin (2006) explains, "at the root of Indigenous cultures are deeply-held spiritual views based on a profound respect for nature" (p. 77). He explains that an Aboriginal spiritual and traditional view is based on the idea that existence is embedded within nature and within the cosmos (pp. 77-80).

This emphasis on nature in various Aboriginal cultures is born of the recognition that nature has valuable gifts that are produced from the land and resources upon which human beings are completely reliant for survival (Helin, 2006, p. 79). Many Aboriginal beliefs have a holistic view of life that involves viewing existence as enacting within a web of nature; to survive, one must therefore be cautious of how their own individual existence affects nature. Thus, traditional Aboriginal individuals and communities are careful not to exploit or undervalue Mother Earth's great gifts of natural resources, such as water and wildlife. For example, some traditional Aboriginal peoples hold a belief that one must give back to the Creator to maintain a balance when harvesting crops, for example, by replanting what was used.

Trying to understand Aboriginal overrepresentation from a perspective of profound respect for Mother Earth and all her creations yields significantly different results than viewing it from the current, widely held Western outlook. It becomes quite clear that much of the balance, harmony, and circular thinking inherent in Aboriginal teachings and knowledge is not adhered to or internalized in white Westernized Canada. Instead, the current state of the world is very much the result of capitalist ideals such as consumption, consumerism, and, according to some, a complete disrespect for nature (B. McLeod, Elder, Interview with author, October 22, 2009). This is evident by how people in today's world continue to over-consume food and energy as well as many more of the world's limited resources.

Thus, not living in balance and harmony with nature and Mother Earth has created a much different way of life than in the past. With the emphasis on self-interest, the current conditions and economic and social systems dictate a way of life that is divided, centred on greed, and highly individualized (B. McLeod, Elder, Interview with author, October 22, 2009). This system allows a small number of elite people to hold power and misuse the earth resources for their benefit, while disregarding other people and beings.

This current white, Westernized system also creates institutions to maintain this hierarchal order by disciplining and incapacitating those who do not follow "the rules." This is very much the case with the current Euro-Canadian criminal justice system. As criminologists such as Reiman (2007) have explained, the criminal justice system operates to allow wealthy, mainly white people to continue to benefit, while pushing the poor (including Aboriginal people) into deeper poverty and, in many cases, prison, therefore, at the same time upholding an unequal hierarchal system centred on the interests of the powerful.

Indeed, it seems that we are living in a world that not only promotes inequality between people, but one that maintains inequality between all things, the land, peoples, animals, plants, rocks, and everything else – all things human and otherwise. A society that disrespects people and nature to such an extent strives to convert every creation into power and material wealth. And, as according to Sioui (2008), these societal interactions can only result in violent, sexist, and racist activities (p. 83).

Furthermore, the criminal justice system itself is a European white construct, encompassing policing, courts, and correctional institutions all founded on European ideas of deterrence and incapacitation – ideals developed mainly through patriarchal means and, as such, delivered in capitalist societies that seek to uphold inequality.

Father-centeredness vs. Mother-centeredness

Some Aboriginal belief systems would suggest that capitalism, which Canada currently embraces, is a male creation. It is a social and economic mode of exchange keeping people divided, with dominant power structures in charge. In contrast, many traditional Aboriginal ideologies are based on equality – both interactions between individuals in the physical environment and interactions with the environment itself. In fact, when Aboriginal peoples and Europeans first came into contact, Aboriginal people were living in harmony with their physical environment – mostly as hunters and gatherers, but there were also agricultural tribes. Their way of life made little demands on the ecology, and people were even able to drink out of lakes and streams. On the other hand, Europeans were continually developing their technology to achieve control over nature (Frideres & Gadacz, 2001, p. 9). In this Euro-Canadian system everything became the possession of man, including air, water, plants, animals, earth, and rocks. Even women lost their power and high or equal status that they had in circular societies and became man's possession (Huhndorf & Suzack, 2010).

Many traditional Aboriginal societies were organized and operated according to mother-centred principles. Mother-centeredness incorporates a balance between genders, as well as in relation to all creatures in general (Sioui, 2008, p. 138). This does not imply that women must command; rather, it reflects a belief that women have an especially crucial role and a unique ability to teach and to preserve the world (Tarnas, 1991, pp. 443-444). When seeing the world through this aspect of an Aboriginal lens, it becomes apparent that we currently live in a world dominated by patriarchal precedents embracing a more "father-centred" world. According to Sioui (2008, p. 138) father-centred societies are those that embrace linear thinking, where women become servants in the possession of men.

The current domination of patriarchy contrasts with many traditional Aboriginal societal and community structures, (before they were disrupted through the process of colonization), many of which were mother-centered or matriarchal in nature (Givens, 2006, p. 53; Sioui,

2008, p. 138). Even though not all communities were matriarchal, many Aboriginal women played large roles in their communities before European contact, including the areas of family life, marriage, politics, decision making, and the ceremonial life of their people (RCAP, 1996). Many women were responsible for major decisions. For example, in some Aboriginal societies, Aboriginal women were responsible for selecting the men who were to be in leadership positions (Eppler, 2007, p. 170). Some Aboriginal women have argued that both Aboriginal men and women were equal and that gender equality was in place before white Western society and religion came into being. Since European contact there has been a concerted effort to diminish the role of Aboriginal women (see Eppler, 2007, p. 172).

In many traditional Aboriginal nations, a person's identity traditionally followed his or her mother's line (i.e., matrilineal descent). However, since European contact, the patrilineage system was imposed on Aboriginal communities (Jacobs & Williams, 2008, p. 123). Such a move increased the power and authority of men at the expense of women. As a result, there were major disruptions within "traditional kinship systems, matrilineal descent patterns, and matrilocal, post-martial residency patterns" (Stevenson, 1996, p. 68 qtd. in Jacobs & Williams, 2008, p. 123). Moreover, such practices in turn forced the rule that Aboriginal women and their children, similar to European women and their children, would be subject to their fathers' and husbands' domination (Stevenson, 1996, 68 as cited by Jacobs & Williams, 2008, p. 123).

Viewing the world through a lens which sees all people as equals, including women, brings to light the fact that the current system is rife with inequalities and, to some extent, quite regressive compared to traditional Aboriginal social systems. A system built upon such inequality can have detrimental effects on people stuck at the low end of this imposed hierarchical structure. When viewing the current world as unequal and structured on patriarchal precedents, it becomes clear that high rates of crime and violence affecting Aboriginal people may very well be a result of such a system, as inequality, reinforced and intensified by capitalism, keeps Aboriginal people near the lower ends of the hierarchy.

Aboriginal people have been relegated to the lowest echelons of the hierarchy. Throughout history, there have been initiatives trying to eliminate any Aboriginal presence (for example, through residential schools). This also includes assimilation policies such as White Paper on Indian Policy proposed by the Pierre Trudeau government in 1969. This White Paper was written primarily by Jean Chrétien, who was the minister of Indian affairs at the time. It proposed to eliminate the Indian Act and thus, "get out of the Indian Business." This was a deliberate effort by the federal government to one-sidedly try to enact Aboriginal peoples into extermination through the revoking of any Indian rights and status.

These types of policies and strategies such as the White Paper and residential schools are aimed at assimilation and eradication. They are acts of colonial violence against Aboriginal peoples. Such acts uphold a society that maintains large disparities in the distribution of opportunity, wealth, and power. Such an unequal system provides profits to individuals and institutions that hold the power, and it inflicts adverse and damaging repercussions on those lacking power. Numerous Aboriginal people hold less power and are offered fewer opportunities. Many are "othered," abjected, and put into positions of relentless struggle with this inequitable, unbalanced, and male-dominated system. As a result, Aboriginal peoples become targets of an unequal criminal justice system that works against Aboriginal people rather than for Aboriginal people.

Inequality vs. Equality

In fact, the current criminal justice system is a perfect example of the inequality inherent in the current male-dominated Western hierarchal social system in which Canada currently operates. As Reiman (2007) argues, the criminal justice system itself operates in a way that benefits the rich and penalizes the poor. Recognition of the harmful acts of the elite are ignored, and the public is provided with an image of the "threat of crime as a threat from the poor" (Reiman, 2007, p. 1). This misrepresentation that the danger of crime originates from the poor has powerful repercussions.

First, danger to society is thought to be "the work of the poor, an image that serves the interests of the powerful" (Reiman, 2007, p. 8). Second, these portrayals imply that people are in poverty because they haven't done what they should to prevent it, not because of a greater social injustice. And third, these portrayals imply that people are in poverty because "of their own shortcomings, particularly moral shortcomings such as incontinence and indolence" (Reiman, 2007, p. 183). This type of distorted thinking and categorization of entire groups of people foster a conservative perspective that accepts a society with substantial inequalities of wealth, power, and opportunity and dissuades progressive demands for equality. It also maintains and supports the cycle of inequality and retains the desired hierarchal order in place. It is a system that gives a false appearance of equality, and actually creates inequality by allowing an elite group to maintain their power over everyone else, and over all of Mother Earth's creations. A society that functions in such a way clearly contributes to people being abused by a criminal justice system that operates to support the Western hierarchal order.

Some Aboriginal scholars have noted the need to move away from such a patriarchal and linear thinking system, stating that change is needed to address many of the problems that have been brought about by these male-dominated capitalist systems over the years (M. Saavedra-Vargas, Indigenous Studies Professor, Aboriginal Studies Program, University of Ottawa, conversation with the author, September 2, 2009). Some Aboriginal women have argued that women are more collaborative and that they bring a different type of sensitivity to leadership (see Eppler, 2007, p. 172). This idea is something also relayed by a female Cherokee chief who describes an Aboriginal prophecy, which explains that there will be a time when a switch to feminine approaches will need to take place:

> In September 1993 Cherokee Chief Wilma Mankiller cited "One Native prophecy," which foretold that "this is the 'time of the women,' a time when women's leadership skills are needed." Noting the differences in male and female approaches, she added, "Women, by and large, bring to leadership a greater sense of collaboration, an ability to view social, political and personal concerns in a uniquely interconnected, female way." (as cited by Eppler, 2007, p. 167)

Finally, it is clear that there is an inherent hegemony implicit within Western traditions. Yet this is not to say that forms of leadership do not exist in traditional Aboriginal systems. For example, chiefs existed, and still exist, who act as leaders. However, the difference in the ways leadership is understood is apparent when one considers the following example: a leader, in many traditional Aboriginal societies and understandings does not ask, "What can I control?" but rather, "What am I responsible for?"; a leader does not ask, "What do I get?" but instead, "What can I contribute?" (Eppler, 2007, p. 147).

Conclusion: Next Steps

Contextualizing this issue of Aboriginal people's high rates of violence and crime through an Aboriginal lens assists in providing a much more broadened understanding of the issue. The criminal justice system itself is part of an unequal male-dominated hierarchal social structure, resulting from the domination of European interests based on inequality.

By viewing Aboriginal people's overrepresentation as victims and offenders of crime and violence through an Aboriginal lens, this chapter suggests the need for a reframing of the question. No longer is the question, what do Aboriginal peoples need to change in order to reduce their overrepresentation as victims and offenders of crime and violence? Rather, what does the current system have to change to become more equal and balanced?

It is important to continue to contextualize this issue through such a lens, as this frame of thinking could be the basis for moving forward towards solutions. Aboriginal traditional knowledge has revealed the importance of maintaining balance, equality, and respect between all things, and this is something that should be more thoroughly considered, pressed, and embraced.

Family-focused social and cultural programming, which seeks to tackle the risk factors and acknowledge history and intergenerational legacies of colonization, could be a productive first step forward. There are many programs that seek to do just that – and are by and for Aboriginal people. These programs can be found operating out of Aboriginal Friendship Centres and other Aboriginal organizations or grassroots agencies across Canada. The support and further recognition of these Aboriginal-specific programs could pose as a useful starting point, especially since many operate on their own Aboriginal guiding principles and worldviews.

The Prince Albert Outreach Program Agency in Prince George, British Columbia provides the Youth Alliance Against Gang Violence Project, also referred to as the Warrior Spirit Walking Project (WSW). The WSW program is targeted to reducing gang violence and involvement. The foundation of the program is based on Lakota Sioux youth-care expert Martin Brokenleg's circle of courage approach (Brendtro, Brokenleg & Van Bockern, 2002). This approach is rooted in traditional Aboriginal child rearing philosophies, as well as research in child psychology and resilience. It utilizes a medicine wheel framework, and centres on four central values: belonging, mastery, independence, and generosity. In order to have one's circle of courage complete, and thus live a life in balance, all four components must be present in one's life. Individuals must belong to a social support network. They need to master personal goals and gain personal satisfaction. Individuals must also have individual freedom, and the autonomy to make choices. Finally, they must be generous, embrace a value system of simplicity, and experience the fulfilment of being able to give freely (Brendtro, Brokenleg & Van Bockern, 2002, p. 57).

Following this circle of courage framework, the WSW program offers a variety of programs and services to youth aged 12 to 21, who are at high risk of joining a gang, or whom where already gang involved (Totten & Dunn, 2012, p. 7). Services include crisis counselling, employment counselling, substance abuse counselling, community school-based counselling, and female assistance group counselling (Totten & Dunn, 2012, p. 20). Under the supervision and assistance of staff members, a team of previous gang members provide presentations to youth at risk with the aim to teach them about the dangers of gangs, violence, and bullying

(Totten & Dunn, 2012, p. 21). These presentations are all rooted in traditional cultural teachings, and incorporate their personal stories, hip-hop, recreational activities, and others. Additional program activities include employment training, recreational, outreach, and cultural activities, among others.

The WSW program underwent an evaluation, showing that among the youth who were gang members at the start of the program, all had left the gangs by the 24 month follow-up of the evaluation (Totten & Dunn, 2012, p. 69). In a comparison between a control group and program group, the youth receiving the programming were found to have more positive outcomes, including better attachment to teachers, parents, and school (Totten & Dunn, 2012, p. 108.) Some were shown to have better acceptance of their ethnic identity, and have reduced levels of substance abuse as compared to the control group (Totten & Dunn, 2012, p. 108).

Ultimately, understanding violence affecting Aboriginal peoples in a variety of ways, more specifically, through a broader lens based on equality, respect, balance, and more circular way of thinking, may aid in the eventual attainment of more in-depth answers to the question of high rates of victimization and offending and its eventual reduction. The chapter has sought to be a part of creating a much-needed new discourse that may move this problem towards possible solutions. By using Aboriginal knowledge and viewpoints to more fully understand problems and issues facing Canada, Aboriginal peoples can hopefully begin to be looked to as being part of a solution, rather than existing as part of a "problem." Finally, this discourse will hopefully play a small part in leading the way to becoming more harmonious and in peace with sacred Mother Earth.

Keywords

Circular thinking, linear thinking, assimilation, genocide, doctrines of discovery, genocidal policies, residential schools, intergenerational trauma, mother-centeredness, father-centeredness.

Review Questions

1. How might explanations for violence be explained when examining it through a circular lens, versus a linear lens?
2. Why it is important to acknowledge residential school experiences when examining violence that affects Aboriginal peoples today?
3. How and in what ways might patriarchy play a role in the violence experienced by Aboriginal peoples?
4. Why might some describe the Canadian criminal justice system as a system of injustice?
5. What might be some promising solutions to reducing violence affecting Aboriginal peoples?

Suggested Readings

Cote, H., & Schissel, W. (2008). Damaged children and broken spirits: A residential school survivor story. In C. Brooks & B. Schissel (Eds.), *Marginality and condemnation: An introduction to critical criminology* (2nd ed.) (pp. 220-237). Black Point, NS: Fernwood Publishing.
Human Rights Watch. (2013). *Those who take us away: Abusive policing and failures in protection of Indigenous women and girls in Northern British Columbia, Canada*. United States: Human Rights Watch.

Monture-Angus, P. A. (1998). Lessons in decolonization: Aboriginal overrepresentation in Canadian criminal justice. In D. Long & O. P. Dickason (Eds.), *Visions of the heart: Canadian Aboriginal issues* (pp. 361-386). Scarborough, ON: Thomson Nelson.

Perreault, S. (2011). Violent victimization of Aboriginal people in the Canadian provinces, 2009. *Juristat, 30*(4), 1-35.

Totten, M. (2009). Aboriginal youth and violent gang involvement in Canada: Quality prevention strategies. *IPC Review, 3,* 135-156.

References

Absolon, K., & Willett, C. (2004). Aboriginal research: Berry picking and hunting in the 21st century. *First Peoples Child and Family Review, 1*(1), 5-17.

Amnesty International. (2004). *Stolen sisters: A Human rights response to discrimination and violence against Indigenous women in Canada*. Ottawa: Amnesty International.

Atkinson, J. (2002). *Trauma trails: Recreating song lines: The transgenerational effects of trauma in Indigenous Australia*. North Melborne: Spinifex Press Pty Ltd.

Backhouse, C. (1999). *Colour-coded: A legal history of racism in Canada, 1900-1950*. Toronto: University of Toronto Press.

Berkhofer Jr., R. R. (1978). *The white man's Indian: Images of the American Indian from Columbus to present*. New York: Random House Vintage Books.

Brendtro, L. K., Brokenleg, M., & Van Bockern, S. (2002). *Reclaiming youth at risk: Our hope for the future*. Bloomington, IN: Solution Tree Press.

Brennan, S. (2011). *Violent victimization of Aboriginal women in the Canadian provinces, 2009*. Ottawa: Ministry of Industry.

Brzozowski, J. A., Taylor-Butts, A., & Johnson, S. (2006). Victimization and offending among the Aboriginal population in Canada. *Juristat, 26*(3), 1-31.

Chansonneuve, D. (2007). *Addictive behaviours among Aboriginal people in Canada*. Ottawa: Aboriginal Healing Foundation.

Chrisjohn, R., Young, S., & Maraun, M. (2006). *The circle game: Shadows and substance in the indian residential school experience in Canada* (Rev. ed.). Penticton, BC: Theytus Books.

Comack, E., Deane, L., Morrissette, L., & Silver, J. (2009). *If you want to change violence in the 'hood, you have to change the 'hood: Violence and street gangs in Winnipeg's inner city*. Winnipeg, MB: Canadian Centre for Policy Alternatives.

Corrado, R. R., and Cohen, I. M. (2003). *Mental health profiles for a sample of British Columbia's Aboriginal survivors of the Canadian residential school system*. Ottawa: Aboriginal Healing Foundation.

Couture, J. (1998). The role of Native elders: Emergent issues. In D. Long & O. P. Dickason (Eds.), *Visions of the heart: Canadian Aboriginal issues* (2nd ed.) (pp. 31-48). Scarborough, ON: Thomson Nelson.

Cote, H., & Schissel, W. (2002). Damaged children and broken spirits: A residential school survivor's story. In C. Brooks & B. Schissel (Eds.), *Marginality and condemnation: An introduction to critical criminology* (2nd ed.) (pp. 175-192). Black Point, NS: Fernwood Publishing.

Dickason, O. P. (2002). *Canada's First Nations: A history of founding peoples from earliest times* (3rd ed.). Don Mills, ON: Oxford University Press.

Dickson-Gilmore, J. and LaPrairie, C. (2005). *Will the circle be unbroken? Aboriginal communities, restorative justice, and the challenges of conflict and change.* Toronto: University of Toronto Press.

Eppler, S. J. (2007). *Beloved women: The political lives of LaDonna Harris and Wilma Mankiller.* DeKalb, IL: Northern Illinois University Press.

Fitzgerald, R. T., Carrington, P. J. (2008). The neighbourhood context of urban Aboriginal crime. *Canadian Journal of Criminology and Criminal Justice, 50*(5), 523-557.

Fixico, D. (2009). *The American Indian mind in a linear world: American Indian studies and traditional knowledge.* Binghamton, NY: Routledge.

Fleras, A. (2004). Researching together differently: Bridging the research paradigm gap. *Native Studies Review, 15*(2), 117-129.

Fournier, S., & Crey, E. (1997). *Stolen from our embrace: The abduction of First Nations children and restoration of Aboriginal communities.* Vancouver: Douglas & McIntyre.

Fournier, S., & Crey, E. (2006). "Killing the Indian in the child": Four centuries of church-run schools. In R. C. A. Maaka & C. Anderson (Eds.), *The Indigenous experience: Global perspectives* (pp. 141-149). Toronto: Canadian Scholars' Press.

Frideres, J. S., & Gadacz, R. R. (2001). *Aboriginal peoples in Canada: Contemporary conflicts* (6th ed.). Toronto: Prentice Hall.

Furniss, E. (1995). *The victims of benevolence: The dark legacy of the Williams Lake Residential School.* Vancouver: Arsenal Pulp Press.

Furniss, E. (1999). *The burden of history: Colonialism and the frontier myth in a rural community.* Vancouver: University of British Columbia Press.

Gagné, M.-A. (1998). The role of dependency and colonialism in generating trauma in First Nations citizens: The James Bay Cree. In Y. Danieli (Ed.), *International handbook of multigenerational legacies of trauma* (pp. 355-372). New York: Plenum.

Givens, K. M. (2006). Weeping for the lost matriarchy. In B. A. Mann (Ed.), *Daughters of mother earth: The wisdom of Native American women* (pp. 53-68). Westport, CT: Praeger Publishers.

Grant, A. (1996). *No end of grief: Indian residential schools in Canada.* Winnipeg, MB: Pemmican Publications.

Hawkins, J.D., Catalano, R.F., Morrison, D.M., O'Donnell, J., Abbott, R.D., & Day, L.E. (1992). The Seattle Social Development Project: Effects of the first four years on protective factors and problem behaviors. In J. McCord & R.E. Tremblay (Eds.), *Preventing adolescent antisocial behavior: Interventions from birth through adolescence* (pp. 139-161). New York: Guilford Press.

Helin, C. (2006). *Dances with dependency: Indigenous success through self-reliance.* Vancouver: Orca Spirit Publishing & Communication.

Huhndorf, S. M., & Suzack, C. (2010). Indigenous feminism: Theorizing the issues. In C. Suzack, S. M. Huhndorf, J. Perreault, & J. Barman (Eds.), *Indigenous women and feminism: Politics, activism, culture* (pp. 1-17). Vancouver: University of British Columbia Press.

Human Rights Watch. (2013). *Those who take us away: Abusive policing and failures in protection of Indigenous women and girls in Northern British Columbia, Canada.* United States: Human Rights Watch.

Hylton, J. D. (with the assistance of M. Bird, N. Eddy, H. Sinclair, & Stenerson, H.). (2002). *Aboriginal sexual offending in Canada.* Ottawa: Aboriginal Healing Foundation.

Jacobs, B., & Williams, A. J. (2008). Legacy of residential schools: Missing and murdered Aboriginal women. In M. B. Castellano, L. Archibald, & M. DeGagné (Eds.), *From truth to reconciliation: Transforming the legacy of residential schools* (pp. 119-140). Ottawa: Aboriginal Healing Foundation.

Kelly, F. (2008). Confession of a born again pagan. In M. B. Castellano, L. Archibald, & M. DeGagné (Eds.), *From truth to reconciliation: Transforming the legacy of residential schools* (pp. 11-40). Ottawa: Aboriginal Healing Foundation.

Kirmayer, L. J., Brass, G. M., Holton, T., Paul, K., Simpson, C., & Tait, C. (2007). *Suicide among Aboriginal people in Canada*. Ottawa: Aboriginal Healing Foundation.

La Prairie, C. (1992). *Dimensions of aboriginal over-representation in correctional institutions and implications for crime prevention*. Ottawa: Aboriginal Peoples Collection, Solicitor General of Canada.

La Prairie, C. (1994). *Seen but not heard: Native people in the inner city*. Ottawa: Department of Justice.

La Prairie, C. (2002). Aboriginal over-representation in the criminal justice system: A tale of nine cities. *Canadian Journal of Criminology, 44*(2), 181-208.

La Prairie, C., & Stenning, P. (2003). Exile on Main Street: Some thoughts on Aboriginal over-representation in the criminal justice system. In D. Newhouse & E. Peters (Eds.), *Not strangers in these parts: Urban Aboriginal peoples* (pp. 179-193). Ottawa: Policy Research Initiative.

Maté, G. (2012). *In the realm of hungry ghosts: Close encounters with addiction*. Toronto: Vintage Canada.

Milloy, J. S. (1999). *A national crime: The Canadian government and the residential school system 1879 to 1986*. Winnipeg: University of Manitoba Press.

Monture-Angus, P. A. (1998). Lessons in decolonization: Aboriginal overrepresentation in Canadian criminal justice. In D. Long & O. P. Dickason (Eds.), *Visions of the heart: Canadian Aboriginal issues* (pp. 361-386). Scarborough, ON: Thomson Nelson.

National Crime Prevention Centre. (2012). *A statistical snapshot of youth at risk and youth offending in Canada*. Ottawa: Public Safety Canada.

Native Women's Association of Canada. (2010). *What their stories tell us: Research findings from the Sisters in Spirit initiative*. Ohsweken, ON: Native Women's Association of Canada.

Newhouse, D. (2004). Indigenous knowledge in a multicultural world. *Native Studies Review, 15*(2), 139-154.

O'Donnell, V., & Wallace, S. (2011). *Women in Canada: A gender-based statistical report: First Nations, Métis and Inuit Women*. Ottawa: Ministry of Industry, Statistics Canada.

Pearce, M. (2013). *An awkward silence: Missing and murdered vulnerable women and the Canadian justice system (Doctoral dissertation)*. University of Ottawa, Ottawa.

Perreault, S. (2009). The incarceration of Aboriginal people in adult correctional services. *Juristat, 29*(3), 1-27.

Perreault, S. (2011). Violent victimization of Aboriginal people in the Canadian provinces, 2009. *Juristat, 30*(4), 1-35.

Reiman, J. (2007). *The rich get richer and the poor get prison: Ideology, class, and criminal justice*. Boston, MA: Allyn and Bacon.

Rice, B., & Snyder, A. (2008). Reconciliation in the context of a settler Society: Healing the legacy of colonialism in Canada. In M. B. Castellano, L. Archibald, & M. DeGagné (Eds.),

From truth to reconciliation: Transforming the legacy of residential schools (pp. 43-61). Ottawa: Aboriginal Healing Foundation.

Rodriguez, J. P. (1997). *The historical encyclopedia of world slavery (Vol. 2.)* Santa Barbara, CA: ABC-CLIO Inc.

Royal Commission on Aboriginal Peoples (RCAP). (1996). *Bridging the cultural divide: A report on Aboriginal people and criminal justice in Canada,* Ottawa: Minister of Supply and Services Canada.

Sampson, R. J., & Laub, J. H. (1993). *Crime in the making: Pathways and turning points through life.* Cambridge, MA: Harvard University Press.

Sellers, B. (2013). *They called me number one: Secrets and survival at Indian residential school.* Vancouver: Talonbooks.

Sioui, G. (2008). *Histoires de Kanatha: Vues et contées: Histories of Kanatha: Seen and Told.* Ottawa: University of Ottawa Press.

Smith, A. (2005). *Conquest: sexual violence and American Indian genocide.* Cambridge, MA: South End Press.

Söchting, I., Corrado, R., Cohen, I. M., Ley, R. G., & Brasfield, C. (2007). Traumatic pasts in Canadian Aboriginal people: Further support for a complex trauma conceptualization? *BC Medical Journal, 49*(6), 320-326.

Statistics Canada. (2008). *Aboriginal People in Canada in 2006: Inuit, Métis, and First Nations, 2006 census.* Ottawa: Canadian Centre for Justice Statistics.

Statistics Canada. (2013). *Aboriginal Peoples in Canada: First Nations People, Métis, and Inuit, National Household Survey, 2011.* Ottawa: Statistics Canada.

Tarnas, R. (1991). *The passion of the Western Mind: Understanding the ideas that have shaped our world view.* New York: Harmony Books.

Royal Canadian Mounted Police. (2014). *Missing and murdered Aboriginal women: A national operational overview.* Ottawa: Her Majesty the Queen in Right of Canada.

Totten, M. (2009). Aboriginal youth and violent gang involvement in Canada: Quality prevention strategies. *IPC Review, 3,* 135-156.

Totten, M., & Dunn, S. (2012). *Final evaluation report for the Prince Alberta Outreach Program Inc. Youth Alliance Against Gang Violence Project.* Gatineau: QC: Totten and Associates.

Trevethan, S., Moore, J. P., & Rastin, C. J. (2002). A profile of Aboriginal offenders in federal facilities and serving time in the community. *FORUM on Corrections Research, 14*(3), 17-19.

Venne, S. (1997). Understanding Treaty 6: An Indigenous perspective. In M. Asch (Ed.), *Aboriginal and Treaty Rights in Canada: Essays on Law, Equality, and Respect for Difference* (pp. 173-207). Vancouver: University of British Columbia Press.

Venne, S. H. (1998). *Our Elders understand our rights: Evolving international law regarding Indigenous people.* Penticton, BC: Theytus Books.

Wesley-Esquimaux, C. C., & Smolewski, M. (2004). *Historic trauma and Aboriginal healing.* Ottawa: Aboriginal Healing Foundation.

World Health Organization. (2010). *Violence prevention: The evidence.* Geneva: WHO Press.

PART 3

Violence in the Home, Family, and Society

Family Violence and Abuse within a Canadian Context

Learning Objectives

In this chapter you will...

▶ articulate the complexity family violence and abuse within a Canadian context

▶ describe some of the main trends and patterns of family violence and abuse in Canada

▶ learn about some of the main legislation that relates to family violence and abuse in Canada

▶ gain an understanding how history and the growing diversity of Canada's demographics have impacted traditional understanding of family violence and abuse in Canada

Chapter 8

Monica Pauls and
John Winterdyk

Introduction

Family violence is as ancient a crime as any crime known to human kind (Malley-Morrison, 2004). However, as an area of study and research, it is a comparatively new field of study and is often fraught with operational, definitional, and quantification challenges (Hackler, 2006). By way of example, the year 2011 marked only the eleventh year that Statistics Canada has produced a report on family-centred violence in Canada. And although we might have a general understanding of what family violence and abuse (V&A) means in Canada, in her book of family violence and abuse, Malley-Morrison (2004) points out that it can mean different things depending on ones' culture and historical experience. For example, what constitutes family violence and abuse is commonly related to the role that women and children play in different cultures. Therefore, while this chapter will focus on the topic within a Canadian context, we will conclude the chapter with an example of family violence and abuse that historically was not part of the Canadian culture. We are referring to honour killings.

Since the early 1980s, Canada has been witness to a range of studies and reports that have focused exclusively on family violence and abuse. In its family violence overview paper the Department of Justice (2009) provides examples of some of the benchmark studies and surveys, which include "the 1984 Badgley Report on Child Sexual Abuse, the 1993 Violence Against Women Survey, the 1993 Canadian Panel on Violence Against Women and the 1996 Royal Commission on Aboriginal Peoples. National surveys, such as the General Social Survey (GSS), the Canadian Incidence Study of Reported Child Abuse and Neglect, and the Uniform Crime Reporting Survey, provide valuable information on victimization and crime trends related to many forms of family violence" (p. 8).

The family unit is considered one of the most important social units of the life of a child as they develop their personality, their sense of self-worth, and a sense of security, as well as the role modeling for their behaviour. Although there are many expressions that reflect the importance of family (e.g., "your family is your most important social bond," "we do anything for a family member," and one's "children get unconditional love"), a major problem in the world today are the challenges that characterize many family units. For example, high divorce rates and the negative impact that family breakups have on children – especially younger children and their sense of security – and shrinking family time due to economic demands of longer work hours often mark family discord.[1,2,3] There is no shortage of literature and academic research that focuses on the family, child rearing, and, more recently, the elderly. However, the focus of this chapter is family violence. The Department of Justice (2009) website describes "family violence" as including "many different forms of abuse that adults or children may experience in their intimate, kinship or dependent relationships. Family violence also includes being mistreated or being neglected by these members."

Perhaps upon first reflection one might think that the meaning of what constitutes a family is pretty straightforward. To most Canadians, a family consists of a father, a mother, and one or more children. However, upon closer reflection, we can likely readily identify how limiting the configuration is. A number of years ago, Queen's University law professor Nicolas Bala (1994) noted how the Charter of Rights in 1984 extended the traditional historical definition of a Canadian family to one that is more pluralistic and functional. Bala points out that step-parents and other types of unions (e.g., same-gender relationships) have gained legal status. Along with the social, legal, and cultural shift in the meaning of a family, it is more challenging and limiting to examine family violence and abuse only within the historical traditional frame-work. For example, in Alberta, family law also covers intimate partner relationships where there is no marriage. In Alberta, the legal term is "adult interdependent relationship" and it falls under the *Adult Interdependent Relationships Act* (Law Central Alberta, 2014).

Hence, just as the concept of crime is complex (Winterdyk, 2004), so too is the subject of family violence and abuse. Aside from family composition issues, family V&A can express itself in a number of ways and has been explained in a number of different ways. For example, the Department of Justice (2009) website identifies the following types of family violence:

- ► physical abuse;
- ► sexual abuse and exploitation (being used for a sexual purpose); neglect;
- ► psychological or emotional abuse; and
- ► economic or financial abuse.

These are rather broad types of potential V&A, but they serve to illustrate the diversity of family violence. In addition to being a complex and diverse concept, explanations as to why family V&A occurs span the range from internally motivated explanations to the less deterministic model of life-course theory (see, generally, Green, 2010).

Defining Family Violence

It should be noted at the onset that within the *Canadian Criminal Code* there is no specific offence for "family violence" per se. Instead, the potential offences that may be attributable to family violence include offences such as:

- ► assault (causing bodily harm, with a weapon and aggravated assault);
- ► sexual offences against children and youth;
- ► sexual assault;
- ► criminal harassment (often called "stalking");
- ► making threats against someone; and
- ► homicide – murder, attempted murder, infanticide, and manslaughter (Department of Justice, 2011).

Just as there are no specific sections in the *Criminal Code* that specifically refer to family violence offences, there are no specific offences that relate to victims of family violence or abuse. However, the *Criminal Code* does include provisions intended to help prevent family violence.

Before we embark on an overview of some specific types of family violence, we will review some of the trends and patterns of family violence in Canada.

The Prevalence of Family Violence and Abuse in Canada

Within criminology there is a well-known concept referred to as the "dark figure" of crime. Coined in the 1970s by the British criminologist Richard Sparks, it refers to the fact that, for some types of crimes, the detection, recording, and/or reporting incident rate is very low. Such is the case with family violence. According to the Department of Justice (n.d.), family V&A often remains hidden or unreported. The reasons for not reporting this violence include: age and/or developmental stage of the victim, physical frailty or limited cognitive disability to be able to effectively communicate, geographic or social isolation, and victims' lack of knowledge about how to report an act of violence or abuse that has been directed at them (Department of Justice Canada, 2009). Fortunately, however, with growing public awareness, academic interest, and special interest groups, we are beginning to gain an increasingly richer under-standing of the nature, extent, and etiology of the many different expressions of family violence and abuse.

In Canada, there are four primary sources where one can begin to gain insight into some of these indicators. The sources include: (1) victimization data; (2) police-reported spousal abuse in Canada; (3) police-reported family violence against children and youth; and (4) family homicides (see Department of Justice, 2009).

The Department of Justice (2009) report, "*Family violence: Department of Justice Canada overview paper,*" provides a snapshot of findings on family violence and its relative distribution:

- ► Femicide (the killing of women) is more common within intimate and/or family situa-tions;
- ► Women are significantly more likely to killed by a spouse/partner than are men;
- ► An estimated 7% of Canadian women and men aged 15 years and over who were in a current or previous marital or common-law relationship experienced some form of spousal violence in the five years prior to the 2004 GSS;
- ► The 2004 GSS indicates that Aboriginal people were three times more likely than non-Aboriginals to be victims of spousal violence;
- ► The rate for non-Aboriginal people to be victims of spousal violence was 7%;
- ► In 2006, almost one-quarter (22%) of all the incidents of reported violent crime involved

family violence. The majority (83%) of the reports involved spousal violence and female victims; and

▶ Two percent of all victims of violent crime in 2005 were older adults, aged 65 and older.

Why Does It Happen?

While it is considered helpful to be able to describe the nature and extent of the different forms of family violence, from an intervention and prevention perspective, it is important to be able to understanding the causes of family violence. The first thing that should be noted is that no one, regardless of age, gender, socioeconomic status, religion, occupation, and so on is immune to the risk of being either a victim or perpetrator of family violence or abuse. Therefore, while there are some commonly accepted theories, the range of explanations are considered quite diverse. Perhaps one of the most common explanations is that violence and abuse is linked to a power imbalance in the relationship and inequalities either within the relationship setting or the community itself. Another common explanatory approach focuses on socio-psychological factors of the individuals involved. Finally, life-course theory suggests that living in an environment being exposed to violence and abuse, literacy barriers, discrimination, and so on pose potential risks. We will explore some of the explanations as they relate to certain types of victims.

Family Abuse

Elder Abuse

Elder abuse in Canada stems from a history of social conditions that ultimately affect the position of elderly people in society (Harbison et al., 2012). Forced retirement, assumed declining capabilities, and financial reliance on the government are just some examples of conditions that led to the idea that older people are vulnerable and in need of protection (Harbison et al., 2012). As the senior population in Canada continues to grow (it is estimated that by 2031, adults 65 years and older will make up 25% of the population [Statistics Canada, 2007]), it is expected that the demand for caregiving of this group will also increase, as will elder abuse, mistreatment, and neglect (Walsh & Yon, 2012; Fulmer et al., 2000). This is due, in part, to societal perceptions of the elderly, but also as a result of numerous risk factors (e.g., low social support, social isolation, prior traumatic events, and low income) converging to increase the likelihood of abuse (Anetzberger, 2005).

Very few attempts to measure the prevalence of elder abuse and neglect at a national level have been made in Canada (Poole & Rietschlin, 2012; Harbison et al., 2012). As noted in a study conducted by Podnieks (1992), it was found that an estimated 4% of older adults in Canada had been victim to one or more types of abuse in their home, from a partner, relative, or significant other. According to the GSS on victimization (2009), over 2,400 seniors (65 years and older) were victims of violent crime perpetrated by a family member; this makes up one-third of all violent incidents committed against older adults that year (Statistics Canada, 2011).

Explanations of elder abuse. One of the most challenging aspects of understanding and ultimately responding to elder abuse and neglect is the lack of a universal definition of the phenomenon (Anetzberger, 2005). Because the issue is made up of a number of different problems and encompasses a broad spectrum of actions, individuals, contexts, and settings, it is difficult to develop a comprehensive definition (Walsh & Yon, 2012). For example, spiritual or systemic medical abuse may not be incorporated into definitions of elder abuse conceptualized as physical, sexual, financial or neglect by a perpetrator who is in a trusting relationship with an older person. Perceptions of abuse differ among cultures, age groups and environmental settings (institutional vs. community), and there are unclear boundaries between elder abuse and ageism (the systemic process of discrimination and stereotyping based on age) (Walsh & Yon, 2012). Harbison et al. (2012) point out that even housing elder abuse within the family violence framework may be problematic in that it suggests the issue involves only family members and caregivers, yet we know elder abuse occurs within the external community, in institutions, and through exploitation and discrimination in the wider society. Despite these challenges, it is important to create a common definition in order to be able to accurately measure its' prevalence, generalize findings, facilitate comparisons, and develop appropriate assessment tools, intervention strategies, and effective policies.

The same issue exists when considering theoretical explanations of elder abuse and neglect. Some theories come from the family violence literature, explaining elder abuse in line with explanations of abuse against other vulnerable populations, such as children. This perspective includes explanations such as social learning, fitness theory (abuse caused by the stress of caring for an impaired individual) and societal attitudes. Other theories come from research and empirical studies, making it difficult to find one theory that could explain all forms of elder abuse in all contexts (Anetzberger, 2005). Rather, much research has focused on characterizing the victim and the perpetrator through the identification of risk factors (Poole & Rietschlin, 2012). For example, characteristics of the victim (e.g., poor health) and the perpetrator (e.g., addiction), environmental factors (e.g., social isolation), and negative societal attitudes towards the elderly are considered risk factors that increase the likelihood of, and opportunity for, abuse. It is important to note that risk factors do not necessarily cause elder abuse but rather increase the possibility of abuse when correlated with other risk factors. So, an elderly person in poor health in a supported living environment is less at risk of being abused than an elderly person in poor health living with an adult child who has substance abuse issues. As the risk factors compound, so does the likelihood of abuse.

Considering elder abuse from the perspective that each situation is unique, it is not enough to consider only one component or system as an explanation for elder abuse and neglect, but rather one must examine how various factors converge or correlate to create a situation of abuse. Particularly in the context of family violence, it is important to understand how internal (i.e., characteristics of the victim and perpetrator) and external factors (i.e., environmental and societal characteristics) intermingle to influence the relationship within which the abuse takes place. While elder abuse often takes place within the family, it is not just a family issue.

Intervention: Reporting, investigation, and criminal charges. Definition rears its ugly head once again in regards to intervention. The lack of a single definition of elder abuse to provide a foundation for Canadian law leads to formal responses that vary among provinces and territories, as most aspects of health and family life fall within the respective governments (Harbison et al., 2012). Similarly, one's legal obligation to report concerns of elder abuse, neglect, or risk depends on the province or territory within which the incident occurs (Canadian Centre for Elder Law, 2011). Sectors of health, social services, and adult guardianship are all provincially and territorially governed; while some jurisdictions have domestic violence laws that pertain, in part, to elder abuse, others have laws focused on persons in care, vulnerable persons, and neglected adults (Canadian Centre for Elder Law, 2011).

Adult protection legislation throughout Canada approaches the issue of elder abuse from various standpoints on a continuum between intervening to protect the individual and respecting an individual's autonomy and independence (Canadian Centre for Elder Law, 2011; Coughlan et al., 1995). However, while there is no specific crime of elder abuse in Canada, sometimes criminal charges under the Criminal Code are applied regardless of the age of the victim.

Child Abuse

As is the case with elder abuse, historical values and societal perceptions deeply influence the issue of child maltreatment. How we should treat children has been redefined many times over the years, ranging from viewing children as property to recognizing children as human beings with individual rights (Tower, 1989). The recognition that children are potentially an at-risk population did not happen until the late 1800s, and even though child welfare legislation and practice has been developing throughout the last century, the study of child abuse and neglect in Canada is still in its infancy (Trocme et al., 2011; Ward & Bennett, 2003).

Family function (and dysfunction): Taking a look at abusive families. Examining child maltreatment in the context of family violence requires consideration of family functioning. The family is considered the primary tool for socialization and ultimately prepares children for experiences later in life (Kelly & Totten, 2002). And while the underlying purpose of the family may not have changed, as noted above, the family as an institution has changed significantly over the years (Tower, 1989). For example, increased societal pressures, economic stressors, career demands, alternative definitions of family, and life events can challenge the family system in its functioning. If the family is not meeting expectations and reflecting what society wants to promote, society feels the right to intervene (Tower, 1989).

Societal perceptions have laid a somewhat shaky foundation for families who do not meet expectations; yet this does not determine the occurrence of child maltreatment. Child abuse and neglect are precipitated by many social and environmental factors, such as poverty, substance abuse, inadequate social supports, educational deficits, and environmental stressors (Collins & Collins, 2005). These factors in themselves do not cause child abuse and neglect; rather, they put families at risk. While many abusive parents want to be healthy and nurturing towards their children, a lack of resources, supports, and education can trigger stressors and impair coping abilities and the overall functioning of the family system (Collins & Collins, 2005; Tower, 1989). In this context, child maltreatment is more than a family violence problem; this is a systemic issue that needs a societal response (Collins & Collins, 2005).

The relationship between being abused and perpetrating abuse later in life. While not a direct correlation, being a child victim of abuse (whether directly experiencing or witnessing violence) does increase the likelihood of perpetrating later in life. Maltreated children experience emotional harm that puts them at risk for developing negative behavioural responses. Victims of child abuse and neglect have a distorted perception of how express their thoughts and emotions. These types of behaviours put children at risk of being further victimized and of using violence against others as they grow-up (Kelly & Totten, 2002; Collins & Collins, 2005).

Considering Aboriginal Peoples and family abuse. Aboriginal children are overrepresented in the child welfare and foster care systems. Although exact numbers are unknown, a rough estimate suggests that 30% to 40% of children in out-of-home care are Aboriginal (Public Health Agency of Canada, 2010; Farris-Manning & Zandstra, 2003). In 2008, the third cycle of monitoring the Canadian Incidence Study of Reported Child Abuse and Neglect reported that 22% of the 85,440 substantiated cases of child maltreatment in Canada involved children of Aboriginal heritage (Public Health Agency of Canada, 2010). While First Nations and Aboriginal communities have been motivated to develop their own child and family service agencies, on the whole there has been little effort by the Canadian government to understand the root cause of child maltreatment in Aboriginal communities. Aboriginal families are faced with an overwhelming number of risk factors, such as high rates of suicide, incarceration, low education, and poor living conditions, which stem from environmental stressors such as poverty, unemployment, and a lack of culturally appropriate supports and services. Addressing child maltreatment within First Nations communities needs to include recognition of these factors, as well as legitimization of Aboriginal systems of care (Blackstock et al., 2004).

Child protection in Canada. Like other family violence issues, researchers are challenged to measure the true prevalence of child maltreatment in Canada (Ward & Bennett, 2003). Lack of consistent definitions across the country and variations in reporting and investigation make it difficult to get an accurate picture of what is going on (Trocme et al., 2003; Ward & Bennett, 2003). Child welfare legislation and services in Canada are organized at the provincial and territorial level (Trocme et al., 2003; Khoo, Hyvonen, & Lennart, 2002; Public Health Agency of Canada, 2010). While child welfare is mandated across the country and all systems share some common characteristics, there are still many differences in how the systems are organized. For example, some provinces have a centralized government-run child welfare system, while others have implemented decentralized models run by private agencies. Many provinces and territories are also developing fully mandated Aboriginal agencies (Trocme et al., 2003; Public Health Agency of Canada, 2010). Child welfare statues vary across Canada with respect to the scope of intervention permitted, age of the children involved, and forms of maltreatment covered (Trocme et al., 2011).

The *Canadian Incidence Study of Reported Child Abuse and Neglect (CIS)* in 1998, and the follow-up cycles in 2003 and 2008, provide the most comprehensive data on child maltreatment in Canada. Up until this study, there was no source of national statistics on children and families investigated for suspected child abuse and neglect (Trocme et al., 2003). The *Uniform Crime Report (UCR2)* collects data on police-reported violence against children and youth, but this only includes sexual offences and physical assaults that have been reported to and substantiated by Canadian police services, which represents approximately 48% of the national volume of reported crime (Trocme et al., 2003; Statistics Canada, 2011).

According to the *CIS 2008*, there were 85,440 substantiated cases of child maltreatment in Canada. In a further 18,867 cases, there was insufficient evidence to substantiate, but child abuse and/or neglect was still suspected by the worker at the end of the investigation. In 11,792 cases, the worker thought there was risk of future maltreatment. The two most frequently occurring types of maltreatment were exposure to intimate partner violence (in 34% of cases) and neglect (in 34% of cases), and in 20% of cases, the primary form of abuse was physical.

Sibling Abuse

Kids will be kids: Is sibling abuse a serious issue? Historical attitudes in society towards sibling abuse have kept the issue undercover. The idea of family life as a private matter helped hide the seriousness and pervasiveness of sibling maltreatment (Kiselica & Morrill-Richards, 2007). Even more recently, as attention has been drawn to issues of family violence, the focus has remained on the parent-child relationship. Sibling abuse continues to be thought of as a common characteristic of family life, and very few cases are brought to the attention of authorities (Caffaro & Conn-Caffaro, 2004). However, sibling maltreatment is a real issue and can have serious and devastating effects. In fact, violence between siblings may be even more common than that of parent to child (Kiselica & Morrill-Richards, 2007). For example, an American study by Straus and Gelles (1990) found that 53% of children aged 3 to 17 had committed acts of serious violence towards a sibling, compared to 2.3% of parents (as cited in Kiselica & Morrill-Richards, 2007).

Keep it in the family: Identification, reporting and intervention. Identification of sibling maltreatment is a tentative exercise in that it is often difficult to distinguish between the normal developmental behaviours of siblings and actual abuse (Kiselica & Morrill-Richards, 2007). Positive sibling relationships do include rivalry and moderate conflict; these are not considered harmful and are, in fact, a healthy part of family functioning. Sibling interactions help children share and think for themselves, building self-esteem and personal identity (Caffaro & Conn-Caffaro, 2004). In order to identify a sibling relationship that has become abusive, severity, motivation, intent of the act, and emotional impact must be taken into consideration (Kiselica & Morrill-Richards, 2007).

At the time of preparing this chapter, no prevalence studies of sibling abuse have been conducted in Canada, and statistics around the issue within the context of family violence are extremely limited. Statistical profiles of family violence in Canada, produced by Statistics Canada, do report on perpetrators of physical and sexual abuse towards children, but these are based on criminal incidents that have been reported to and substantiated by Canadian police services (Statistics Canada, 2011). According to Statistics Canada (2011), in 2009 there were 2,866 assaults against children perpetrated by siblings (a rate of 41 per 100,000 children). There is a tremendous gap in research, reporting, and intervention in this area that needs to be addressed.

Domestic Violence

Like the other forms of family violence discussed in this chapter, the definition of domestic violence or spousal abuse continues to evolve as the issue becomes better understood (Department of Justice Canada, 2009). Historically thought of as a private issue due to the nature and intimacy of the relationship involved, domestic violence has gained public attention with the recognition of the need to protect and support victims. Along with greater public recognition, there has been a strong effort to criminalize domestic violence under the *Criminal Code* (Department of Justice Canada, 2003).

It has been difficult to accurately assess the prevalence of domestic violence across Canada (Flaherty, 2010). National data collection tools include the *Uniform Crime Report (UCR2)*, the *General Social Survey on Victimization (GSS)*, the *1993 Violence Against Women*

Survey and the *Homicide Survey*. While there are pros and cons to each of these, most statistics are taken from the *GSS*, as this survey collects data on the experiences of victimization (Department of Justice Canada, 2003; Statistics Canada, 2011). However, the *GSS 2009* reported that only 22% of victims of spousal violence reported the incidents to the police (Statistics Canada, 2011).

The *2009 GSS* reported that of the 19 million respondents who identified as having a current or former spouse that year, 6% had been physically or sexually victimized by their partner in the five years prior to completing the survey; 2% reported being abused in 12 months prior to completing the survey. Although respondents were asked about emotional and financial abuse, these responses were not included in the overall calculation of domestic violence victims. Females reported more serious offences than males, and 57% of females reported recurring incidents of abuse in the five years prior to completing the survey. Findings indicated that people aged 25 to 34 years, those involved in common-law relationships, and those living in blended families were more likely to report being victims of domestic violence. (Statistics Canada, 2011).

Children witnessing family violence. Perhaps one of the most tragic consequences of domestic violence is the impact it has on children in the home. Findings from the *GSS 2004* showed that 33% of victims of spousal violence reported that children saw or heard the violence (Department of Justice Canada, 2009). Children may be affected in several ways, from witnessing the violence to becoming direct victims themselves. Children may hear verbal altercations or see incidents of abuse, may be ignored by parents (perpetrator or victim) who feel the need to focus on their personal situation, and can feel torn between their loyalty to their parents and feelings of fear (Flaherty, 2010). Children who are exposed to violence in the family may experience serious emotional, developmental, behavioural, and academic difficulties, even if they are not directly harmed (Ward & Bennett, 2003; Department of Justice Canada, n.d.). However, a study by Fantuzzo and Mohr (1999) found that 45% to 70% of children exposed to domestic violence are also victims of physical abuse. The *Canadian Incidence Study of Reported Child Abuse and Neglect* (2008) reported that 34% of the 85,440 substantiated cases of child maltreatment involved exposure to intimate partner violence (Public Health Agency of Canada, 2010). Exposure to violence also increases the risk that children will become part of a generational cycle of abuse, either as a perpetrator or as a victim (Department of Justice Canada, 2003; Statistics Canada, 2011).

Honour Killing: The case of Zainab Shafia. As noted at the outset of this chapter, Canada has become a multicultural and multi-ethnic country with ever increasing social dynamics within the family context that present new challenges to family violence and abuse. One such form is what is referred to as "honour killing"(Atlasshrugs, 2010). Honour killing has been described as involving "cases in which women were killed for becoming pregnant outside of wedlock or through incest, for committing adultery, or merely for being the subject of community gossip" (Dale, 2009). We will limit our discussion to the recent case of 19-year-old Zainab Shafia.

In June of 2009, Zainab, along with two of her younger sisters and first wife (Rona Amir Mohammed, who was reported to be infertile) of Zainab's father, were found dead inside a car that was discovered underwater by the Kingston Mills lock of the Rideau Canal in Ontario.

Not only were the parents and their son found guilty on all four counts of murder in January 2012, but the murders were characterized as the first honour type killings to be successfully prosecuted in Canada.

Although the case involved the killing of four women and captured the national and international attention, it is ironic that there has been a lack of outrage from any feminist groups in Canada. This speaks to a possible void in the Canadian conscience about such violence or an uncertainty about how to respond (Freeze, 2012; Carlson, 2010). But, the case has at least drawn light to the diversity and complexity of cultural values and practices that can be found in Canada today.

Intervention: Reporting, investigation, and prevention of family V&A. In the past, physical and sexual assaults by a stranger have often received more legal and social attention than those by a spouse or common-law partner (Canadian Centre for Justice Studies, 2005). However, recognition that domestic violence is also human rights issue, and acknowledgement that this issue affects all people on a personal, relational, and societal level, has brought about change in Canada (Flaherty, 2010). The Family Violence Initiative of the federal government is working to implement legal reform, increase education, further research in the field, and strengthen support for program and services (Department of Justice Canada, n.d.).

The biggest legislative reform in Canada has been the push to criminalize spousal abuse through "pro-charging" and "pro-prosecution" policies (Department of Justice Canada, 2003). These types of policies advocate that the decision to charge and/or prosecute the perpetrator in domestic violence cases be made independent of the victim's wishes (providing there is sufficient evidence to proceed). 1981 saw the first Canadian police agency in London, Ontario implement a charging policy for spousal assault. By the early '90s, all jurisdictions were revising directives to expand policies and address specific issues. And while all jurisdictions in Canada now support a pro- or mandatory response to domestic violence, how this plays out in individual provinces and territories can vary tremendously. Several jurisdictions have family and domestic violence legislation that specifically addresses certain issues, and many have developed domestic violence courts and service and treatment programs (Department of Justice, 2003). However, Canada still lacks consistency and comprehensiveness in addressing this issue effectively.

Conclusion

In this chapter we have provided a sweeping overview of the issue of family violence within a Canadian context. While we have attempted to acknowledge some of the key and emerging forms of family violence, areas such as infanticide (i.e., killing of one's children) were not addressed. Family violence and abuse remains a serious issue and one that clearly is in need of further study to not only better understand and prevent such crimes, but to also identify and introduce protective strategies and legislation that better assist prospective perpetrators and victims.

Keywords

Femicide, honour killing, dark figure of crime, family violence, elder abuse, child abuse, domestic violence, human rights

Review Questions

1. Despite is prevalence, why is family V&A so difficult to articulate and study?
2. What are some of the main trends and patterns of family V&A? Are there any forms of family violence that appear to be emerging in Canada?
3. How does 'honour' based violence compare/differ from family based violence? What type of solutions are offered in the chapter? What do think is the 'best' method/means for addressing honour based violence?
4. Describe some of the main legislation as it relates to family violence? How effective do you think it is?
5. What impact does the growing diversity within Canada present in terms of family violence and abuse? Do you think Canada is being proactive or reactive in responding to the potential issues?
6. Describe some of the main intervention and prevention strategies for family violence.

Notes

[1] Although in 2012, Statistics Canada reported that divorce rates had declined for the third straight year, the trend is off-set by the fact that common-law unions are becoming more common (Zamon, 2012).

[2] A 2009 study in UK reported that in one-third of family break-ups the children lose contact with their biological fathers. The study places the blame on the inadequacies of the family court system (Bingham, 2009).

[3] According to Statistics Canada, in 2006 the average age of a women given birth was 29.7 and compared to 1979 when 54.7% of first time mothers were between the ages of 25 to 34, by 2004 the proportion had climbed to 61.1% (Statistics Canada, 2006).

References

Anetzberger, G. J. (2000). Caregiving: Primary cause of elder abuse? *Generations, 24*(2), 46-51.

Anetzberger, G. J. (2005). The reality of elder abuse. *Clinical Gerontologist, 28*(1/2), 1-25.

Atlasshrugs. (2010). *Honor Killings*. Retrieved from http://atlasshrugs2000.typepad.com/honor_killings/

Bala, N. (1994). The evolving Canadian definition of the family: Towards a pluralistic and functional approach. *International Journal of Law, Policy and the Family, 8*(3), 293-318.

Bingham, J. (2009, 11, 16). Third of family break-up children lose contact with fathers in 'failing' court system, poll. *The Telegraph*. Retrieved from http://www.telegraph.co.uk/relationships/divorce/6575997/Third-of-family-break-up-children-lose-contact-with-fathers-in-failing-court-system-poll.html

Blackstock, C., Trocme, N., & Bennett, M. (2004). Child maltreatment investigations among Aboriginal and non-Aboriginal families in Canada. *Violence Against Women, 10*(8), 901-916.

Caffaro, J. V., & Conn-Caffaro, A. (2004). Treating sibling abuse families. *Aggression and Violent Behaviour, 10,* 604-623.

Canadian Centre for Elder Law. (2011). *A practical guide to elder abuse and neglect law in Canada*. Retrieved from http://www.bcli.org/sites/default/files/Practical_Guide_English_Rev_JULY_2011.pdf

Canadian Centre for Justice Studies. (2005). Family violence in Canada: A statistical profile 2005. Retrieved from http://www.statcan.gc.ca/pub/85-224-x/85-224-x2005000-eng.pdf

Carlson, K.B. (2010, 07, 12). Update: Minister's 'honour killings' misstep. *National Post*. Retrieved from http://news.nationalpost.com/2010/07/12/rona-ambrose-honour-killings-will-not-be-tolerated-in-canada/

Collins, B. G., & Collins, T. M. (2005). *Crisis and trauma: Developmental-ecological intervention*. Boston: MA: Lahaska Press.

Coughlan, S., Downe-Wamboldt, B. D., Elgie, R. G., Harbison, J., Melanson, P. M., & Morrow, M. (1995). *Mistreating elderly people: Questioning the response to elder abuse and neglect. Volume 1: Legal responses to elder abuse and neglect*. Halifax, NS: Dalhousie University, Health Law Institute.

Dale, D. (2009, July 25). Shining a light on honour killings' dark corner. *Toronto Star*. Retrieved from http://www.thestar.com/news/canada/article/671779

Department of Justice Canada. (2003). *Spousal abuse policies and legislation*. Final Report of the Ad Hoc Federal-Provincial-Territorial Working Group. Retrieved from http://www.justice.gc.ca/eng/pi/fv-vf/rep-rap/spo_e-con_a.pdf

Department of Justice Canada. (2009). *Family violence: Department of Justice Canada overview paper*. Retrieved from http://www.justice.gc.ca/eng/pi/fv-vf/facts-info/fv-vf/fv-vf.pdf

Department of Justice Canada. (2011). *Family violence initiative*. Retrieved from http://www.justice. gc.ca/eng/pi/fv-vf/laws-lois.html

Department of Justice Canada. (n.d.). *Spousal abuse: A fact sheet from the Department of Justice Canada*. Retrieved from http://www.justice.gc.ca/eng/pi/fv-vf/facts-info/sa-vc.pdf

Fantuzzo, J. W., & Mohr, W. K. (1999). Prevalence and effects of child exposure to domestic violence. *The Future of Children. Special Issue: Domestic Violence and Children, 9*(3), 21-32.

Farris-Manning, C., & Zandstra, M. (2003). *Children in care in Canada: A summary of current issues and trends with recommendations for future research*. Policy paper for the Child Welfare League of Canada. Retrieved from http://www.nationalchildrensalliance.com/nca/pubs/2003/Children_in_Care_March_2003.pdf

Flaherty, M. (2010). Constructing a world beyond intimate partner abuse. *Affilia: Journal of Women and Social Work, 25*(3), 224-235.

Freeze, C. (2012, 01, 31). Canada looks for ways to prevent honour killings in wake of Shafia trial. *The Globe and Mail*. Retrieved from http://www.theglobeandmail.com/news/national/canada-looks-for-ways-to-prevent-honour-killings-in-wake-of-shafia-trial/article542501/

Fulmer, T., Paveza, G., Abraham, I., & Fairchild, S. (2000). Elder neglect assessment in the emergency department. *Journal of Emergency Nursing, 26,* 436-443.

Green, L. (2010). *Understanding the life course*. Hoboken, NJ: Wiley.

Hackler, J. (2006). *Canadian criminology: Strategies and perspectives* (2nd ed.). Scarborough, ON: Prentice-Hall.

Harbison, J., Coughlan, S., Beaulieu, M., Karabanow, J., VanderPlaat, M., Wildeman, S., & Wexler, E. (2012). Understanding "elder abuse and neglect": A critique of assumptions underpinning responses to the mistreatment and neglect of older people. *Journal of Elder Abuse and Neglect, 24*(2), 88-103.

Kelly, K. D., & Totten, M. (2002). *When children kill: A social-psychological study of youth homicide.* Peterborough, ON: Broadview Press.

Khoo, E., Hyvonen, U., & Lennart, N. (2002). Child welfare or child protection: Uncovering Swedish and Canadian orientations to social intervention in child maltreatment. *Qualitative Social Work, 1*(4), 451-471.

Kiselica, M. S., & Morrill-Richards, M. (2007). Sibling maltreatment: The forgotten abuse. *Journal of Counseling and Development, 85,* 148-160.

Law Central Alberta. (2014). Retrieved from http://www.lawcentralalberta.ca/learn/adult_inter-dependent.aspx

Malley-Morrison, K. (Ed.). (2004). *International perspectives on family violence and abuse: A cognitive ecological approach.* Mahwah, NJ: Lawrence Erlbaum and Associates.

Podnieks, E. (1992). National survey on abuse of the elderly in Canada. *Journal of Elder Abuse and Neglect, 4*(1/2), 5-58.

Poole, C., & Rietschlin, J. (2012). Intimate partner victimization among adults aged 60 and older: An analysis of the 1999 and 2004 general social survey. *Journal of Elder Abuse and Neglect, 24*(2), 120-137.

Public Health Agency of Canada. (2010). *Canadian incidence study of reported child abuse and neglect – 2008: Major findings.* Retrieved from http://www.phac-aspc.gc.ca/cm-vee/csca-ecve/2008/assets/pdf/cis-2008_report_eng.pdf

Statistics Canada. (2006). *Births.* Retrieved from http://www.statcan.gc.ca/daily-quoti-dien/060731/dq060731b-eng.htm

Statistics Canada. (2007). *Canada's population future.* Retrieved from http://www 41.statcan.gc.ca/2007/3867/ceb3867_001-eng.htm

Statistics Canada. (2011). *Family violence in Canada: A statistical profile.* Retrieved from http://www.statcan.gc.ca/pub/85-224-x/85-224-x2010000-eng.pdf

Steinmetz, S., & Straus, M. (1974). *Violence in the family.* New York: Harper and Row.

Tower, C.C. (1989). *Understanding child abuse and neglect.* Boston, MA: Allyn and Bacon.

Trocme, N., Fallon, B., MacLaurin, B., Chamberland, C., Chabot, M., & Esposito, T. (2011). Shifting definitions of emotional maltreatment: An analysis of child welfare investigation laws and practices in Canada. *Child Abuse and Neglect, 35,* 831-840.

Trocme, N., Tourigny, M., MacLaurin, B., & Fallon, B. (2003). Major findings from the Canadian Incidence Study of Reported Child Abuse and Neglect. *Child Abuse and Neglect, 27,* 1427-1439.

Walsh, C., & Yon, Y. (2012). Developing an empirical profile for elder abuse research in Canada. *Journal of Elder Abuse and Neglect, 24*(2), 104-119.

Ward, M. G. K., & Bennett, S. (2003). Studying child abuse and neglect in Canada: We are just at the beginning. *Canadian Medical Association Journal, 169*(9), 919-920.

Winterdyk, J. (2004). *Canadian criminology* (2nd ed.). Scarborough, ON: Pearson.

Zamon, R. (2012, 03, 29). Divorce rates in Canada on decline: StatsCan numbers show fewer cases. *The Huffington Post Canada.* Retrieved from http://www.huffingtonpost.ca/2012/03/29/divorce-rates-in-canada-decline_n_1387979.html

Aboriginal Women and Violence: The Pickton Serial Murders

Chapter 9

Learning Objectives

In this chapter you will...

Patricia O'Reilly
and Thomas Fleming

► gain an understanding of the nature of cultural issues that lead to violence against Aboriginal women

► learn about the police investigation of the Pickton murders, particularly in the case of Aboriginal women

► examine the nature of danger and violence associated with Aboriginal street sex trade work

► consider prevailing views of Aboriginal women as invisible victims of violence

► explore how policing organizations can provide effective protection of Aboriginal women

---

Introduction

Violence against Aboriginal women is, unfortunately, an all too often reported problem in Canadian society. This phenomenon has given rise to various organizations of Aboriginal women. They have attempted to educate the public about the extent of violence and to bring forth justice for victims and their families. One such organization, Stolen Sisters, is recognized for its advocacy concerning the large number of Aboriginal women who are either missing or murdered. Their estimate places this number at 500 individuals. Some advocates for Aboriginal women have pointed out that if 500 women across Canada from the dominant culture were missing or murdered, there would be massive public outcry and demand for action from policing organizations (Amnesty International, 2004). There have also been key cases involving violence against Aboriginal women and emerging cases of Aboriginal women as victims of a serial predator that have prompted critical investigation, criticism, and highlighted issues of discrimination and its part in violence (Amnesty International, 2004; Comack & Seshia, 2010). But the most disturbing and certainly most blatant example of violence towards Aboriginal women remains that of the murder of 13 women at the hands of serial murderer Robert Pickton (Fleming & O'Reilly, 2010a, 2010b, 2010c). Aboriginal women accounted for almost half of the known victims of Pickton, who was able to take human life for a period of over 20 years without being apprehended by the police. In this chapter we will explore the Pickton case in detail focusing on the murder of his Aboriginal victims and the police response to their disappearance. We will examine the experience of Aboriginal families in their dealings with police agents and agencies during the course of the cases. We have avoided using the term "investigation" in referring to the conduct of police with regard to the case of what has been termed "the lower east side missing women" (Rossmo, 2009, 2011) because we have serious criticisms of their handling of the case and the families of the missing (Fleming & O'Reilly, 2010a, 2010b, 2010c; O'Reilly & Fleming, 2011). We assert that violence directed against Aboriginal women occurs in a number of distinct contexts, but that an exploration of the Pickton victims and their families' treatment highlights many of the recurring claims of Aboriginal groups concerning their interaction with police services. Further, it is important to understand that violence is not merely perpetrated through assault and murder but that it is also done to victims and their families through societal inaction, discrimination, and systemic racism. Furthermore, the extent of violence toward Aboriginal women has been both neglected and underestimated because violence may go unreported in certain contexts, is ignored, not considered important, or is not pursued effectively by investigative agencies (Amnesty International, 2004). The Pickton case offers an opportunity to develop insights in the challenges facing Aboriginal women, most clearly those engaged in sex trade work in urban settings, but we argue it also offers lessons on violence towards Aboriginal women in other social contexts. The devaluing of Aboriginal women involved in the sex trade, which renders them dispensable by serial killers, as we shall argue, reflects Aboriginal views of societal attitudes toward Aboriginal women and girls as "just another Indian" (Goulding, 2001; Chartrand et al, 1999).

It is important to clarify for readers that we are not making an argument that all Aboriginal women are at risk of violence or, indeed, that the majority of Aboriginal women engaged in their daily life are imminently at risk. Our chapter looks specifically at sex trade workers who also were drug addicted. However, we also ask our readers to refrain from assigning these women a "master status" (Fleming, 1981) based upon their involvement in a marginal and "risky" lifestyle. Rather, we position them as human beings; sisters, mothers, daughters, aunts, and so on, whose lives are accorded the same value as any other Canadians and whose work and lives on the street were but a small portion of their entire self.

Aboriginal Women and the Challenges of the Urban Environment

The greatest portion of Canada's current Aboriginal population, contrary to widely held perceptions, do not live on reserves with over 70 percent living off reserve.

The urban experience of Aboriginal persons will be quite diverse, and only recently have sustained efforts been made to study these communities spanning wide range of social, cultural, economic, political, and legal issues. Our knowledge of the conditions which confront these individuals has been expanded through research, (The Urban Aboriginal Task Force, 2007). The broadening of Aboriginal efforts in the field of television through the Aboriginal Peoples Television Network (APTN) and The National Film Board (NFB), for example, had made an important contribution assisting us in contextualizing the plight of those Aboriginal peoples, including those living both on and off the reserve.

The adaptation of Aboriginal peoples from reserve settings ensconced in Canada's rural areas to the urban interstices is concisely documented by James Frideres (1974), a well-respected researcher from the University of Calgary. He found that while federal levels of government encouraged immigration to urban settings, municipal governments were ill-prepared to deliver the types of ground-level services and assistance needed to ease the transition of Aboriginal peoples. As pressure towards assimilation mounted under the government of Pierre Trudeau, and the grim realities of life on some reserves confronted Aboriginal peoples, a large percentage of these individuals moved to Canada's major cities for a more promising future. Frideres (1974) argues that the urban settings that greeted Aboriginal peoples was an "alien" environment where discrimination was accentuated by the separation from white society so that, while existing beside the dominant culture, many found that acceptance was not forthcoming. For some, and we emphasize this is but a small fraction of Aboriginal women, problems adapting to this way of life lead to the street, a transient existence, the selling of their bodies, and the use of "heavy" street drugs. Again, it is important to remember that the majority of Aboriginal women live their lives without the notice of authorities. We are not arguing here that violence against Aboriginal women is confined to those living on the street, since there is considerable evidence that Aboriginal women are subject to violence in domestic situations like their non-Aboriginal counterparts (Amnesty International, 2004). They are also more likely to experience violence in the home and to be the victims of street violence (RCMP, 2014). The RCMP report (2014) on missing and murdered Aboriginal women asserts that there are 225 unsolved cases of missing or murdered Aboriginal women in Canada. Further, they argue that Aboriginal women are "over represented" as victims of violence and homicide.

There is considerable research data on the issue of the barriers facing women regarding integration into city life (Abbott, 2004; Balakrishnan & Jurdi, 2007) and the many types of discrimination that occur when Aboriginal women attempt to obtain decent housing (Cohen & Corrado, 2004). Cora Voyageur's (2011) research has further added to our knowledge of this subject in demarcating the types of issues that confront Aboriginal women in our society including discrimination in housing, employment and interactions with society generally. Fleming's (1993) research explored the condition of homeless persons in Canada and found that the social capital of some Aboriginal women provided little resource to prompt integration into urban cultures. Social capital refers to the forms of preferential treatment that members of groups can expect given their membership in that group. When one is a member of a minority group they often find they cannot obtain the economic benefits, for example, which others may enjoy. They may experience discrimination in attempting to find employment or a place to live. This can have serious implications for one's economic well-being and health.

Robert Pickton and the Pig Farm Murders

To place the murders of Aboriginal victims of Robert Pickton in perspective, it is important to have an understanding of the case and some of the investigative failures that have led to a negative view of the conduct of the case by Aboriginal leaders as well as Amnesty International and others (Rossmo, 2009, 2011). The Pickton case is very significant in the history of Canadian murders. First, is the serial murder case with the greatest number of recorded victims. Identifying personal effects, pieces of identification, and DNA samples confirmed the presence of 27 victims on Pickton's farm located on the outskirts of Vancouver. Eventually, Pickton would be charged in all of these murders, except one where the victim could not be identified as any known missing person. Second, the murders covered a span of two decades beginning in the 1980s and ending with his arrest in February 2002.

The lower east side of Vancouver is an area well known for its drug culture, street prostitution, and criminal activities. Street life is, by its nature, dangerous (Fleming, 1993b), and sex trade work leaves women vulnerable to violence. Contrasting the working life of women prostituting on the street versus those working from condominiums, doing outcalls to hotel clients, or employed by massage parlours, there is a considerable daily risk of violence associated with conducting business (Lowman, 1998, 2000). When we consider the frequent use of "hard" drugs, including crack and crystal meth, by street prostitutes, and the role of alcohol in increasing the potential targeting of street prostitutes, one can understand to some measure the dangerous world they inhabit. All of the prostitutes who disappeared from Vancouver's street over these decades were known to have problems with drug use or addiction (Rossmo, 2009, 2011). The escalating rate of disappearance of women from the lower east side during the 1990s should have induced the police to allocate considerable resources to the investigation. Consider the factors involved in these unique disappearances. Normally, there is no specific patterning to missing persons cases in terms of the geographic area from which individuals disappear. Persons go missing from all areas of any urban centre. However, in the case we are examining, all of the victims exhibited the following characteristics:

1. They all disappeared from a very small, specific area of Vancouver comprising a limited number of blocks;
2. They were all working in the sex trade;
3. They were all women;
4. They were all heavy drug users; and
5. More than half were Aboriginal.

If we were to change the location of the disappearances and the characteristics of the missing, we can assume that if two dozen white middle-class women went missing from a several block urban area, a massive police effort would have been underway to discover what happened to them. Further, we can speculate that it would have taken far less than a dozen women missing from a small middle-class enclave to bring intense familial, legal, and political pressure to bear upon investigative efforts. It is incredible, and disturbing, that investigative efforts were so fruitless and, as we shall learn, that police continued to deny the possible existence of a serial killer up until the apprehension of Pickton in 2002.

Even more disturbingly, a number of groups, including Amnesty International and various Aboriginal groups, had pressured the Vancouver Police and the RCMP to consider these women as murder victims. What further adds to our criticism of police attitudes in these women's cases is that a Vancouver police detective had prepared a report in 1999, some three years before Pickton was arrested, indicating clearly that all of the missing women were dead. Rossmo (2011), who at the time was completing a PhD in criminology, developed a computer program to identify serial offenders and now is a professor. He trains police across the globe in his Rigel system of offender identification. Rossmo found there was no evidence whatsoever to support the contention that the missing women were alive. They had not cashed a cheque, gone to a bank, been in contact with police or social service agencies, and most importantly, had not been in touch with their families. While street persons are not known for their dependability, the families of the missing Aboriginal victims indicated that their family member would contact them, perhaps *infrequently*, it was clear that they were not following their regular pattern of contact. Police tried to explain the women's' disappearances to their

Aboriginal families in the following terms:

1. They were on the prostitution circuit. The circuit includes Vancouver, Seattle, and Calgary. Police suggested they were likely in one of the other cities and would soon return.
2. They did not want to be found by their relatives.
3. They were on a reserve and again, didn't want to speak to their families.
4. They were more heavily involved in drug use and weren't interested in contacting their families. (Rossmo, 2011)

We can only imagine the frustration of Aboriginal families, as documented by Amnesty International (2004), in attempting to convince police to pursue the cases of their missing loved ones.

When Pickton was finally arrested in February 2002, a massive forensic dig of his farm property ensued. While we cannot accurately gauge the final costs associated with his case, consider that the forensic excavation of his property cost $70 million and produced 100,000 exhibits (Rossmo, 2009). It is a gruesome fact that Pickton's victims were murdered and then fed to his pigs. This, in turn, meant that their skeletal remains were scattered over a wide swath of his lands. Given that the disappearance of women commenced in the 1980s, as far as police knowledge of the case indicated, it was necessary to excavate down over 12 feet in order to ensure that all possible victims were identified. The Herculean task of sifting through massive amounts of soil with the accuracy of an archaeological dig was necessary to make sure that no victims went unidentified. When we add to this the costs of prosecution incurred when the Crown prosecutor tried Pickton on six cases, we can add considerably to the final costs.

The number of identified victims (26) and the number included in the court case (6) might confuse some readers. Only those cases with the strongest possibility of conviction, in other words, cases in which the Crown felt there was more than sufficient hard evidence to convict and no possibility of reasonable doubt arising, were pursued. While promises were made that the cases of the remaining victims would be prosecuted, this did not occur because from a legal standpoint, Pickton could not be given any further prison time than his 25 year sentence which was the maximum sentence permitted by law for the murder of a human being.[1] Given his age and the length of his sentence, Pickton will never be released, and so this made more prosecutions not only fruitless from the point of view of extracting justice but financially indefensible. To end this section, we ask readers to consider that fully eleven of the thirteen missing women murdered after Rossmo's 1999 report were victims of Pickton as a means to highlight the flaws in the police investigation of these crimes.

Aboriginal Women, Police, and the Dangers of Street Work

In this section of the chapter, we turn our attention to the issue of the vulnerability of Aboriginal (and all other) women working in the sex trade and try to situate our explanation of the weaknesses in police investigation of the women within the context of research knowledge on policing and the issue of serial murder. Since the mid-1980s considerable academic research in the field of victim selection by serial murderers and their patterns of target acquisition have been explored by a number of criminologists (Leyton, 1986; Fleming & O'Reilly, 2010a, 2010b, 2010c; Hickey, 2006; Holmes & Holmes, 2010). Most of us are unaware of Aboriginal street sex workers; they are essentially "invisible," as are many of the homeless in our marginal urban areas (Davis & Shaffer, 2004; Fleming, 1993a; Shaver, 1997).

It is not difficult to understand the qualities of the majority of the victims for the serial killer. The existing research reveals several distinct groups as the preferred victims of serial killers, forming part of what Egger (1990, 2001) has termed, the "less dead," as we previously indicated. His is a term which can be understood to describe groups whose murder elicits far less sympathetic public support for concentrated investigation and whom police have relegated to a low priority status in comparison with other murder investigation (Hickey, 2006). Specifically, these groups include prostitutes, visible minorities, and gay men. To these we must add Aboriginal women working the street sex trade, given the Pickton case. The "less dead" are of less value in the eyes of society and police investigators. They are chosen as victims because serial killers understand that less police resources will be expended in attempting to find their killers. Research by Egger (2001) and Jenkins (1994) has provided both historical and cross-cultural evidence that serial killers choose victims who are easy prey on a repetitive basis. Jack the Ripper, for example, murdered prostitutes in London's east end. Likewise in America, as two of many examples, both Gary Ridgway, the Green River Killer, and Arthur Shawcross preferred prostitutes as victims. Despite common reassurances that police "thoroughly" investigate all homicide cases no matter who the victim is, research has consistently shown this not to be the case. A review of the Dahmer and Gacy cases in the United States or the Nielson case in Great Britain clearly demonstrates the priority given to victims drawn from the less dead (Fleming, 2006; Hickey, 2006). Given that police budgets are limited, it is natural that detectives must choose which cases to pursue most vigorously. Traditionally, this has meant that those victims drawn from the upper socioeconomic strata will have relatives in a position to exert pressure on police and politicians, and, in turn, politicians will turn to chiefs of police to take action (Fleming, 2006; Fleming & O'Reilly, 2010a, 2010b, 2010c).

Thompson (2010) informs us that one view of the Aboriginal community confirms the results of the research cited above; "My Aboriginal sisters are not perfect victims in the eyes of the police and the courts, especially when they're considered vagrant, addicted and sex workers" (p.1). Victim selection also reflects the vulnerability of Aboriginal sex workers on the street; they are easily accessible, will accompany men to out-of-the-way places, and are somewhat transient so that killers recognize that family and friends do not expect them to check in on a regular basis. We also understand that serial rapists and serial killers educate themselves to select victims who are more vulnerable because they are under the influence of drugs or alcohol. They may provide or use such substances to render the victim more pliable so that they can get them into what is referred to as their "control" zone, where the victim has no chance of escape. This could be a car with childproof locks, a specially constructed bunker or hidden room, or a secluded location in a rural area.

The nature of serial killing, which most typically involves stranger-to-stranger encounters, poses considerable investigative challenges for detectives in contrast to murders committed in everyday life (Leyton, 2005b) where a connection typically exists between offender and victim. Investigators who conduct murder investigations as part of their police duties are well versed in this latter form of murder, but this does not translate into skills that will solve a serial murder. Second, chiefs of police are reticent to declare a serial murder is operating in their jurisdiction since they are in a catch-22 situation; if they announce a serial killer is murdering, they must get results and identify a suspect to be successful. However, if they do not apprehend a perpetrator, they risk losing their authority and being the subject of criticism or even dismissal. Finally, if they commit to an investigation, it means that a large amount of any police budget will be dedicated to the investigative effort and, as such, other areas of police service will suffer (O'Reilly & Fleming, 2011).

The disparity between police interest in the murder of white women versus Aboriginal women has been commented upon by Aboriginal writers such as Sherry Lewis, who wrote that that it took the disappearance of one non-Aboriginal woman after five Aboriginal women had disappeared on British Columbia's "Highway of Tears," an 800 km section of Highway 16 which connects Prince Rupert and Prince George, before there was a "media frenzy" (qtd in d'Entremont, 2004). We have previously argued that the "three-pronged" nature of Aboriginal sex trade workers' lives made them extremely vulnerable to Pickton, specifically their Aboriginal status, drug use, and involvement in the sex trade (O'Reilly & Fleming, 2011). Egger's (1990) admonition that the status of serial murder victims places them in a position where they "unable to alert authorities to their plight" (p.2), and thus remain powerless in terms of access to protection makes them extremely vulnerable to extreme violence. In 2013, Canadian sex trade workers have successfully challenged the legality of prostitution laws that place them in jeopardy of being arrested when they call police for assistance.

The Canadian Supreme Court found that this places sex trade workers in an untenable and dangerous predicament in violation of their *Charter* right to security of the person. At present, the Federal government is contemplating changes to the laws governing the sale of sex in order to respond to the court's decision. Hickey (2010) argues that society often sees such victims as losers who "get what they deserve" (p.303). Although the Vancouver Police, in their report on the investigation of the case (LePard, 2010), contends that they treated the case of the missing women no differently than any other investigation, the Amnesty International Report (2004) "No More Stolen Sisters: Justice for the missing and murdered Indigenous women of Canada" provides contrary evidence. First, Aboriginal families in the Amnesty Report have asserted they were not treated with dignity and respected when they sought more information on their missing relatives or asked police to ramp up their investigative efforts. Some measure of their dissatisfaction with police efforts and their treatment is reflected in pending civil cases launched by families of the victims against the RCMP. By August of 2013, six civil lawsuits had been registered against the RCMP and Pickton for "failing to properly investigate reports of missing sex workers or warn the public of a potential serial killer" (Canadian Press, 2013). The RCMP, it is important to understand, are responsible for policing the province outside of Vancouver whereas the Vancouver Police Department polices the city. This may pose some difficulty for the law suits since ascertaining which police service(s) may have failed in their duties according to the plaintiffs, will require determining whether there is a failure where the sex trade workers were picked up, or where they were murdered, which covers two distinct police jurisdictions. If we accepted that the investigations were no different than any others, then there is also a problem since the number of women missing from such a small geographic area would require much more than the (normal) effort expended on missing persons cases where foul play is suspected by the families of the victim. One key question has to be considered is: would these police services have dared to stall investigative efforts and dismiss families concerns about their loved ones if they were not drawn largely from the Aboriginal community?

Societal Views of Aboriginal Women: Some Voices

Warren Goulding (2001) penned a book on serial killer John Martin Crawford, responsible for the murder of three Aboriginal women. In another case, Shawn Lamb, a drug user with a record of over 109 convictions was accused of murdering three Aboriginal sex trade workers in Winnipeg, eventually pleading guilty to two counts of second degree murder, and was sentenced to twenty years in prison (McIntyre, 2012; cbc.ca, 2013). Goulding argues that the general public does not care about missing or murdered Aboriginal women. He views it as an attitude of indifference to their plight. Moreover, he believes that Aboriginal women are viewed as being of less value than a white person. The vastness of Canada plays some part in this which must be acknowledged. The sheer size of our country, and the general lack of interest in murder cases occurring outside of our own city or province means that individuals in one province will generally not be aware of murders committed in another province. Murder cases are not generally reported on national news or in national newspapers, and remain isolated in news coverage to a specific province. Serial murders, mass murders, murders involving famous individuals, and those with bizarre elements will, of course, be the subject of national interest. Thus there is a significant disconnect between local murders and national coverage of these cases. Goulding's view echoes that of The Aboriginal Justice Inquiry and Implementation Commission that suggested Aboriginal peoples are the subject of intense policing efforts that are contrasted to very little effort being expended by the police to protect them (Chartrand et al., 1999). Their view is that Aboriginal peoples are viewed by many as a danger from which society must be protected (Amnesty International, 2004). Others have commented on how the media constructs Aboriginal sex workers as victims not deserving of societal sympathy since they are written about or portrayed as though their involvement in the sex trade and their substance abuse rendered them unworthy of concern (Travis, 2006). As Travis (2006) and Harding (2006) note, their characterization as marginal persons existing outside of the mainstream had the effect of making them into social pariahs. The power of media to construct pervasive images has been well documented in the criminological literature on the portrayal of crime in the media (Fleming, 1981, 2011), and, given the lack of public familiarity with Aboriginal sex trade workers, there is little that they can do to combat this image despite academic research in these field. The recent victory in the Canada of sex trade workers challenging the constitutionality of prostitution and sex-trade related laws (*Attorney General v. Bedford*, 2013, SCC72) should have had a significant impact on public knowledge of the dangers of sex trade work.

We also acknowledge the problems inherent in Aboriginals dealings with the police. The Oka Crisis, the murder of Dudley George in the Ipperwash land dispute, the push to assimilate Aboriginal peoples into Canadian society, the failure of successive governments to settle land claims, and the discrimination suffered by Aboriginal peoples across so many aspects of their existence have combined to cause distrust of police services, which, in the opinion of many Aboriginal critics, appear to criminalize rather than assist. The attitude of police towards the families of the missing Aboriginal women in the Pickton case are not, therefore, unique. Aside from the report by Amnesty International (2004), we could also cite the work of Audrey Huntley, a CBC associate producer, who, in her investigation of missing Aboriginal women and girls, found police agencies indifferent (Travis, 2006).

Racism and discrimination on the part of official agencies in dealing with Aboriginal women is not a new phenomenon. The Aboriginal Justice Inquiry conducted in Manitoba during the 1990s identified racist and sexist stereotypes that had dispersed throughout society, echoing our assessment of the impact of media constructions in the absence of alternative sources of information. More telling perhaps is one of the conclusions of the Amnesty International Report (2004) which found that sexism and racism were contributing factors to the presumption of those men who inflicted violence on Aboriginal women that society actually condoned their actions. The report also found that Aboriginal people were not receiving policing available to other Canadians. Consider these concluding statements: "police failed to act promptly when their sisters or daughters went missing, treated the families disrespectfully, or kept the family in the dark about how the investigation-if any-was proceeding" (Amnesty International, 2004, p.12). The Amnesty investigators also found that "despite the concern of family members that a missing sister or daughter was in serious danger, police failed to take basic steps such as promptly interviewing family and friends or appealing to the public for information" (p.12). Both the Vancouver Police Department (LePard, 2010) and the RCMP (Williams & Simmill, 2006) have produced reports documenting their response to criticisms of their performance in the Pickton case. The Vancouver Police report (LePard, 2010) is lengthy and detailed. However, in the end it finds fault in the performance of individual officers in particular, and several other investigative flaws. A plethora of research has demonstrated that while "bad apples" may exist, there is more blame to be directed towards the "bad barrel" in other words, the policing organizations (Ericson, 1993). The Vancouver Police and the RCMP also argue that there were insufficient personnel, both sworn and civilian, and a lack of resources to carry out an efficient and timely investigation.

Rossmo's 1999 report as a detective with the Vancouver Police Department which contended that the missing women were dead was ignored by senior officers (Rossmo, 2009). LePard (2010) also acknowledges that the investigation *prior* to Pickton's arrest was not sufficient and flawed. The disturbing irony of the commitment of the police to the recovery of dead victim's identifying DNA and identification cards after Pickton's arrest is more pronounced in light of Rossmo's report and his constructive dismissal from the Vancouver Police Department. There seemed to be no limit to the budget for recovery in comparison to the inadequacy of resources for investigation of the missing Aboriginal women and other sex trade workers. Also consider the money available for the production of police reports on the case, the Oppal Inquiry examining the police investigation, and the costs associated with defending law cases brought by victims' families for damages. The inability of police services to learn from previous inquiries into serial murder cases, most notably the Campbell Inquiry (1996) into police handling of the Bernardo-Homolka murders, and apply those lessons to their own investigation led to the same type of systemic errors that recur in serial murder cases from that of Clifford Olson in 1980 to Pickton in 2002.

The Aftermath of the Murders

Following the discovery of the bodies on Pickton's farm and his successful prosecution for six of the murders, Aboriginal leaders, victims' families, and others began to seek justice in what they viewed as a failure of police agencies to take seriously the case of the missing women. For many Aboriginal people in Canada, racism is the overwhelming factor in the disrespectful attitude taken towards victims' families by the police. Racism, according to Chartrand et al. (1999) encourages and excuses violence towards Aboriginal people. When we presented a paper on this topic at the Urban Aboriginal Conference in 2011, we were approached by a contingent of Aboriginal women from the audience who heard our paper and told us that, for them, the behaviour of the police could only be understood in the context of racism. We thank them, as family members who have lost loved ones to homicide, for their insight. Despite calls from Rossmo in 2002 and others (Kines & Bolan, 2002), no inquiry was called into the case until nine years after Pickton was arrested. In 2011, the Oppal Inquiry began its deliberations and issued its five volume report. Volumes IIa and IIb are instructive considering their titles, "Nobodies: How and Why We Failed the Missing and Murdered Women" (Oppal, 2013). However, there has been severe criticism of the inquiry on several grounds:

1. Mr. Oppal served as Attorney General of British Columbia at the time of the disappearance of the women (Mulgrew, 2010);
2. No Chiefs, Elders, or Aboriginal leaders are included as decision making members of the Inquiry;
3. Aboriginal groups were barred from receiving government funding to be represented at the inquiry (Keller, 2011; Sahajpal, 2011);
4. The inquiry limited its scope to police actions from 1999 to 2002 rather than examining the history of the entire police investigation, or lack thereof;
5. The inquiry will not examine the fate of 32 unsolved murders on the Highway of Tears;
6. The public sessions held as information gathering were not being documented (see Matas, 2011a, 2011b, 2011c, 2011d).

Given the RCMP's depiction of their actions as an excellent investigation, the disappearances and their claims to have exhausted all leads (Williams & Simmill, 2002) and the stance of the Vancouver Police that the RCMP have responsibility for the events that unfolded, it is no wonder that this inquiry took so long to convene, and that Aboriginal people are skeptical that any positive change can be forthcoming. The Oppal Inquiry (2013) found that "the missing and murdered women were forsaken twice, once by society and again by the police" (p.160). However, given the limited institutional memory of policing institutions, it is unlikely that the Oppal report will have any substantive effect on future investigations. Inquiries into police failures in Canadian serial murder cases are important and do provide clear recommendations for positive change, but are quickly forgotten as the repetitive nature of police errors in these investigations demonstrates (Fleming & O'Reilly, 2010a). Sahajpal (2011) argues that the lack of effective representation of Aboriginal peoples at the inquiry means that they have effectively been silenced once again. It is little wonder that Aboriginal peoples have such little faith in the "justice" being delivered to them in Canada.

Conclusions

In this chapter, we have explored violence towards Aboriginal sex trade workers in the Robert Pickton case. Our objective has been to inform readers about the reality and dangers of street sex trade work faced by Aboriginal women and the vulnerable position in which it left the women who disappeared from the streets of Vancouver during a twenty-year period. Our analysis examined the challenges urban living poses for some Aboriginal women and how this impacts the ability of some to survive in our society. The reluctance of police agencies to give credence to and respect the families of Aboriginal victims regarding their concerns about the whereabouts of their loved ones, and, later, their conviction that these women were dead was examined. In a society where the effects of racism are an everyday reality for Aboriginal peoples, Amnesty International's (2004) "Stolen Sisters" report highlights the helplessness felt by victims' families and underscores Aboriginal mistrust and lack of faith in policing authorities.

Finally, we explored the serious concerns regarding police inaction in investigating the case of the missing women and the criticisms of the Oppal Inquiry which recently reported on police failures. The recurring phenomenon of Aboriginal women as victims of serial violence is a grave concern that deserves further study. Despite calls for a national inquiry on missing and murdered women by the Aboriginal community, the federal government has refused to go this route, opting instead to issue a RCMP report in 2014. Given that the Oppal Inquiry cited police failures we would ask readers why Aboriginal peoples would trust them to produce a report on this issue? Given the number of unsolved cases documented in the report there appears to be more than enough evidence that a national inquiry conducted with Aboriginal persons as decision makers is warranted. We have examined these murders and police response to them to demonstrate the end point of a continuum of violence against Aboriginal women in Canada. Their plight has only received nationwide attention in recent years due to the Pickton case and the advocacy work of organizations such as Stolen Sisters and research by criminologists and others. We hope that systemic change can occur in the policing of violence towards Aboriginal women, particularly, though not exclusively, for those who live lives punctuated by risk. We also suggest that education for police officers in Aboriginal culture, issues of respect, and the need to learn from past investigations of this type is pursued. Finally, we suggest that Aboriginal Chiefs and Elders must become part of this process of education of the police and society to shine a light on, and eliminate systemic neglect and abuse of Aboriginal women victims of violence and their families.

Keywords

Aboriginal women, police investigative failures, urban, Amnesty International, serial murder

Review Quetions

1. What factors in the urban environment have contributed to the violent victimization of Aboriginal sex trade workers?
2. What are three failures of police investigative efforts in the Pickton case and how might they have contribute to violence against Aboriginal women?
3. How can society change widely held views of Aboriginal women as victims of crime?
4. What steps could the federal government take to initiate a response to calls by the National Chief and the Stolen Sisters organization to investigate the disappearance and murders of many Aboriginal women?
5. How can we prevent violence towards Aboriginal women engaged in the sex trade?
6. Consider the recent legal appeal of sex trade workers to the Supreme Court of Canada to laws criminalizing solicitation and communication for the purposes of prostitution. Does this violate their *Charter* rights to security of the person?

Note

1. The law on first degree murder was amended by the federal government in 2014 to allow for consecutive sentences for individual victims, thus permitting sentences of 50 years for 2 victims, 75 for three victims, and so on. Pickton would now be eligible for a sentence of 125 years.

References

Abbott, K.L. (2004). Urban Aboriginal women in British Columbia and the impacts of matrimonial real property regime. In J. P. White, P. Maxim, and D. Beaven, (Eds.), *Aboriginal policy research: Setting the agenda for change* (Vol.2) (pp.165-182).Toronto: Thompson Educational Publishing.

Amnesty International. (2004). *Stolen Sisters: A human rights response to discrimination and violence against Indigenous Women in Canada.* Retrieved from http://www.amnesty .org/en/library/asset/AMR20/003/2004/en/cc99816-d57b-11dd-b24-1fb85fe8fa05/amr 200032004en.html

Balakrishnan, T. R., & Jurdi, R. (2007). Spatial residential patterns of Aboriginals and their socio-economic integration in selected Canadian cities. In J. P. White, S. Wingert, D. Beavon, & P. Maxim (Eds.), *Aboriginal policy research* (Vol.4) (pp.263-274).Toronto: Thompson Educational Publishing.

Campbell, A. (1996). *Bernardo investigation review.* Government of Ontario. Toronto: Government Printing Office.

Cbcnews. (2013, November 14). Shawn Lamb sentenced to twenty years for 2 slayings. Retrieved from www.cbc.ca

Chartrand, P., et al. (1999). *The Aboriginal justice implementation commission* (Vol. 1). Manitoba: Manitoba Statutory Publications Office.

Cohen, L., & Felson, M. (1979). Social change and crime rate trends: A routine activity approach. *American Sociological Review, 44,* 488-608.

Cohen, I., & Corrado, R. (2004). Housing discrimination among a sample of Aboriginal people in Winnipeg and Thompson, Manitoba. In J.P. White, P.Maxim and D. Bevan (Eds.), *Aboriginal policy and research: Setting the agenda for change* (Vol.1) (pp. 113-126). Toronto: Thompson Educational Publishing.

Comack, E., & Seshia, M. (2010). Bad dates and street hassles: Violence in the Winnipeg Street sex trade. *Canadian Journal of Criminology and Criminal Justice, 52*(2), 203-214.

Davis, S., & Shaffer, M. (2004). *Prostitution in Canada: The invisible menace or the menace of invisibility?* Retrieved from http://www.walnet.org/csis/papers

D'Entremont, D. (2006). Seeking justice for Canada's 500 missing Native women. *Cultural survival.* Retrieved from http://www.culturalsurvival.org//seeking-justice-canada-s-500-missing-native-women

Egger, K. (1999). Preliminary data base on serial killers from 1900-1999. In S. Egger. *The killers among us: An examination of serial murder and its investigation* (pp.38-73). Upper Saddle River, NJ: Prentice Hall.

Egger, S. (1990). *Serial murder: An elusive phenomenon.* New York: Praeger.

Egger, S. (2001). *The killers among us: An examination of serial murder and its investigation.* Upper Saddle River, NJ: Prentice Hall.

Ericson, R. (1993). *Making Crime: A study of detective work*. Toronto: University of Toronto Press.

Fleming, T. (1981). The bawdy house 'boys': Some notes on media, sporadic moral crusades and moral panics. *Canadian Criminology Forum*.

Fleming. T. (1993a). *Down and out in Canada: Homeless Canadians*. Toronto: Canadian Scholars Press.

Fleming, T. (1993b). Policing serial murder: The politics of negligence. In L. Visano and K. McCormick (Eds.), *Understanding Policing* (pp. 323-346). Toronto: Canadian Scholars' Press.

Fleming, T. (Ed.). (2006). *Serial and mass murder: Theory, policy and research*. Toronto: Canadian Scholars' Press.

Fleming, T. (2008). Victims lost: Recurring investigative errors in Canada's serial murder mega cases. Paper presented at *Canadian Society of Criminology National Conference*. Toronto, May.

Fleming, T. & O'Reilly, P. (2010a; February 5). History repeats itself: Recurring errors in Canadian serial murder investigation. Paper presented at the *Western Society of Criminology*. Honolulu, Hawaii.

Fleming, T. & O'Reilly, P. (2010b, February 3). The value of victims: Police treatment of victims' families in the Lower East Side missing women (Pickton) case. Paper presented at the *Western Society of Criminology*. Honolulu, Hawaii.

Fleming, T. & O'Reilly, P. (2011, March 1-5). Police investigative failures in the Pickton investigation. Paper presented at the *Academy of Criminal Justice Sciences*, 48th Annual Meeting. Toronto.

Frideres, J. (1974). *Canada's Indians: Contemporary conflicts*. Toronto: Prentice Hall.

Goulding, W. (2001). *Just another Indian: A serial killer and Canada's indifference*. Calgary: Fifth House.

Guelph Mercury. (2013, August 1). Children of missing women files 6th lawsuit vs. Pickton and police. Retrieved from http://www.insideHalton.ca

Harding, R. (2006). Historical representations of Aboriginal people in the Canadian news nedia. *Discourse and Society, 17*(2), 205-235.

Hickey, E. (2006). *Serial murderers and their victims* (4th Ed.). Belmont, CA : Wadsworth.

Holmes, R., & Holmes, S. (2010). *Serial murder* (3rd ed.). London: Sage.

Jenkins, P. (1994). *Using murder: The social construction of serial homicide*. New York: Aldine de Gruyter.

Keller, J. (2011, May 24). Province denies funding for sex workers, Aboriginal groups at Pickton Inquiry. *Canadian Press* (Vancouver).

Kines, L., Culbert, L., & Bolan, K. (1999, September 26). BC slow to adopt lessons of Bernardo: Police face obstacles tracking down serial predators. *Vancouver Sun*.

LePard, D. (2010). *Missing women: Investigation review*. Vancouver Police Department.

Leyton, E. (2005a). *Hunting humans: The rise of the modern multiple murder*. Toronto: McClelland and Stewart.

Leyton, E. (2005b). *Men of blood: Murder in everyday life*. Toronto: McClelland and Stewart.

Lowman, J. (1998). Prostitution law reform in Canada. Retrieved from http://24.85.225.7/lowman_prostitution/ProLaw/prolawcan.htm

Lowman, J. (2000). Violence and the outlaw status of (street) prostitution in Canada. *Violence Against Women, 6*(9), 987-1011.

Matas, R. (2011a, January 18). In aftermath of Pickton case, BC's missing women commission to begin inquiry. *Globe and Mail* (Toronto).

Matas, R. (2011b, January 21). Mounties acknowledge shortcomings on Pickton case. *Globe and Mail* (Toronto).

Matas, R. (2011c, January 26). Internal report praised RCMP investigation into Pickton killings. *Globe and Mail* (Toronto).

Matas, R. (2011d, March 3). Oppal seeks to expand scope of missing-women inquiry. *Globe and Mail (Toronto).*

McIntyre, M. (2012, June 29). *Accused serial killer- Shawn Lamb denies links to dozens.* Winnipeg Free Press.

Oppal, W. (2013). *Missing women – Commission of Inquiry.* British Columbia: Province of British Columbia.

O'Reilly, P., & Fleming, T. (2011:February 23-24). Kept in the dark: Reforming police practices in communicating with Aboriginal families in the aftermath of the case of the Lower East Side missing women (Pickton) case. Paper presented at *Fostering Biimaadiziwin, National Research Conference on Urban Aboriginal Peoples.* Delta Chelsea, Toronto.

Purdy, C. (2003, November 26). Serial killer who roamed Saskatoon met with indifference by police, media: Journalist-author accepts award for book about slain Aboriginal women. *Edmonton Journal.*

RCMP. (2014). *Missing and murdered Aboriginal women: A national operation inquiry.* Ottawa: Government of Canada.

Rossmo, D. K. (2009). *Criminal investigative failures.* Boca Raton, FL: CRC Press.

Rossmo, D. K. (2011, March 1-5). Criminal investigative failures in the missing women/pig farm serial murder case. Paper presented at the *Academy of Criminal Justice Sciences,* 48th Annual Meeting. Toronto.

Sahajpal, R. (2011, June). Discrimination in BC? No funding for advocacy groups in Pickton inquiry. *McClung's Magazine.* Retrieved from http://mcclungs.ca/2011/06/

Shaver, F. (1997). Prostitution: On the dark side of the service industry. in T. Fleming (Ed.), *Post-critical criminology* (pp.42-65). Scarborough, ON: Prentice Hall Canada.

Thompson, K. (2010, August 25). Everybody failed Pickton victims: Women's shelter. *Metro Vancouver.*

Travis, H. (2006). Pickton Trial: Who were the victims?" *The Tyee.* Retrieved from http://thetyee.ca/

Urban Aboriginal Task Force. Final Report, Commissioned by The Ontario Federation of Indian Friendship Centres. The Ontario Metis Aboriginal Association and The Ontario Native Women's Association. 2007.

Voyageur, C. (2011). First Nations women in Canada. In D. Long & O.P. Dickason (Eds.), *Visions of the heart: Canadian Aboriginal issues* (3rd Ed.) (pp.213-235). Toronto: Oxford University Press.

Williams, R. J., & Simmill, K. W. (2006). *Re: Joesbury vs. Her Majesty The Queen (Project Evenhanded - Request For Assistance, External Review File: 2002e-3220).* Royal Canadian Mounted Police.

Wyld, A. (2011, March31). Top court will hear prostitution law challenge. *Canadian Press.* Retrieved from http://www.cbc.ca/news/canada/british-columbia/story/2011/03/31/bc-prostitution.html

Violence towards Nonhuman Animals

Learning Objectives

In this chapter you will...

▶ gain an understanding of intertwined oppression and violence against all animals, including human animals

▶ explore the importance of the examination of structural violence

▶ consider the political and economic analysis of violence

▶ reflect on the need to re-evaluate the status of nonhuman animals in our society

▶ critically assess and analyze everyday socially accepted violence

Chapter 10

Atsuko Matsuoka and John Sorenson

Introduction

In 2010, Mary Bale became "one of the most hated women in the world" when CCTV video showing her trapping a cat in a trash bin in Coventry, England was broadcast on the Internet (Trowbridge, 2010a). Bale became the target of public outrage. She was compared to Hitler and over 10,000 people joined the Mary Bale Hate Group on Facebook. After Lola the cat spent 15 hours in the bin, Bale was identified from video images and laughed about the incident saying, "I did it as a joke because I thought it would be funny" and wondering, "what everyone is getting so excited about – it's just a cat" (Trowbridge, 2010b).

In 2012, Percy Love expressed similar surprise when Chicago police charged him with animal cruelty after seeing him kick a kitten through football posts and then raise his arms to signal a field goal. Like Bale, Love protested, "it's just a cat" (*Huffington Post*, 2012). Bale and Love were minor monsters compared to Canadians Jesse Powers, Anthony Wennekers, and Matthew Kaczorowski, who were convicted of disemboweling a cat with dental tools and skinning her alive in 2001, although their punishment was light under Canada's outdated cruelty laws. A more recent case is that of Zhou Yang in Shanghai, who reportedly killed hundreds of cats she had adopted. In May 2012, a crowd of 50 "animal lovers" stormed her apartment and found three headless kittens in the trash; cleaning staff said they often found decapitated cats there. Many in the group had given kittens to Zhou on the understanding that she would care for them. Confronted by the group, Zhou said they were her cats and she could do whatever she wanted with them. She later went into hiding but faces no penalties since China has no law against cruelty to small animals. In contrast, police charged the "animal lovers" with trespassing but later released them with a warning not to bother Zhou (Moore, 2012).

These incidents, merely a sample from a constant stream of media reports on abuse, are indicative of how widespread the phenomenon is, the disregard that abusers have for the lives of other animals, the weakness of laws protecting those animals, and the powerful public emotions that can be aroused by their abuse. Furthermore, these incidents exist in a context of institutionalized violence towards other animals as they are exploited for profit. Due its pervasiveness, human violence against other animals is deserving of more sustained academic attention. Nevertheless, some are even offended by concern for other animals, seeing this as trivial, misplaced, and misguided. Such aggrieved dismissals of other animals' suffering suggest that resistance to examining these issues reflects efforts to maintain a firm boundary between them and ourselves (Arluke, 2006). Singer (2002) refers to this phenomenon as speciesism: "a prejudice or attitude of bias in favor of the interests of members of one's own species and against those of members of other species" (p.6). Arluke (2006) further argues that such a speciesist stance stems from fears that too much concern for others will degrade what it means to be human.

Studies of violence toward other animals have focused largely on the idea of cruelty. Ascione (1993) defines cruelty to animals as "socially unacceptable behaviour that intentionally causes unnecessary pain, suffering or distress to and/or death of an animal" (p. 228). He specifically excludes "socially approved practices related to the treatment or use of animals in veterinary practices and livestock production (including humane slaughter) or other animal husbandry practices … hunting and in laboratory research" (p. 228).

Looking at violence towards other animals only in terms of cruelty has the effect of overlooking the vast majority of harms inflicted on them and their systemic character. We may contrast Ascione's definition of cruelty with the World Health Organization's definition of violence: "the intentional use of physical force or power, threatened or actual, against oneself, another person, or against a group or community that either results in or has a high likelihood of resulting in injury, death, psychological harm, maldevelopment or deprivation" (Krug, Dahlberg, Mercy, Zwai & Lozano, 2002, p. 5). The WHO's definition emphasizes intentionality but also addresses the idea of socially acceptable violence. Certain behaviours, such as physical discipline of children, may be socially acceptable in some cultures but the WHO defines violence in relation to the well-being of individuals. Similarly, in looking at violence toward other animals, we should be concerned about the effect upon those individuals rather than the fact that certain harmful practices are widely accepted because they benefit humans. Definitions that are not bound to social values help to unveil practices and social relations that are considered normal and help us to see violence as a part of oppression. The new field of animal studies has directed more attention to the significance of other animals in their relation to human society. While much of this work remains abstract and does not challenge their exploitation for food, clothing, experimental purposes, or entertainment, a few do adopt a critical animal studies approach, one that is explicitly political and committed to an animal rights perspective (e.g., Davis, 2009; Nibert, 2002; Nocella, Sorenson, Socha & Matsuoka, 2014; Sanbonmatsu, 2011; Sorenson, 2010, 2014). This chapter utilizes a critical animal studies approach to examine violence against nonhuman/other animals and adopts Iris Marion Young's (2010) framework of social justice, which considers violence as a form of oppression that creates social injustice. Seeing violence and cultural imperialism as aspects of oppression and matters of social injustice, Young (2010) contends that exploitation, marginalization, and powerlessness stem from social divisions of labour, "structural and institutional relations that delimit people's material lives, including … the concrete opportunities they have or do not have to develop and exercise their capacities" (p. 58). While Young limits her discussion to human oppression, much of it is directly applicable to other animals as well. Violence against marginalized Others is frequent but goes unrecognized by theorists of social justice because they consider these the actions of particular individuals, often by the disturbed, rather than seeing these as institutional issues and matters of social injustice. Young (2010) states:

> What makes violence a face of oppression is less the particular acts themselves, though these are often utterly horrible, than the social context surrounding them, which makes them possible and even acceptable. What makes violence a phenomenon of social injustice, and not merely an individual wrong, is its systemic character, its existence as a social practice. (pp. 61-62)

By integrating Young's ideas about social justice into a critical animal studies approach, we interrogate violence against other animals.

The link between Violence or Cruelty to Animals and Violence against People

A database search on work related to cruelty to other animals reveals a record extending back to the nineteenth century, and discussions of violence against animals go back to the eighteenth century. Most studies of violence against other animals in the twentieth and twenty-first centuries focus on individual acts of cruelty against companion animals. There is a "relatively well-documented" connection between violence toward nonhuman animals and other forms of domestic violence (McPhedran, 2009a, p. 41). Nonhuman animals are convenient targets because they are both "property" and "members of the family" (p. 42). Abusers may harm other animals because such actions are considered trivial under the law, while at the same time they can have tremendous emotional impact, sometimes more painful than physical assault. Thus, perpetrators can control those they abuse by threatening to kill a family pet. Trollinger (2001) suggests that up to 40% of women stay with perpetrators because they fear what may happen to their companion animals if they leave. Some are skeptical; for example, Piper (2003) questions the link with violence towards other animals, suggesting that abused women's statements about their husbands' abuse of family pets may be exaggerated because they want to portray them as monsters in order to claim the family house and so on (Hinch & DeKeseredy, 1991).

Despite such criticism, individual abuse of companion animals is gruesome and deserving of moral concern, and research that can inform action to protect these animals and reduce such violence is certainly worthwhile. However, we cannot overlook the fact that the focus of most of this research is not on violence inflicted on these animals themselves but rather on the degree to which this is a marker of current or future violence towards humans. For example, psychiatrist John MacDonald (1961) identified animal abuse as one element in a triad of behaviours (along with bed-wetting and obsession with fire) that could be indicative of future aggression, including homicide, although this connection derived from a sample of convicted murderers. Anthropologist Margaret Mead (1964) stated that abuse of other animals in childhood suggested a violent personality that, if left untreated, could possibly result in the murder of another person. The American Psychiatric Association (1987) identifies nonhuman animal abuse as an indicator of conduct disorder. The FBI identified significant connections between abuse of nonhuman animals and other violent crimes after interviewing a sample of several dozen serial killers in the 1970s (Lockwood & Church, 1996). McPhedran (2009a) cites research that finds a lack of empathy among violent criminals, sex offenders, and nonhuman animal abusers. Various studies find that violent criminals are more likely to have abused and killed nonhuman animals than were nonviolent criminals and noncriminals (Kellert & Felthous, 1985; Merz-Perze, Heide, & Silverman, 2001; Tingle et al., 1986). Researchers increasingly recognize cruelty to other animals as a form of psychological disturbance and an indication of dysfunction within families. Yet violence towards nonhuman animals is mainly seen as an indicator of more serious crimes that may occur in the future.

Seeking to theorize the relationship, Ascione and Shapiro (2009) suggest that the link between harming nonhuman animals and harming humans is a "byproduct" of the development of urban modernism in which certain nonhuman animals are seen as companions. Based on their analysis of case histories of serial killers, Wright and Hensley (2003) endorse the "graduation hypothesis," suggesting progression from violence against nonhuman animals to violence against humans. Peterson and Farrington (2007) cite the graduation hypothesis as a major explanation of nonhuman animal abuse, along with strain theory (in which nonhuman animals are used as scapegoats or safe targets for discharging aggression) and social learning theory (in which nonhuman animal abuse is seen as a learned behavior adopted by children exposed to family violence and sexual abuse). Others challenge existence of the link between violence against other animals and against humans (Arluke, 2006) and note that many abuse nonhuman animals and do not become serial killers of humans (Piper, 2003). Bierne (2004) challenges the idea of a progression from harming nonhuman animals to harming humans on both conceptual and methodological grounds, citing gaps and discrepancies in research. However, Bierne suggests that rather than focusing on matters of individual psychology, more scholarly attention should be directed towards institutional practices in which violence towards animals is considered acceptable.

Structural Violence

Definitions of abuse or cruelty typically specify that the harm inflicted on nonhuman animals should be intentional, unnecessary, and socially unacceptable (Ascione, 1993; Ascione & Shapiro, 2009; Flynn, 2001; Kellert & Felthous, 1985). As Flynn (2001) notes, Ascione's widely accepted definition of cruelty exempts "humane killing of farm animals, hunting, and the use of animals in research" (p. 72). These exemptions are not random acts of individuals but rather actions integrated into everyday life; yet they inflict harm on individual animals.

Few sociologists consider how other animals' lives are affected by structural violence. Structural violence describes various constraints placed upon humans by political and economic structures that created poverty and unequal access to resources and services such as education and medical care (Galtung, 1969). Yet investigations into the violence of everyday life (e.g. Farmer, 1996; Scheper-Hughes, 1993), in which structural violence is made invisible and normalized through institutions, practices, and discourses that make inequality seem natural, ordinary, and expected, ignore other animals. Just as the global economy of military production creates structural violence on an extensive scale, so does the global meat industry create structural violence that affects other animals most directly but also has negative impacts on humans. There are good reasons to challenge the widely accepted exceptions in theories about cruelty to animals, including the treatment of farmed animals, hunting, entertainment, use of animals in experiments, and other forms of exploitation.

Humane Killing, or Cruelty and Systemic Violence?: Farm Animals

Some consider it humane to kill others, including humans, if they are incurably ill and suffering, although even these decisions are contested (BBC, 2012; Marcoux, Mishara & Durand, 2007; Nantais & Kuczewski, 2004). The idea of "humane killing" is problematic. In the case of so-called farm animals the terminology does a kind of violence to other animals since it is a mass term that denies them individuality and suggests that their very existence is defined only in terms of their instrumental value to humans. However, these are young, healthy individuals who are killed, not to spare them unendurable pain but rather to profit from their death (Adams, 2007). Even if we accept that killing can be done mercifully, it is questionable to what degree such procedures truly are painless (Davis, 2011). In the context of commercialized slaughter on an industrial scale, where the drive for profit necessitates ever-greater speed and efficiency, it is clear that violations of even the existing inadequate standards are not an exception and that many animals suffer excruciating pain (Grandin, 1988; Rifkin, 1992; Webster, 2005). Animals are beaten, whipped, and electrically shocked to force them into slaughterhouses where the speed of processing means many are boiled alive or dismembered while conscious (Warrick, 2001). Another example is the organization Mercy For Animals' (2010) exposure of abuse in the dairy industry with undercover video from Conklin Dairy in Ohio: workers beating cows with crowbars, stabbing them with pitchforks, and punching them in their heads. Farm owner Gary Conklin characterized this as the behaviour of one sadistic employee, Billy Joe Gregg Jr., who was fired and charged with animal cruelty. But these abuses, and worse, are standard practice.

A grim undercover video captured everyday practice at an Iowa chicken plant, Hy-Line Hatchery, where thousands of unwanted male chicks are thrown alive into a grinder (Mercy for Animals, 2009). Thus, animals are not killed "humanely," as industry propaganda suggests. We also need to understand that quite often workers in industrialized slaughterhouses are non-unionized, uninsured, and poorly paid (Human Rights Watch, 2005; Winders & Nibert, 2004), and in some situations they are undocumented foreign workers who would not report inhumane conditions (Human Rights Watch, 2005). Therefore, cruelty to factory-farmed animals is not simply random acts of individuals but the predictable outcomes of the poor working conditions and the systems that allow them and that commodify other animals.

It is estimated that 56.5 billion nonhuman animals worldwide were killed for food in 2007 (Compassion in World Farming, 2009). Many species have been intensively bred to grow larger and faster, which creates deformity and pain, exacerbated by close confinement that thwarts all natural behavior and repeated impregnation (Canadian Coalition for Farm Animals, 2005; Lancet, 2003; Singer et al., 2003). Intensive confinement is increasing for the sake of efficiency and profitability as global demands for cheap meat grow (Food and Agricultural Organization of the United Nations, 2009). For example, reporting on the call for an expansion of mega farms in the UK by Peter Kendall, president of the National Farmers Union, the Guardian noted it was "not uncommon" for US farms to contain 10,000 pigs and that Saudi Arabia had a "super dairy" containing 37,000 cows (Jowit, 2012). In such a system, nonhuman animals are mere commodities, not sentient individuals, and they are treated as such. We would recognize systemic forced confinement, repeated impregnation, and other forms of suffering as violence if these were committed against humans, but we do not acknowledge them as such simply because they are inflicted upon other animals. This is a form of speciesism. The growing global demand for meat leads to more extensive violence towards nonhuman animals, legitimized by such ideologies.

Sport or Cruelty?: Hunting

Ascione's widely used definition of cruelty to animals excludes hunting, considering this as another socially acceptable practice. Yet the practice of deliberately setting out to kill other animals is clearly violent and, where it is unnecessary for human survival, indicative of attitudes that we normally consider coldhearted and psychopathic. It is a sign of moral progress that the popularity of this practice is declining. However, those who take pleasure in destroying life still engage in killing for sport, joining organizations such as the Safari Club that organize competitions for wealthy hunters to kill rare and endangered species in exotic locations, and promote retrograde and brutal constructions of masculinity (Anahita & Mix, 2006; Kalof, Fitzgerald, & Baralt, 2004). Sport hunters engage in stalking activities similar to those described by serial killers of humans. Many enjoy posing and photographing themselves with the corpses of those they have killed and some keep body parts as grisly souvenirs. As do serial killers of humans, hunters describe experiencing sexual thrills from killing other animals (Luke, 1998). Although these particular killers may be psychologically disturbed in some way, these are not simply individual acts; rather, they are part of an extensive industry, involving a wide variety of businesses involving accommodations, transportation, restaurants, outfitters, guides, and governments that collect fees from the hunters/killers and license them. Thus, like the meat industry, hunting is institutionalized violence.

Science or Cruelty?: Vivisection, Experimentations

As for the idea that the term *cruelty* does not describe what is inflicted on other animals in research, this is no more convincing than the other exclusions. Defenders of vivisection insist it is necessary to save humans from deadly diseases. Yet most vivisection is "glaringly non-medical" (Dunayer, 1993, p. 58); instead, it involves testing of mundane commercial products such as oven cleaners and deodorants and is conducted to provide corporations with legal protection (Doctors and Lawyers for Responsible Medicine, n.d.; Irish Antivivisection Society, 2011). It is clearly cruel to hurt and kill others for trivial purposes. An extra dimension of cruelty is added in military testing: here, nonhuman animals are deliberately wounded and killed in order to develop deadlier weapons, including biological and chemical poisons, and devise more terrible ways to kill humans. Even where medical testing is involved, much of this is redundant, as corporations seek to develop their own brand names of existing drugs. Rather than saving human lives, medical testing often produces misleading results and human deaths, since humans and other animals do not respond in the same way to various chemicals, and even temperatures at which animals are confined can drastically affect results of chemical tests (Knight, 2007a, 2007b; *Science Daily*, 2012). In other cases, violence inflicted on other animals for human medical treatments produces substances that actually are harmful instead. For example, Asia's bear farms confine these animals in tiny cages for years, with tubes inserted into their abdomens to drain the bile from their gall bladders, for use in traditional medicine (Animals Asia, 2010). In addition to physical and psychological stress, the bears suffer infections and cancers. Bile extracted from sick bears can poison those people who ingest it in the hope of curing their own health problems (Parry, 2010). In the vivisection industry, nonhuman animals are confined, deliberately infected with diseases, burned, and poisoned – procedures that would be considered torture if performed outside a laboratory. Academic and corporate researchers build careers on animal testing, funded by public money, government grants, and fundraising campaigns. This structured violence is fundamental to food, chemical, medical, pharmaceutical, and military industries and to the various other industries that supply feed, cages, restraining devices, surgical tools, and other equipment. Although some may argue some form of animal testing is necessary, greater efforts need to be made to change this structure of violence.

Cruelty and Entertainment

Typically, when we use other animals for entertainment we force them into spectacles of torture. In Spain, bullfighting is the best known form of brutalizing nonhuman animals for public entertainment; other traditions have included throwing live goats out of towers or attaching flaming torches to terrified animals and chasing them through the streets. Although Spain banned some of these festivities after an international campaign, many continue. Canada also allows such primitive practices. The Calgary Stampede is one example of animal abuse presented as entertainment; each year animals are killed in racing and roping events. Other entertainment industries also consider nonhuman animals disposable property. For example, following a slump in tourism after the 2010 Winter Olympic games, the company Howling Dog Tours, owned by Outdoor Adventures Whistler, decided to get rid of 100 unwanted sled dogs by shooting them and slashing their throats and dumping them, some still alive, in a mass grave. These events came to light when Robert Fawcett, the person who killed the dogs was awarded compensation on the grounds that he experienced post-traumatic stress disorder (Zelman, 2011). Although a charge of cruelty was laid and stronger penalties were introduced, along with a new Sled Dog Code of Practice, animal protection groups such as the Humane Society and Lifeforce questioned why the new code of practice included instructions on how to properly shoot unwanted dogs. The SPCA pointed out that the government did not provide funding for cruelty investigations and that, without resources, the regulations would remain "just a book on a shelf without the ability to actually enforce it" (Indian Country Today Media Network, 2012).

Cruelty and Clothes or Fashion

Atrocities are also built in to industries that exploit other animals for clothing. The fur industry, confines nonhuman animals in barren wire cages, factory-farm style, where they endure psychological torment before they are strangled, anally electrocuted, or skinned alive (as shown in undercover videos of the Chinese fur industry). The documentary film *Skin Trade* (Keith, Stolar, Blalock, & Feldman, 2010) exposes the grotesque depravity of the fur industry. But even when they are spared confinement and are taken from the wild, many animals do not experience a quick death in the traps set for them but instead are wounded and left to die slowly. In Canada, thousands of baby seals are clubbed and hacked to death each spring to obtain their skins. This is called a hunt, although the practice is more properly described as a massacre: the killers merely walk directly up to the helpless animals and attack them (Sea Shepherd, n.d.).

Cruelty and Pet-keeping

Even activities that may seem compassionate towards other animals, such as pet-keeping, involve the suffering of millions of individuals. For example, many pets are produced in puppy farms, in which dogs are confined in filthy conditions where diseases are rampant. Overbreeding to produce a desirable appearance creates serious health problems for the animals themselves, such as respiratory problems, deafness, and cancer (Allan, 2010; Calboli et al., 2008). The pet industry has become a lucrative one, and those animals we claim to love as our pets are taken from their own families, isolated, mutilated, sterilized, or bred selectively to produce other animals who have certain desirable characteristics, often with extremely detrimental consequences for their own health. They may be trained with harsh methods and beaten and punished for disobeying rules devised by individuals of other species. Many are frustrated from lack of exercise and stimulation, and they can be abandoned and killed when considered inconvenient. Thus, pet-keeping, which seems to be among the most benign practices toward other animals, is in fact a part of the structure of violence that affects other animals. Many people consider pets disposable, and those who are no longer wanted are deposited in so-called shelters. Millions of nonhuman animals are killed each year in institutions we describe as "shelters" but that actually serve as killing-centres for what are essentially waste products of the pet-keeping industry. Most shelters do not have no-kill policies, and many pets are killed simply because of lack of space and the funds to provide food, shelter, and medical care. While millions of these disposable animals are killed each year, pet dealers have widened their operations through the use of social media, often depicting the living commodities they sell as having come from individual homes rather than from industrial breeding operations. In September 2013, the US Department of Agriculture announced that it would close an existing loophole in the Animal Welfare Act that had allowed unlicenced breeders to sell animals over the Internet (Pacelle, 2013). However, in Canada while some online services such as Craigslist have stopped facilitating pet sales, Kijiji still runs advertisements for thousands of animals (Edmiston, 2013).

Clearly, definitions that emphasize social acceptability have the effect of excluding from consideration the vast majority of violence inflicted on nonhuman animals in raising them for food, vivisection, hunting and trapping, and various forms of entertainment in which nonhuman animals are forced to perform stunts, race, or fight one another. Certainly the harms done to nonhuman animals in these institutionalized forms of exploitation are serious ones. The scale of commercial, institutionalized violence towards nonhuman animals far surpasses that of individual abuse and cruelty, and we should not underestimate how common these forms of violence are.

Why Does Violence Continue?

How can we explain the fact that Mary Bale's actions in trapping a cat in a rubbish bin caused international outrage and inspired thousands to join a campaign against her while millions of people readily participate in actions that cause much greater harm, including death, to nonhuman animals?

To some degree, people engage in these actions out of ignorance of the effects. They are helped in remaining ignorant by, for example, industry propaganda such as meat and dairy industries that seek to maintain secrecy about conditions in factory farms and slaughter-houses, and instead present images of laughing cows and pigs dancing with knives and forks, as if the victims could imagine no greater joy than to be confined, mutilated, killed, and consumed. Advertising presents the consumption of animals' flesh as necessary, nutritious, and delightful, a source of masculine strength or motherly concern. Flesh itself is packaged and euphemistically renamed. Animal exploitation industries also present themselves as being concerned with the welfare of nonhuman animals. Indeed, many industries that are based on killing animals claim that the welfare of these animals is their highest priority (e.g., McDonald's, n.d.; National Farm Animal Care Council, 2012; National Farmers' Federation, 2012).

Our attitudes about violence are confused. We find it more comfortable to think of animal abusers as deranged and sadistic individuals than to recognize that the majority of violence committed against other animals is carried out by normal people who support these actions through their unquestioned economic activities. In this situation, the concept of the banality of evil is quite appropriate (Arendt, 1995). People do not wish to see themselves as monsters but participate in monstrous actions through daily activities.

In order for us to better understand the nature of human violence toward other animals, we should reject the narrow definition of cruelty that is used by most researchers. It may be more comfortable for academic researchers to focus on these individualized acts of violence than to challenge powerful corporate interests that are based upon the exploitation of nonhuman animals. Virtually everyone agrees that we should not harm other animals "unnecessarily" so concentrating on the actions of individual abusers is uncontroversial, especially when the approach is based on an appeal to help humans by exploring the connection between violence toward other animals and toward humans. Making a case for the importance of studying violence towards nonhuman animals themselves is more difficult because it challenges the centrality of human beings.

Pointing out the incoherence of generally accepted views about nonhuman animals means challenging the selective outrage that allows people to define themselves as "caring" individuals while continuing to engage in the exploitation of other animals. It also puts researchers at odds with prevailing anthropocentric views and with interests of major corporations. Challenging the common sense instrumentalist views that other animals exist to serve humans and that we can do as we please with them is a radical stance that puts one outside accepted boundaries. One risks being seen as an "animal rights fanatic."

Profiting from Violence (Economic Incentives)

Certain forms of violence toward nonhuman animals are considered socially acceptable because someone profits from them. It is the fact that someone profits from the harm caused to animals that makes such violence "necessary." For example, the pharmaceutical industry in China is a defender of bear bile production. Similarly, livestock producers profit directly from violence towards animals, although they may also claim that they are contributing towards the welfare of their own species by providing nutritious food or useful knowledge about disease. In many instances, these claims are false, since meat and dairy products are linked to a wide assortment of serious illnesses such as cancer, diabetes, heart disease, and stroke as well as obesity with further serious health risks created by water pollution from industrial production methods (Burkholder et al., 2006).

Furthermore, the meat and dairy industries have been strong proponents of the so-called Ag-Gag laws in the United States that would prevent animal activists from exposing conditions on factory farms. Iowa, Kansas, Montana, North Dakota, and Utah all have laws making it illegal for animal welfare groups to conduct undercover operations to expose cruelty in animal agriculture (Flynn, 2012). Nathan Runkle, spokesman for Mercy for Animals, which has conducted numerous such investigations of cruelty in agribusiness, stated that "legislators should be ashamed of themselves for bowing to pressure from corporate interests while turning a blind eye to American consumers and animal abuse" (qtd. in Galli, 2012). Under these laws, journalists who take undercover assignments can be convicted of a crime; thus, these laws not only undermine animal welfare but freedom of speech (Smith, 2012). While Florida, Illinois, and Indiana rejected similar proposed laws, the agriculture lobby is pressing forward with legislation in Minnesota, Missouri, Nebraska, New York, and Tennessee (Flynn, 2012). Undeniably, the oppression of other animals is structured by the economic interests of powerful industries that exploit them for profit.

Moral Conviction and Tradition

Underlying widespread violence towards nonhuman animals is a conviction that this is acceptable, that other animals are less worthy of moral consideration. One source of moral conviction can be found in religious ideas that see humans as uniquely privileged possessors of divine souls. Although dissident currents existed, this has been the dominant tendency in Western religious and philosophical thought, with various capacities such as reason, language, tool-use, or self-reflection serving as a marker of human uniqueness and exceptionalism. Advances in knowledge about other animals have undermined the basis for these beliefs but the speciesist moral convictions are still widespread.

Violence is often defended on the grounds of tradition, surely among the weakest of all arguments. For example, on the eve of Yom Kippur some Orthodox Jews follow the practice of kapparot. They believe that by swinging a live chicken above their heads and reciting a prayer, their sins are transferred to the chicken, who is then slaughtered (United Poultry Concerns, n.d.). Other Jewish religious leaders dismiss this as foolish superstition and cruelty to animals, and some suggest that the traditional use of chickens can be replaced with money (Gersholm & Schwartz, n.d.; Schwartz n.d.).

Violence as a Marker of Power and Status

In some cases, violence against other animals continues because it is celebrated as a marker of power and status. Killing certain types of animals or keeping exotic pets is also a means of asserting one's own power or charisma. In many societies, masculine identity in particular has been demonstrated by the domination or killing of other animals (Flynn, 2001). Wearing the skin of or eating certain types of animals is regarded as a marker of elite status. In many cases, the desirability of foods is linked directly to the amount of violence inflicted on animals. For example, Canada is a major producer of foie gras, widely considered an epicurean delight. It is produced by force-feeding geese and ducks, using a tube rammed down their throats several times each day, in order to create a bloated, fatty liver. Typically, the birds are confined in small cages and many choke to death or suffer from infections and ruptured organs. Although foie gras has been banned in a number of countries because of the obvious cruelty, many celebrity chefs and expensive restaurants defend it (Weise, 2012). Similarly, shark-fin soup is a status symbol and tradition for special events such as weddings (CBC, 2012); however, producing this involves hacking off the sharks' fins and, typically, their bodies are thrown back into the ocean, leaving the animals to die a slow death. Because of such cruelty, a global movement to ban shark-fin soup has developed but many restaurant owners protest this because the soup is considered a lucrative delicacy. Here status symbols and profits are intertwined.

We may also note that violence towards nonhuman animals continues because there are few negative consequences for perpetuating it. The flipside of this is that power rests on the side of perpetrators of systemic violence. While individuals like Mary Bale sometimes are singled out for condemnation, institutional abusers are protected by law (Bisgould, King, & Stopford, 2001). Even when they are convicted of violating the few protections that are given to other animals, as they are merely property (Francione, 2000), the penalties are minimal and can be dismissed as a cost of doing business (CBS News, 2011; Humane Society of the United States, 2009; Laino, & Ruoff, 2012; New England Anti-Vivisection Society, 2012). Policies and laws are reflections of dominant values and ideology. The ideology that supports such power is speciesism.

Speciesism and Property Status

The ideology of speciesism allows this structural violence to continue as other animals are excluded from the sphere of moral consideration and relegated to the status of property, commodities, resources, mere things rather than sentient beings with their own interests and intrinsic worth. Monotheistic religions as well as the major currents of Western philosophy have emphasized human exceptionalism and superiority, relegating other animals to the status of property and resources that exist to serve us. Normalization of violence towards other animals not only encourages us to find it acceptable to kill tens of billions of other animals every year but allows us to refrain from thinking about such practices in the first place. While propaganda from the food and fashion industries present the products of this violence as desirable, delicious, and luxurious, the violence that is required to create them is concealed. Killing is conducted out of sight; industries not only hire security forces to patrol their operations but spend large amounts of money on lobbying efforts to shape legislation to suit their purposes, such as the Ag-Gag laws passed or proposed in the United States that make it a criminal offence to take photographs of animals used in industrial agriculture, as noted above. Animal exploitation industries hide the routine torture and murder of billions of animals and provide "necessary illusions" by inventing images of contented animals who can imagine no happier future than to be killed for our benefit. Yet there is a kind of unspoken collusion here. They do everything they can to hide the atrocities that continue in factory farms, vivisection laboratories, and slaughterhouses, and we do everything we can not to find out and to remain ignorant to speciesism. Similar processes of distancing oneself from those one exploits have been common in relation to violence against human animals throughout history; the utility of the ideology of racism for systems of slavery is just one example. Similarly, ecofeminists point out gendered aspects of violence towards nonhuman animals and inter-twined oppression of sexism and speciesism (Adams, 2000; Cudworth, 2008; Gruen, 2007).

This is perpetuated through pornographic language and imagery in hunting and in meat and dairy industries, especially through the socially accepted exploitation of female bodies for milk, eggs, and reproduction.

Cultural Imperialism

Another factor at play is cultural imperialism, in which the values and structures of a dominant system are imposed on others. Many actions that would be seen as abuse and cruelty if performed by individuals are accepted as standard practices by animal exploitation industries. These industries subject nonhuman animals to a cycle of activities that include the abduction of infants and violation of family structures, confinement, mutilation, repeated forced reproduction, and, ultimately, killing. The public supports these activities through the purchase of the industry's products. In some cases, it is considered acceptable to inflict certain types of violence on individuals of certain categories ("farm animals") but not others ("pets"). Since the categorization of other animals is not consistent across cultures, it is not uncommon to regard the practices of others as barbaric. For example, many Canadians are appalled by the fact that dogs are considered edible livestock in some Asian societies but are quite willing to place chickens, cows, pigs, sheep, and other animals in that category. This is ethically inconsistent but provides a convenient opportunity to reinforce the boundaries of group identity by condemning the practices of others. While different treatment of nonhuman animals may be used by racists to attack others, industry and governments may also attempt to manipulate these cultural differences in violence towards other animals. For example, after the European Union banned the sale of seal products because of the widespread cruelties associated with the seal hunt, the Canadian government responded with legal challenges and a propaganda campaign that showcased Inuit traditions of hunting these animals, suggesting that the ban on seal products was ill-informed and discriminatory. However, the Inuit traditionally hunted on a subsistence basis, not a commercial one, and most opponents of the seal hunt specifically made exceptions for subsistence practices. The Canadian government's determination to prop up the commercial seal hunt led it to campaign vigorously for an agreement with China to import seal products as a means to offset the European ban. However, after the agreement had been reached, over 40 Chinese organizations protested it as a racist and imperialistic deal to dump unwanted products. Professor Lu Di, director of the China Small Animal Protection Association, pointed out that the majority of North Americans and Europeans have rejected seal products and suggested that "the perception of Canada's sealing industry that the Chinese eat everything and the Chinese people do not care about animal suffering is indicative of the racist and cultural imperialistic attitude towards non-western societies still held by some Canadians" (Watts, 2011). Cases such as this, in which the utility of speciesism for the practice of cultural imperialism is clear, demonstrate the mutually reinforcing nature of different forms of prejudice and violence.

Conclusion

By looking at violence against animals, it becomes plain that we tend to look at individual levels of violence but tend to overlook structural violence, which makes very clear the systemic nature of violence. This brief overview of violence against other animals leads to the need to seriously reevaluate the status of nonhuman animals in our society. The fact that individual animal abusers do spark public outrage offers a somewhat reassuring message about human concern for those who are helpless and victimized. We should rightly condemn the cruelty of these individuals who abuse animals for their own peculiar pleasures. Yet, rather than seeing perpetrators as aberrations, we should recognize that they have internalized various forms of socially accepted violence (Duffy & Momirov, 1997), and while condemning acts of individual gratuitous cruelty, we should also refuse to accept structural violence against other animals on a much broader scale. Prevailing definitions of nonhuman animal cruelty are too narrow to understand the systemic nature of violence (Agnew, 1998; Bierne, 2004) and ill-equipped to understand the complex social relations involved. In order to challenge structural violence, we need to reject the narrow definition of cruelty we questioned in this chapter. As we begin to understand that violence continues because of our ideology of speciesism, we need to realize the importance of adopting an anti-speciesist approach that recognizes them as sentient beings whose interests should be protected. This means not only taking seriously violence towards nonhuman animals in terms of individual companion animals but reviewing the entire ethical basis of our society, challenging the normalization of systemic violence towards other animals, and working for changes in public attitudes, practices, and policies.

Structural violence provides a context for individual abusers to hurt other animals as we discussed in the section on factory-farmed animals. Food, biomedical, pet, hunting, and fashion industries provide the social context where structural violence against other animals is allowed as this is seen as necessary or mundane everyday practice. As Young (2010) rightly points out, such systemic violence against a group (in this case nonhuman animals) makes this type of social practice oppression and a matter of social injustice that we need to challenge. The thousands of people who were properly outraged by Mary Bale's behaviour should be equally moved by the plight of these other animal victims. In the compassionate, humane, and just world that we should all strive to build, we should do our best to condemn and abolish such atrocities.

Keywords

Cruelty, humane killing, hunting, pet-keeping, structural violence, systemic violence, vivisection

Review Questions

1. Form a 4-6 person groups with your classmates and view the video "Earthlings" http://video.google.ca/videoplay?docid=6361872964130308142
2. Discuss how the definition of violence as "socially unacceptable behaviour that intentionally causes unnecessary pain, suffering or distress to and/or death of an animal" (Ascione, 1993, p.228) presented in this chapter, helps or does not help to prevent the atrocities depicted in this video.
3. Check the belongings you have today and make a list of those of which you consider to be products of nonhuman animals. Are these items essential to you? Do alternatives exist?
4. Discuss how we can minimize our dependency on nonhuman animals and end violence against them in our everyday life.
5. Discuss how speciesism relates to other forms of systemic oppression and social injustice. Some of these systemic oppressions can be remembered as an acronym: GRACES. Here, G stands for gender based oppression i.e. sexism, R stands for racism, A stands for

ageism and ableism, C stands for classism, E notes ethnocentricism, and S stands for oppression based on sexual identities, for instance, heterosexism.

References

Adams, C. J. (2000). *The sexual politics of meat*. New York: Continuum.

Adams, C. J. (2007). The war on compassion. In J. Donovan & C. J. Adams (Eds.), *The feminist care tradition in animal ethics* (pp. 21-36). New York: Columbia University Press.

Agnew, R. (1998). The causes of animal abuse: A social-psychological analysis. *Theoretical Criminology, 2*(2),177-209.

Allan, C. (2010, May 20). The purebred paradox. Humane Society of the United States. Retrieved from http://www.humanesociety.org/news/magazines/2010/05-06/the_purebred_paradox.html

American Psychiatric Association. (1987). *Diagnostic and statistical manual of mental disorders* (3rd rev. ed.). Washington: DC.

Anahita, S., & Mix, T. L. (2006). Retrofitting frontier masculinity for Alaska's war against wolves. *Gender & Society, 20*(3), 332-353.

Animals Asia. (2010, July 21). Vietnam's top traditional medicine doctor warns bear bile tonics can kill. Retrieved from http://www.animalsasia.org/index.php?UID=9BAOL4V7OL7

Arendt, H. (1995). *Eichmann in Jerusalem*. New York: Penguin.

Arluke, A. (2006). *Just a dog*. Philadelphia: Temple University Press.

Ascione, F. R. (1993). Children who are cruel to animals: a review of research and implications for developmental psychopathology. *Anthrozoos, 6*(4), 236-247.

Ascione, F. R., & Shapiro, K. (2009). People and animals, kindness and cruelty: Research directions and policy implications. *Journal of Social Issues, 65*(3), 569-587.

BBC. (2012). Ethics guide euthanasia and physician assisted suicide. Retrieved from http://www.bbc.co.uk/ethics/euthanasia/

Bierne, P. (2004). From animal abuse to interhuman violence? A critical review of the progression thesis. *Society and Animals, 12*(1), 39-65.

Bisgould, L., King, W., & Stopford, J. (2001). Anything goes: An overview of Canada's legal approach to animals on factory farms. Toronto: Animal Alliance. Retrieved from http://www.environmentvoters.org/report%20-%20Anything%20Goes.pdf

Burkholder, J., Libra, B. , Weyer, P., Heathcote, S. , Kolpin, D., Thorne, P.S., & Michael Wichman, M. (2006). Impacts of waste from concentrated animal feeding operations on water quality. *Environmental Health Perspectives, 115*(2), 308-312.

Calboli, F. C. F., Sampson, J., Fretwell, N., & Balding, D. J. (2008). Population structure and inbreeding from pedigree analysis of purebred dogs. *Genetics, 179*(1), 593-601.

Canadian Coalition for Farm Animals. (2005). Battery cages and the welfare of hens in Canada: A summary of the scientific literature. Retrieved from http://www.humanefood.ca/pdf%20links/BatteryReport.pdf

CBC News. (2012, July 9). Shark-fin ban sought in Richmond, BC. Retrieved from http://www.cbc.ca/news/canada/british-columbia/story/2012/07/09/bc-richmond-shark-fin-ban-proposal.html

CBS News. (2011, November 29). Ringling circus agrees to $270K fine. Retrieved from http://www.cbsnews.com/8301-201_162-57332597/ringling-circus-agrees-to-$270k-fine/

Compassion in World Farming. (2009, December). *Slaughter fact sheet.* Retrieved from http://www.ciwf.org.uk/includes/documents/cm_docs/2010/s/slaughter_fact_sheet_feb_2010.pdf

Corso, P. S., Kramer, M. H., Blair, K. A., Addiss, D. G., Davis, J. P., & Haddix, A. C. (2003). Costs of illness in the 1993 waterborne cryptosporidium outbreak, Milwaukee, Wisconsin. *Emerging Infectious Diseases, 9*(4), 426-431. Retrieved from http://wwwnc.cdc.gov/eid/article/9/4/02-0417_article.htm

CTV News. (2011, January 12). China to import seal meat and oil from Canada. Retrieved from http://www.ctvnews.ca/china-to-import-seal-meat-and-oil-from-canada-1.595358#ixzz1z1ByzNoC

Cudworth, E. (2008). "Most farmers prefer blondes": Social intersectionality and species relations. In B. Carter & N. Charles (Eds.), *Human and other animals: Critical perspectives* (pp.153-172). Houndmills, Basingstoke: Palgrave MacMillan.

Davis, K. (2009). *Prisoned chickens, poisoned eggs.* Summertown, TN: Book Publishing.

Davis, K. (2011, April 28). Decompression: A new way to torture chickens and turkeys to death. *United Poultry Concerns.* Retrieved from www.upc-online.org/slaughter/decompression

Doctors and Lawyers for Responsible Medicine. (n.d.). The human victims: Animal-based medical research. Retrieved from http://www.dlrm.org/resources/victims.htm

Duffy, A. & Momirov, J. (1997). *Family violence.* Toronto: Lorimer.

Dunayer, J. (1993, April). Censored: Faculty who oppose vivisection. *Z Magazine,* 57-60. Retrieved from http://www.peta2.com/takecharge/prj-Vivisection.pdf

Edmiston, J. (2013, August 9). Montreal dog walker launches petition urging Kijiji to ban online pet sales in bid to end puppy mills. *National Post.* Retrieved from http://news.national-post.com/2013/09/08/montreal-dog-walker-launches-petition-urging-kijiji-to-ban-online-pet-sales-in-bid-to-end-puppy-mills/

Farmer, P. (1996). On suffering and structural violence: A view from below. *Daedalus, 125*(1), 261-283.

Flynn, C. P. (2001). Acknowledging the "zoological connection": A sociological analysis of animal cruelty. *Society and Animals, 9*(1), 71-87.

Flynn, D. (2012, March 26). Five states now have Ag Gag laws on the books. *Food Safety News.* Retrieved from http://www.foodsafetynews.com/2012/03/five-states-now-have-ag-gag-laws-on-the-books/

Food and Agricultural Organization of the United Nations. (2009, September 7). Meat consumption. Animal Production and Health. Retrieved from http://www.fao.org/AG/AGAINFO/themes/en/meat/background.html

Francione, G. L. (2000). *Introduction to animal rights: Your child or the dog?* Philadelphia: Temple University Press.

Galli, C. (2012, February 29). "Ag Gag" bills would stop undercover animal abuse investigations. *ABC News.* Retrieved from http://abcnews.go.com/Blotter/ag-gag-bills-stop-under-cover-animal-abuse-investigations/story?id=15816805

Galtung, J. (1969). Violence, peace and peace research. *Journal of Peace Research, 6*(3), 167-191.

Gershom, Y., & Schwartz, R. (n.d.). The custom of Kapparot in the Jewish tradition. Jewish vegetarians of North America. *The Schwartz collection on judaism, vegetarianism, and animal rights.* Retrieved from http://jewishveg.com/schwartz/kapparot.html

Grandin, T. (1988). Behavior of slaughter plant and auction employees toward the animals. *Anthrozoos, 1,* 205-213.

Gruen, L. (2007). Empathy and vegetarian commitments. In J. Donovan & C. J. Adams (Eds.), *The feminist care tradition in animal ethics* (pp. 333-343). New York: Columbia University Press.

Hinch, W., & DeKeseredy, R. (1991). *Woman abuse.* Toronto: Thompson Educational.

Huffington Post. (2012, February 3). Percy Love sentenced to jail time for kicking kitten, signaling field goal. Retrieved from http://www.huffingtonpost.com/2012/03/02/percy-love-sentenced-to-j_n_1316221.html

Human Rights Watch. (2005). Blood, sweat, and fear: Workers' rights in US meat and poultry plants. Retrieved from http://www.hrw.org/node/11869/section/5

Humane Society International. (2011, March 15). HSI Canada commends the National People's Congress of China for steps to ban seal product trade. Retrieved from http://www.hsi.org/world/canada/news/releases/2011/03/china_seal_proposals_031511.html

Humane Society of the United States. (2009, November 2). Dogfighting fact sheet. Retrieved from http://www.humanesociety.org/issues/dogfighting/facts/dogfighting_fact_sheet.html

Indian Country Today Media Network. (2012, February 23). Legacy of whistler sled dog massacre is new, controversial code. Retrieved from http://indiancountrytodaymedianetwork.com/2012/02/23/legacy-of-whistler-sled-dog-massacre-is-new-controversial-code-99449#ixzz1wxTaHKcl

Irish Antiviisection Society. (2011). *2011 Irish animal experimentation statistics.* Retrieved from http://www.irishantivivisection.org/statistics.html

Jowit, J. (2012, June 5). Super farms are needed in the UK, says leader of National Farmers Union. *Guardian.* Retrieved from http://www.guardian.co.uk/environment/2012/jun/05/uk-needs-super-farms-says-nfu

Kalof, L., Fitzgerald, A., & Baralt, L. (2004). Animals, women and weapons: Blurred sexual boundaries in the discourse of sport hunting. *Society and Animals, 12*(3), 237-251.

Keith, S., Stolar, S., Blalock, G. & Feldman, J. (Producers), & Keith, S. (Director), (2010). *Skin trade* [Motion Picture]. (Available from ARME 4804 Laurel Canyon Boulevard, Valley Village, CA, USA 91607.

Kellert, S., & Felthous, A. (1985). Childhood cruelty towards animals among criminals and noncriminals. *Human Relations, 38,* 113-129.

Knight, A. (2007a). Systematic reviews of animal experiments demonstrate poor human clinical and toxicological utility. *ATLA: Alternatives to Laboratory Animals, 35*(6), 641-659.

Knight, A. (2007b). The poor contribution of chimpanzee experiments to biomedical progress. *Journal of Applied Animal Welfare Science, 10*(4), 281-308.

Krug, E., Dahlberg, L., Mercy, J.A.. Zwai, A.B. & Lozano, R. (Eds.). (2002). *World Report on Violence and Health.* Geneva: World Health Organization.

Laino, T., & Ruoff, A. (2012, May 3). Circus headed for Frederick settles on animal cruelty charges. *Gazette.Net Maryland Community News Online.* Retrieved from http://www.gazette.net/article/20120503/NEWS/705039973/1009/circus-headed-for-frederick-settles-on-animal-cruelty-charges&template=gazette

Lancet (2003). To ban or not to ban? *The Lancet Infectious Diseases, 3*(1), 1. Retrieved from http://www.thelancet.com/journals/laninf/article/PIIS1473-3099(03)00496-1/fulltext

Lockwood, R., & Church, A. (1996, Fall). Deadly serious: An FBI perspective on animal cruelty. *Humane Society News, 27-30.*

Luke, B. (1998). Violent love: Hunting, heterosexuality and the erotics of men's predation. *Feminist studies, 24*(3), 627-655.

MacDonald, J. (1961). *The murderer and his victim.* Springfield, IL: Charles C. Thomas.

Marcoux, I., Mishara, B. L., & Durand, C. (2007). Confusion between euthanasia and other end-of-life decisions: Influences on public opinion poll results. *Canadian Journal of Public Health, 98*(3), 235-239.

McDonald's, (n.d.). *McDonald's animal welfare.* Retrieved from http://www.aboutmcdonalds. com/content/dam/AboutMcDonalds/Sustainability/Sustainability%20Library/McD_Animal-WelfareGuidingPrinciples.pdf

McPhedran, S. (2009a). Animal abuse, family violence and child wellbeing: A review. *Journal of Family Violence, 24*(1), 41-52.

McPhedran, S. (2009b). A review of the evidence for associations between empathy, violence, and animal cruelty. *Aggression and Violent Behaviour, 14*(1), 1-4.

Mead, M. (1964). Cultural factors in the cause of pathological homicide. *Bulletin of the Menninger Clinic, 28,* 11-22.

Mercy For Animals. (2009). *Hatchery horrors.* Retrieved from http://www.mercyforanimals.org /hatchery/

Mercy For Animals. (2010). *Ohio dairy farm brutality.* Retrieved from http://www.mercyforanimals.org/ohdairy/

Merz-Perez, L., Heide, K. M., & Silverman, I. J. (2001). Childhood cruelty to animals and subsequent violence against humans. *International Journal of Offender Therapy and Comparative Criminology, 45,* 556-573.

Moore, M. (2012, May 25). Cat "House of Horrors" discovered in Shanghai. *Telegraph.* Retrieved from http://www.telegraph.co.uk/news/worldnews/asia/china/9289661/Cat-house-of-horrors-discovered-in-Shanghai.html

Nantais, D., & Kuczewski, M. (2004). Quality of life: The contested rhetoric of resource allocation and end-of-life decision making. *Journal of Medicine and Philosophy, 29*(6), 651-664.

National Anti-Vivisection Society. (2012, July 9). Animals suffering in labs rises – predicted to rise again. Retrieved from http://www.navs.org.uk/about_vivisection/27/46/2735/

National Farm Animal Care Council. (2012). *Codes of practice for the care and handling of farm animals.* Retrieved from http://www.nfacc.ca/codes-of-practice

National Farmers' Federation. (2012, June 15). Animal welfare the priority for Australia's farmers. Retrieved from http://www.nff.org.au/read/2874/animal-welfare-priority-for-australias-farmers.html

New England Anti-Vivisection Society. (2012). Animals in research law and regulations. Retrieved from http://www.neavs.org/research/laws

Nibert, D. (2002). *Animal rights, human rights.* Lanham, MD: Rowman & Littlefield.

Nocella, A., Sorenson, J., Socha, K., & Matsuoka, A. (Eds.). (2014). *Defining critical animal studies: An intersectional social justice approach to liberation.* New York: Peter Lang.

Pacelle, W. (2013, September 10). USDA announces landmark rule to crack down on online puppy mills. A Humane Nation. Humane Society of the United States. Retrieved from http://hsus.typepad.com/wayne/2013/09/usda-announces-puppy-mill-rule.html

Parry, S. (2010, December 2). The deadly souvenirs. *China Daily*. Retrieved from http://www.chinadaily.com.cn/hkedition/2010-12/02/content_11639882.htm

Peterson, M. L., & Farrington, D. P. (2007). Cruelty to animals and violence to people. *Victims and Offenders, 2,* 21-43.

Piper, H. (2003). The linkage of animal abuse with interpersonal violence: A sheep in wolf's clothing? *Journal of Social Work, 3*(2), 161-177.

Rifkin, J. (1992). *Beyond beef: The rise and fall of the cattle culture.* New York: Plume Book.

Sanbonmatsu, J. (2011). *Critical theory and animal liberation.* Lanham, MD: Rowman & Littlefield.

Scheper-Hughes, N. (1993). *Death without weeping.* Berkeley: University of California Press.

Schwartz, R. H. (n.d.) Why perform a rite that kills chickens as a way to seek God's compassion? Jewish Vegetarians of North America. *The schwartz collection on judaism, vegetarianism, and animal rights.* Retrieved from http://jewishveg.com/schwartz/WhyPerform RiteQ.html

Science Daily. (2012, March 30). Comfy mice lead to better science: Are cold mice affecting drug testing? Retrieved from http://www.sciencedaily.com/releases/2012/03/120330205 921.htm

Sea Shepherd. (n.d.). Stop the Canadian seal slaughter. Retrieved from http://www.seashepherd.org/seals/

Singer, P. (2002). *Animal liberation.* New York: Ecco.

Singer, R. S., Finch, R., Wegener, H. C., Bywater, R. Walters, J., & Lipsitch, M. (2003). Antibiotic resistance: The interplay between antibiotic use in animals and human beings. *The Lancet Infectious Diseases, 3*(1), 47-51.

Smith, S. E. (2012, June 6). Agriculture gag laws are violating press freedom in the US. *Guardian.* Retrieved from http://www.guardian.co.uk/commentisfree/2012/jun/06/agriculture-gag-laws-press-freedom

Sorenson, J. (2010). *Animal rights.* Halifax, NS: Fernwood.

Sorenson, J. (Ed.). (2014). *Critical animal studies: Thinking the unthinkable.* Toronto: Canadian Scholars Press.

Tingle, D., Barnard, G., Robbins, G., Newman, G., & Hutchinson, D. (1986). Childhood and adolescent characteristics of pedophiles and rapists. *International Journal of Law and Psychiatry, 9,* 103-116.

Trollinger, M. (2001). The link among animal abuse, child abuse, and domestic violence. *The Colorado Lawyer, 30*(9), 29-32.

Trowbridge, L. (2010a, August 26). UK woman who dumped cat in garbage may face charges, prison time. *Digital Journal.* Retrieved from http://digitaljournal.com/article/296617

Trowbridge, L. (2010b, August 28). UK cat-dumping woman may now lose her bank job due to outcry. *Digital Journal.* Retrieved from http://www.digitaljournal.com/article/296709

United Poultry Concerns. (n.d.). A wing & a prayer: The kapparot chicken-swinging ritual. Retrieved from http://www.upc-online.org/kaparos/a_wing_and_a_prayer.html

Watts, J. (2011, January 13). Canada 'racist' for selling China seal meat, say Chinese activists. *Guardian.* Retrieved from http://www.guardian.co.uk/environment/2011/jan/13/canada-selling-china-seal-meat

Warrick, J. (2001, April 10). They die piece by piece. *Washington Post.* Retrieved from https://www.uta.edu/philosophy/faculty/burgess-jackson/Warrick,%20They%20Die%20Piece%20by%20Piece%20(2001).pdf

Webster, J. (2005). *Animal welfare: Limping towards Eden*. Oxford: Blackwell Publishing.

Weise, E. (2012, May 24). Chefs lead fight against Calif. ban on foie gras delicacy. *USA Today*. Retrieved from http://www.usatoday.com/news/nation/story/2012-05-22/foie-gras-california-ban-humane/55143812/1

Winders, B., & Nibert, D. (2004). Consuming the surplus: Expanding "meat" consumption and animal oppression. *International Journal of Sociology and Social Policy, 24*(9), 76-96.

Wright, J., & Hensley, C. (2003). From animal cruelty to serial murder: Applying the graduation hypothesis. *International Journal of Offender Therapy and Comparative Criminology, 47*(1), 71-88.

Young, I.M. (2010). *Justice and the politics of difference*. Princeton: Princeton University Press.

Zelman, J. (2011, January 31). 100 Sled Dogs Killed in British Columbia Due to Slump in Tourism. *Huffington Post*. Retrieved from http://www.huffingtonpost.com/2011/01/31/100-sled-dogs-slaughtered_n_816462.html

Unecessary Roughness: Violence in Sports

Chapter 11

Kenneth Dowler

Learning Objectives

In this chapter you will...

► discuss why violence in sports is ambiguous

► describe the nature of violence in sport within the game itself

► learn about the theories of criminal conduct and violence by athletes

► compare the different types of violence committed by sports fans

► explore how violence impacts youth sport

I went to a fight the other night and a hockey game broke out.
–Rodney Dangerfield

Introduction

Within a civilized society, violence is generally viewed as shameful, dishonorable, and impermissible. Those that "do violence" are norm violators who are ostracized and punished. Yet, within the world of sport, athletes that do violence are considered heroic figures who gain respect, admiration, fame, and fortune. Sports violence is celebrated by fans, commentators, and athletes as an essential "part of the game" that propels athletes to victory and glory. Paradoxically, sports violence is also loathed, condemned, and considered the height of bad sportsmanship. As such, the relationship between violence and sport is very ambiguous. With this background, the purpose of this chapter is to explore the nature of violence in sport. The first part of the chapter will examine the consequences of sport violence. The second part of the chapter will explore sport violence in terms of (1) the game, (2) the athlete, and (3) the spectator/fan. The third part of the chapter will discuss issues arising from violence and youth sport.

From Gladiator Games to The Hunger Games

The film *The Hunger Games* (2012) depicts a futuristic world in which teenage combatants enter an arena with the sole purpose to kill the other competitors (tributes) and be crowned the victor. The film takes us to a dystopian world in which violence in the name of sport is both celebrated and used as a means of oppression by totalitarian governments. In a sense, it is a return to the Roman Empire, in which gladiators would fight to the death to appease and titillate bloodthirsty crowds.

Of course, within contemporary sports, the death of an athlete is not celebrated or advocated. Although relatively rare, fatalities in sport generally provide the impetus for rule changes to make the respective sport safer. For example, on August 17, 1920, the Cleveland Naps were playing the New York Yankees. The Yankees' pitcher Carl Mays threw the ball and it hit Ray Chapman on the head. Fans thought that the sound of the ball hitting his skull was the sound of it hitting his bat. Chapman was taken to the hospital and died 12 hours later. His death emphasized why players need to wear batting helmets (Lawless, 2012).

Similarly, on January 15, 1968, Minnesota North Stars player Bill Masterton died after his head hit the ice after an innocuous hit. After his death, there was an immediate call to require mandatory helmets for all players, which at the time were rarely used. In fact, players who wore helmets were often chastised by other teammates, other players, and fans. Despite the tragic death of Masterton, the only NHL player to die as a result of an on-ice play, the NHL did not require mandatory helmets until 1979, at which time the majority of players (70%) were already wearing helmets (Gutkin, 2011).

Without question, the most violent sports are boxing and mixed martial arts, in which there have been numerous fatalities. It is estimated that over 1,600 boxers have died as a result of fighting injuries (Svinth, 2007). In fact, boxing is considered by some to be so dangerous that numerous medical organizations, including the Canadian Medical Association (CMA), have called for boxing and mixed martial arts to be banned (Ball & Dixon, 2011).

In one of the most famous incidents, South Korean boxer Duk Koo Kim died after he fought Ray Mancini for the lightweight championship on November 13, 1982. Kim fought valiantly for 14 rounds, until the referee declared that Mancini had won with a TKO (Technical Knockout), after which Kim collapsed in the ring, went into a coma, had emergency brain surgery, and succumbed to his injuries four days later. Two weeks after the death of Kim, heavyweight champion Larry Holmes pummeled a clearly outmatched Randal "Tex" Cobb for 15 rounds. In the later rounds, the legendary broadcaster, Howard Cosell condemned professional boxing with his negative anti-boxing commentary, in which he retorted, "I wonder if that referee understands that he is constructing an advertisement for the abolition of the very sport that he's a part of?" Cosell, further claimed that if the referee did not stop the fight, he would never announce another professional boxing match again, which he never did (Ribowsky, 2011).

"Getting Your Bell Rung": Concussions and Sport

Despite the relatively low risk for death during an actual competition, the physical burden of violence in sports takes a heavy toll on the future health of athletes. Athletes that have participated in violent sports may experience a variety chronic ailments, such as knee and joint problems and increased risk of arthritis. Some former professional athletes acknowledge that the rewards of competing at a high level and attaining fame and fortune outweigh the risk of chronic, yet manageable, pain. Conversely, for many former and current athletes, the dangers associated with head injuries is frightening, especially in light of some very high profile cases of athletes who have been diagnosed with chronic traumatic encephalopathy (CTE). CTE is a neurological degenerative disease that has been found in individuals who have experienced multiple incidents of brain trauma or concussions. It is more likely to be found in professional athletes who have participated in contact sports, such as boxing, football, hockey, and professional wrestling, in which repetitive brain trauma occurs frequently. Unfortunately, the condition can only be diagnosed post-mortem, which means that current and former athletes may not be aware that they have CTE. Nonetheless, symptoms of CTE include dementia, memory loss, aggression, confusion, and depression, which generally manifest years or decades after the trauma (McKee et al., 2009).

One of the most tragic incidents that may have involved CTE was the Chris Benoit double murder-suicide. Benoit, a highly acclaimed professional wrestler, committed suicide after he murdered his wife and seven-year-old son. Initially, theories revolved around extensive steroid abuse or "roid rage," a failing marriage, a history of domestic violence, and alcohol abuse. However, a study of Benoit's brain revealed that he suffered from CTE and some speculate that may have caused his violent outburst (Muchnick, 2009). Nonetheless, as the research is in its infancy, some researchers argue that there are no studies that conclusively show a link between CTE and psychiatric or mental health issues, alcohol and drug use, and suicide (McCrory et al., 2013).

The highly acclaimed PBS Frontline documentary *League of Denial* (2013) examined the NFL response to the concussion debate. Based on the book *League of Denial*, written by Mark Fainaru-Wada and Steve Fainaru (2013), the documentary powerfully and convincingly argues that the National Football League has carefully avoided the link between football and brain injuries. Simply, since 1994, the NFL has pretended to care about the link between football and concussions, yet has attempted to push the issue off the table with stacked committees and discounting of credible medical evidence. As a consequence of the league's complicity, players received false reassurances that their sport was safe and parents received no warning that participation in football may put their kids at risk for brain injury. In fact, the league settled a $765 million settlement of a concussion suit brought by former players, yet admitted no liability (Shaw, 2013).

The Structure of Violence in Sport

As mentioned in the introduction, the discussion of violence in sport will be separated into three distinct areas, which include (1) the game (2) the athlete and (3) the fan/spectator.

(1) The Game

In the "real world," the use of unsanctioned violence is considered a rejection of social norms and punished accordingly. Yet, within a "game," sanctioned violence is celebrated, glorified, and often justified as a "means to an end" – that is, to win the game. Even unsanctioned violence, such as illegal hits, fights, and poor sportsmanship are excused as a "part of the game," something that is inevitable in competitive sport amongst "passionate" players.

In professional hockey, there are countless examples of dirty play, cheap shots, and poor sportsmanship. Interestingly, in Canada, hockey is often connected to a sense of national identity and pride. For example, the 1972 summit series, in which Team Canada, featuring NHL stars, defeated the Soviet national team is often referred to as a landmark moment in the formation of a Canadian identity. At the time, Canada was in the midst of a renewed sense of nationalism, with the centennial birthday (Expo 67) and a new national flag. The series was broadly intertwined with both social, cultural and political forces (K. Kennedy, 2011; Holman, 2009). The image of Paul Henderson's game-winning goal is forever cemented within the Canadian identity, and the series is celebrated as a great Canadian achievement. Yet one of the dirtiest and most unsportsmanlike plays occurred in game six. Bobby Clarke, who gained notoriety with the "Broad Street" Bullies, the infamous 1970s era Philadelphia Flyers, intentionally broke Valeri Kharlamov's ankle with a vicious two-handed slash. Kharlamov, the most talented player on the Soviet team, missed the seventh game and was largely ineffective in the eighth and final game (K. Kennedy, 2011). Canadian perspective of the incident is muted, as some justify the attack on Kharlamov as either retaliation for "dirty stickwork" or as a necessary measure than enabled the Canadians to win the series (Cormack & Cosgrave, 2013). Conversely, if a Soviet player had slashed a Canadian in the same manner, there would been a collective sense of outrage and condemnation. However, with national pride on the line, the slash has often been both celebrated and minimized.

Yet dirty play is generally followed by outrage by various stakeholders, especially media pundits. Although some media pundits, such as Don Cherry, may excuse a transgression, the majority denounce the offence and call for action to curb unnecessary violence. Remarkably, every year there appears to be an ongoing debate about the problem of violence in hockey, with a pattern of a high-profile, egregious incident followed by outrage and calls for stiffer penalties. The only thing that really changes, however, is the names of the players.

Two very high profile incidents include Todd Bertuzzi on Steve Moore and Marty McSorley on Donald Brashear. In 2004, Bertuzzi chased Moore around the ice trying to start a fight; Moore refused to fight. After Moore turned away, Bertuzzi grabbed Moore by the jersey and punched him in the back of the head. Both fell and Moore's head hit the ice hard under the weight of the two bodies. Moore suffered three fractured vertebrae, a concussion, and ligament and nerve damage. His career was over, and Bertuzzi was suspended for what amounted to 20 games (see Kerr, 2006, for sociological analysis of the incident). In 2000, McSorley challenged Brashear to a fight and was refused. With a few seconds left in the game, he approached Brashear from behind and delivered a two-handed swing of his stick to Brashear's temple. Brashear fell and hit his head on the ice, suffering a concussion. McSorley was charged with and subsequently found guilty of assault. The NHL suspended him for a year and he subsequently retired (see Atkinson & Young, 2008 and Smith, Stuart, & Fish, 2000, for a sociological and psychosocial analysis of the incident).

Anecdotes aside, there are very few academic studies that attempt to explain on-the-field violence among players. Sociologist Mike Smith (1983) identified four categories of violence in sports:

1. Brutal body contact. This includes physical practices that are typical in some sports and accepted by athletes as part of the sport. For example, collisions, hits, tackles, blocks, and body checks that fall within the rules of the sport. It is not defined as either illegal or criminal.
2. Borderline violence. This includes practices that violate the rules of the game but are recognized by most players and coaches as consistent with the norms of the sport ethic and as useful competitive strategies. Examples include the "brushback" pitch in baseball, fighting in hockey, and "hard foul" in basketball. Despite increasing public pressure to increase sanctions, the official sanctions in terms of penalties, suspensions, and/or fines are usually not severe.
3. Quasi-criminal violence. This includes practices that violate the formal rules of the game, public laws, and even informal norms among players. Examples include cheap

shots, late hits, sucker punches, and flagrant fouls. These incidents generally result in either suspensions and/or fines.

4. Criminal violence. This includes practices that are clearly outside the law to the point that athletes condemn them without question and law enforcement officials may prosecute them as crimes. Examples are assaults that occur before, during, and after the game that appear to be premeditated and severe enough to seriously injure an opponent. In these incidents, the offender clearly crosses the line of acceptable conduct and breaches the norms of the sport.

Although, the Smith typology is useful, Atkinson and Young (2008) argue that the differences between the categories shift over time, as norms change within both sports and society. Moreover, the typology fails to address the origins of violence within the sport ethic. Space limitations preclude a thorough theoretical examination of the reasons for violence in sport. Nonetheless, the ambiguous nature of the relationship between the sport ethic and violence can best be illustrated with a brief discussion of "the Code" and "Bounty Gate."

"The Code." A culture of violence permeates the sport of hockey. In fact, amongst professional team sports, hockey is the only sport that condones and, some would argue, promotes fighting. Statistics from the 2011-12 NHL season reveal that there were 546 fights in 1,230 games played, an average of 0.44 fights per game. There were 423 games (34%) that had at least one fight and 98 games with more than one fight. From the year 2001-02 to 2011-12, there have been 6,526 fights, which is an average of 0.46 fights per game. In same time period, approximately 37% of games featured at least one fight (Singer, 2014). Granted, in other professional sports, there is the occasional fight that breaks out during the heat of the game. Although relatively rare, there is a long tradition of bench clearing brawls in baseball. In other professional sports such as basketball, soccer, football, and even race car driving, athletes sometimes resort to fights to settle scores during or after the heat of battle.

However, unlike hockey, players who engage in fights are usually automatically ejected and suspended for future games. Yet within hockey, the penalties for fighting are minimal and generally are not a deterrent. According to the official rules, a player who engages in a fight receives a five-minute penalty, with the possibility of an extra two minutes if he instigates the fight. In attempt to make fighting "safer," the NHL has supplementary penalties (game misconduct and possible suspension) for "aggressors." An aggressor is a player who attempts to inflict punishment on an opponent who is in a defenseless position or who is an unwilling combatant (NHL, 2014). In addition, the NHL will suspend a player for 10 games if he leaves the bench to engage in a fight. This rule was instituted to eliminate the bench clearing brawls that were a staple of the past.

In his book *The Code: The Unwritten Rules of Fighting and Retaliation*, Ross Bernstein (2006) argues that, to navigate the culture of fighting in hockey, players are socialized to adhere to an unwritten "code of honor," known simply as "the Code." Bernstein (2006) writes

As mysterious as it is sacred, the Code is an unwritten set of rules, the bible of hockey sportsmanship if you will, that has been handed down from generation to generation. The Code picks up where the rulebook leaves off and fills in the gaps, all in an effort to govern the game and its players - allowing them to compete in a manner deemed fair and respectful.

A proponent of fighting, Bernstein (2006) interviewed fifty NHL players (both current and former), coaches, and media personalities. Bernstein (2006) claims,

> The Code is much, much bigger than any one individual or team. Simply put, you don't break the rules of the Code, because if you do, then there will be hell to pay – period. There is a chain of accountability in pro hockey and it's been that way for more than 100 years. It is about keeping a sense of equality when it comes to big players competing against little players. It is about keeping the game on an equal playing field with regards to everything from cheap shots, to high sticks, to slashing, to fighting. That is what the Code is all about – respect, accountability, pride and honor.

Critics of fighting in hockey argue that "the Code" does not really exist, that it simply legitimizes fighting and maintains the status quo. Many opponents of fighting argue that many fights are not the result of pent up emotions during the normal course of play; they are, in fact, staged events involving "enforcers" whose only role is to fight. According to the opponents of fighting, the solution is to ban fighting, however, in reality it is not that easy. There is large percentage of fans, players, and league's administrators and owners who believe that the game and, more importantly, the business is better off with fighting than without it. For example, annual polls of NHL players reveal consistent support for fighting, whilst some fans and media pundits have romanticized fighting to the point where it becomes a defining characteristic of the sport.

Despite the glorification of fighting and the accompanying hero worship of "tough guys" or "goons," there are dozens of stories of enforcers who live troubled off-ice lives, filled with anxiety, depression and drug, alcohol, and steroid abuse. These enforcers have a marginal existence within the NHL; their only real value is their ability to fight, which means that they are often challenged by younger and sometimes bigger opponents. They are subjected to increased risk of concussion and permanent brain damage. To ease the pain associated with the role, they may also abuse painkillers and sleep aids. For example, the highly acclaimed documentary, *The Last Gladiators* (2011) examines the troubling role of the enforcer in hockey. The documentary features Chris Nilan, a former enforcer for the Montreal Canadians, who penned the book, *Fighting Back: The Chris Nilan Story* (2013), in which he documents his off-ice struggles with drug and alcohol addiction.

Moreover, a watershed moment in the debate over the role of the enforcer arose when three NHL enforcers died within four months in 2011. Derek Boogaard died of an overdose of painkillers and alcohol, while Rick Rypien and Wade Belak allegedly committed suicide. These high-profile fatalities caused a stir within the hockey community, with various commentators claiming that the NHL and NHLPA should provide counselling to enforcers, while others strongly urging that fighting be banned altogether. Moreover, the tragic death of 21-year-old Don Sanderson in a semi-professional hockey game in Brantford, Ontario led to intense public scrutiny surrounding the role of fighting in hockey. Both critics and supporters used the untimely death as a sounding board for the debate about fighting in hockey. Yet, in the large picture, a young man died playing a "game" (Elcombe, 2010).

"Bounty Gate." Similar to "the Code", there are a series of unwritten rules that permeate both professional and amateur sport. These unwritten rules provide a set of norms that enable players to make sense of the violence that they are inflicting on their opponents. One such rule is that players do not "intentionally" attempt to injure or end the career of an opposing player. Of course, it seems somewhat illogical, as in many violent sports the objective is to hit other players with great ferocity. It also appears that there is an ambiguous line between unintentional and intentional actions that cause injury.

The NFL had to deal with this issue, with the so-called Bounty Gate scandal. In sum, the New Orleans Saints were found to have operated a bounty system in which players were paid bonuses for, among other things, hard hits and deliberately injuring opposing players. The system was in place from 2009 (their Super Bowl-winning season) to 2011, and it was alleged that up to 27 Saints players participated in the program. The NFL investigation found that defensive coordinator Gregg Williams and his players pooled money to pay out bonuses over the three seasons. Both head coach Sean Payton and general manager Mickey Loomis were aware of the program but neither put a stop to the program, even though Saints owner Tom Benson ordered it to end.

As a result of the investigation, the NFL suspended the general manager and several coaches and players. Head coach Sean Payton was suspended for one year without pay, while the ringleader, defensive coordinator, Gregg Williams was suspended indefinitely. Many pundits believed that Williams would never coach again in the NFL, as a particularly virulent audiotape had surfaced in which Williams was heard instructing his defence to target/injure several players on the San Francisco 49ers prior to a divisional playoff game in 2012. This outraged some players (current and past), as Williams had specifically targeted two players that had histories of knee and concussion issues. Despite the outrage, the NFL reinstated Williams after the 2012 season, and he was hired as a defensive coach with the Tennessee Titans.

(2) The Athlete

Within the game, athletes engage in illegal violent acts, and, for the most part, their transgressions are either forgiven or excused due to the "nature of the "game." A growing body of literature examines criminal activities of athletes outside of the game (Benedict, 1997; Otto, 2009). Although extremely rare, when athletes (current or former) are accused of homicide, national media attention ensues (see O.J Simpson, Oscar Pistorius, Aaron Hernandez, and Rae Carruth as prominent examples). Kadence Otto (2009) examined the convictions of 88 athletes in a professional and college sports. She reports that the athletes were charged with 146 offences, ranging from sex crime (32%), rape (27%), assault/battery (12%), drugs and/or weapons (11%), and homicide (4%). Similarly, in their analysis of NFL players, Benedict and Yaeger (1998) report that one out of every five NFL players had been charged with a serious crime, including 30% that were charged with assault and/or battery and 14% with sex crimes.

There are numerous highly publicized cases in which male athletes have been accused and/or convicted of sexual assault. These cases involve both amateur and professional athletes and the victims are often discredited within the media (Hnida, 2006; Dowler, 2006). Certainly, there are some cases in which athletes are unjustly accused because of their celebrity status. Anecdotal evidence, however, suggests that the social worlds of male athletes who are involved in violent sport are characterized by disregard for women as little more than a "game" to be pursued and conquered (Curry, 1991; Lefkowitz, 1997; Messner & Stevens, 2002). In their study of student athletes, Smith and Stewart (2003) found that male athletes in contact sports that had higher levels of competitiveness reported more sexually aggressive attitudes toward women. Moreover, Crosset, Benedict, and McDonald (1995) report that men in sex-segregated groups (sports teams) are more likely to engage in group sexual offences such as gang rape. Conversely, sport sociologist Todd Crosset (1999) conducted a review of published research on sexual assaults by male athletes. Although, intercollegiate athletes are involved in more sexual assaults compared to other male students, the results were not statistically significant, and the association between participating in violent sport and violence toward women was not supported. Aside from the inherent problem with causality, Crosset (1999) concluded that any discussion of violence against women by athletes must be placed into the context of societal, cultural, patriarchal, and ideological concerns.

Theories of Violent and Criminal Behaviour by Athletes

Otto (2009) argues that there are three reasons why male athletes commit crime: (1) adherence to win-at-all cost mentality; (2) male dominance and entitlement; and (3) celebrity status. The win-at-all costs mentality involves an overly aggressive and intimidating persona, which some athletes believe gives them a competitive advantage in sport. In effect, these attitudes and behaviours are carried over into non-sport settings (Coakley, 2009). The carryover effect or spillover theory posits that the violence used in sport is carried over into athlete's lives off the field. A survey of amateur hockey players found some support for the cultural spillover theory of hockey violence, in which violence in hockey spills over into violence in other social settings. Players in highly competitive select leagues were more likely to approve of violence and act violently in other social settings than less competitive players and non-players (Bloom & Smith, 1993).

In addition, studies of college and high-school athletes reveal that they are more likely to engage in abusive behaviours (Chandler, Johnson, & Carroll, 1999). For example, research on 13- to 17-year-olds in US schools reveals that sport participation, especially for young men in contact sports, is associated with fighting and delinquency off the field (Kreager, 2007; Wright & Fitzpatrick, 2006). Moreover, the status dynamics inherent within sport team membership amplifies the differences between youths. Essentially, a social hierarchy is sustained, in which harassment, bullying, and fighting is more likely to be carried out by athletes involved in contact sports (Wright & Fitzpatrick, 2006).

Nonetheless, research on the carryover effect is very difficult to conduct, and the results are often plagued by methodological issues. Most importantly, statistical correlations that show a relationship between playing certain sports and violent activity cannot establish causality. We cannot say that playing violent sports causes violence off the field. In addition, people with a propensity for violence may choose to engage in violent sports. Finally, off-the-field violence may be the result of exceptional situational factors that are unrelated to the sport. In addition, the carryover effect assumes that violence in sport is unregulated. However, athletes in the violent sports may learn self-control, patience, and responsibility. For example, French sociologist Loic Wacquant (1995) found that participation in the boxing taught marginalized youngsters to control their aggression and violence. Similarly, Trulson (1986) found that aggressive tendencies of juvenile delinquents decreased after they received training in martial arts.

Otto (2009) claims that the second reason for criminal activity amongst male athletes is male dominance and entitlement. Some males are socialized to believe that traditional forms of masculinity, such as aggression and dominance, are worthy of respect and should be encouraged. In the hypermasculine environment of a male locker room, these values may be magnified, which may result in increased violence in the real world. Although, violence in sport is not limited to men, critical feminist theorists posit that an understanding of gender ideology and masculinity is necessary to explain violence in sports. Messner (1992) argues,

> Young males come to sport with identities that lead them to define their athletic experience differently than females do. Despite the fact, that few males truly enjoy hitting and being hit, and that one has to be socialized into participating in much of the violence common-place in sport, males often view aggression, within the rule-bound structure of sport, as legitimate and "natural." (p. 67)

Essentially, participation in sport has become a salient way to demonstrate masculinity. Boys that engage in violent sport learn that they will be judged according to traditional mascu-line norms and values, in which physical skills, including violent acts, are assessed by their peers. These youngsters learn that "real men" participate in violent sport and that the ability to be violent becomes a cornerstone of masculinity. Unfortunately, many boys that do not effectively engage in violent sports are labelled with derogatory and emasculating terms, such as *pussy*, *girl*, *fag*, *wimp*, and *sissy* (Ingham et al., 1999). Moreover, an important review of the literature found that boys or young men that avoid so-called power or performance sports risk estrangement from male peers (White & Young, 1997).

Finally, Otto (2009) claims that celebrity status may encourage athletes to perceive that they are above the law. In effect, even at an early age athletes are placed on a pedestal and are granted high privileged status. Transgressions are often overlooked or unpunished. As such, the athlete may have little respect for law and potential victims (Benedict, 1997). Histor-ically speaking, Otto (2009) argues that professional leagues (NBA, NFL, MLB, and NHL) preferred to deal with criminal activity in-house" in which perpetrators rarely received discipli-nary action and misdeeds were often covered up. As a result, the athlete's notion of invincibility in terms of law violations is maintained and reinforced. Currently, the major professional sports are more likely to suspend a player for off-the-field violations. There are two reasons for this shift in policy. First, the media is more likely to report on player misdeeds. In the past, beat writers would not report activities for fear that they would not be allowed access to the players. Second, the professional leagues now recognize the importance of public relations and the huge profits that come with positive attention.

(3) The Spectator/Fan

Violence in sport is not limited to the game or the athlete, in some instances the fan or spec-tator can incite or participate in violent actions and behaviours. Spectators can either watch the sporting event on television (either at home or in a bar) or can physically attend the sport-ing event. It is impossible to assess the relationship between watching sports on television and violence. Fans that watch their favourite team lose may experience feelings of anger, resentment, and bitterness. They may verbally lash out at players, referees, and or coaches. It is entirely possible that for some fans these bad feelings may spill over to relationships with friends and families, which may subsequently lead to a violent outburst.

Some economists argue that there is a relationship between family violence and viewing football games on television. Card and Dahl (2011) found a 10% increase in the rate of at-home violence by men against wives and girlfriends shortly after an upset loss by the home team. Quite simply, they argue that fans of teams that are expected to win become angry after a loss and engage in acts of domestic violence. Nonetheless, this research suffers from the ecological fallacy, in which aggregate data is used to explain individual level behaviour. Domestic violence may statistically increase during those particular times but that does not indicate causation; nor does it take into account other factors that lead to family violence.

Obviously, there are distinct differences between fans that attend sporting events and fans that choose to watch the event on television at home. The chance for misbehaviour may increase, as spectators that attend sporting events may be influenced by the dynamics of crowd behaviour and the consumption of alcohol. In fact, the sport riot is the subject of numerous research articles (Young, 2010).

The Sports Riot

Vancouver and Montreal are all too familiar with the damaging consequences of sport riots. Aside from the potential for fatalities and serious injuries, there have been millions of dollars in property damages, and the reputations of both the cities and their police are tarnished after a sports riot occurs. Mann (1989) developed the most useful typology for classifying sport riots – the so-called FORCE typology, which includes:

1. **Frustration:** Riots that are based in frustration may include acts motivated by either deprivation (a fan waiting for hours to receive a ticket that is not available) or perceived injustice (a fan favorite being suspended).
2. **Outlawry:** This involves unruly groups of people that do battle (actual or symbolic) near a sports site (a staging ground) with the purpose of gaining attention.
3. **Remonstrance:** These riots have their origins in long standing ideological conflicts, in which a particular social or political cause attempts to gain media attention.
4. **Confrontation:** These involve groups that have a long and bitter history of conflict. These conflicts have long-standing issues rooted in racial, religious, class, or economic injustices.
5. **Expressive:** These are strictly post-event disorders that stem from extreme emotional state of highly aroused fans whose team has either won or been defeated.

Misbehaving fans often receive positive reinforcement from other fans. For example, hecklers receive reinforcement when other spectators laugh at their antics, whilst more violent behaviour (such throwing a beer bottle) may draw cheers. In fact, the environment at major sporting events, allows, and even encourages, many behaviors that are well outside the norm. Moreover, in a review of social-psychological research relating to sport riots, Russell (2004) found that situational, environmental, social, and cognitive variables are associated with spectator violence. Situational factors may include crowd size, number of fouls and disputed penalties, extent of "home" versus "away" supporters' involvement, and position of contending teams in league standings. Environmental factors may include temperature, darkness, and noise. Cognitive factors suggest that rioters are more likely to be angry, physically aggressive, impulsive, sensation seeking, and antisocial.

Hooliganism. In Europe, sport riots often associated with the phenomenon of hooliganism. Football hooliganism refers to unruly, violent, and destructive behaviour by overzealous supporters of football (soccer) clubs, including brawling, vandalism, and intimidation.

Football hooliganism usually involves clashes between gangs, often known as football firms (British slang for a criminal gang), created for the specific purpose of intimidating and physically attacking supporters of other teams. Certain clubs have long-standing rivalries with other clubs, and hooliganism associated with matches between them is more likely to be more severe. Conflict may take place before, during, or after matches. Participants often select locations away from the stadium to avoid arrest by the police, but conflict can also erupt spontaneously inside the stadium or in the surrounding streets. In such cases, shop windows may be smashed, garbage bins set on fire, and police cars may be overturned. In extreme cases, hooligans, police, and bystanders have been killed, and riot police need to intervene to quell the disturbance (Kerr, 1994).

The Special Case of Violence and Youth Sport

It is estimated that 51% of youth (ages 5 to 14) participate in organized sport activities, and on average these sport activities take place about 2.6 times per week during their sports season (Ifedi, 2008). There are obvious benefits for participation in sports, such as improved mental and physical health, increased social and life skills, and an overall enhanced well-being, which may include improved self-confidence and self-esteem (Janssen & LeBlanc, 2010). Sports participation can also be a deterrent to negative behaviour by providing youth with an opportunity for pro-social activities (Davis & Menard, 2012). Yet there is a darker side to youth involvement in sport, in which children are victimized in a variety of ways, including emotional, verbal, physical, and sexual abuse.

David (2004) argues that physical abuse against youth athletes can be manifested in four ways: (1) excessive intensive training; (2) violence due to participating in competitions; (3) peer violence; and (4) physical violence by adults. Stafford, Alexander, and Fry (2013) claim that "undergoing training as a child athlete can have serious implications for physical, physiological and psychological health" (p. 289). Estimates suggest that 55% of youth athletes report that they continued training for sport even when they were injured or exhausted. Coaches and peers employ a combination of sanctions and guilt to maintain an ethic of excessive training within sport. For example, approximately 9,000 high school athletes are annually treated for exertional heat illness. Tragically, the National Centre for Catastrophic Sport Injury Research reports that from 1960 to 2012, 133 football players have died from heat stroke (Kerr et al., 2013). Regrettably, with appropriate procedures and precautions, these fatalities were totally preventable. There is absolutely no reason or justification for youth athlete to be placed a risk for the sake of a game.

Similar to professional athletes, youth athletes are also exposed to violence within the game. In fact, Stafford Alexander, and Fry (2013) found that youth athletes believed that physical aggression and violence was to be expected in sport as "part of the game." Conversely, other youth athletes found it repressive and difficult to manage, with some claiming that excessive violence and bullying was the reason that they decided to quit the sport altogether.

Peer violence is also a troublesome concern within youth sport, whether it is the result of sports training and practice or external activities related to team membership. Youth athletes that are involved in violent sports such as hockey or football will experience physical aggression or hostility within the practice environment. Although coaches regulate the environment (especially with the star players), fights will break out, violent hits will be delivered, and injuries will occur.

The phenomenon of bullying has become a major social issue recently, especially within the school environment. Yet, within organized sports, bullying appears to be normative behaviour that is rarely regulated. Within a team sport, it is pretty standard for teammates to ridicule and mock teammates. This offensive behaviour is often expressed as "pranks" or "jokes" and is often defended as a team building exercise. Even within professional sports, grown men can succumb to the degradation of constant bullying and rejection. The majority of parents would not want their children exposed to verbal and emotional abuse at the hands of their teammates. Unfortunately, hazing occurs quite frequently within high-school-aged athletes.

Hazing

Hazing denotes any activity expected of someone who is joining a group (or to maintain full status in a group) that humiliates, degrades, or risks emotional and/or physical harm, regardless of the person's willingness to participate. Historically, hazing actions were normally considered harmless pranks or comical pranks associated with young men in college fraternities. Currently, the activities associated with hazing are considered to be physically abusive, hazardous, and/or sexually violating. The specific behaviours or activities within these types differ extensively among participants, groups, and settings. While alcohol use is common in many types of hazing, other examples of typical hazing practices include personal slavery, shouting at and insulting new members/rookies, being required to dress in embarrassing or humiliating apparel in public, consumption and/or smearing of disgusting substances, physical beatings, binge drinking and drinking games, sexual simulation and sexual assault (Fields, Collins, & Comstock, 2010; Nuwer, 2001).

The issue of hazing within team sports is particularly troublesome. Hazing is often shaped by power dynamics that operate within a group or organization. Studies reveal that approximately 80% of college athletes have experienced hazing (McGlone, 2010). Yet the vast majority of incidents in high school, college, and professional sport go unreported. Nonetheless, anecdotal evidence is plentiful, with numerous media reports about youth athletes being exposed to mental, physical, and sexual abuse in the name of "team harmony."

Sexual Violence in Sports

Sexual abuse is considered a "hidden crime" in that it often goes unreported and unpunished. Despite some very high-profile incidents within the sports community, sexual abuse is largely concealed. Not surprisingly, the vast majority of perpetrators are coaches or trainers. It is within this environment that youth athletes are vulnerable (Hartill, 2013). Unfortunately, space limitations preclude an extensive examination of sexual violence within sports. However, there are some very high-profile incidents within the sporting community.

"We are Penn." The sporting world was shocked when legendary football coach Joe Paterno was fired on November 5, 2011. Just four days earlier, Jerry Sandusky, a former assistant coach, was indicted on 52 counts of child molestation dating from 1994 to 2009. Sandusky founded the Second Mile, a charity that was formed as a group foster home dedicated to helping troubled boys and eventually grew into a charity dedicated to helping children with absent or dysfunctional families. Unfortunately, Sandusky used his position as a respected football coach to lure the young boys into the Penn State facilities, where he sexually assaulted the boys in the shower. It was alleged that university officials, including Paterno covered up the assaults to ensure that the reputation of the program would not be tarnished. The Freeh report found that university officials, including Paterno, were complicit in conceal[ing] "Sandusky's activities from the Board of Trustees, the University community and authorities" and that they "failed to protect against a child sexual predator harming children for over a decade" (Freeh, Sporkin, & Sullivan, 2012, p. 14).

Although, some students held vigils for the victims, there was overwhelming support for Paterno, who many claim was not culpable in his complicity. In a shameless example of hero worship, the students at Penn State rioted after news of Paterno's dismissal. In light of the Freeh report, university officials removed the statue of Paterno and the National Collegiate Athletic Association (NCAA) imposed numerous sanctions on the football program.

Canada's Dirty Little Secret. The media frenzy that accompanied the Penn State scandal highlighted the problem of sexual abuse within the sporting environment. Yet, within Canada, the issue of sexual abuse and sport had appeared fifteen years earlier, when former NHLer Sheldon Kennedy and another unnamed player bravely came forward with complaints about sexual abuse they had suffered between 1984 and 1995. Graham James, a high profile coach for the Western Hockey League's Moose Jaw Warriors pled guilty to over 350 assaults and was sentenced to three and half years in jail (S. Kennedy, 2011). Around the same time, in 1997, Martin Kruze publicly admitted that he had been molested at the venerable Maple Leaf Gardens. After going public, dozens of other victims came forward telling stories of employees sexual abusing young boys during the 1970s and 1980s. At least four other employees were linked to the assaults, using their positions to lure young boys into the Gardens to commit these atrocities. One of the abusers, Gordon Stuckless, plead guilty to sexually assaulting 24 boys and only received a sentence of two years less a day. Tragically, a distraught Kruze committed suicide three days after the sentence (Donnelly, 1999).

More recently, the problem of sexual abuse in hockey was further amplified after Theo Fleury admitted that he, like Kennedy was also molested by Graham James. A former NHL all-star with a troubled past, Fleury had long denied any allegations of abuse by his former coach. However, in his memoir, *Playing with Fire: The Theo Fleury Story*, Fleury courageously documents abuse that was perpetrated against him starting from the age of 14, after he had joined the Moose Jaw Warriors (Fleury & Day, 2010). After the book's release, Fleury filed a criminal complaint against James, who once again pled guilty and received a sentence of two years. Although, some criticized Fleury for not coming forward sooner, like Sheldon Kennedy, Fleury has become a prominent and important spokesperson for the victims of sexual abuse.

Conclusion

This chapter has demonstrated the ambiguous and contradictory nature of sports violence. The chapter has provided an overview of major forms of sports violence, in terms of the game, the athlete, and the spectator. The chapter has also introduced the problem of violence in youth sports. Finally, this chapter introduced the reader to several issues within sport violence, such as fighting, concussions, sports riots, hazing, and sexual violence.

Keywords

Sports, fighting, concussions, the code, masculinity, riots, hooliganism, youth sport, hazing, sexual violence

Review Questions

1. Please define and describe CTE. Also discuss the impact that CTE has on both professional and amateur sports.
2. Sociologist Mike Smith identified four categories of violence in sport, please identify and describe.
3. Please define and describe the "Code". What are some critiques of the "code"?
4. According to Otto (2009) there are three reasons why male athletes commit off-the field crime. Please identify and discuss these reasons.
5. Please identify and describe the so-called FORCE typology. Please provide examples for each category.
6. According to David (2004) there are four ways in which youth athletes experience violence. Please identify and discuss.

References

Atkinson, M., & Young, K. (2008). *Deviance and social control in sport*. Windsor, Ontario: Human Kinetics.

Ball, C. G., & Dixon, E. (2011). The consensus statement on mixed martial arts: Emotion, not evidence-based. *Canadian Journal of Surgery, 54*(1), E1.

Benedict, J. (1997). *Public heroes, private felons: Athletes and crimes against women*. Boston, MA: Northeastern University Press.

Benedict, J., & Yaeger, D. (1998). *Pros and cons: The criminals who play in the NFL*. New York: Warner Books.

Bernstein, R. (2006). The code: The unwritten rules of fighting and retaliation in the NHL. Retrieved from http://www.bernsteinbooks.com/books/hockey_code.aspx

Bloom, G. A., & Smith, M. D. (1993). *Hockey violence: A test of cultural spillover theory*. Toronto: York University.

Card, D., & Dahl, G. B. (2011). Family violence and football: The effect of unexpected emotional cues on violent behavior. *Quarterly Journal of Economics, 126*(1), 103-143.

Chandler, S. B., Johnson, D. J., & Carroll, P. S. (1999). Abusive behaviors of college athletes. *College Student Journal, 33*(4), 638-645.

Coakley, J. (2009). *Sports in society: Issues and controversies*. Boston: McGraw Hill.

Cormack, P. & Cosgrave, J.F. (2013). *Desiring Canada: CBC contests, hockey violence and other stately pleasures*. Toronto: University of Toronto Press.

Crosset, T. (1999). Male athletes' violence against women: A critical assessment of the athletic affiliation, violence against women debate. *Quest, 51*(3), 244-257.

Crosset, T. W., Benedict, J. R., & McDonald, M. A. (1995). Male student-athletes reported for sexual assault: A survey of campus police departments and judicial affairs offices. *Journal of Sport & Social Issues, 19*(2), 126-140.

Curry, T. J. (1991). Fraternal bonding in the locker room: A profeminist analysis of talk about competition and women. *Sociology of Sport Journal, 8*(2), 119-135.

David, P. (2004). *Human rights in youth sport: A critical review of children's rights in competitive sport*. New York: Routledge.

Davis, B. S., & Menard, S. (2012). Long term impact of youth sports participation on illegal behavior. *Social Science Journal, 50*(1), 34-44.

Donnelly, P. (1999). Who's fair game? Sport, sexual harassment and abuse. In P. White & K. Young, (Eds.), *Sport and gender in Canada* (pp. 107-128). Toronto: Oxford University Press.

Dowler, K. (2006). Sex, lies, and videotape: The presentation of sex crime in local television news. *Journal of Criminal Justice, 34*(4), 383-392.

Elcombe, T. (2010). The moral equivalent of "Don Cherry." *Journal of Canadian Studies/Revue d'études canadiennes, 44*(2), 194-218.

Fainaru-Wada, M., & Fainaru, S. (2013). *League of denial: The NFL, concussions and the battle for truth*. New York: Random House LLC.

Fields, S. K., Collins, C. L., & Comstock, R. D. (2010). Violence in youth sports: Hazing, brawling and foul play. *British Journal of Sports Medicine, 44*(1), 32-37.

Fleury, T., & Day, K. M. (2010). *Playing with fire: The highest highs and lowest lows of Theo Fleury*. Toronto: Harper Collins.

Freeh, S., Sporkin, F, & Sullivan, LLP (2012). *Report of the special investigative counsel regarding the actions of Pennsylvania State University related to the child sexual abuse committed by Gerald A. Sandusky*. Retrieved from http://progress.psu.edu/the-freeh-report

Gibney, A. (Producer & Director). (2011). The Last Gladiators [Motion picture]. USA: Locomotion Pictures.

Gutkin, C. (2011). A head-injured society? *Canadian Family Physician, 57*(8), 968.

Hartill, M. (2013). Concealment of child sexual abuse in sports. *Quest, 65*(2), 241-254.

Hnida, K. (2006). *Still kicking: My journey as the first woman to play division I college football*. New York: Scribner.

Holman, A. C. (Ed.). (2009). *Canada's game: Hockey and identity*. Montreal and Kingston: McGill-Queen's Press.

Ifedi, F. (2008). *Sport participation in Canada, 2005*. Ottawa: Statistics Canada, Culture, Tourism and the Centre for Education Statistics.

Ingham, A. G., Dewar, A., Coakley, J., & Donnelly, P. (1999). Through the eyes of youth: "Deep play" in PeeWee ice hockey. *Inside sports,* 17-27.

Janssen, I., & LeBlanc, A. G. (2010). Systematic review of the health benefits of physical activity and fitness in school-aged children and youth. *International Journal of Behavioral Nutrition and Physical Activity, 7*(40), 1-16.

Kennedy, K. (2011). Forward. In Sports Illustrated (ed.) *Sports Illustrated hockey talk: From hat tricks to headshots and everything in-between* (pp. xi-vii). Plattsburgh, NY: McClelland & Stewart Ltd.

Kennedy, S. (2011). *Why I Didn't Say Anything*. Toronto: Insomniac Press.

Kerr, J. H. (1994). *Understanding soccer hooliganism*. Buckingham: Open University Press.

Kerr, J. H. (2006). Examining the Bertuzzi–Moore NHL ice hockey incident: Crossing the line between sanctioned and unsanctioned violence in sport. *Aggression and Violent Behavior, 11*(4), 313-322.

Kerr, Z. Y., Casa, D. J., Marshall, S. W., & Comstock, R. D. (2013). Epidemiology of exertional heat illness among US high school athletes. *American Journal of Preventive Medicine, 44*(1), 8-14.

Kreager, D. A. (2007). Unnecessary roughness? School sports, peer networks, and male adolescent violence. *American Sociological Review, 72*(5), 705-724.

Lawless, M. (2012). *Hit by pitch: Ray Chapman, Carl Mays and the fatal fastball*. Jefferson, NC: McFarland.

Lefkowitz, B. (1997). *Our guys: The Glen Ridge rape and the secret life of the perfect suburb*. Berkeley: University of California Press.

Mann, L. (1989). Sports crowds and the collective behavior perspective. In J. Goldstein (Ed), *Sport, games and play: Social and psychological viewpoints*, (pp. 229-327). Hillsdale, NJ: Laurence Earlbaum.

Messner, M. A. (1992). *Power at play: Sports and the problem of masculinity*. Boston: Beacon Press.

Messner, M. A., & Stevens, M. A. (2002). Scoring without consent: Confronting male athletes' violence against women. In M. Gatz, A. Messner, & S.J. Ball-Rokeach (Eds,), *Paradoxes of youth and sport* (pp. 225-239). Albany: State University of New York Press.

McCrory, P., Meeuwisse, W. H., Kutcher, J. S., Jordan, B. D., & Gardner, A. (2013). What is the evidence for chronic concussion-related changes in retired athletes?: Behavioural, pathological and clinical outcomes. *British Journal of Sports Medicine, 47*(5), 327-330.

McGlone, C. A. (2010). Hazy viewpoints: Administrators' perceptions of hazing. *International Journal of Sport Management and Marketing, 7*(1), 119-131.

McKee, A. C., Cantu, R. C., Nowinski, C. J., Hedley-Whyte, E. T., Gavett, B. E., Budson, A. E., & Stern, R. A. (2009). Chronic traumatic encephalopathy in athletes: progressive tauopathy following repetitive head injury. *Journal of Neuropathology and Experimental Neurology, 68*(7), 709-735.

Muchnick, I. (2009). *Chris and Nancy: The true story of the Benoit murder-suicide and pro wrestling's cocktail of death*. Toronto: ECW Press.

NHL. (2014). *NHL.com*. Retrieved from http://nhl.com

Nilan, C. (2013). *Fighting back: The Chris Nilan story*. New York: HarperCollins.

Nuwer, H. (2001). *Wrongs of passage: Fraternities, sororities, hazing and binge drinking*. Bloomington, IN: Indiana University Press.

Otto, K. A. (2009). Criminal athletes: An analysis for charges, reduced charges and sentences. *Journal of Legal Aspects Sport, 19*, 67-102.

Ribowsky, M. (2011). *Howard Cosell: The man, the myth, and the transformation of American sports*. New York: W.W. Norton & Company.

Russell, G. W. (2004). Sport riots: A social-psychological review. *Aggression and Violent Behavior, 9*(4), 353-378.

Shaw, G. (2013). The concussion crisis – A 'Frontline' documentary: What did the NFL know and when and what could neurology have done? *Neurology Today, 13*(20), 1-16.

Singer, D.M. (2014). *Hockeyfights.com*. Retrieved from http://www.hockeyfights.com

Smith, M. D. (1983). *Violence and sport*. Toronto: Butterworths.

Smith, D., & Stewart, S. (2003). Sexual aggression and sports participation. *Journal of Sport Behavior, 26*(4), 384-395.

Smith, A. M., Stuart, M. J., & Fish, K. (2000). A psychosocial perspective of aggression in ice hockey. *Safety in Ice Hockey, 3*, 199-215.

Stafford, A., Alexander, K., & Fry, D. (2013). Playing through pain: Children and young people's experiences of physical aggression and violence in sport. *Child Abuse Review, 22*(4), 287-299.

Svinth, J. R. (2007). Death under the spotlight: The Manuel Velazquez boxing fatality collection. *Journal of Combative Sport*, 1-20.

Trulson, M. E. (1986). Martial arts training: A novel "cure" for juvenile delinquency. *Human Relations, 39*(12), 1131-1140.

Wacquant, L. J. (1995). The pugilistic point of view: How boxers think and feel about their trade. *Theory and Society, 24*(4), 489-535.

White, P., & Young, K. (1997). Masculinity, sport, and the injury process: A review of Canadian and international evidence. *Avante, 3*(2), 1-30.

Wright, D. R., & Fitzpatrick, K. M. (2006). Violence and minority youth: The effects of risk and asset factors on fighting among African American children and adolescents. *Adolescence, 41*(162), 251.

Young, K. (2010). *Sport, violence and society*. New York: Routledge, Taylor & Francis.

Criminal Justice Responses to Domestic Violence against Women: Feminist Activism and the Canadian State

Chapter 12

Jennifer Fraser

Learning Objectives

In this chapter you will...

▶ gain an understanding of the context in which domestic violence emerged as a social problem in Canada

▶ consider the influence of social construction on social problems claims-making

▶ identify the three main types of mobilization engaged in by the battered women's movement

▶ explore the effect of sociopolitical factors on activism

▶ learn about "what matters" to domestic violence victims when seeking justice

Introduction

Aggressive criminal justice policies and processes for domestic violence against women, including mandatory arrest policies, pro-prosecution policies, specialized domestic violence courts, and Partner Assault Response (PAR) programs, began to emerge in Canada in the early 1980s. A variety of factors contributed to these responses, including the high visibility of the battered women's movement in the 1970s. Since the 1980s, government interventions into domestic violence have proliferated, though they have largely focused on the criminal justice system, despite the sparse evidence to suggest that these measures are effective at reducing levels of domestic violence, keeping women safe, or recognizing the diverse needs of women who experience violence.

Women's consciousness raising in the 1970s uncovered the widespread prevalence of violence committed against women by their male partners. As many activists within the battered women's movement recognized the role governments should have in addressing the problem of "wife battering," they used the narrative of the "helpless battered woman" to garner public sympathy for the problem (Loseke, 2003). To ensure widespread public support for, community ownership of, and government intervention into the issue, feminist activists strategically framed the problem of "wife battering" using this narrative. However, through research and experience providing services to women who had experienced violence, feminist activists became increasingly aware of the multiple forms of violence that women experience in intimate relationships that did not fit the "helpless battered woman" narrative (Fraser, 2013).

In addition to, and as a consequence of, the gender-neutral reframing of the issue from "wife battering" to "domestic violence," the criminal justice system was emphasized as a site of response. There have been a number of unintended consequences because of this shift. In some instances when police are called, both partners will be charged, women may be charged instead of their abusive partner, or children may be removed by social services because of the difficulty in determining the primary aggressor or based on the behaviour of each person upon police arrival at the scene (Durfee, 2012). The use of the "helpless battered woman" construct in the criminal justice system has led to a concentration on physical abuse largely to the exclusion of other forms of violence, including psychological, emotional, sexual, and financial abuse, which can have similarly damaging consequences (see Forrestor, 2011). There is also a dearth of responses in other social institutions, such as education, health, and social services, that might be just as well, if not better, suited to address the problem of domestic violence.

This chapter will examine the evolving strategies for domestic violence activism and the parallel growth of aggressive criminal justice responses in Canada to explore the relationship between feminist activists and the Canadian state. Using a feminist historical lens helps us make sense of the current primacy given to criminal justice interventions for domestic violence. The actions and responses of both feminist activists and Canadian governments will be situated within the respective sociopolitical contexts of the time. The intention of the chapter is to highlight the evolving and increasing sophistication of feminist claims-making concerning domestic violence alongside the simultaneous decline in state recognition of feminist expertise on, and ownership of, the issue (see Best, 2013; Spector & Kitsuse, 2009). First, this chapter will overview the evolution of feminist thought and activism on domestic violence and the different approaches to engaging the Canadian state for recognition and response to an evolving social problem. Next, the predominant Canadian state response to domestic violence – criminal justice interventions – will be reviewed and evaluated based on existing criminological research. The final section will reflect on feminist strategies and government responses given what we know now. The conclusion will consider the situation of feminist advocacy, service provision, and research given the current sociopolitical climate, which is characterized by backlash and a decline in recognition of feminist expertise and ownership over the issue of domestic violence.

Feminist Activism and Engagement with the Canadian State

Colette Parent and Cécile Coderre (2004) identify three distinct moments in the battered women's movement: the discovery of the problem; the documentation of women's stories revealing the widespread victimization of women within and beyond the marital unit; and, the recognition of the diversity of women victims and the inadequacy of criminal justice responses. Before the 1970s, while violence against women certainly existed, it was a problem with no name, a private family matter, and widely socially accepted as long as men's abuse did not exceed unspoken limits (Backhouse, 1991; DeKeseredy & Hinch, 1991; DeKeseredy &

MacLeod, 1997; Dobash & Dobash, 1979). Women in feminist consciousness-raising groups of the 1970s began to discover that the violence they experienced at the hands of their male partners was not unique, and they began to connect this experience to women's overall inequality in other spheres of social life. Women also recognized that their experiences of victimization were largely minimized or medicalized by formal services, such as the police and healthcare professionals, who often saw women as deserving of violence in some way (Matthews, 1994; Schechter, 1982). With no specialized public services being available, feminists began opening up their own homes to women fleeing abusive husbands (Jones & Cook, 2008). These services were rooted in feminist philosophies of women's empowerment and autonomy and operated as non-hierarchical, volunteer-based collectives (Macy, Giattina, Parish, & Crosby, 2010).

Evidence from an analysis of documents stored at the Canadian Women's Movement Archives (CWMA) at the University of Ottawa suggests that early feminist conceptualizations of violence against women were complex, integrating discourses of human rights, sociostructural issues, community dynamics, individual maladaptive behaviour, and crime (Fraser, 2013). This suggests that feminist groups have long recognized the multidimensionality of violence against women – that it is perpetrated and perpetuated by individual men who may or may not have mental health issues, anger management, and stress-related problems, or addictions. However, they also suggest that this violence occurs within a social context that implicitly and explicitly reinforces abusive behaviour through male-dominated or patriarchal social structures and socialization processes that undermine women's equality and autonomy. This connection to the social has seemingly long included a desire for domestic violence to be recognized as a crime like other forms of assault, but that this recognition would be one component of a broad, multifaceted social response, recognizing a continuum of violence against women and the overlap in perpetration and effects on victims of different types of domestic and sexual violence (see WHO & London School of Hygiene and Tropical Medicine, 2010). A complex understanding of violence against women informed a multipronged and coordinated feminist response to the problem, incorporating increasingly sophisticated feminist service provision in shelters and women's centres for women who had experienced violence, advocacy aimed at increasing public awareness of the problem, research conducted at every level from the grassroots to the academy, and engagement with the Canadian state for an official government response (Fraser, 2013).

Before wife battering was recognized by the Canadian criminal justice system and after, due to the reluctance of many women to report their victimizations to police, feminist groups referred to it as a "silent crime" in their advocacy. The use of this claims-making technique in the 1980s involved some feminist groups calling on police to recognize and treat wife battering like any other crime as part of a comprehensive social solution. This comprehensive solution was also meant include government support of feminist service provision, widespread public education aimed at changing attitudes, and legislative change to guarantee women's substantive equality. It was also at this time when Canada's first national study on wife battering was conducted by Linda MacLeod over a six-week period and released in 1980 under the title, *Wife Battering in Canada: The Vicious Circle*. MacLeod (1980) collected the first statistics in Canada on wife battering by contacting individual shelters and transition homes, as well as police departments, court offices, and hospitals, though she discovered that these public services did not collect specific information on wife battering at the time. With a background in math and statistics, MacLeod (1980) constructed the first statistic on the prevalence of wife battering in Canada: "Every year, 1 in 10 Canadian women who are married or in a relationship with a live-in lover are battered" (MacLeod, 1980, p. 21). This statistic is cited in nearly every pamphlet or brochure housed in the CWMA after 1980 and before Statistics Canada's first and only Violence Against Women Survey in 1993[1] (see Johnson, 1996; Johnson & Sacco, 1995).

MacLeod's (1980) study galvanized and provided evidence to support the work of the battered women's movement in Canada in the 1980s. However, when it was used to inform the Report of the Standing Committee on Health, Welfare, and Social Affairs on wife battering presented to the House of Commons in 1982, the idea that wife battering was prevalent in Canada was considered preposterous and even humorous to many members of Parliament (Dawson, 1994; Pierson, 1993). The need to assuage what came to be perceived as a political gaffe was just one factor that contributed to the shift of wife battering from a private issue to a public problem. Other factors that would hold this response predominantly within a criminal justice gaze included influential social science research like the Minneapolis Domestic Violence Experiment and a similar study in London, Ontario that found arrest, and not mediation or "cooling off" periods, to be the strongest predictor of lower repeat arrests in a six-month follow-up with violent male partners (Jaffe, Wolfe, Telford, & Austin, 1986; Sherman & Berk, 1984) and high-profile lawsuits in the United States where women sued police departments for failing to protect them from domestic violence (Buzawa & Buzawa, 2003; Mills, 1999). Despite subsequent research that has produced conflicting results on the effectiveness of arrest in reducing future assaults or keeping women safe (Maxwell, Garner, & Fagan, 2001; Sherman, 1992; Sheptycki, 1991), various criminal justice interventions for domestic violence have proliferated since this time.

As a result of these factors, as well as mobilization at the provincial level, between 1983 and 1986 the Federal Solicitor General and provincial Attorneys General called on police within their jurisdictions to adopt mandatory arrest policies in cases of wife battering. Pro-prosecution policies and specialized domestic violence courts soon followed to deal with the influx of cases into the system. The problem of physical domestic violence against women was one easily incorporated into the existing criminal justice understanding of crimes as individual transgressions against the state that can be arbitrated through an adversarial system. Aggressive strategies are now deeply embedded as a part of the increasingly neoliberal Canadian state's "tough on crime" approach that is centred on the premise that engaging strong and punitive crime control responses will denounce violence by naming it as a social wrong and hold individual offenders accountable for the crimes they commit.

Criminal Justice Responses to Domestic Violence

Advocates for the aggressive criminalization of domestic violence provide a number of arguments to support their case. They argue that these policies demonstrate a clear societal commitment to treat domestic violence as a serious crime by providing a credible threat of prosecution for the offender. Additionally, some research has found that specialized domestic violence policies result in speedier court processing and greater consistency in sentencing. Many advocates also believe that these policies will protect women from retaliation if the abuser perceives the decision to prosecute is out of her hands (Corsilles, 1994; Eley, 2005; Hanna, 1996). Despite the entrenchment of criminal justice responses to domestic violence as the dominant way to address this problem in Canada, most evaluations of these interventions have focused on procedural indicators of effectiveness – for example, number of cases processed, number of offenders attending, and completing Partner Assault Response (PAR) programs, or number of re-arrests (e.g., Dinovitzer & Dawson, 2007; Prairie Research Associates (PAR), 2006; Ursel, Tutty, & leMaistre, 2008). These evaluations have shown some promising results in terms of domestic violence case processing in the criminal justice system, including a rise in the number of cases reported to the police; more offenders pleading guilty; fewer cases being dropped by the police or prosecution; and, more supports available for victims within the system (Dugan, Nagin, & Rosenfeld, 1999; Hornick, Boyes, Tutty, & White, 2008; Tutty, McNichol, & Christensen, 2008; Ursel & Hagyard, 2008). However, there is little evidence to suggest that criminalization is effective at keeping women safe from violence, promoting women's sense of justice, or addressing the complexity of women's experiences of violence.

Procedural indicators of criminal justice effectiveness are insufficient to measure the extent to which various criminal justice interventions for domestic violence keep women safe from violence. Most domestic violence-related offences prosecuted in court involve charges of physical assault. Other types of violence can be difficult to prosecute when little physical evidence is present or are seen as less serious if there is no physical injury (see Forrestor, 2011). Since the Criminal Code of Canada (1985) does not have a specific prohibition against domestic violence, related offences are subsumed under existing offences that can result in an incongruence between police officers' understandings of offences or their charging practices and women's experiences of domestic violence (see Hoyle, 1998).[2] In addition, the number of cases processed through the system or the number of individuals completing PAR programs cannot speak to any future violence committed by offenders if follow-ups are not conducted with both the convicted offender and their current or former partners. Arrest and re-arrest rates are an inadequate measure because many women who experience domestic violence do not report their victimizations to the police. Statistics Canada's 2009 General Social Survey (GSS) on Victimization found that only 23% of women who experienced domestic violence contacted the police (Brennan, 2011a). If, as research suggests, women tend to contact the police after a particularly severe incident of violence or after their partner "crosses the line" (Grauwiler, 2008; Holder, 2008), relatively less serious incidents of violence committed after the abuser has already been processed through the criminal justice system would likely not reach the attention of police. Any instances of unreported violence would then not be reflected in re-arrest rates, giving a potentially false sense of criminal justice effectiveness if an offender has not been re-arrested for domestic violence.

Research on "what matters" to women who have experienced intimate partner violence has found that women who call the police are usually looking for protection and an immediate stop to a particular incident of violence; many are not committed to long-term involvement with the criminal justice system (Holder, 2008; Holder & Mayo, 2003; Landau, 2000). When women call the police they want the violent man removed, advice, and information about their short- and long-term options, and someone to talk to who will be supportive and non-judgmental and who will not insist on prosecution (Hoyle, 1998). Women identify the need to be believed and have their experiences validated, to have immediate protection from violence, and to secure their children's well-being (Minaker, 2001). Many survivors of domestic violence speak of wanting "justice," but they do not always see that as something the criminal justice system can deliver, and, in fact, engaging the justice system can often result in negative consequences, such as dual charging and loss of children (Minaker, 2001).

Women who contact the criminal justice system may be looking for something entirely different than punishment and retribution. Studies find that the most important resolution victims of violence want is validation of their experiences and for family and friends to take an unequivocal stance in support of them and in condemnation of the perpetrator's violence (Herman, 2005). Victims express a desire for healing and rebuilding and to feel safe throughout and as result of this process. While many individuals have faith in the criminal justice system, overall most do not see it is a solution to their situation or a guarantee of safety (Barata, 2007). Many women worry that involving the criminal justice system will make their situation worse in terms of their future financial and personal well-being. Women may be afraid of their partner, but feel frustrated and confused about the criminal justice process and conflicted over whether or not they want him criminalized (Bennett, Goodman, & Dutton, 1999). Many women express a desire for their partners to be rehabilitated rather than punished (Cretney & Davis, 1997; Robinson, 2008).

Further, the ability of some women to access the Canadian criminal justice system is limited by a number of social factors, including being a visible minority, having a mental or physical disability, speaking neither English nor French, experiencing violence in a same-sex relationship, or having a low income (Barrett & St. Pierre, 2011). While it is widely documented that violence against Aboriginal women in Canada is disproportionately higher than violence against non-Aboriginal women (Brennan, 2011b), this violence is often not considered within the lens of Aboriginal peoples' experiences of historical and ongoing colonization (Farley, Lynne, & Cotton, 2005; Native Women's Association of Canada, 2010; Weaver, 2009). In an Australian study, Indigenous women were more likely than non-Indigenous women to see the criminal justice system as a tool of oppression and a facilitator of violence against them and their communities than as a mechanism for advancing the status of women. As a result of this view, Indigenous women tended to prefer alternative interventions, like restorative justice, that prioritize relationships and community well-being over state-defined solutions to violence (Nancarrow, 2007). However, alternative solutions that emphasize the needs of victims are rarely available. Wherever Aboriginal women live, whether in rural or urban settings, it is often difficult for them to access services if they have limited resources and when specialized services are so few and far between (Warrington, 2001).

The increasing diversity of Canadian society means that a "one size fits all" justice system is unable to account for the different meanings women attach to the violence they experience and their abilities to secure safety. For example, women who immigrate to Canada from another country may be following a husband or coming as a refugee; thus, they may not be freely choosing to leave their home country. This move can be isolating if ties are cut with family in their home country to live somewhere where most people speak a different language and practise a different culture (Rojas-Viger, 2008). Upon arrival, many women face other challenges, including unrecognized educational achievements, difficulty accessing education and jobs, and social exclusion and marginalization. A woman who is a newcomer to Canada and also experiences domestic violence faces a dilemma between the values of Canadian society, which encourage women to leave an abusive partner, and familial, religious, and cultural pressures that may discourage her from disclosing victimization or leaving her husband (Alaggia, Regehr, & Rishchynski, 2009; Miedema & Wachholz, 1998). Since women may find the justice system difficult to navigate, the power of the husband may be bolstered with the potential for violence to manifest in different forms (Alaggia & Maiter, 2006; Rojas-Viger, 2008). For example, immigrant women's vulnerability is increased if they are financially dependent on their partner, as in the case of women who are sponsored by a husband who has already achieved permanent residency status in Canada or if she is unaware of Canadian laws against domestic violence and the social supports available for victims (Côté, Kérisit, & Côté, 2001; Pontel & Demczuk, 2007).

From this body of literature three main themes can be gleaned. First, there seems to be a disconnect between the goals of the criminal justice system and the goals of women when they make first contact with the criminal justice system through the police. What is considered an "effective" criminal justice response may not be what women would consider an effective process and outcome of that interaction. Second, women who experience violence tend to conceptualize violence differently than the assumption underpinning the operation of the criminal justice system: women tend to want validation of their experiences and support for their and their children's long-term well-being, while the criminal justice system emphasizes punishment of individual offenders for a transgression against the state. Finally, a rigid criminal justice system is not able to account for the diverse and complex experiences of women who experience abuse.

Feminist Activism and Government Responses to Domestic Violence

Given the variety of solutions proposed by feminist groups in the 1970s and 1980s, it is curious that the public response to domestic violence has centred on criminal justice interventions largely to the exclusion of attending to activists' other proposals. Feminists have urged governments to provide adequate funding to support feminist social service provision and public education. They wanted the government to ensure equal opportunities for men and women in terms of education, employment, participation in political life, and overall well-being. Instead, governments have responded to domestic violence through an individualized lens that focuses on isolated acts, rather than from a perspective that recognizes the systemic nature and women's dynamic and ongoing experiences of domestic violence. To explain how this happened, we need to look at the evolution of the battered women's movement's claims-making techniques and the multiple social constructions that exist to make sense of domestic violence (see Best, 2013; Spector & Kitsuse, 2009).

In the early years, the battered women's movement had to strategically work to frame wife battering as a social problem – and not just a women's problem – in order for it to be palatable to the general public and governments who were asked to respond (Dobash & Dobash, 1992; Schneider, 2000). The earliest advocates in the 1970s used what Donileen Loseke (2003) terms "formula stories" to raise public consciousness that there was a problem and to reinforce the severity of the problem. These formula stories were based on the recognizable figure of the helpless battered woman and the abusive man who exerts physical control over his wife.[3] The narrative of the "helpless battered woman" reinforced what it meant to be a victim and perpetrator of domestic violence, but provided only one social construction of intimate partner violence – one that emphasized extreme physical violence and a helpless woman victim who has developed psychological pathologies. This characterization of wife battering, which did indeed describe some women's experiences, was useful to garner sympathy for the problem in the early years of the battered women's movement. However, this was not the view with which feminists were operating in their service provision to victims of violence. Through their experience providing services to victims, and later due to research evidence, feminists were aware of the widespread prevalence and the complex dynamics of domestic violence. They also knew that not all women were "helpless"; indeed, they recognized women as active agents who could take control over their own lives (Fraser, 2013). Thus, the narrow narrative of the "helpless battered woman" could not account for all women's experiences of violence.

Other feminists have also criticized the movement's early and continued reliance on the battered woman-as-victim archetype (e.g., Comack, 1993; Randall, 2004), but it has been difficult to maneuver out of the path it has carved. Feminist legal scholar Melanie Randall (2004) argues that early conceptualizations of wife battering have influenced the social and legal responses to intimate partner violence by stereotyping women's experiences and responses to abuse. Specifically, she highlights how the "battered woman syndrome" and the conceptualization of the "uncooperative witness" fail to acknowledge that women "may be making decisions which are both reasonable and rational when grasped within the particular circumstances of their lives and the social conditions which shape those circumstances" (Randall, 2004, p. 108). Because the early feminist narrative of the battered woman was picked up and integrated into the crime discourse that is predicated on an identifiable victim and perpetrator, feminists have had to negotiate their evolving and increasingly nuanced conceptualizations of intimate partner violence with the multiplying criminal justice interventions for domestic violence based on an obsolete construction of the problem.

While the story of the "battered woman" may have been the image the battered women's movement was projecting to the general public and governments in the early years, it was certainly not their assumption of women who had experienced violence. Feminist groups demonstrated a clear recognition of women's agency. Thus, a juxtaposition was produced between the public image of how the battered women's movement conceptualized wife battering (i.e., helpless victims, monstrous perpetrators) and the way in which many feminist groups were actually working with women who had experienced abuse (i.e., women as active agents in their own lives) (Fraser, 2013). Nuance is not easily captured when an issue gets taken up in another social arena with an alternate lens through which social problems are articulated and negotiated. This is not to suggest, as some feminists have argued, that there has been an active co-optation of feminist agendas by government crime control agendas (see Bumiller, 2008; Gotell, 1998, 2010), but that working with institutions that are largely coming from a non-feminist perspective inevitably leads to a degree of reinterpretation, or a "watering down" of nuanced, feminist analysis. Thus, the issue of physical domestic violence – which could easily be incorporated into existing crime legislation and discourse without the need for nuanced, feminist revisions – emerged as the predominant type of domestic violence to be addressed by the Canadian state.

Conclusion

The reality today is that feminists of all stripes are increasingly facing backlash due to the turn toward social conservative values advocating punishment and the traditional family (see Chesney-Lind, 2006; Chunn, Boyd, & Lessard, 2007; DeKeseredy, 1999; Dragiewicz, 2008), as well as neoliberal governing strategies stressing individual responsibility for the prevention of victimization (see Bumiller, 2008; Gotell, 1998, 2010). Activists within the battered women's movement, who have been providing services for decades to women experiencing violence, have been decreasingly considered by governments to be experts on the issue of violence against women.[4] This is evidenced by the gradual decline in government consultations with progressive women's groups, along with the formal acknowledgement of the conservative group REAL Women of Canada, who oppose many of the advances that have been made to women's status in Canada since the 1970s. The dissolution of national level feminist organizations has meant that feminist groups across the country no longer have access to formal mechanisms that facilitate communication with Canadian governments.[5] The mandate of the federal agency Status of Women Canada has been narrowed and no longer funds research and advocacy activities but action-oriented projects.[6] Feminist service providers, while always struggling for funding, increasingly have to resort to "innovative," project-based grants to sustain their services, when what they really need is stable, operational funding to guarantee that the women who need safe spaces, information, and emotional support will be able to access these services. Feminist activism and research on domestic violence has been further undermined by men's and fathers' rights groups using methodologically problematic "family conflict" research to argue that women are as violent as men in intimate partnerships (see Loseke & Kurz, 2005; Straus, 2005). A host of other discouraging sociopolitical factors leave many feminist activists and domestic violence service providers asking, where do we go from here?[7]

While there has been an observable decline in the value afforded to research and the influence of feminist research on government policy making, as well as a loss of formal feminist lobby groups and government consultations, promising activism is still emerging and reaching a public consciousness. The rapid expansion of an event like Slutwalk demonstrates a global recognition that women's rights and autonomy continue to be undermined by deeply entrenched sexist attitudes – but also a continued willingness for mass groups of individuals to agitate at the grassroots for social change.[8] The story of the battered women's movement, from its early influence to its declining impact, is complex, incorporating multiple factors for why the criminal justice response to domestic violence emerged and proliferated as it did. Clearly, feminist activism, from service provision to advocacy to research, does not exist in a vacuum. Sociopolitical contexts have played a significant role in the extent to which feminist expertise has been recognized and valued in the public realm at different points during the last 40 years. While focusing on domestic violence in particular, this chapter has highlighted the importance of considering context in social problem claims-making and the value of looking to history to see how we got to where we are today. Future activism can build on lessons learned from the past by considering the utility of strategically reframing issues to bolster political relevancy in light of what is lost in terms of core social movement values.

Keywords

Domestic violence, feminist activism, social construction

Review Questions

1. What do you think are some of the reasons that feminist activism on domestic violence exploded in the 1970s?
2. What do you think are appropriate measures of "effectiveness" when evaluating criminal justice interventions?
3. Consider the Canadian criminal justice system's overall use of evidence-based practice. How does the response to domestic violence fit into the broader theoretical orientation of criminal justice in Canada?
4. What are some of the other issues feminist activists were mobilizing around starting in the 1970s? How have those issues been responded to by Canadian governments?
5. How might we alternatively conceptualize "justice"?

Notes

[1] In addition to collating police-reported crime rates, Statistics Canada now measures spousal assault and sexual assault victimization rates through their General Social Survey (GSS) on Victimization conducted every five years. Data is currently available from 1999, 2004, and 2009.

[2] The most common domestic violence-related charges include common assault; assault with a weapon or causing bodily harm; breaches of peace bonds, restraining orders, or probation/parole; uttering threats; and, mischief (Forrestor, 2011).

[3] Early feminist activism on domestic violence tended to focus on violence within the husband-wife relationship, but it has since evolved to recognize violence within common law partnerships, dating partnerships, and same-sex partnerships.

[4] The battered woman syndrome, based on Walker's (1979) theory of learned helplessness, was an early feminist explanation for why women stay in abusive relationships and is available as a possible defence in cases where women have killed their abusive partners. It was most famously used in Canada in *R. v. Lavallee* [1990]. The concept of the "uncooperative witness" is a non-feminist archetype that has emerged since the proliferation of aggressive criminal justice policies and the influx of domestic violence cases seen in court. It refers to women who may not want to participate in the criminal prosecution of their abuser, for a variety of reasons.

[5] For about a decade, from the late 1970s to the late 1980s, women's groups across Canada, represented by the National Action Committee on the Status of Women (NAC), were consulted by all federal political parties at an annual lobby on Parliament Hill. Beginning in the late 1980s, some political parties refused to consult with "special interest groups" and by the mid-1990s, the NAC no longer had the funding to sustain their national network. Women's groups continue to be sporadically consulted, albeit on an ad hoc basis. For example, a group of representatives from women's groups across the country were consulted as experts by then Minister of Justice Kim Campbell in 1991 concerning Bill C-49, the "No means No" law, that was passed the following year (see McIntrye, 1994). This

law clarified when sexual history evidence could be admissible in the prosecution of sexual assault. It also defined consent and made changes to the defence of an "honest but mistaken" belief in consent. More recently, women's groups were consulted at the provincial level in Ontario concerning the Sexual Violence Action Plan, released in 2011.

[6] The Canadian Advisory Council on the Status of Women, an arms-length advisory body to the federal government, was dismantled by the Prime Minister Jean Chrétien in 1995. The National Action Committee on the Status of Women, which acted as the national lobby group for English Canada's women's movement from the 1970s until the 1990s, crumbled amid funding cuts to Status of Women in the late 1990s (see Anderson, 1996; Landsberg, 2011; Rebick, 2005).

[7] Action-oriented projects typically refer to the one-time implementation of an "innovative" initiative or campaign. Status of Women Canada funds projects that can be planned and implemented in three years or less by organizations at the local, regional, or national level (see Status of Women Canada's website: http://www.swc-cfc.gc.ca/index-eng.html).

[8] Other sociopolitical factors contributing to a climate of uncertainty around the future status of women in Canada include the reopening of the "abortion debate" in the House of Commons and the dismantling of the long-gun registry in early 2012, the discontinuation of federal funding for research on missing and murdered Aboriginal women and girls in 2010, and the 2006 cancellation by newly-elected Conservative Prime Minister Stephen Harper of a national childcare program developed by the previously governing Liberal Party.

[9] Slutwalk was born in 2011 in response to comments made by a Toronto police officer to a group of Osgoode Hall Law School students that women could avoid getting raped if they did not dress like "sluts."

References

Alaggia, R., & Maiter, S. (2006). Domestic violence and child abuse: Issues for immigrant and refugee families. In R. Alaggia & C. Vine (Eds.), *Cruel but not unusual: Violence in Canadian families* (pp. 371-396). Waterloo, ON: Wilfrid Laurier University Press.

Alaggia, R., Regehr, C., & Rishchynski, G. (2009). Intimate partner violence and immigration laws in Canada: How far have we come? *International Journal of Law and Psychiatry, 32,* 335-341.

Anderson, D. (1996). *Rebel daughter: An autobiography.* Toronto: Key Porter Books.

Backhouse, C. (1991). *Petticoats and prejudice: Women and law in nineteenth century Canada.* Toronto: Women's Press.

Barata, P. C. (2007). Abused women's perspectives on the criminal justice system's response to domestic violence. *Psychology of Women Quarterly, 31*(2), 202-215.

Barrett, B. J., & St. Pierre, M. (2011). Variations in women's help seeking in response to intimate partner violence: Findings from a Canadian population-based study. *Violence Against Women, 17*(1), 47-70.

Bennett, L., Goodman, L., & Dutton, M. A. (1999). Systemic obstacles to the criminal prosecution of a battering partner. *Journal of Interpersonal Violence, 14*(7), 761-772.

Best, J. (2013). *Social problems* (2nd ed.). New York: W.W. Norton & Company.

Brennan, S. (2011a). Self-reported spousal violence, 2009. *Family Violence in Canada: A Statistical Profile.* (Catalogue no. 85-224-X). Ottawa: Statistics Canada.

Brennan, S. (2011b). Violent victimization of Aboriginal women in the Canadian provinces, 2009. *Juristat* (no. 85-002-X). Ottawa: Statistics Canada.

Bumiller, K. (2008). *In an abusive state: How neoliberalism appropriated the feminist movement against sexual violence.* Durham, NC: Duke University Press.

Buzawa, E. S., & Buzawa, C. G. (2003). *Domestic violence: The criminal justice response.* Thousand Oaks, CA: Sage.

Chunn, D.E., Boyd, S.B., & Lessard, H. (2007). *Reaction and resistance: Feminism, law, and social change.* Vancouver: UBC Press.

Comack, E. (1993). Feminist engagement with the law: The legal recognition of the battered woman syndrome. *CRIAW Papers 31.*

Corsilles, A. (1994). No-drop policies in the prosecution of domestic violence cases: Guarantee to action or dangerous solution? *Fordham Law Review, 63,* 853-881.

Côté, A., Kérisit, M., & Côté, M. (2001). *Qui prend pays— l'impact du parrainagesur les droits à l'égalité des femmes immigrantes.* Ottawa: Condition féminine Canada.

Cretney, A., & Davis, G. (1997). Prosecuting domestic assault: Victims failing courts or courts failing victims? *Howard Journal of Criminal Justice, 36*(2), 146-157.

Dawson, T. B. (1994). *Relating to law: A chronology of women and law in Canada* (2nd ed.). Concord, ON: Captus Press.

DeKeseredy, W.S. (1999). Tactics of the antifeminist backlash against Canadian national violence against women surveys. *Violence Against Women, 5*(11), 1258-1276.

DeKeseredy, W. S., & Hinch, R. O. (1991). *Woman abuse: Sociological perspectives.* Toronto: Thompson Educational Publishing.

DeKeseredy, W. S., & MacLeod, L. (1997). *Woman abuse: A sociological story.* Toronto: Harcourt Brace & Company.

Dinovitzer, R., & Dawson, M. (2007). Family-based justice in the sentencing of domestic violence. *British Journal of Criminology, 47,* 655-670.

Dobash, R. E., & Dobash, R. (1979). *Violence against wives: A case against the patriarchy.* New York: Free Press.

Dobash, R. E., & Dobash, R.P. (1992). *Women, violence and social change.* London: Routledge.

Dragiewicz, M. (2008). Patriarchy reasserted: Fathers' rights and anti-VAWA activism. *Feminist Criminology, 3*(2), 121-144.

Dugan, L., Nagin, D. S., & Rosenfeld, R. (1999). Explaining the decline in intimate partner homicide: The effects of changing domesticity, women's status, and domestic violence resources. *Homicide Studies, 3*(3), 187-214.

Durfee, A. (2012). Situational ambiguity and gendered patterns of arrest for intimate partner violence. *Violence Against Women, 18*(1), 64-84.

Eley, S. (2005). Changing practices: The specialised domestic violence court process. *The Howard Journal, 44*(2), 113-124.

Farley, M., Lynne, J., & Cotton, A. (2005). Prostitution in Vancouver: Violence and colonization of First Nations women. *Trans Cultural Psychiatry, 42*(2), 242-271.

Forrestor, T. (2011). *Hidden from sight volume II: A profile of violence against women in Ottawa.* Ottawa: Ottawa Coalition to End Violence Against Women.

Fraser, J. (2013). Claims-making in context: Forty years of Canadian feminist activism on violence against women. (Unpublished doctoral dissertation). Department of Criminology, University of Ottawa, Ottawa.

Gotell, L. (1998). A critical look at state discourse on "violence against women": Some implications for feminist politics and women's citizenship. In M. Tremblay & C. Andrew (Eds.), *Women and political representation in Canada* (pp. 39-84). Ottawa: University of Ottawa Press.

Gotell, L. (2010). Canadian sexual assault law: Neoliberalism and the erosion of feminist inspired law reform. In C. McGlynn & V. E. Munro (Eds.), *Rethinking rape law: International and comparative perspectives* (pp. 209-223). London: Routledge.

Grauwiler, P. (2008). Voices of women: Perspectives on decision-making and the management of partner violence. *Children and Youth Services Review, 30*(3), 311-322.

Hanna, C. (1996). No right to choose: Mandated victim participation in domestic violence prosecutions. *Harvard Law Review, 109*(8), 1849-1910.

Herman, J. L. (2005). Justice from the victim's perspective. *Violence against Women, 11*(5), 571-602.

Holder, R. (2008). Catch-22: Exploring victim interests in a specialist family violence jurisdiction. *International Journal of Comparative and Applied Criminal Justice, 32*(2), 265-290.

Holder, R., & Mayo, N. (2003). What do women want? Prosecuting family violence in the ACT. *Current Issues in Criminal Justice, 15*(1), 5-25.

Hornick, J. P., Boyes, M., Tutty, L. M., & White, L. (2008). The Yukon's domestic violence treatment option: An evaluation. In J. Ursel, L. M. Tutty, & J. leMaistre (Eds.).*What's law got to do with it? The law, specialized courts and domestic violence in Canada* (pp. 172-193). Toronto: Cormorant Books.

Hoyle, C. (1998). *Negotiating domestic violence: Police, criminal justice and victims.* Oxford: Oxford University Press.

Jaffe, P., Wolfe, D. A., Telford, A., & Austin, G. (1986). The impact of police charges in incidents of wife abuse. *Journal of Family Violence, 1*(1), 37-49.

Johnson, H. (1996). *Dangerous domains: Violence against women in Canada.* Toronto: Nelson Canada.

Johnson, H., & Fraser. J. (2011). *Specialized domestic violence courts: Do they make women safer? Community report: Phase 1.* Ottawa: Department of Criminology, University of Ottawa.

Johnson, H., & Sacco, V. F. (1995). Researching violence against women: Statistic Canada's national survey. *Canadian Journal of Criminology, 37*(3), 281-304.

Jones, H., & Cook, K. (2008). *Rape crisis: Responding to sexual violence.* Dorset: Russell House Publishing.

Landau, T. C. (2000). Women's experiences with mandatory charging for wife assault in Ontario Canada: A case against the prosecution. *International Review of Victimology, 7,* 141-157.

Landsberg, M. (2011). *Writing the revolution.* Ottawa: Feminist History Society.

Loseke, D. R. (2003). Formula stories and support groups for battered women. In D. R. Loseke & J. Best (Eds.), *Social problems: Constructionist readings* (pp. 241-247). New York: Aldine de Gruyter.

Loseke, D. R., & Kurz, D. (2005). Men's violence toward women is the serious social problem. In D. R. Loseke, R. J. Gelles, & M. M. Cavanaugh (Eds.), *Current controversies on family violence* (pp. 79-95). Thousand Oaks, CA: Sage.

MacLeod, L. (1980). *Wife battering in Canada: The vicious circle.* Ottawa: Minister of Supply and Services Canada.

Macy, R. J., Giattina, M. C., Parish, S. L., & Crosby, C. (2010). Domestic violence and sexual assault services: Historical concerns and contemporary challenges. *Journal of Interpersonal Violence, 25*(1), 3-32.

Matthews, N. A. (1994). *Confronting rape: The feminist anti-rape movement and the state*. New York: Routledge.

Maxwell, C. D., Garner, J. H., & Fagan, J. S. (2001). *The effects of arrest on intimate partner violence: New evidence from the spouse assault replication program*. Washington, DC: Department of Justice, National Institute of Justice.

McIntyre, S. (1994). Redefining reformism: The consultations that shaped Bill C-49. In J. V. Roberts & R. M. Mohr (Eds.). *Confronting sexual assault: A decade of legal and social change* (pp. 293-314). Toronto: University of Toronto Press.

Miedema, B., & Wachholz, S. (1998). *Une toile complexe: L'accès au système de justice pour les femmes immigrantes victimes de violence au Nouveau-Brunswick*. Ottawa: Condition féminine Canada.

Mills, L. G. (1999). Killing her softly: Intimate abuse and the violence of state intervention. *Harvard Law Review, 113*, 550-613.

Minaker, J. C. (2001). Evaluating criminal justice responses to intimate abuse through the lens of women's needs. *Canadian Journal of Women and the Law, 13*(1), 74-106.

Nancarrow, H. (2007). In search of justice for domestic and family violence: Indigenous and non-Indigenous Australian women's perspectives. *Theoretical Criminology, 10*(1), 87-106.

Native Women's Association of Canada. (2010). *What their stories tell us: Research findings from the Sisters in Spirit initiative*. Ohsweken, ON: Native Women's Association of Canada.

Parent, C., & Coderre, C. (2004). Paradoxes des théories féministes sur la violence contre les conjointes. *La Revue Nouvelle, 11*, 36-45.

Pierson, R. R. (1993). The politics of the body. In R. R. Pierson, M. G. Cohen, P. Bourne, & P. Masters (Eds.), *Canadian women's issues, volume 1: Strong voices* (pp. 98-185). Toronto: James Lorimer & Company.

Pontel, M., & Demczuk, I. (2007). *Répondre aux besoins des femmes immigrantes et des communautés ethnoculturelles*. Montréal: Fédération de ressources d'hébergement pour femmes violentées et en difficulté du Québec.

Prairie Research Associates (PRA). (2006). *Evaluation of the domestic violence court program*. Ottawa: Ontario Ministry of the Attorney General.

Randall, M. (2004). Domestic violence and the construction of "ideal victims": Assaulted women's "image problems" in law. *St Louis University Public Law Review, 23*, 107-154.

Rebick, J. (2005). *Ten thousand roses: The making of a feminist revolution*. Toronto: Penguin Canada.

Robinson, A. L. (2008). Measuring what matters in specialist domestic violence courts. *Cardiff School of Social Sciences Working Paper 102*. Retrieved from http://www.cardiff.ac.uk/socsi/ resources/wp102.pdf

Rojas-Viger, C. (2008). L'impact des violences structurelle et conjugale en contexte migratoire: perceptions d'intervenants pour le contrer. *Nouvelles pratiques sociales, 20*(2), 124-141.

Schechter, S. (1982). *Women and male violence: The visions and struggles of the battered women's movement*. Boston: South End.

Schneider, E. M. (2000). *Battered women & feminist lawmaking*. New Haven: Yale University Press.

Sheptycki, L. W. G. (1991). Using the state to change society: The example of domestic violence. *Journal of Human Justice, 3*(1), 47-66.

Sherman, L. W. (1992). The influence of criminology on criminal law: Evaluating arrests for misdemeanor domestic violence. *Journal of Criminal Law and Criminology, 83*(1), 1-45.

Sherman, L. W., & Berk, R. A. (1984). *The Minneapolis domestic violence experiment.* Washington: Police Foundation.

Spector, M., & Kitsuse, J. (2009). *Constructing social problems.* New Brunswick, NJ: Transaction.

Straus, M. A. (2005). Women's violence toward men is a serious social problem. In D. R. Loseke, R. J. Gelles, & M. M. Cavanaugh (Eds.), *Current controversies on family violence* (pp. 55-77). Thousand Oaks, CA: Sage.

Tutty, L., McNichol, K., & Christensen, J. (2008). Calgary's HomeFront specialized domestic violence court. In J. Ursel, L. M. Tutty, & J. leMaistre (Eds.), *What's law got to do with it? The law, specialized courts and domestic violence in Canada* (pp. 152-171). Toronto: Cormorant Books.

Ursel, J., & Hagyard, C. (2008). The Winnipeg family violence court. In J. Ursel, L. M. Tutty, & J. leMaistre (Eds.), *What's law got to do with it? The law, specialized courts and domestic violence in Canada* (pp. 95-119). Toronto: Cormorant Books.

Ursel, J., Tutty, L. M., & leMaistre, J. (2008). *What's law got to do with it? The law, specialized courts and domestic violence in Canada.* Toronto: Cormorant Books.

Walker, L. (1979). *The battered woman.* New York: Harper & Row.

Warrington, M. (2001). "I must get out": The geographies of domestic violence. *Transactions of the Institute of British Geographers, 26*(3), 365-381.

Weaver, H. (2009). The colonial context of violence: Reflections on violence in the lives of Native American women. *Journal of Interpersonal Violence, 24*(9), 1552-1563.

WHO & London School of Hygiene and Tropical Medicine. (2010). *Preventing intimate partner and sexual violence against women: Taking action and generating evidence.* Geneva: WHO.

PART 4

STATE VIOLENCE AND CONTROL: TERRORISM, PROTEST, AND GENOCIDE

Canadian Responses to Terrorism: Attitudes and Actions

Learning Objectives

In this chapter you will...

► examine the importance of the problems associated with defining terrorism

► assess the nature differing interpretations of Canadian political culture

► compare and contrast Canadian government responses to the October Crisis of 1970 and the events of 9/11

► describe the Canadian people's reactions to authoritarian measures

► appraise the tendency of law enforcement to use surveillance and data mining technology for purposes more expansive than necessary anti-terrorist measures

Chapter 13

Howard A. Doughty

Toward a Definition of Terrorism

Academic treatments of controversial political topics often begin with careful definitions. This is sometimes tiresome and needlessly pedantic. In the case of terrorism, however, it is less so. Terrorism is what W. B. Gallie (1956) famously called an "essentially contested concept," which is to say that discussions about it – like beauty, justice, democracy and evil – depend less on empirical evidence or logical argument than upon definitions. Such terms are evaluative, complex, imprecise, and generally resistant to empirical description and verification. We fight over what we think the word means.

A less lethal example than terrorism is the concept of art. Whether we like realistic paintings by Cornelius Krieghoff and J. J. Audubon or abstract works by Jackson Pollock and Lawren Harris depends a great deal on whether we define art as a faithful representation of reality or as an expression of feelings. Such definitions affect our opinions not only about particular artists, but also about our aesthetic sensibilities generally and how we interpret beauty.

So it is with terrorism and how we view politics. Just as specific artistic styles are followed in the pursuit of beauty and the expression of human identity, so terrorism is a tactic in the conduct of conflict, but it is also more. It not only poses an immediate threat to civilians, law enforcement officers and soldiers, all in the name of advancing some political cause, but it also invites existential questions of what defines our humanity and what moral values do or should regulate our behaviour.

No one has yet supplied an unambiguous and comprehensive meaning for terrorism of the sort that would be useful in defining it as a legally binding basis for domestic or international crime. Terrorism is generally understood as the use of violence by non-state actors seeking to intimidate the general public or specific minority groups. The terrorists' main aim may either be to maim or kill specific targets or it may be to undermine the authority of the state by demonstrating that the government is unable to exercise its most basic function – the task of upholding public order and ensuring the safety of its citizens. In the latter case, the objective is to provoke a crisis of legitimacy as a crucial step toward the overthrow of authority and thereby of the social power structure.

Of course, there are also ample instances of state-sponsored terrorism. Examples are the so-called paramilitary "death squads" that once terrorized numbers of countries in Latin America. They sought to frighten political dissidents, often with the tacit support of national governments. As well, sometimes governments in "police states" have used terror to suppress dissent or, in a recent, odious euphemism, to promote "ethnic cleansing." Whether acts by small groups of assassins, guerrilla organizations aiming to overthrow a government, governments that want to control rebellious elements, or ethno-religious communities nursing ancient hatreds, anyone studying terrorism knows that it's complicated.

Even the most well-intentioned and methodical attempts by the United Nations to define terrorism have failed, mainly due to different political opinion about who is and who is not a terrorist. In the 1970s, for instance, Nelson Mandela was described by the Government of Canada as a terrorist, but he was made an honourary citizen of Canada in 1991 and awarded the Nobel Peace Prize in 1993.

Likewise, combatants and their supporters in the Near East, Latin America, Africa, Asia, and elsewhere have disagreed violently about which side is the terrorist in various conflicts. So, similar tactics were employed by future Israeli Prime Minister Menachem Begin's Irgun group in their battle for independence from the United Kingdom to those later employed by the Palestine Liberation Organization under Yasser Arafat against Israel to win a Palestinian homeland.

As well, in Nicaragua, the Sandinista National Liberation Army was declared a terrorist organization by the United States when it fought against the dictatorship of Anastasia Somoza (1961-1979); when, however, the Sandinistas ousted Somoza, the United States promptly (and illegally) funded the "Contras," a coalition of Somoza supporters. The Sandinista government (1979-1990) survived the Contra's violence and voluntarily yielded power after a democratic election. Throughout almost forty years of suffering, who were really the terrorists?

Terrorism is an emotion-laden term that goes far beyond the cliché that one person's "terrorist" is another's "freedom-fighter." Defining terrorism is more than a dispassionate matter of classification. It tests the boundaries of what we are pleased to call civilized life.

Aristotle (384-322 BCE) called our species *zoon politikon* (political animals). He meant that we are inherently social creatures and that an essential part of human nature is our participation in our communities. The "polis" was the ancient Greek city-state, the primary form of government and organized social affairs. Aristotle believed that politics – involvement community affairs – was our most ennobling vocation and our highest secular calling. In contrast, in 1832, Carl von Clausewitz (1968, p. 119) said that war was merely carrying on politics by other means.

Echoing Aristotle and opposing von Clausewitz, the French philosopher Étienne Balibar (2008) explained that war is not an extension of politics but its *subversion*: "the use of violent means," he said, "reacts upon politics itself, or modifies politics. Politics cannot make use of the violent means of war without being transformed itself by the use of these means, and perhaps radically transformed, denatured."

Now, just as von Clausewitz's phrasing seemed to normalize nineteenth-century warfare, those who are currently composing a footnote to von Clausewitz are coming close to normalizing terrorism. They appear to be placing it within the category of understandable and potentially acceptable human actions. The prospect does not come easily to Canadians.

Canadian Political Culture

Citizens of Canada, regardless of their political opinions, have long indulged in the conceit that Canada is, as William Kilbourn (1970) described it, a "peaceable kingdom." It has been commonly accepted that Canada is largely defined by its differences from the United States. Canadians think of themselves as a more orderly country in which regard for established institutions and respect for law is deeply engrained. No simpler symbol of the difference can be found in two well-known encapsulations of the attitudes of each country – at least in their beginnings. In 1776, the *American Declaration of Independence* proclaimed that the new nation would be committed to the protection of individual "life, liberty and the pursuit of happiness." The first ten Amendments to the *Constitution of the United States* were ratified in 1791 and expanded personal liberties in their "Bill of Rights." Canada was more modest. In section 91 of the *British North America Act* (1867), Canadians were not guaranteed individual rights. That had to wait for the *Canadian Bill of Rights* (1961) and the fundamental law – the *Charter of Rights and Freedoms* (1982). Instead of an inventory of liberties, early Canadians were assured that they would enjoy "peace, order and good government."

There have been a number of approaches to the study of Canadian political culture. For our purposes, they can usefully be divided into four roughly distinct camps. First, in the mid-twentieth century, Harold A. Innis (1950, 1951, 1956; Easterbrook & Watkins, 1984) and his colleagues at the University of Toronto advanced the "staples thesis," which explained how a reliance on the export of natural resources shaped the attitudes of colonial Canadians. Though a political economist, his insights inspired studies of culture and communications – not least those of media guru Marshall McLuhan. Innis outlined a culture that was economically dependent, culturally derivative, and mainly interested in promoting wealth and stability by trade with large partners – in order, France, the United Kingdom, and the United States.

Second, George P. Grant (1918-1988), a devout Christian and political conservative, critically analyzed the emergence of the United States as a vast technological empire, the largest and most powerful in history. Grant judged that the Canadian project of building a conservative alternative to American society was destined to fail and wrote as much in his obituary for Canada, *Lament for a Nation* (1965). Somewhat paradoxically, it was Grant's work that led a number of radical young academics to re-examine Canadian culture in relation to its dependence on the American political economy. They combined Innis's economic analysis with Grant's moral fervour and, in some cases, became political activists in the "New Left" and worked for an independent socialist Canada (Lumsden, 1970; LaPierre et al., 1971; Teeple, 1972; Laxer, 1973). Grant, who respected the righteousness of their cause and sympathized with some of their objectives, was alternately approving, amused, and appalled.

Third, while ostensible socialists were pushing Grant's perspective to the left, some Canadian scholars were taking their cue from the American historian Louis Hartz (1964). They debated the question of how and to what degree the Hartzian thesis could be used to explain Canadian political culture. Hartz reckoned that every formerly colonial society could be understood best in terms of the culture from which it emerged in its "point of departure" from Europe. Each new society, he said, carried with it the political culture at the time of separation. Hence, French Canada was a "feudal fragment" of pre-revolutionary France, whereas the United States was mainly a product of the classical Lockean liberalism that dominated eighteenth-century Britain – except for the slave-owning South, which, in the century after its defeat in the Civil War, gradually gave up its traditions and, like the people of Quebec, sloughed off their customary constraints, embraced industrialism, and CNN to integrate with modernity or, perhaps in Quebec's case, postmodernity.

Hartz's point was not that new societies ossified, but that their pattern of ideological development and their founding institutions strongly reflected the attitudes of people who were in power when the nation gained self-government. So, the United States replicated the bourgeois values and formed what George Grant (1966) described as a country with "no history before the age of progress" (p. 125). As for Canada, at least since Confederation and excluding the Riel Rebellions in the latter third of the nineteenth century, its self-image and reputation is as a society that exhibits exemplary politeness, deference to authority and, perhaps, a little stodginess. Demands for social change are managed almost completely within the framework of legitimate parliamentary politics.

Canada has had no shortage of reformers, but there has been a distinct absence of revolutionaries. Assassinations (D'Arcy McGee in 1868) and the inchoate insurrections (the Winnipeg General Strike of 1919) have occurred, but they punctuate rather than write the national narrative. That narrative, of course, is a human convention and needs occasional revision; See (1997), for instance, reminds us that "the peaceable kingdom notion … suits 20th-century Canada far better than it does its 19th-century predecessor, when collective violence often erupted and Canadian communities experienced traumatic episodes that equaled in magnitude, if not frequency, various riots that rocked American cities" (p. 36); it is the received wisdom and current opinion.

Finally, we can turn to pointedly empirical studies by social scientists who have used the tools of their trade to decide how much respect for authority and the law actually characterizes Canadian life (Lipset, 1969, 1989; Truman, 1971, 1977; Adams, 2003). Foremost among the early analysts was the American sociologist Seymour Martin Lipset, who studied Canadian normative patterns with emphasis on elitism, populism, individualism, statism, and so on. By examining all aspects of Canadian and American society from government structures to entrepreneurs, trade unionists, religious and literary figures, he summed up a version of Canada's collective consciousness, the shared experiences, prevalent values, and common sentiments in the land. The result was a plausible reproduction of the notion of the peaceable kingdom. Canada, for instance, still has an appointed senate and homicide rate roughly one-third that of the United States. Still, there were accusations that Lipset's work was methodologically thin. As Truman (1971) boldly states, "Lipset's numbers are simply erroneous" (p. 497). Meantime, work by Michael Adams (2003) claimed that fundamental attitudes of Canadians are not merely different than those of Americans, but are growing further apart, as though Canada is changing and evolving, but the United States is not. If the hoary old question of the "Canadian identity" is raised, there is at least a credible case that it remains ill-expressed, but remains strong.

Attitudes into Actions I: The *War Measures Act*

To test the Canada's alleged deferential elitism and lack of liberal individualism, it is worthwhile exploring institutional responses to actual cases of terrorism. In Canada, the principal case concerns the Front de libération du Québec (FLQ), which was active from 1963 to 1970 and precipitated (not for the first time) the imposition of the *War Measures Act* upon Canadians; however, the jihadist attack on the United States in 2001 brought terrorism home to Americans, but also had a formidable impact on Canada.

In the past, Canadians had been concerned about subversion, and its government had acted swiftly. In September, 1945, Igor Gouzenko, a cipher clerk in the Embassy of the Union of Soviet Socialist Republics, defected. He revealed an operating spy network some say was the opening event in the Cold War. In response, Prime Minister William Lyon Mackenzie King signed a secret Order in Council activating the *War Measures Act*, an instrument that curtailed personal liberties while availing law enforcement agencies of almost unlimited powers of arrest, detention, and deportation. The critical facts about this extraordinary event concern the secrecy that surrounded it. King was worried, in part, that the existence of a Soviet spy ring would sabotage delicate negotiations at the United Nations and elsewhere. He also worried that there was insufficient evidence to convict the targeted spies. Accordingly, although arrests and trials followed, there was a marked difference between King's handling of the matter and that of Pierre Trudeau.

By 1970, circumstances had changed a great deal. Although there was still a fear of allegedly monolithic communist subversion at home and aggression abroad, Canadians were feeling a little more independent. Canada had annoyed the United States by declining to break relations with Cuba after Fidel Castro came to power. Prime Minister Lester B. Pearson had upset President Lyndon B. Johnson not only by refusing to commit Canadian soldiers to the military incursion into Vietnam, but also by openly criticizing American actions – especially the massive but ultimately ineffective bombing of North Vietnam. Also exasperating was Canada's welcome to United States' "draft dodgers" throughout the undeclared war.

In the process, anti-American feelings, which had been present to some degree since the American Revolution, were rekindled. A rather smug Canadian sense of moral superiority had been on display during the American civil rights movement as well as the Vietnamese adventure. It was joined by the personal popularity of Trudeau and, at least in parts of English-speaking Canada, a growing frustration with Quebec. Meantime, seeking full Quebec independence, the FLQ practised "the propaganda of the deed," which consisted of over 150 violent actions that killed eight people and injured many more. Bombs exploded in federal government symbols, notably postal boxes. There were well-publicized attacks on the Montreal Stock Exchange and the home of Montreal's mayor. When, therefore, an FLQ cell kidnapper British Trade Commissioner James Cross, the stage was set for dramatic action.

Cross was kidnapped on October 5, 1970. Quebec Labour Minister Pierre Laporte was kidnapped on October 10. On October 16, Prime Minister Trudeau invoked the *War Measures Act*, claiming an "apprehended insurrection" was taking place. The next day, Laporte was found dead. Importantly and contentiously, official documents not released until 2010 admit what the FLQ had contended – namely, that Laporte had died accidentally and had not been murdered (Radio-Canada, 2010).

The October Crisis, as this series of events came to be known, was controversial. There were accusations of weakness against Robert Bourassa, the Premier of Quebec, and Jean Drapeau, the mayor of Montreal, both of whom pleaded for federal intervention. Prime Minister Trudeau was accused of turning the event into a melodrama, not to save Cross and Laporte but to permanently crush the separatist movement. In fact, it has become clear that there was no compelling evidence of an apprehended insurrection, that Trudeau ignored advice he was given by law enforcement professionals, and that, "from a Machiavellian standpoint, Trudeau skillfully manipulated a crisis not of his making to effect an end that was in the national interest" (Whitaker, 2013, p. 250).

When the *War Measures Act* came before the House of Commons for a vote, New Democratic Party leader Tommy Douglas and most NDP members of Parliament voted against it, insisting that Canada faced criminal actions, not terrorism much less an apprehended insurrection. Robert Stanfield, the leader of the opposition and all but one Progressive Conservative voted in favour. The Canadian people approved; as historian Ramsay Cook baldly put it, Canadians "like peace and they like order … I don't think this has ever been a country that had an enormous interest in civil rights" (qtd. in Valpy, 2005, October 5). Later, further anti-separatist actions would be taken. The Royal Canadian Mounted Police (RCMP) would engage in illegal actions, including arson, in the effort to do away with the FLQ, and FLQ leader François Mario Bachand would be assassinated in Paris, apparently by members of the RCMP (McLoughlin, 1998).

During and in the immediate aftermath of the events of October 1970, public opinion polls showed that between 80% and 90% of Quebeckers supported the *War Measures Act* with even higher proportions in English-speaking Canada (Torrance, 2006, p. 39). Tommy Douglas openly and proudly opposed Trudeau's action, claiming that the prime minister had "used a sledgehammer to crack a peanut" (qtd. in Gray, 2000). Even thirty years later, his critics did not forgive his willingness to put civil liberties above Trudeau's theatrics. Robert Stanfield ultimately conceded that his decision to support the *War Measures Act* had been "the only regret of his long political career" (qtd. in McQueen, 2004). In time, public opinion would change as well … but not much. Many Canadians (or at least many of those who remember those events and recall cheering the government on) have altered their opinions, but the tendency to acquiesce that compromised freedom remained, especially before the *Charter of Rights and Freedoms* was passed to become an important Canadian symbol for newer generations.

Attitudes into Actions II: The *Anti-Terrorism Act*

Canadians may have had second thoughts about invocation of the *War Measures Act* in 1970 but the images of the collapse of the World Trade Center and the contention that the perpetrators were engaged in a jihad against Western civilization turned vague suspicions of non-Western cultures into resentment and rage. The events of September 11, 2001, known as 9/11, may not have "changed the world" as American politicians, print and broadcast media contend, but they certainly and significantly altered North Americans attitudes for a time.

Just as the United States rushed to pass the *Patriot Act*, which spawned the creation of the largest and most invasive domestic surveillance system in history, the *Canadian Anti-*

Terrorism Act was enacted quickly (and some now say thoughtlessly) in 2001. Even in later iterations, it permitted *in-camera* trials, pre-emptive detention, and expanded security and surveillance powers. The Liberal government of the day said that it was taking care to maintain a balance between public safety and civil rights; however, the few political figures such as federal NDP leader Alexa McDonough, who urged restraint and openly worried about the loss of privacy and political liberty, were openly hectored. Again, a majority of Canadians agreed that public protection outweighed concerns about individual liberties and due process of law; still, the rate of approval was barely half of what it had been in 1970 when pollsters had also invited public opinion on matters such as police powers to detain citizens without charge (Valpy, 2010).

What had happened? York University legal scholar Bruce Ryder explained that the willingness to defer to authority has been part of Canada's "tory" tradition from the beginning, but others such as Craig Forcese at the University of Ottawa pointed to the decline, saying that the *Charter of Rights and Freedoms* has become an important Canadian value and that rights are taken "more seriously" than in the past (Valpy, 2010). Interpreting the changes in Canadian attitudes is not easy. Some say that Canadians are becoming more "Americanized" and are therefore standing up for personal liberty more consistently. At the same time, however, both the governments of George W. Bush and Barack Obama have enabled a mass surveillance system and even a "kill list" of Americans suspected of terrorism. So, some suggest that Americans are becoming more deferential or are at least less effective in making their protests plain.

In Canada, moreover, there is growing skepticism about the credibility of the authorities Canadians used to implicitly trust. Disclosure of the falsehoods of the Trudeau administration, a series of well-publicized incidents of apparent police abuse of power at the APEC Summit in Vancouver in 1997 and the G20 meeting in Toronto in 2010, the consideration given to the ordeal of Maher Arar who was "renditioned" for torture in Egypt and Syria (Government of Canada, 2006), and even the fate of Canadian "child soldier" Omar Khadr in Guantánamo Bay, Cuba have added to concerns about the promise of "good government" as well as peace and order. Three other factors merit consideration. They are the changing Canadian demographic, the vast power of new information technology, and the culture that it insinuates into large organizations.

First, while there is merit in the argument that Canada's founding institutions and ideology fostered a combination of awe and obsequiousness in the face of political and social elites, the past fifty years of immigration have brought multiculturalism as a sociological fact of Canadian life. Recent migrants from China, India, the Philippines and the Caribbean cannot be expected to share the same values as seventeenth-century habitants or eighteenth-century United Empire Loyalists.

Second, as psychologist Abraham Maslow said, "to a man with a hammer, everything looks like a nail"; so, to people with easy access to information, everything becomes data to be used regardless of the purpose. In more forbidding terms, there is a "technological imperative" that suggests: if it can be done, it will be done, and it must be done. One response to terrorism is to try to apprehend terrorists, preferably before they commit hideous deeds. Unfortunately, the development of the means to do so ensures that the technologies may be used for other purposes.

Even after more than a decade, the pall of 9/11 has not wholly diminished. The events of that day, however, have not changed the world so much as the North American reaction has changed both the United States and Canada. The effects of massive increases in funding, the proliferation of agencies tasked with collecting and analyzing "big data," and the enormous development of "the national security state" have created a political atmosphere in which routine investigations have rendered the right to privacy almost obsolete. Torin Monahan's (2011) helpful definition of surveillance as "the systematic monitoring of people or groups in order to regulate their behavior" (p. 198) pushes the study of such practices well beyond Foucault's (1977) meditations on the "panopticon" far into the background. No longer is surveillance limited to people incarcerated in criminal or mental health facilities; surveillance is now pervasive as well as invasive, and we are all inmates in the prison and asylum of modernity.

Enormous corporate institutions – both public and private – and the all-encompassing "social media" make it clear that almost no interaction with others can, is, or will not be monitored whether in closed-circuit security television, online financial transactions, or voluntary posts on Facebook. In this atmosphere of high technology communications exchange, storage, and retrieval, the expectation that governments can and will monitor personal behaviour makes a truism of the old joke "if you're not paranoid, you don't know half of what they're doing to you." The sheer technological capacity to scrutinize activity or to create alternate realities with altered records and documents is beyond most people's capacity to imagine, let alone to control.

Third, deploying information gathering devices and processes allows for governments to watch anyone it chooses; it is therefore likely to expand its range of sight. Defining the public interest to be anything that serves the needs or desires of the government in power, it is possible for dissident political groups to be infiltrated without the need for a police or intelligence officer to physically join a peace group, an Aboriginal group, a student group, or what you will. So, the ease, economy, and efficiency of spying on citizens is enormously expanded (although, to be fair, "fifth columnists" have not yet been robotized). As Shawn McCarthy (2013) reports, the "Harper government has lashed out at radical environmental groups that seek to block resource development, and use funding from foreign sources to undermine what the government sees as Canada's national interest." By naming Greenpeace, for instance, an extremist or a terrorist group, the government is able to use anti-terrorism to mold public attitudes. Jeffrey Monahan and Kevin Walby (2012) go on to explain that security and police have invented, conflated, and then unnecessarily amplified "threat categories" in an arbitrary process of "net-widening" that confuses and ultimately incapacitates law enforcement. And, finally, as former Solicitor-General Warren Allmand (2013) has reiterated, the call from the Public Safety Committee and from the head of the Arar inquiry to create a parliamentary standing committee "to ensure more robust transparency and genuine political accountability over the CSE and other national security agencies" should be heeded.

So, to return to the beginning: what is terrorism? It is unlikely to be defined satisfactorily; instead, it continues to be politically contentious. It will be temporarily defined for practical purposees. The definition will normally be determined by the rulers and more or less accepted by the ruled. From time to time, however, opportunities arise for political action in formal democracies. Knowledge can be powerful. Understanding elite behaviour is susceptible to scrutiny by citizens with the courage and the energy to live their lives as "political animals" in their own interest but also the best interests of their communities. Although finding out what governments and corporations are doing is not always easy, the demand for transparency is justified and the rewards of discovery are of immense value to anyone willing to accept the responsibilities and rewards of citizenship. Privacy concerns, absence of parliamentary oversight and threats to due process are just some of the issues that worry citizens about federal legislative initiatives as Canada becomes more deeply involved in North African, Near and Middle Eastern conflicts. The time is right for Canadians to reflect on past values, consider their relevance to present conditions, and make some decisions about the kind of culture they want to build. Absent such initiatives, the power of the corporate state may bring about consequences that seem remarkably like terrorism.

Keywords

Terrorism, political culture, War Measures Act, Anti-Terrorism Act

Review Questions

1. Is it important to grapple with the theoretical problems of defining complex concepts before making practical suggestions?
2. Is there a core Canadian value system that permits citizens to debate critical social issues in a constructive and civil fashion?
3. What criteria are important in striking a balance between individual freedom and public safety?
4. Is technology now more important than political principles in determining what society will be like in the twenty-first century?
5. Can democratic participation ensure that the authorities in government, business, science, and education act in the interest of the people they are entrusted to serve?

References

Adams, M. (2003). *Fire and ice: The United States, Canada and the myth of converging Values*. Toronto: Penguin.

Allmand, W. (2013, September 4). Canadians need answers on domestic spying powers. *Toronto Star*. Retrieved from www.thestar.com/opinion/commentary/2013/09/04/canadians_need_answers_on_domestic_spying_powers.html

Balibar, É. (2008). *Politics as war, war as politics. Post-Clausewitzian variations*. Centre International D'Étude de la Philosophie Francaise Contemporaine. Retrieved from http://www.ciepfc.fr/spip.php?auteur5

Easterbrook, W., & Watkins, M. (1984). The staple approach. In W. Easterbrook & M. Watkins. (Eds.), *Approaches to Canadian Economic History* (pp. 1-98). Ottawa: Carleton University Press.

Foucault, M. (1977). *Discipline and punish: The birth of the prison*. New York: Vintage.

Gallie, W. (1956). Essentially contested concepts. *Proceedings of the Aristotelian Society*, *56*, 167-198.

Government of Canada. (2006). Commission of inquiry into the actions of Canadian officials in relation to Maher Arar. *Report of the events relating to Maher Arar: Analysis and recommendations*. Retrieved from http://epe.lac-bac.gc.ca

Grant, G. (1965). *Lament for a nation: The defeat of Canadian nationalism.* Toronto: McClelland & Stewart.

Grant, G. (1966). Protest and technology. In C. Hanly (Ed.), *Revolution and response: Selections from the Toronto international teach-in* (pp. 122-125). Toronto: McClelland & Stewart.

Gray, J. (2000, September 30). How Trudeau halted the reign of terror thirty years later. *Globe and Mail* (Toronto). Retrieved from http://v1.theglobeandmail.com/series/trudeau/jgray2_sep30.html

Hartz, L. (1964). *The founding of new societies: Studies in the history of the United States, Latin America, South Africa, Canada and Australia.* New York: Harcourt, Brace & World.

Innis, H. (1950). *Empire and communication.* Oxford: Clarendon Press.

Innis, H. (1951). *The bias of communication.* Toronto: University of Toronto Press.

Innis, H. (1956). *The fur trade in Canada: An introduction to Canadian economic history* (Rev. ed.). Toronto: University of Toronto Press.

Kilbourn, W. (Ed.) (1970). *A guide to the peaceable kingdom.* Toronto: Macmaillan.

LaPierre, L., McLeod, J., Taylor, C., & Young, W. (1971). *Essays on the left: Essays in honour of T. C. Douglas.* Toronto: McClelland & Stewart.

Laxer, R. (1973). *(Canada) Ltd: The political economy of dependency.* Toronto: McClelland & Stewart.

Lipset, S. (1969). Revolution and counter-revolution: The United States and Canada. In *Revolution and counter-revolution: Change and persistence in social structures* (pp. 37-76). New York: Anchor Books.

Lipset, S. (1989). *Continental divide: The values and institutions of the United States and Canada.* New York: Routledge.

Lumsden, I. (1970). *Close the 49th parallel etc.: The Americanization of Canada.* Toronto: University of Toronto Press.

McCarthy, S. (2013, June 10). Opposition, privacy watchdog question spy agency's metadata collection. *Globe and Mail* (Toronto). Retrieved from http://www.theglobeandmail.com/news.politics/privacy-watchdog-on-spy-agencys-data-collection-we-want-to-find-out-more/article12459998/

McLoughlin, M. (1998). *Last stop, Paris: the assassination of Mario Bachand and the death of the FLQ.* Toronto: Viking.

McQueen, R. (2004, February). Remembering Robert Stanfield: A good humoured and gallant man. *Policy Options.* Retrieved from http://www.irpp.org/en/po/canadascities/remembering-robert-stanfield-a-good-humoured-and-gallant-man/

Monahan, J., & Walby, K. (2012). "…They attacked the city": Security intelligence, the sociology of protest policing and the anarchist threat at the 2010 G-20 Summit. *Current Sociology, 60*(5), 653-671.

Monahan, T. (2011). Surveillance as cultural practice. *Sociological Quarterly, 52,* 495-508.

Radio-Canada. (2010, September 24). "Révélations sur la mort de Pierre Laporte" [Revelations on the Death of Pierre Laporte]. *Radio-Canada* (in French). Retrieved from http://www.radio-canada.ca/nouvelles/Politique/2010/09/23/006-flq-mort-laporte.shtml

See, S. (1997). Nineteenth-century collective violence: Toward a North American context. *Labour/Le Travail, 39,* 13-38.

Teeple, G. (1972). *Capitalism and the national question in Canada.* Toronto: University of Toronto Press.

Torrance, J. (2006). *Public violence in Canada, 1867-1982*. Montreal and Kingston: McGill-Queen's University Press.

Truman, T. (1971). A critique of Seymour M. Lipset's article, "Value differences, absolute or relative": The English-speaking democracies. *Canadian Journal of Political Science, 4*(4), 497-525.

Truman, T. (1977). A scale for measuring a Tory streak in Canada and the United States. *Canadian Journal of Political Science, 10*(4), 597-614.

Valpy, M. (2010, Oct. 5) 40 years later: Security and the FLQ. *Globe and Mail*.

Von Clausewitz, C. (1968). *On war*. London: Penguin.

Whitaker, R. (2003). Keeping up with the neighbours? Canadian responses to 9/11 in historical and comparative context. *Osgoode Hall Law Journal, 41*(2 & 3).

Genocide in Canada? The Crimes against Humanity and War Crimes Act

Learning Objectives

In this chapter you will...

▶ gain an understanding of Canada's international treaty obligations regarding genocide

▶ consider the definition of genocide as it is applied in Canada

▶ recognize the key aspects of the debate regarding genocide in the context of Canada's Aboriginal Peoples

▶ identify Canada's response to the violence committed against Aboriginal Peoples

Chapter 14

Nicholas A. Jones and John A. Winterdyk

Introduction

Genocide, the act of committing (mass) violent crimes against group(s) with the intent to destroy the existence of the group(s), is not a new phenomenon. According to Chalk and Jonassohn (1990), its history can be traced back to the earliest formations of human societies during the early conflicts between city-states in the time of antiquity. Given the scale of the violence associated with genocide, one might assume it is worthy of garnering widespread attention and scrutiny when accusations of its occurrence both past and present arise – even, arguably, within a Canadian context. However, Winterdyk (2009) observes that, although a major human rights violation, genocide is a seldom-explored topic in criminology. Furthermore, Woolford and Thomas (2011) note that genocide in the context of the colonial experiences of Canadian Aboriginal peoples garners "little academic and even less public discussion" (p. 61).

Following the 2006 Indian Residential School Settlement Agreement (IRSSA) and Prime Minister Harper's resulting public apology to the former students of the residential school system there have been many questions raised as to the use of the term *genocide* to describe the plight of Aboriginal Peoples in colonial times (Woolford, 2013). In this chapter, we examine the subject of genocide within a Canadian context.

Definition of Genocide in Canada

Within a Canadian context, the definition of genocide is the result of a lengthy process that encapsulates the intertwining and interpretation of aspects of both international and domestic law. The definition that we use has a decidedly legalistic orientation.[1] The framework for the legal definition in Canada is derived from a number of international legal instruments, themselves the result of negotiation, collaboration, and compromise (Aust, 2010). MacDonald and Hudson (2011) refer to this process as "subject to a certain degree of horse-trading" (p. 10) – in other words – as a politically driven process, the various parties arrived at a compromise definition wherein the different parties negotiated based on their own interests. However, it is important to note that the existing legal definition, and therefore its interpretation, is much narrower than other definitions proffered. As Schabas (2006) notes, "the definition of genocide adopted by the UN General Assembly in December 1948 represents a dilution of a relatively broad concept proposed by Raphael Lemkin four years earlier" (p. 102). Significant within this "diluting process" is the omission of a variety of categories of protected groups and what might be considered within the realm of actual crimes, particularly, cultural genocide. The definition of genocide continues to evolve internationally with the creation of the international criminal tribunals for the former Yugoslavia and Rwanda, a number of "hybrid courts,"[2] and of the creation of the Statute of the International Criminal Court (Rome Statute) in 2002. This evolution has affected Canada's legal definition of genocide and the assessment of the case for genocide against Canada's Aboriginal peoples.

Although domestic courts were permitted to undertake prosecutions for genocide based on a state's signatory status to the UN Convention for the Prevention and Punishment of Genocide (UNGC), it is typically required that they have domestic legislation in place before proceeding. It was not until the crafting and enactment of the Rome Statute that countries began to reflect their signatory status within their own domestic laws (Rikhof, 2009).[3] Canada became a signatory to the Rome Statute in 1998. Although the convention was technically not in force until 2002, between the time when Canada signed on to the convention and its entry into force, they were obliged to refrain from any actions that would be considered to be in "bad faith," that is, undermine the purpose of the treaty. In addition, they were obliged to begin the process of drafting domestic legislation in congruence with the treaty. Canada fulfilled one aspect of their obligations by passing the Crimes against Humanity and War Crimes Act (CAHWC Act), on October 23, 2000. This legislation permits Canadian courts to "prosecute such crimes … committed both within and outside Canada" (Currie & Stancu, 2010, p. 834).

International Treaty Obligations

Canada's domestic judicial approach to addressing genocide has been shaped by various international treaty obligations. Canada ratified the UN Convention on the Prevention and Punishment of Genocide (UNGC) on September 3, 1952. Canada's signatory status to the UNGC effectively provided domestic recognition of the crime of genocide. However, it was not until 1985 that genocide was officially criminalized in Canadian law (see the Canadian Criminal Code section 318, "Advocating genocide." Unfortunately, as reported by MacDonald and Hudson (2011), the backdrop and rationalizations surrounding the amendments did not give any consideration to the array of crimes committed against First Nations people. Instead, the rational focused on the events that transpired in Europe during the Second World War. This change to the Criminal Code did provide an initial, albeit very restricted, definition of genocide. Section 318(2) of the Criminal Code states that "genocide means any of the following acts committed with intent to destroy in whole or in part any identifiable group, namely,

(a) killing members of the group; or (b) deliberately inflicting on the group conditions of life calculated to bring about its physical destruction." Additionally, the amendment focused solely on advocating, or promoting, genocide and not on the commission of any defined acts constituting the crime of genocide. Although broadening the UNGC's concept of "identifiable group," to include sexual orientation consistent with the *Charter of Rights and Freedoms,* the crimes of genocide were limited to killing and/or the physical destruction of the group. MacDonald and Hudson (2011) argue that the "deliberates and disingenuous" omissions of certain components of the UNGC in the amendments to the *Criminal Code* "have important ramifications for what Aboriginal peoples can claim as genocide in Canadian courts" (p. 12).

War Crimes and Crimes against Humanity Act

The enactment of the CAHWC Act is the result of a long and arduous process that reflects its international obligations and its stated policy of combating impunity for international crimes and addresses deficiencies in previously enacted Canadian law (Currie & Stancu, 2010). The Rome Statue is widely regarded as the "most contemporary formulation of the international law pertaining to [genocide, war crimes and crimes against humanity]" (Rikhof, 2009, p. 5). The implementation of the CAHWC Act meets the requirement set forward in the statute under Section 88 whereby: "State Parties shall ensure that there are procedures available under their national law for all forms of cooperation which are specified under this Part." Although the policy demonstrates Canada's commitment to the international fight against impunity, it is important to note that the focus of this policy emanated from, and is directed toward, crimes committed outside of Canada. In fact, as we shall encounter later in the chapter, "when dealing with genocidal acts committed within Canada, genocide is considered to have been a crime under international customary law only *following* the international adoption of the *Rome Statute* i.e., July 17, 1998" (MacDonald & Hudson, 2011, p. 13, italics in original).

In addition to the aforementioned treaty obligations, problems with Canadian legislation hampered the prosecution in four prominent Canadian cases. Of these cases *R v. Finta* was the source for the greatest criticisms, providing the "hardest and final blow to what has been a long overdue but laudable effort by Canada to address the issue of impunity" (Lafontaine, 2010, p. 271). The impact of the court decision sent the Canadian government "back to the drawing board, emerging with a re-calibrated approach in the new CAHWC Act" (Currie & Stancu, 2010, p. 835). Thus, the CAHWC Act defines genocide, as applicable in Canadian courts as:

> an act or omission committed with the intent to destroy, in whole or in part, an identifiable group of persons, as such, that, at the time and place of its commission, constitutes genocide according to customary international law or conventional international law or by virtue of its being criminal according to the general principles of law recognized by the community of nations, whether or not it constitutes a contravention of the law in force at the time of and in the place of its commission. (CAHWC Act, Article 4(3))

Furthermore, in accordance with Article 6 of the Rome Statute, the following acts are considered the constituent acts of genocide:

(a) Killing members of the group;
(b) Causing serious bodily or mental harm to members of the group;

(c) Deliberating inflicting on members of the group conditions of life calculated to bring about its physical destruction in whole or in part;

(d) Imposing measures intended to prevent births within the group; and

(e) Forcibly transferring children of the group to another group.

Having provided the background for and the definition of genocide in Canada, we turn our attention to the application of the law prohibiting genocide, particularly with regard to the well-documented "crimes" committed against Canada's Aboriginal peoples.

Is Genocide an Appropriate Legal Term in the Context of Canada's Aboriginal Peoples?

The operation and findings of the Truth and Reconciliation Commission of Canada (TRC) revived questions surrounding the use of the term *genocide* in relation to Aboriginal peoples in Canada. As noted by MacDonald and Hudson (2011), the idea of genocide has "merited close attention as a descriptor for what happened in Residential Schools" (p. 1). The debate over the use of the term *genocide* as it relates to Indigenous populations in general and Canada's Aboriginal peoples is centered on issues of "genocide definition, cultural destruction, and colonial genocide [each of which has] great bearing on the question of genocide(s) in Canada" (Woolford & Thomas, 2011, p. 62). Furthermore, the debate has been plagued by a lack of consideration given to Indigenous perspectives, focussing rather on applying Euro-centric comprehensions of genocide that relegating Indigenous understandings to the "borders" of genocide research (Bischoping & Fingerhut, 2006). Specifically, the authors argued that the "ambiguity of the genocide definition that complicates the classification of indigenous peoples' experiences; the limitations of genocide typologies in which indigenous genocides are separated from other cases; and the current emphasis in genocide research on prevention and prediction of new genocides, which entails a focus on perpetrators' motivations rather than on victims' experiences" (Bischoping & Fingerhut, 2006, p. 482) has shunted Indigenous perspectives out of the consciousness of genocide research. Finally, the oft-made distinction between "genocide" (pertaining to physical destruction) and "cultural genocide" (pertaining to cultural destruction) muddy the waters when giving consideration to Aboriginal perspectives. These concepts are not "ideal tools for undertaking this scrutiny" (Woolford, 2013, p. 16). As, Chrisjohn and Young (2006) argue, "even the phrase 'cultural genocide' is an unnecessary ellipsis: cultural genocide is genocide" (p. 63).

The discussion surrounding genocide in Canada is framed with the notion of "settler colonialism" wherein "policies of extermination and/or exploitation unto death were most pronounced in areas where Europeans sought to conquer indigenous territories and both displace and supplant their native populations" (Jones, 2006, p. 106). It is within the context of colonialism that the genocide question is explored. This context, however, provides substantial challenges when attempting to arrive at a definitive conclusion. The challenges stem from issues surrounding the diversity of experiences experienced by Aboriginal peoples over time (see Woolford, 2009). Given that the work of the TRC is ongoing and a final report remains in process, we are cognizant that, like MacDonald and Hudson (2011), "our knowledge about the IRS [Indian Residential School] system is evolving," and therefore our analysis is restricted as "any claims about genocide [are] based on 'facts' … on shifting sands" (p. 3).

Keeping these issues at the forefront, we now endeavour to explore the genocide question in Canada through the lens of the CAHWC Act.

Application of the Crimes against Humanity and War Crimes Act

In 2006, the Canadian government and the Assembly of First Nations negotiated the Indian Residential School Settlement Agreement (IRSSA) to redress the residential school experiences. With the exception of individualized accounts of survivors' experiences and a wider discussion of the potential for the use of the term *genocide*, the term itself is not present in any of the official documentation. Instead, individual abuses surrounding physical and sexual harms and the broader notion of damage to Aboriginal communities is recognized (Woolford, 2013).

A number of authors have written extensively on the colonial experiences of Aboriginal people in Canada, particularly with respect to the Indian residential school system and applied the UNGC in relation to these experiences (see Grant, 1996; Annett, 2001; Chrisjohn & Young, 2006; MacDonald & Hudson, 2011).[4] As we address the experience within the framework of the CAHWC Act, we remind the reader that the CAHWC Act is a true reflection of those identified in the UNGC. Therefore, the applicability of the five crimes elucidated in the CAHWC Act has been examined by these same authors and only a brief summary will be provided. The application represents a rather sweeping generalization that does not necessarily account for regional differential experiences. Nonetheless, in some locales, each of the constituting crimes of genocide has been demonstrably identified by various authors. As MacDonald (2012) notes, the cumulative effect of these claims is more than simply suggestive of the occurrence of genocide against Canada's Aboriginal peoples.

When trying to establish criminal responsibility for a crime, the prosecution must prove beyond a reasonable doubt the two required components of an offence, the *actus reus* (physical element) and *mens rea* (mental element). In abiding by the principle *actus non facit reum nisi mens sit rea*, the act alone is not sufficient in and of itself for a finding of guilt – the "guilty mind" must also be present.

Actus Reus – The Acts Constituting Genocide

1. "Killing members of the group." This first constituting crime linked to colonial and residential school policies that resulted in a grievous mortality rate associated with European diseases ravaging many Aboriginal communities and many residential schools in particular, where these children were essentially wards of the state and, therefore, under state care. Citing a report from Dr. Peter Bryce, Annett (2001) states, "the mortality level in Residential Schools averaged 40%, or more than 50,000 native children across Canada" (p. 14). In addition to deaths resulting from disease, many Aboriginal children died as a result of beatings. Whether these deaths were "intentional" is debated (Grant, 1996). Nevertheless, Chrisjohn and Young (2006) argue that, "on the basis of the calculated underfunding of the Churches and the failure to provide health care as specified in the numbered treaties, a case could be made that Canada did bring about the deaths of Aboriginal Peoples" (p. 60).

In a "modernist interpretation" (see Woolford, 2009), there is a hybridized separation between deaths arising from "natural" causes and those otherwise resulting. The implication is that death from disease is the result of natural causes and therefore not the same thing as deliberate killing. Given the statement above from Annett, and considering the notion of criminal negligence in Canadian law, we agree with Woolford's (2009) assertion that "any claim that this was simply 'natural' is exposed as disingenuous at best" (p. 91).

2. "Causing serious bodily or mental harm to members of the group." Once again, it is clear that a multitude of acts committed within the confines of residential schools confirms the existence of these crimes (see Macdonald & Hudson, 2011). Meanwhile, Grant (1996) argues that "the greatest abuse ... consisted of mental and psychological abuse which destroyed the bond between children and their parents, culture and language" (p. 272). The impact of these crimes was experienced beyond the walls of the residential schools, permeating into the communities from which these children were removed. The assault on Aboriginal culture wherein "all things associated with Indigenous life are presented as profane, dirty, backward, and an obstacle to survival" (Woolford, 2013, p. 25) severely impacted Aboriginal self-identity for generations. Former students no longer "belonged" in their own communities; nor did they belong in the wider society, and this sense of non-belonging manifested itself "as a more general inability to form and maintain human relationships" (Woolford, 2013, p. 25). Beyond the confines of the residential school system, the widespread attempted destruction of Aboriginal culture through the legal banning of culturally significant traditions, such as the potlatch and sun dance, eroded a sense of Aboriginal identity (Woolford, 2009). This has resulted in "continuing cycles of emotional, physical, and sexual abuse, as well as addiction, suicide, and other markers of intergenerational trauma, within Aboriginal communities" (Woolford, 2009, p. 85).

3. "Deliberately inflicting on members of the group conditions of life calculated to bring about its physical destruction." According to Woolford (2013), by ignoring Aboriginal perspectives, this focus has resulted in a determination of genocide focussed on the destructions of "lives within a group" rather than the destruction of "group life" (p. 29). Nevertheless, there is evidence pertaining to the existence of both. The governmental policy of assimilation described by Grant (1996) as "designed to eradicate all traces of their Indianness" (p. 273) certainly speaks to the destruction of group life, that is, any vestige of Aboriginal culture including traditions, language, and identity. Woolford (2013) further notes the importance of the erosion of Aboriginal rights and self-governance and loss of land as contributing to the erosion of group life.

The physical destruction of Aboriginal peoples is evident in relation to the "killing of members of the group" previously discussed. Primary among the "conditions created" is the transmission of disease to Aboriginal peoples whether through arguably negligent treatment within residential schools or more widely (MacDonald & Hudson, 2011). Annett (2001) cites a 1953 article in the *Globe and Mail* wherein he recalled the statement made by Trevor Jones (an official in the Anglican Church) that it was "the federal government's practice of 'not hospitalizing Indians and Eskimos with tuberculosis' because of an 'unofficial attitude ... that they were dying races and wouldn't last long'" (p. 38).

4. "Imposing measures intended to prevent births within the group." Grant (1996) posits that this genocidal act was not directly evident within the residential school but existed in a broader sense in the forced sterilizations of Aboriginal women. Annett (2001) provides evidence of laws passed in Canada that facilitated these acts. Although not specifically directed at Aboriginal peoples in that they applied to "any inmate of a penitentiary, mental institute, or 'industrial School' ... any Aboriginal child or youth in Canada could legally undergo sexual sterilization at the whim of one man, the School principal – and thousands of native people were subsequently sterilized under these laws" (Annett, 2001, p. 44). In addition to forced sterilization, forced abortions were "more prevalent than sterilizations ... [and] common practice" (Annett, 2001, p. 46), and many of these procedures resulted in the additional deaths due to unsound medical practices.

5. "Forcibly transferring children of the group to another group." The residential school system was the result of the federal government's exercise of "plenary constitutional power" under the *British North America Act* (Jago, 1998, p. 40). This power, not clearly articulated at any time during the signing of the various treaties with respect to the colonial enterprise, provided the federal government with control over the education of Aboriginal youth (Jago, 1998). This same power was exercised in the in the creation of the *Indian Act,* which, through amendment, made Aboriginal youth education at residential schools mandatory by 1920. The amendment further made it criminal for children not to attend residential schools or for parents to prevent their attendance (Jago, 1998; Woolford, 2013). Another example that extends beyond the experience of that of residential schools is what has been referred to as the "'60's scoop," wherein as a result of legislative changes to the *Indian Act* Aboriginal children were removed from their homes and adopted by non-Aboriginal families (Blackstock, 2011).

Although the above discussion presented a broad generalization of acts that transpired over the course of colonial history and geographical locales, this discussion is not exhaustive; nor does it reflect the differential experiences of the array of Canada's Aboriginal groups. Nevertheless, the evidence suggests that, indeed, all of the crimes that fall under the CAHWC Act that constitute the commission of genocide are present in some form at some time. We now proceed to the second element required for successfully prosecuting genocide, the proof of *mens rea*, the guilty mind.

Mens Rea - The Dolus Specialus (Intent) for Genocide

In the *Prosecutor v. Akayesu*, the Trial Chamber at the International Criminal Tribunal for Rwanda (ICTR) stated, "genocide is distinct from other crimes as it embodies a special intent or *dolus specialus* ...Thus, the special intent in the crime of genocide lies in 'the intent to destroy, in whole or in part'" (Para. 498). It is this special intent that differentiates genocide from the individual crimes that may constitute it. In essence, genocide is defined more in reference to its intention than it is to the actions that constitute it (MacDonald, 2012).

In order to prove the existence of the genocide, "the prosecutor must place the actions and intentions of the accused within the wider context of the entire event" (Jones, 2010, p. 134). The difficulty of proving the "special intent" of genocide has repeatedly been the primary stumbling block in achieving convictions for the "crime of crimes" across many cases.[5] This is especially evident in the "context of colonial injustices" (MacDonald & Hudson, 2011, p. 16).

One issue facing the analysis of *mens rea* is the difficulty of the expansive time and geographical space covered by colonialism and the residential school system. Unlike in other cases such as in Rwanda or Srebrenica (Bosnia), wherein the mass violence was an isolated event in time and location, colonial and residential school system violence existed over many decades and across vast geographic spaces, and, most importantly, was not experienced in the same manner in all places and times. Furthermore, as Woolford (2009) notes, "it would be difficult to legally prove the existence of a formal plan of annihilation" (p. 86). This becomes even more uncertain when, as Grant explains (1996), "it would be a mistake to leave the impression that nothing beneficial came out of the Residential School system or that there were no good people in the Schools" (p. 275). While recognizing the atrocities that took place at some schools, it is clear that the implementation of the residential school policy varied across locations. This could be construed as undermining the establishment of the genocidal intent. However, the policy of assimilation and components of the *Indian Act* were clear in their intention.

Furthermore, the policy was premised upon a foundation that it disregarded the humanity of Aboriginal people. In a manner similar to that observed in Australia, Woolford (2009) explains, "the source of destruction may lie less in an unambiguous 'intent to destroy' a human group, than in the presumption that there was not much to destroy" (p. 92). The definition of what constitutes a "group" could be viewed as problematic given the diversity of the Aboriginal peoples in Canada. However, the fact that the policies created by the federal government ascribe a singular group status should be sufficient to dispel any concerns of this nature.

Second, the oft-recorded "intent" of the residential school system was humanitarian-based, with the "best interests" of the Aboriginal people at the very heart of the process (MacDonald, 2012; Woolford, 2009, 2013).[6] This "civilizing project" (Woolford, 2009) and its intended "moral uplift" (Woolford, 2013) appear benign when considering the intentions of the residential school system. However, does this excuse those involved from any sense of culpability given the outcomes? The case of the *Prosecutor v. Akayesu* may be informative in that genocidal intent was inferred from the consequences of the actions undertaken (Jones, 2010). If, as observed in the genocide case of *R v. Munyaneza* (2009), Canadian courts are both able and willing to look to international jurisprudence for guidance, the conceptualization of inferred intent may be relevant in Canada, further supporting the establishment of the *mens rea* in the case of the crimes against Aboriginal peoples.

The politics surrounding the means by which crimes committed against Aboriginal peoples are addressed have resulted in a bifurcated response to genocide in Canada. In the case of foreign nationals (i.e., Finta, Munyaneza, and Mungwarere) the primary avenue for addressing alleged international crimes, including genocide, has been prosecution. However, despite the CAHWC Act representing Canada's adoption of the Rome Statute, only in cases where genocide was allegedly committed outside Canadian borders can the law be applied retroactively. As MacDonald and Hudson (2011) observe, "when dealing with genocidal acts committed within Canada, genocide is only considered to have been a crime under international customary law only *following* the international adoption of the *Rome Statute*." (p. 13). As such, the crimes committed within Canadian borders prior to 1998 are excluded from genocide prosecutions.[7] In response to "certain harms and abuses" committed against Aboriginal children at residential schools, on May 8, 2006 the Government of Canada entered into the Indian Residential Schools Settlement Agreement.

The IRSSA - Truth and Reconciliation Commission for Aboriginal Peoples

Yacoubian (2003) notes, "the international community has relied on five ways of responding to violations of international criminal law: (1) doing nothing; (2) granting amnesty; (3) creating a truth commission; (4) domestic prosecutions; and (5) creating ad hoc international tribunals"

(p. 135). What may account for the different mechanisms employed in addressing these crimes is the different end goal of each process dependent on its contextual relevance.

Unlike the criminal prosecutions of foreign nationals in Canadian courts, designed to contribute to international efforts to eradicate the culture of impunity, reduce the safe havens available to perpetrators, and add to international jurisprudence, the IRSSA seeks a "fair, comprehensive and lasting resolution of the legacy of Indian Residential Schools" (IRSSA, 2006, p. 6). The process by which it seeks to achieve these aims is multifaceted. It identifies the following mechanisms for redress:[8]

(i) to settle the Class Actions and the Cloud Class Action, ...;
(ii) to provide for payment by Canada of the Designated Amount to the Trustee for the Common Experience Payment;
(iii) to provide for the Independent Assessment Process;
(iv) to establish a Truth and Reconciliation Commission;
(v) to provide an endowment to the Aboriginal Healing Foundation to fund healing programmes addressing the legacy of harms suffered at Indian Residential Schools including the intergenerational effects; and
(vi) to provide funding for the commemoration of the legacy of Indian Residential Schools. (IRSSA, 2006, pp. 6-7)

In addition to the specifics of the IRSSA, Prime Minister Harper presented an apology in the House of Commons on June 11, 2008. In the apology, he formally recognized that the policy of assimilation and the objectives designed to achieve them were wrong and caused great harm; and the apology called for forgiveness and healing (Prime Minister, June 11, 2008). Absent from the apology is any reference to genocide. However, the apology "goes well beyond the narrow framing of the 1996 'statement of regret,' ... [and] acknowledges not simply physical and sexual harms, but also the harm of forced assimilation and its impact on Indigenous communities" (Woolford, 2013, p. 9).

While criminal prosecutions for genocide are clearly absent, and unlikely to ever occur, this does not, however, exclude the concept of accountability for what transpired. For example, research following the mass violence in Bosnia and Herzegovina observed that "active responsibility," defined as demonstrating remorse through confession and apology, was positively correlated with dialogical-based processes (where victims are provided the opportunity to share their experiences), as well as demonstrating a stronger relationship with trust and reconciliation than "imposed obligations" (where perpetrators are judicially required to make amends for their wrongdoings (Jones, Parmentier, & Weitekamp, 2012). It appears that the processes outlined in the IRSSA have the potential to facilitate the achievement of its stated goals, primary among which is reconciliation. Additionally, the provision of testimony, wherein survivors are provided an opportunity to share their experiences, "while painful, is often the beginning of healing that is important in properly dealing with the residential school experience" (Assembly of First Nations, 2002, p. 5).

However, to be truly transformative, the work of the TRC must fully acknowledge the experiences of Aboriginal peoples in the broadest sense possible. It must avoid the trap of asserting itself and its outcomes from a colonialist perspective. As Woolford (2013) observes, "unfortunately, so many of our redress processes are directed toward inserting the Indigenous person into the reaffirmed colonial universe, where practices of economic, symbolic, and linguistic domination sit unchallenged" (p. 29).

Of noted significance in progressing in a truly transformative manner, are the challenges faced in the (re)construction of collective memories, especially the recognition of genocide (MacDonald, 2012; Woolford, 2013). The label attached to the atrocities committed against Aboriginal peoples in the residential schools and beyond has significance. The disparity between what Aboriginal people experienced and what is more widely accepted in the broader Canadian society remains an issue that the TRC must face. As MacDonald (2012) suggests, "a full engagement implies seeing the residential schools as embedded within the colonial history of the country, and contextualizing this engagement within the current relationships" (p. 13). It is vital that the process of the TRC remain open to, and inclusive of, the Aboriginal perspective – and not "shape" and "manage" the experiences in a manner that reflects the colonial perspective, thereby relegating the Aboriginal understanding to the margins.

Conclusion

Although most readers might not have initially thought that the subject matter of genocide is something of particular interest or importance to Canadians, we trust that this chapter has raised the question about whether Canada may have been complicit in what could legally be defined as genocide (mass violence) against its First Nations people. And even though it has never been legally established in court that Canada officially engaged in genocide,[9] this chapter has served to question whether Canada's Indigenous peoples were the intentional subject of mass violence. We have attempted to show that, in accordance with the legal criteria and even without a formal acknowledgement of genocide at this time, Canadians did engage in a crime that speaks to the much larger issue of the humanity of people.

Finally, although mass violence is a true rarity in Canada, the Canadian TRC demonstrates the potential for healing, which may in turn reduce the amount of external and internal violence of our First Nations people continue to experience as a result of the past. How a nation deals with its past, especially in the event of mass atrocities, is crucial in determining how it approaches its future. As Prime Minister Harper stated in his apology, the TRC is a:

> positive step in forging a new relationship between Aboriginal peoples and other Canadians, a relationship based on the knowledge of our shared history, a respect for each other and a desire to move forward together with a renewed understanding that strong families, strong communities and vibrant cultures and traditions will contribute to a stronger Canada for all of us. (Prime Minister, 2008)

In order to achieve this laudable goal, Aboriginal voices must be heard and their perspectives allowed to resonate in the (re)construction of our national history.

Keywords

Genocide, cultural genocide, international treaties, assimilation, residential school system

Review Questions

1. Consider discussing, in class, how the study of crimes of humanity and genocide might represent an important role within a criminological and/or criminal justice context.
2. Perhaps in a small group format, consider examining the 1984 UN Genocide Convention and then commenting on what the major features, ambiguities, and controversial aspects are.
3. Although this chapter only focused on the possibility of genocide being committed against our Indigenous people, examine and explain why so many other genocides have been committed against Indigenous people worldwide. What lessons might we be able to learn from having an understanding of the reason why these atrocities occur in terms of prevention of any future violence of this nature?
4. The chapter includes a brief discussion on impunity and reconciliation. Consider whether within a Canadian context one can talk about seeking "justice" in cases of genocide. Compare and contrast internal vs. international cases.

Notes

[1] The authors recognize that the decision to employ a "legalistic" definition is not without its issues. Many other definitions of genocide exist that would have broader implications for the overall discussion.

[2] See Rikhof (2009) for a more in depth discussion of the hybrid tribunals.

[3] See MacDonald and Hudson (2011) for a discussion regarding how monism, dualism, and "persuasive authority" influenced the model used for crafting the CAHWC Act.

[4] The focus on the UNGC is partially attributable to the omission in Canadian law to various components of the UNGC prior to the creation of the CAHWC Act. The aforementioned 1987 amendments to the *Criminal Code* were deemed insufficient for an exploration of genocide against Aboriginal peoples in Canada despite Canada's signatory status to the UNGC.

[5] Given the difficulty in establishing the *dolus specialus*, a prosecutor recalled that one of his greatest fears was that the entire world, other than the Trial Chamber at the ICTR, would know that there had been genocide in Rwanda (Jones, 2010).

[6] An interesting parallel is presented in the Australian case of *Kruger v. Commonwealth* wherein this argument was accepted by their High Court (MacDonald & Hudson, 2011, p. 16).

[7] Many criminal cases have been launched as a result of crimes that took place at residential schools. However, in all cases these were not "genocide cases" but rather cases of sexual assault or crimes already within the *Criminal Code*.

[8] See the IRSSA (2006) for a complete description of each of the individual mechanisms and Woolford (2013) for a detailed analysis of the mechanisms.

[9] The reader is reminded that the events occurred well before there was any formal recognition of genocide or crimes against humanity.

References

Annett, K. (2001). *Hidden from history: The Canadian holocaust – The untold story of the genocide of Aboriginal peoples by Church and State in Canada. The Truth Commission into Genocide in Canada.* Retrieved from http://canadiangenocide.nativeweb.org/genocide.pdf

Assembly of First Nations. (2002, November 21). *Human rights report to non-governmental organizations: Redress for cultural genocide – Canadian residential schools.* Retrieved from http://www.turtleisland.org/news/afnrezschools.pdf

Aust, A. (2010). *Handbook of international law* (2nd ed.). New York: Cambridge University Press.

Bischoping, K., & Fingerhut, N. (2006). Border lines: Indigenous peoples in genocide studies. *Canadian Review of Sociology and Anthropology, 33*(4), 481-506.

Blackstock, C. (2011). The Canadian Human Rights Tribunal on First Nations child welfare: Why if Canada wins, equality and justice lose. *Children and Youth Services Review, 33,* 187-194.

Chalk, F. R., & Jonassohn, K. (1990). *The history and sociology of genocide.* New Haven: Yale University Press.

Chrisjohn, R. D., & Young, S. L. (2006). *The circle game: Shadows and substance in the Indian Residential school experience in Canada.* Penticton, BC: Theytus Books.

Currie, R. J., & Stancu, I. (2010). *R. v. Munyaneza*: Pondering Canada's first core crimes conviction. *International Criminal Law Review, 10,* 829-853.

Deschênes, The Honourable J. (1986). *Commission of inquiry on war criminals report: Part 1: Public.* Ottawa: Minister of Supply and Services.

Grant, A. (1996). *No end of grief: Indian residential schools in Canada.* Toronto: Pemmican Publications Inc.

Jago, J. M. (1998). *Genocide, culture, law: Aboriginal child removals in Australia and Canada.* (Unpublished master's thesis). University of British Columbia, Vancouver, BC.

Jones, A. (2006). *Genocide: A comprehensive introduction.* New York: Routledge.

Jones, N. A. (2010). *The courts of genocide: Politics and the rule of law in Rwanda and Arusha.* New York: Routledge.

Jones, N. A., Parmentier, S., & Weitekamp, E. M. (2012). Dealing with international crimes in post-war Bosnia: A look through the lens of the affected population. *European Journal of Criminology, Special Issue on Atrocity Crimes and Transitional Justice,* (5), 533- 564.

Lafontaine, F. (2010). Canada's Crimes against Humanity and War Crimes Act on trial: An analysis of the *Munyaneza* case. *Journals of International Criminal Justice, 8,* 269-288.

MacDonald, D. B., & Hudson, G. (2011, May). The genocide question and Indian residential schools in Canada - Draft. Paper presented for the Canadian Political Science Association Annual Conference, Waterloo, ON. [Cited with permission of authors.]

MacDonald, D. B. (2012, June). Reconciliation after genocide? Reinterpreting the UNGC through Indian Residential Schools - Draft. Paper presented for the Canadian Political Science Association Annual Conference, Edmonton, AB. [Cited with permission of author.]

Prime Minister Harper's Statement of Apology. (2008, June 11). *CBC News Canada.* Retrieved from http://www.cbc.ca/news/canada/story/2008/06/11/pm-statement.html

Rikhof, J. (2009). Fewer places to hide? The impact of domestic war crimes prosecutions on international impunity. *Criminal Law Forum, 20,* 1-51.

Schabas, W. A. (2006). "The odious scourge": Evolving interpretations of the crime of genocide. *Genocide Studies and Prevention, 1*(2), 93-106.

Winterdyk, J. (2009). Genocide: international issues and perspectives worthy of criminal justice attention. *International Criminal Justice Review, 19*(2), 101-115.

Woolford, A. (2009). Ontological destruction: Genocide and Canadian Aboriginal peoples. *Genocide Studies and Prevention, 4*(1), 81-97.

Woolford, A. (2013). Nodal repair and networks of destruction: Residential Schools, colonial genocide and redress in Canada. *Settler Colonial Studies, 3*(1), 65-81. .

Woolford, A., & Thomas, J. (2011). Genocide of Canadian First Nations. In S. Totten & R. K. Hitchcock (Eds.), *Genocide of indigenous peoples* (pp. 61-87). New Brunswick, NJ: Transaction Publishers.

Yacoubian Jr., G. S. (2003). Evaluating the efficacy of the International Criminal tribunals for Rwanda and the former Yugoslavia: Implications for criminology and international criminal law. *World Affairs, 165*(3), 133-141.

Legal Citations

Criminal Code, R.S.C., 1985, c. C-46.

Crimes against Humanity and War Crimes Act, S.C. 2000, c. 24.

Indian Residential School Settlement Agreement. (May 8, 2006). Retrieved from http://www.residentialschoolsettlement.ca/english_index.html

Prosecutor v. Akayesu (Jean-Paul), [1998] ICTR-96-4-T.

R v. Finta, [1994] 1 S.C.R. 701.

R v. Munyaneza, 2009 QCCS 2201, leave to appeal to the Quebec Court of Appeal granted 2009 QCCA 1279.

The Statute of the International Criminal Court, U.N. Doc. A/CONF.183/9 17 July 1998, New York: United Nations.

United Nations Convention on the Prevention and Punishment of Genocide, Adopted by Resolution 260 (III) A. 9 December 1948. Entry into force 12 January 1951. New York: United Nations.

State Violence, Anti-Terrorism, and the Criminalization of Dissent

Chapter 15

Jeff Shantz

Learning Objectives

In this chapter you will...

▶ learn about recent policies and practices related to anti-terror concerns in Canada

▶ gain insight into the political character of legislation and impacts on public dissent

▶ learn about important manifestations of political protest in Canada and social concerns of activists

▶ be able to critically assess government policies and practices, and policing practices, in the post-9/11 period

▶ gain insight into different forms of state violence and assess how these might impact democratic practice

Introduction

In the days and weeks following September 11, 2001, the Canadian government, alongside other governments, rushed to show its compliance with the US-initiated "war on terrorism." While the government jumped at the chance to invade and occupy Afghanistan, much of its energy, under both Liberal Party and Conservative Party leadership, has been directed at the "home front," where it has implemented a broad assault on civil liberties. This has played out in the mobilization of police, security, and military forces against a range of community organizers, social movements, and political demonstrators in protests including those against the G8 in Kananaskis, Alberta and the G8/G20 in Toronto (see Adelaide, 2002; Barr 2003; Malleson & Wachsmuth, 2011; Shantz 2010, 2011).

The central and farthest reaching legislation is the *Anti-Terrorism Act* (Bill C-36). Under the *Act* people can be detained without charges. Suspicion can be based on nothing more than use of any symbol or representation associated with a terrorist group. Conditions of release can be placed on people without charges having been laid. The *Act* also allows for secret trials in which accused are denied access to the evidence against them, of course, for "reasons of national security." It is quite telling that these secret trials *were already in place*, since 1990 in fact, for immigration cases.

Despite changes to the *Act* since its introduction, it still covers demonstrations and protests. By including actions that disrupt public services it leaves open the possibility of identifying a range of acts, from strikes to protests, as terrorism. In addition, any behaviour that "threatens economic security" can be considered terrorism. Strikes, sit-ins, blockades, and even boycotts could be captured by this definition (though to this point have not been subjected to the *Anti-Terrorism Act*, as they are still subject to regular policing procedures).

Other pieces of legislation have received less attention but have their own nefarious features. Bill C-35 (to amend the *Foreign Missions and International Organizations Act*) extends state immunity to dignitaries representing international organizations. C-42, the cynically named *Public Safety Act*, and its successors (Bill C-55 and Bill C-17, the *Public Safety Act*, 2002), allows for the declaration of "military security zones" and the suspension of civil liberties on the spot. During the protests against the G8 in Kananaskis, Alberta in 2002, the government threatened protest organizers with the imposition of martial law (Adelaide, 2002; Barr, 2003). As discussed below, this went hand in hand with a full military mobilization against demonstrators, which was justified by supposed concerns for terrorism. All of this has happened in the absence of any credible terrorist threat on Canadian soil.

As many commentators have pointed out, the new legislation, including Bill C-36, the *Anti-Terrorism Act*, has little to do with "fighting terrorism" (which is prohibited by the Criminal Code already). This, and other recent "anti-terrorist" legislation, is really about extending the powers of the state to assist its efforts in quelling dissent and furthering the agenda of capitalist globalization. Anti-capitalist struggles of the past few years have caused a legitimation crisis for governments, and these forces might well account for the eagerness of governments to act (Brabazon, 2006; McNally, 2010). The response has been a range of new legislation directly pointed against opposition to government and business interests, which suggests nothing less than a criminalization of dissent.

The newly implemented prosecutorial and investigative powers introduced through anti-terror measures in Canada include so-called preventive detention, or the right to incarcerate people on the mere suspicion that they might commit a crime, a new police power to compel testimony from anyone believed to have information relevant to a terrorism investigation, closed secret trials, and a right of prosecution to deny an accused and his or her counsel full disclosure of the evidence against them (Legras, 2001; O'Grady, 2007). Perhaps even more troubling has been the ready militarization of policing of political protests. All of this suggests significant shifts in criminal justice systems and legal practice in Canada and the extension of regimes of violence, certainly in terms of regulating political opposition and dissent but also in terms of immigration and border controls. Indeed, these procedural shifts represent abandonment of crucial aspects of due process, the underpinnings of legal systems within liberal democracies.

In order to properly understand the deployment of anti-terrorism discourses, legislation, and practices in Canada it must be remembered that following the Quebec City protests against the Free Trade Area of the Americas (FTAA) in April 2001, the Canadian government was losing the public debate over corporate globalization – and losing it badly. During the anti-FTAA protests, demonstrators went to great lengths to speak with residents and educate people, openly and directly, about their concerns for the FTAA and corporate globalization more broadly. This included daily teach-ins and educational events as well as door-to-door discussions in neighborhoods across Quebec City. In response, the federal government had only violence. The government spent millions of dollars to build a fence around the downtown core and impose security checks for workers trying to access job sites and local residents trying to get home. Thousands of police were deployed to defend the fence, and, over the course of the meetings, thousands of canisters of tear gas were fired not only at protesters but into nearby residential neighborhoods. Water cannons were deployed and rubber bullets were fired into crowds. The public was excluded from the meetings. The contrast between protesters and community organizers who offered open, reasoned dialogue and education and the government and industry, which offered only fences, mass policing, and days of violence, was stark. For many, this was a high water mark in alternative globalization struggles in the Global North. The government and industry in Canada were losing the issue (see Chang et al., 2001).

It is in this context of broader debates and struggles, particularly over capitalist globalization, that the turn to anti-terror legislation and policy in Canada must be situated. This chapter examines developments in government deployment of anti-terrorism discourse, legislation, and practice in relation to alternative globalization protests and social movement actions. Specific pieces of legislation, and threats to liberty contained within, as well as practices of state violence as responses to particular protests, including anti-poverty protests and those against the G8 and G20, are examined.

Acts of (Anti-)Terrorism

Before 9/11 the concept of terrorism or a "terrorist act" had restricted use in Canadian law, notably appearing within the Immigration Act, giving immigration officials the right to expel, or deny entry to, non-Canadians suspected of participation in a terrorist act (Legras, 2001; Shantz, 2010). A reason for limited application has been that officials found it virtually impossible to provide a definition of terrorism that they were confident could withstand a court challenge (Legras, 2001; Brabazon, 2006; O'Grady, 2007). Such definitions ran the risk, precisely, of encompassing a variety of unrelated acts of dissent and protest. Furthermore, the Criminal Code of Canada already criminalizes the offences associated with terrorism, including assassinations, bombings, plane hijackings, and so forth.

The post-9/11 legislation has included within the notion of "terrorist act" a range of specifically political crimes for which the usual limits on state power no longer apply (Legras, 2001; O'Grady, 2007; Shantz, 2010). Conviction for these acts brings an automatic 25-year jail sentence. Critics have noted that the definition of terrorism contained within the legislation is so broad in scope that it could well be used to target, detain, and prosecute trade union members involved in a wildcat strike or political demonstrators participating in civil disobedience (Legras, 2001; Brabazon, 2006).

The centerpiece of the Canadian government's anti-terrorism legislation is the *Anti-Terrorism Act*, also known as Bill C-36. The Act was initiated as an immediate response to 9/11 and contains elements that are similar to those in the *Patriot Act* in the United States. Indeed, the two pieces of legislation emerged in a similar context of heated calls from economic elites and political authorities to act fast to make a public show of new security measures.

The *Anti-Terrorism Act* initiates and institutionalizes a range of exceptional investigative and prosecutorial practices that state agencies can deploy against a variety of activities that they have identified as "terrorist" (Legras, 2001; Brabazon, 2006; O'Grady, 2007). These activities can be as benign and detached from terrorist groups or practices as simple as possessing information or documents about groups that the government has defined as terrorist. Even wearing symbols or signs of groups that have been identified as terrorist could be targeted for prosecution by the state, such as wearing a Tamil Tiger patch on one's coat.

The *Anti-Terrorism Act* defines as a terrorist act "an act or omission, in or outside Canada, that is committed ... for a political, religious or ideological purpose" (Subsections 83.01(1) of the *Criminal Code*). It also includes outcomes such as "substantial property damage" or "serious interference with or serious disruption of an essential service, facility or system, whether public or private." Specifically, part of the Act references threats to the "economic security" of Canada as terroristic. Critics have raised concerns that this could be used against workers or protesters involved in strikes, work-to-rule campaigns, occupations, or walkouts whose activities could be defined as terrorism.

While the government's definition of a terrorist act does manage to exclude legally recognized strikes and demonstrations, it makes this exclusion conditional and ambiguous. Legal activities can potentially drift into the realm of terrorism if they seriously disrupt any essential service. Thus, demonstrations are called into question where they might actually break free of the limits of symbolic, legal, protest to register dissent or disagreement with employers or government and begin to challenge effectively existing structures and practices of injustice or inequality. The *Act* threatens worker and protesters with the suggestion that should their actions begin to upset the established order, and its day-to-day function, they may be subject to provisions of the *Act*, including arrest, detention for an indeterminate period of time, and secret trial. Even more, by specifically referencing legal strikes (those that are compliant with the limited definition of allowable practices within labor law) as exempt from the legislation, the *Act* implicitly opens wildcat strikes or strikes that defy labour laws, such as sympathy strikes, as acts of terrorism (Legras, 2001; Shantz, 2011).

Activities covered by the *Anti-Terrorism Act* go beyond actual commission of an act of terrorism. The *Act* includes within its purview planning to commit an act, threatening to commit and act, and inciting other people to commit an act that is defined as terroristic. Given the broad definition of what is included as an act of terrorism it is possible that someone could be charged with terrorism for calling upon protesters to occupy a public building to disrupt services or publishing a pamphlet that encourages unionists to wildcat. In the words of University of Toronto legal scholar Kent Roach,

> The overboard definition of terrorist activities is then incorporated in new offences such as ... participating in the activities of or harbouring those who commit terrorist activities. These broad offenses, which target activities well in advance of actual terrorism, are in turn expanded by the incorporation of inchoate liability such as conspiracies, attempts, counselling or threats, into the definition of terrorist activities. The overall effect is to lengthen the long reach of the criminal law in a manner that is complex, unclear and unrestrained. (qtd. in Legras, 2001)

Notably, politicians from various stripes, including both those who back and those who oppose the *Act's* definition of a terrorist act, have remarked that, had it then been in force prior to late 2001, the alternative globalization and union demonstrators who mobilized to disrupt the Organization of American States (OAS) Summit of the Americas in Quebec City and the demonstrators, organized by the Ontario Coalition Against Poverty (OCAP), who paralyzed Toronto's financial district with a mass snake march in October of 2001, could well have been prosecuted under its provisions (Legras, 2001; McNally, 2010; Shantz, 2011).

Indeed, OCAP has been named by various media, government, and police officials as a group that they would like to be seen added to the terror list because of its history of successful direct actions against employers and politicians (*Eye*, 2001; Duncan, 2002; Levy, 2013; see also Shantz, 2011).

Along with the implementation of the Anti-Terrorism Act, the government has established a list of groups that it deems to be terrorist organizations. The list of forty targeted groups includes: Aum Shinrikyo, Abu Nidal Organization, Hamas, Hizballah, Kurdistan Workers Party, Liberation Tigers of Tamil Eelam, Palestine Liberation Front, Popular Front for the Liberation of Palestine, Sendero Luminoso, and World Tamil Movement.

The state has authorized itself to seize the assets of all identified organizations and to mobilize legal mechanisms, including arrest and detention, against people presumed to be members and/or supporters of listed organizations. The legislation also empowers the state to seize the assets of all listed organizations in Canada and apply sanctions against members and supporters.

Organizations cannot contest their assignment to the list until after they have been listed. This is, again, a presumption of guilt rather than innocence and forces accused to prove their innocence rather than requiring the government to make a case for guilt. If a hearing occurs to contest the listing, the government is given the right to withhold evidence against the organization of the basis of supposed national security.

The legislation also creates a legal obligation for all banks and other financial institutions to secretly reveal to the state anyone they suspect of having involvement in terrorist activities (McNally, 2010). Failing to do so is liable to a ten-year prison term (Legras, 2001; Brabazon, 2006).

Kananaskis 2002: Anti-Terrorism, Protest, and the Militarization of Public Space

Coming as the first major gathering of global economic and political elites in Canada following 9/11, the Kananaskis, Alberta, G8 summit was framed throughout by the discourses of terrorism and anti-terrorism (Ostrey, 2002; Barr, 2003; Stainsby, 2003). Politicians and media figures raised the specter of a possible terror attack on the summit site, a message that was repeated up to and during the actual conference (Ostrey, 2002; Barr, 2003; Stainsby, 2003).

Then Prime Minister of Canada Jean Chrétien announced the choice of Kananaskis immediately following the previous G8 summit in Genoa. That conference had experienced mass protests involving hundreds of thousands of workers and youth from across Europe and beyond (Adelaide, 2002). It resulted infamously in the killing of one demonstrator, Carlo Giuliani, as well as police raids and assaults that left around 300 injured. Kananaskis was a significant location, given its remoteness as a wilderness site with only one main access road.

In the lead-up to the Kananaskis G8 meetings, the then ruling Liberal government threatened that it would make use of the provision in the proposed anti-terrorist legislation Bill C-42 that would allow the government to declare Kananaskis and the surrounding area a "military security zone" in which martial law was in effect. This threat had its intended effect of discouraging community organizers from mobilizing protests in Kananaskis. In the end, the government did not follow through on this promise but the desired effect had been achieved anyway.

Instead, the government used claims of a terrorist threat to deploy what was then the largest security operation in Canadian history. It would become the most significant homeland mobilization of Canadian troops since the October Crisis in 1970 (Adelaide, 2002; Stainsby, 2003). The result was the enclosure and securitization of the entire town of Kananaskis, what some termed "Fortress Kananaskis."

Government accounts pegged security spending on the summit at US$200 million. Over 6,000 personnel of the Canadian Armed Forced and around 4,500 police were deployed at Kananaskis and the nearest major city to Kananaskis, the city of Calgary. A 6.5 km no-go zone was instituted around Kananaskis Village and a 150 km radius no-fly zone was imposed. The lone road into Kananaskis was stratified with 22 security checkpoints. All seeking land entry into Kananaskis were subjected to repeated security checks and searches of their vehicles. Those allowed passage were escorted by security teams. CF-18 fighter jets monitored air space from the skies, and three anti-aircraft missile batteries were placed to police the skies from the ground.

The post-9/11 state preparation for summits of global capital, such as the G8 meetings in Kananaskis, now included integrated security involving not only local police and the RCMP but the Canadian military (Canadian Forces) as well. As one of the military executors of the integrated security regime at Kananaskis has noted,

Following the terrorist attacks of 11 September 2001, the security concerns surrounding the hosting of the G8 Summit increased dramatically. In addition to the security challenges posed by the forested and mountainous terrain surrounding the Kananaskis site, there was a new threat to consider. The anarchist was no longer the primary concern for the security forces. The terrorist threat, ranging from the lone sniper to bombs to weapons of mass destruction – with an equally wide range of delivery means – was clearly beyond the capability of the Royal Canadian Mounted Police and local law enforcement agencies. The CF was now going to be a key partner in the effort to secure the G8 site from both ground and airborne threats. (Barr, 2003, p. 39)

The threat of terrorism was the central reason presented publicly by security officials to justify the establishment of "Fortress Kananaskis." In the words of Royal Canadian Mounted Police Corporal Jamie Johnston, a G8 security planner, "We plan for the worst-case scenario. Then we allow the intelligence to decide for us whether or not we implement it 100 percent or on a lesser scale ... Everything here is intelligence-driven. We need to be reactive to scale up or scale down" (qtd. in Adelaide, 2002).

Dire warnings were put out publicly by Canadian Forces officials over the months leading up to the summit. Among the more startling claims, certainly designed to frighten potential protesters away, military officials publicly warned that given the heavily wooded environment around Kananaskis, they would not be able to distinguish between protesters and terrorists. The effect of this warning was intensified by the fact that the military had been given shoot to kill orders (Gent, 2003; Stainsby, 2003; Barr, 2003).

Clearly, though, the real motivation, and actual outcome, was the suppression of opposition in the form of mass protests and the stifling of political dissent. Protesters were denied permits to demonstrate even in nearby Calgary. Kanansakis would provide an effective example of how protests could be circumvented simply by holding meetings in inaccessible and remote locations that could be easily closed off to entry by potential activists.

The Toronto 2010 G8 Meetings: "Public Works" and Martial Law

During the summer of 2010, the G8 and G20 Summits were hosted in two Ontario locations – the Muskoka cottage region of Ontario and Toronto, respectively. Widespread public outrage focused on the $1.3 billion security extravagance involved in the events – the fences, security cameras, weapons, vehicles, and mass policing that have become regular features of such gatherings of global capital. While governments of the G8 claim the need for austerity, social spending cuts, and belt tightening for the working classes, they have no shortage of public money to spend on their own comfort (CBC News 2010a, 2010b). The federal Conservative Government of Canada and its corporate sponsors have justified these costs as necessary expenditures in the face of protesters, potential terrorists, and, in the words of then federal Minister of Trade and Treasury Board President Stockwell Day, "anarchist thugs." By the second day in Toronto, police aggression and intimidation had imposed regular random and unlawful searches, requests for identity papers, preemptive arrests of supposed organizers and "leaders," and home invasions. Rubber bullets and tear gas were used against people doing nothing more than sitting outside the main detention center. Once more the media were provided with explanations that included, without accompanying evidence, government concern over possible terrorist threats during the summits (see articles in Malleson & Wachsmuth, 2011).

A key part of the policing of the G20 Summit in Toronto was the imposition of what amounted to conditions of martial law in the city. Under the *Public Works Protection Act*, the provincial government of Ontario was given the capacity to eliminate rights to assemble and remove probable cause before a person or vehicle could be searched.

The *Act* was originally passed in 1939 and later revised in 1990. It originated in the context of the Second World War to address potential terrorist attacks on public buildings and government infrastructure such as courthouses or police stations, railways, or bridges. It was not intended for use against political protests or demonstrations in public space. Under the legislation, the government could decide to designate the area around the summit site and the fence that surrounded the site as a public work. Once these designations are made, the *Act* imposes a series of restrictions upon activity in the area. It works, in effect, to suspend civil rights in the area as in conditions of martial law. Police misinterpreted the law to assert that they could stop, search, and arrest anyone coming within five metres of the summit fence. Yet the law was invoked against people who were well away from the five-metre boundary (Morrow, 2013).

Providing unlimited authority to the government to designate specific areas as a public works facilitated the designation of entire sections of downtown Toronto as a public work at which protests were simply prohibited. Furthermore, the Act empowers not only police officers to enforce its provisions but allows more ambiguous figures identified as "guards" to become empowered with enforcement capacities. In Toronto, this meant that large numbers of security guards, who were not licensed as security in Toronto, were brought to the city and deployed as guards. Without the Act they could never have been employed and worked in the city as guards during the period of the G20 (many could not have been licensed at any point). As designated peace officers, these newly designated guards had the right to arrest and detain and could, in future, hold the right to bear arms (which only exists for police in Canada).

The rights of a guard under the Public Works Protection Act are designated as such:

3(a) A guard or peace officer, (a) may require any person entering or attempting to enter any public work or any approach thereto to furnish his or her name and address, to identify himself or herself and to state the purpose for which he or she desires to enter the public work, in writing or otherwise … [and] … may search, without warrant, any person entering or attempting to enter a public work or a vehicle in the charge or under the control of any such person or which has recently been or is suspected of having been in the charge or under the control of any such person.

This scenario was fully played out during the G20 in Toronto.

Another aspect of the *Act* that came into effect in Toronto during the G20 protests includes the right of guards to "refuse permission to any person to enter a public work and use such force as is necessary to prevent any such person from so entering" (R.S.O. 1990, c. P.55, s. 3). Thus, when people approached the area near the summit site they were subjected to force to keep them away. Notably, the people doing the policing were able to designate spaces blocks away from the summit fence area as prohibited sites, and the police themselves were able to arbitrarily change the designated areas that were off limits. Another provision in the *Act* supported such decisions by stating that a "statement under oath of an officer or employee of the government, board, commission, municipal or other corporation or other person owning, operating or having control of a public work as to the boundaries of the public work is conclusive evidence thereof" (R.S.O. 1990, c. P.55, s. 4). This provision then also removes the fundamental common law right of cross-examination of one's accuser by rendering their statement as "conclusive evidence." This is a fundamental suspension of due process as understood within liberal democracies.

During the G20, police took it upon themselves to compel people to identify themselves simply for being on the street and without any probable cause. They also exercised (perhaps illegally) the authority to search the person without cause. All of this under an *Act* devised to check entrants to public building, like a courthouse. Notably though, the main impetus for the use of the *Act*, as during the G20 protests, was and is to fend off terrorist attacks on public sites.

The deployment of the 1930s anti-terrorism legislation served the government well in 2010 Toronto. Over the course of the G20 Summit, more than 1,100 people were arrested in the largest mass arrest in Canadian history (Seglins, 2012). People were arrested by the dozens simply for being too close to areas arbitrarily designated as public work sites by officers who refused to identify themselves, many of whom were not displaying badge numbers. While investigations are still underway, it is apparent that civil rights were violated en masse. People were routinely compelled to show identification and subjected to searches, both exceptions to Canadian law. Many were stopped and searched by police while undertaking everyday activities like going to or from work or shopping. Still others were detained in makeshift cells in warehouses for days on end. While reports of investigations into police actions during the G20 (including by Gerry McNeilly, head of Ontario's Office of the Independent Police Review Director) have been highly critical of (even "slamming") excessive force, arbitrary search and seizure, and mass arrests by police, there has been virtually no accountability for their actions. Individually, one officer has been convicted for an assault on John Nobody. The *Public Works Act* remains in effect.

From Liberal to Neoliberal Democracy

A cornerstone of criminal justice systems and practices within liberal democracies is the notion of due process. This emerges from classical criminological theories and liberal philosophies, such as those of Cesare Beccaria and Jeremy Bentham (Engelmann, 2003; Held, 2006) and is affirmed as an advance beyond the arbitrary and barbaric practices of punishment as existed under feudal systems. In Canada, for example, aspects of due process include the right to an open and fair trial, the disclosure to the accused of the state's case against him or her and evidence to be used, reasonable time limits for detention before trial, and the right to a defence. Among the most significant features of due process is the presumption of innocence of the accused. This reverses feudal practices that charged people with outlandish activities, such as demonic spells, and then forced them to prove their innocence, an impossible task. The presumption of innocence requires that the state make a case, supported by evidence, to prove the guilt of the accused. The onus is on the state to demonstrate guilt beyond a reasonable doubt in criminal cases. This includes the right to a public trial before a jury of one's (supposed) peers where elected by the accused.

Incredibly, the *Anti-Terrorism Act* subverts and erases these principles of justice within liberal democracies. The *Act*, and the deployment of security certificates, eliminates the requirement of state disclosure of evidence for terrorism suspects. The prosecution is no longer even required to provide specific charges for which the person in question has come to be accused. Within the *Act* prosecution can now withhold – from the accused and the public – central parts of the state's case against an accused with approval of a presiding judge or higher court that such procedure is necessary in the name of national security (Legras, 2001). The prosecution can also withhold how evidence was obtained and the names of witnesses for the prosecution.

Police are given the power under the *Act* to detain people for periods of up to 72 hours simply on suspicion that they might be planning to commit a terrorist act. This is a major move away from the longstanding position of courts in Canada that people cannot be arrested, never mind detained without charge, merely on suspicion that they might, commit a crime; in order for there to be a crime the two elements of a crime, the *actus reus* and the *mens rea* must be present. Previously arrests could not be made without warrant unless police had a reasonable cause to believe a crime had been committed or was imminent (Legras 2001).

The *Act* provides security forces the power to compel testimony from individuals under threat of imprisonment during investigative hearings that are held in secret. While evidence acquired through such secret hearings is not to be used against the individual compelled to give testimony, the process is a serious threat to the important right to silence, a central feature of due process in criminal justice practice. Indeed, given the severity of threats available to security forces this could mean the end of this "right" entirely in Canada, as has occurred in Britain since the 1970s.

For those members of the public concerned about finding out what occurs during anti-terrorism investigations and gaining access to the information gathered during such investigations there are further barriers and impediments. The *Act* gives the federal minister of public safety and emergency preparedness (formerly solicitor-general, responsible for internal security) the power to order those involved in anti-terrorism investigations not to disclose information (Legras, 2001).

These shifts in criminal justice system procedure and practice reflect not simply policy innovations but the institution and implementation of neoliberal regimes of democracy. Neoliberal democracy reverses or eliminates many of the gains made by movements of the working classes and oppressed over decades of struggle in the last half of the twentieth century.

Anti-Terrorism and Movement Building

Given the barriers and challenges to movement building and solidarity posed by anti-terror policies and practices, community organizers and activists have had to redouble their efforts to build bridges and make connections with targeted, criminalized, and marginalized groups. This has, as repression typically does, opened up new opportunities for organizers who have been willing and prepared to take up the challenge. In the Canadian context, among the most significant innovations have been the efforts of No One Is Illegal and other anti-authoritarian migrant defence groups. In addition, activists have begun to recognize the importance of anti-colonial efforts and the need to work in solidarity with Indigenous communities and organizers.

As many commentators have pointed out, this legislation is all about strengthening the government's hand in fighting the globalization struggles at a time when many sensed it was beginning to lose its grip. This is one reason why legislation against activism has gone hand in hand with a clampdown on immigration, the global mobility of labour. Thus, Canadian and US governments are devising joint agreements around border controls and immigration criteria. There has even been chilling talk from some authorities about establishing a continental perimeter, a "Fortress North America."

Event preparation and management since 9/11, from Kananaskis in 2002 to the G8 and G20 in 2010, show the clear militarization and securitization of state responses to protest and dissent. Similar militarization of the policing of protests occurred during the 2010 Winter Olympics in Vancouver. In each case, the explanation provided by governments to legitimize the integration of military and police to regulate protest events has been concern for terrorism. Yet in no case have there been any observable connections to terrorist groups or evidence for terrorist plans during protests against meetings of global capital. Indeed, there have been no such incidents during mass public protests in Canada. While some might suggest a mass security presence has contributed to this, there is no evidence to support the association of terrorism with protests or to suggest any plots have been thwarted.

Keywords

Criminalization, dissent, political violence, protest, repression, resistance, social movements, terrorism

Review Questions

1. What is the nature of violence? Is property destruction during protests an act of violence, or should the term *violence* be reserved for physical harm to life (human or animal)?
2. Liberal political theory suggests the state as a neutral arbitrator of social concerns, weighing claims without prejudice. Do recent state policies and practices, such as those enacted during the G20, call into question notions of state neutrality, i.e., the state taking sides against activists in favour of corporations?
3. Do recent policies and practices, including the militarization of policing, suggest that Canada is becoming a "police state" as some activists would contend?

4. Do preemptive "strikes," either in the form of legislation or mass arrests, as carried out during the G20 in Toronto, represent a violation of fundamental civil rights, such as rights to assembly or rights to speech?

5. Do activists have an obligation to maintain non-violent protest in the face of state violence?

Suggested Readings

Fernandez, L. A. (2008). *Policing dissent: Social control and the anti-globalization movement.* New Brunswick, NJ: Rutgers University Press.

Gordon, T. (2006). *Cops, crime and capitalism: The law-and-order agenda in Canada.* Halifax, NS: Fernwood.

Malleson, T., & Wachsmuth, D. (2011). *Whose streets?: The Toronto G20 and the challenges of summit protests.* Toronto: Between the Lines.

Shantz, J. (Ed.). (2011). *Law against liberty: The criminalization of dissent.* Lake Mary, FL: Vandeplas.

Starr, A., Fernandez, L., & Scholl, C. (2011). *Shutting down the streets: Political violence and social control in the global era.* New York: NYU Press.

References

Adelaide, D. (2002, June 27). G-8 security operation: The stifling and criminalizing of dissent. *World Socialist Website.* Retrieved from http://www.wsws.org/articles/2002/ jun2002/g8-j27.shtml

Barr, D. (2003). The Kananaskis G8 Summit: A case study in interagency cooperation. *Canadian Military Journal, 4*(4), 39-46.

Brabazon, H. (2006). Protecting whose security?: Anti-terrorism legislation and the criminalization of dissent. *YCISS Working Paper 43.* Retrieved from http://yciss.info.yorku.ca /files/2012/06/WP43-Brazabon.pdf

CBC News. (2010a, May 26). Summit costs hit $1.1B. *CBC News.* Retrieved from http://www.cbc.ca/news/politics/summit-costs-hit-1-1b-1.876766

CBC News. (2010b, September 23). G8/G20 costs include $80M for food, lodging. *CBC News.* Retrieved from http://www.cbc.ca/news/politics/g8-g20-costs-include-80m-for-food-lodging-1.884886

Chang, J., Daniels, S., Leroux, D., Or, B., Tharmendran, E., & Tsumura, E. (2001). *Resist!: A Grassroots collection of stories, poetry, photos and analysis from the FTAA protests in québec city and beyond.* Halifax, NS: Fernwood.

Duncan, S. (2002, April 8). Who says it was a riot? *rabble.ca.* Retrieved from http://rabble.ca /news/who-says-it-was-riot

Engelmann, S. G. (2003). "Indirect Legislation": Bentham's Liberal Government. *Polity, 35*(3), 369-388.

Eye. (2001). Fantino, Show Us The Money. November 1. Retrieved from http://contests. eyeweekly.com/eye/issue/issue_11.01.01/news/editorial.php

Gent, A. A. (2003). Newly Developed police tactics to counter direct action at mass demonstrations. *International Advocates for Health Freedom.* Blacksburg, VA: IAHF

Held, D. (2006). *Models of democracy.* London: Polity Press.

Legras, F. (2001, November 20). Canadian "Anti-Terrorism" law attacks democratic rights. *World Socialist Website*. Retrieved from http://www.wsws.org/articles/2001/nov2001/can-n20.shtml

Levy, S.-A. (2013, March 10). "Poverty Terrorists" misguided about homeless issue. *Toronto Sun*. Retrieved from http://www.torontosun.com/2013/03/10/use-money-for-homeless-more-wisely

Malleson, T., & Wachsmuth, D. (2011). *Whose streets? The Toronto G20 and the challenges of summit protests*. Toronto: Between the Lines.

McNally, D. (2010). *Global slump: The economics and politics of crisis and resistance*. Oakland, CA: PM Press.

Morrow, A. (2013, July 16). Ontario yet to scrap expanded police powers used during G20. *Globe and Mail* (Toronto). Retrieved from http://www.theglobeandmail.com/news/politics/despite-promises-ontario-has-yet-to-scrap-public-works-protection-act/article13242018/

O'Grady, W. (2007). *Crime in Canadian context: Debates and controversies*. Toronto: Oxford University Press.

Ostry, S. 2002. Globalization and the G8: Could *Kananaskis* Set a New. Direction? O.D. Skelton Memorial Lecture, University of Toronto.

Seglins, D. (2012, May 16). G20 report slams police for "excessive force. *CBC News*. Retrieved from http://www.cbc.ca/news/canada/g20-report-slams-police-for-excessive-force-1.1137051

Shantz, J. (2010). No one is illegal: Resistance and borders. In J. Shantz (Ed.), *Racism and borders: Representation, repression, resistance* (pp. 157-172). New York: Algora.

Shantz, J. (2011). Introduction. In J. Shantz (Ed.), *Law against liberty: the criminalization of dissent* (pp. 1-9). Lake Mary, FL: Vandeplas.

Stainsby, M. (2003). Neither Trade Talks nor Peace Talks. *Interactivist*. Retrieved from http://interactivist.autonomedia.org/node/2069

Police Use of Force and the Mentally Ill

Chapter 16

Ron Stansfield

Learning Objectives

In this chapter you will...

▶ gain an understanding of the complicated nature of police encounters with persons with mental illness

▶ critically analyze the Use of Force Model used by Canadian police

▶ learn about the three types of responses to police encounters with people with mental illness

▶ explore ways to reduce the risk to police and people with mental illnesses when the two groups interact

Introduction

On February 20, 1997, at approximately 5:25 p.m., 35-year-old Edmund Yu was shot three times and killed by Lou Pasquino. Prior to being shot, Yu committed an unprovoked assault on a female passenger on a bus in Toronto. Yu was at the back of the empty TTC bus and brandishing a hammer when he was shot. Early on the morning of January 12, 2011, 35-year-old Ryan Russell was struck and killed by a snow plow that was being driven by Richard Kachkar. Kachkar stole the parked but running snow plow and drove around Toronto striking several parked cars before striking Russell, who was trying to stop him.

These incidents have two things in common. First, both Kachkar and Yu were experiencing psychotic episodes due to mental illness at the time of these incidents. Second, both Pasquino and Russell were police officers at the time of these incidents. Together these incidents illustrate the complex and potentially dangerous nature for both police and "persons with mental illness" (PMI) when they interact with each other.

As the examples above demonstrate, when police–PMI encounters go wrong the likelihood that someone, sometimes a police officer and sometimes a PMI, will be seriously injured or killed is very high. This makes it incumbent on us to consider what can go wrong with police–PMI encounters and suggest solutions to these problems. We will begin by considering when and under what conditions police are authorized to use force.

Deinstitutionalization, Anti-Psychotics, and PMI

Police encounters with PMI have been increasing since the 1960s when, as a result of the development of anti-psychotic drugs, the deinstitutionalization of psychiatric patients began en masse (Scull, 1985; Mills & Cummins, 1982; Martinez, 2010). The development of anti-psychotic drugs meant that many people with mental illness could lead "normal" lives and did not require ongoing hospitalization; however, significant numbers of PMI refuse to take anti-psychotic medications due to the sometimes serious and unpleasant side effects (Hon, 2012). Others, who do take their medications, still experience often severe symptoms of their illness. The shuttering of many psychiatric institutions at this time, combined with the fact that significant numbers of PMI are episodically mentally ill, ensured that police have become the first responders to conflicts involving PMI in our communities (Teplin & Pruett, 1992).

Police encounters with PMI are inherently dangerous because police are equipped with lethal weapons and authorized to use lethal force, and sometimes PMI behave unpredictably and violently.[1] Together these factors create a potentially volatile mix whenever police encounter PMI. Fortunately, interventions with PMI represent a relatively small proportion of all police interventions (Crocker, Harford, & Heslop, 2009; Hoch et al., 2009). As well, most police interventions with PMI are resolved informally (38.2%) or with a hospital referral (36.0%), and only a minority (30.1%) involve aggressiveness (Charette, Crocker, & Billette, 2011). Also, importantly, police encounters with PMI are typically resolved with less force (Johnson, 2011) and fewer injuries (Kerr, Morabito, & Watson, 2010) than encounters with other citizens. There is no consensus regarding whether police are more (Lawton, 2007; Kesic, Thomas, & Ogloff, 2013) or less (Johnson, 2011; Kaminski, DiGiovanni, & Downs, 2004; Terrill, 2005) likely to threaten or actually use weapons on PMI; however, police were more likely to use electronically controlled devices (ECD)(such as a Taser) (O'Brien et al., 2011) and twice as likely to use pepper spray (Kesic, Thomas, & Ogloff, 2013) on PMI. This may be explained by the fact PMI are more likely to threaten or use weapons on the police (Kesic, Thomas, & Ogloff, 2013).

Police Use of Force

To assist them with their law enforcement mandate, Canadian police are authorized by Section 25 of the Criminal Code of Canada to use force,[2] including lethal force, to resolve conflict. Very simply, Subsection (1) creates a legal justification for individuals, including police officers, who are "required or authorized by law" to use "as much force as necessary" in the "administration or enforcement of the law" if they "act on reasonable grounds." If a police officer is acting under the authority of Subsection (1) and uses force "that is intended to or is likely to cause death or grievous bodily harm," then, to be justified, he or she must believe on "reasonable grounds" that it was necessary for the purpose of preserving himself or herself or someone under his or her protection from "death or grievous bodily harm."

Section 25 of the Code is problematic for several reasons. First, use of the expression "as much force as necessary" creates the impression that the use of force by police to resolve conflict is an expectation. Second, nowhere does this section answer the critical question: how much force is *too much* force? In a much needed attempt to clarify the use of force under Section 25 of the Code, police authorities have developed a "Use of Force Model" (UOFM) to help police decide how much force is appropriate in specific situations (see Figure 1 and Table 1 in the Appendix).

UOFM is an attempt to create a standardized and systematic approach for police to use force. The model is based on the common sense notion that the use of force is on a continuum beginning with little or no violence (e.g., verbal threats), and progresses to extreme physical violence (e.g., lethal assaults). The objective of UOFM is to help police strike a balance between the force being threatened or used by a citizen and the force being threatened or used by police. To accomplish this UOFM offers police a total of five options for resolving conflict. Depending on the level of violence being threatened or used by the citizen, police are encouraged to use more or less force, or perhaps, not to use any force at all. So, for example, if the citizen is being "cooperative," then the officer's appropriate response may be their mere "presence" and "verbal commands." On the other hand, if the citizen is "passively resisting," such as by failing to comply with verbal commands or lying on the ground in protest, then police would be justified to use only their physical "presence" or "tactical communications" to resolve the conflict. Alternatively, if a citizen is being actively resistant, UOFM recommends police use "empty handed techniques" or "soft impact weapons" to resolve the conflict. If, on the other hand, a citizen is being "assaultive," UOFM recommends police use an "aerosol spray" or "hard impact weapon" to resolve the conflict. Finally, if a citizen is threatening to inflict serious bodily harm or death, UOFM recommends police use the "police challenge," an electronically controlled device such as a "Taser" or a "firearm." As a last resort, police would be encouraged to "disengage' from the conflict (Parent & Verdun-Jones, 1998) (Figure 1). While UOFM is an important first step to standardizing the use of force by Canadian police, it has several serious shortcomings.

An implicit feature of UOFM is that police should use a "graduated response" when using force. That is, police should assess the level of force being used or threatened by the citizen and respond with a slightly higher level of force – a "force plus one logic." Also, if at any time, the citizen increases the level of force, police should increase their level of force commensurably.[3] The *intent* of this approach is to ensure that police always have the "upper hand" (i.e., always use or threaten more force than the citizen) in a police–citizen conflict; however, the *result* of this approach may be that the citizen controls the outcome of the encounter. This would be problematic with a rational individual and is even more problematic if the individual suffers from a mental illness that renders them irrational.

The *rational* approach encouraged by the UOFM may be appropriate for mentally healthy individuals but it can be problematic when used with PMI who, by definition, may be behaving *irrationally* at the time they come into conflict with police. For example, by trying to stay one step ahead, police may be forced to escalate the amount of force they use to match the level of force being threatened by a PMI (Kerr, Morabito, & Watson, 2010). Given that PMI may behave irrationally, particularly when encountering police, control of the encounter may be determined by a momentarily "irrational" PMI, not the ostensibly rational police officer. Clearly, this was not the intent of the creators of the UOFM; however, it is equally clear this may be the result. In short, UOFM may have the unintended effect of *escalating* the level of violence in police–PMI encounters – non-violent conflicts may escalate into violent conflicts, and low intensity conflicts may escalate into high intensity conflicts as determined by the PMI not the police (Watson, Corrigan, & Ottati, 2004).

This analysis makes clear the UOFM needs to be revised to be more sensitive to the needs of the PMI. For example, additional versions of the UOFM could be developed just for PMI that include a wider array of non-violent conflict resolution options such as disengagement and stabilization of the situation (Parent, 2011). Also, gender-specific versions of the

UOFM could be developed (Crocker, Harford, & Heslop, 2009). Disengagement could involve police, if it is safe to do so, withdrawing from the PMI to a safe distance until the person calms down. Stabilization might involve controlling the PMI in a contained area until specially trained police could be deployed to interact with the PMI. This last recommendation points out the fact that all police should receive a basic course in how to recognize and appropriately respond to PMI (Kesic, Thomas, & Ogloff, 2013; Parent & Verdun-Jones, 1998).

Importantly, Coleman and Cotton (2014) have recommended all police receive crisis intervention and de-escalation (CID) training. In particular, they propose CID training should augment and complement current use of force training effectively equipping police with a wider range of "tools" to manage potentially violent interactions with PMI. They note British Columbia has one of the "most advanced and promising" CID training programs (p.7).

Police, PMI, and Deadly Force

The worst-case scenario when police encounter PMI is that a police officer or the PMI will be killed. Several studies have investigated the circumstances in which PMI are likely to be killed by police. A study by Parent (2011) analyzed 30 fatal shootings of PMI by police in British Columbia between 2000 and 2009. He found that 26.7% (8) of the decedents either had a documented history of mental illness or were exhibiting signs of mental illness when they were shot by a uniformed patrol officer (UPO). Importantly, all of the decedents were armed at the time they were shot, and, in two cases, the decedent was shot with an ECD prior to being shot with a firearm.[4] Parent (2011) argues that police organizations need a "specialized response" such as a crisis intervention team (CIT) for incidents involving PMI as well as options such as "containment and tactical withdrawal" (p. 69). Finally, he recommends police be provided with more mid-range, less-lethal use of force options such as beanbag shotguns since the existing options such as pepper spray and batons are only effective at close range.

Coleman and Cotton (2005) analyzed 52 fatalities categorized as "death in custody" in Canada between 1992 and 2002. They reported that 21.1% (11) of the decedents in their sample were "apparent" PMI.[5] Ten of the eleven apparent PMI threatened police with a weapon prior to being shot.[6] Also, three police officers tried a less lethal use of force option before they shot the decedent.[7]

Gill and Pasquale-Styles (2009) studied 42 fatal police shootings in New York City between 2003 and 2007. They found that 16.6% of the decedents had a history of psychiatric illness. Similarly, the Toronto Police Service (1998) reported that, between the years 1987 and 1997, their police shot a total of 55 individuals, eight of whom were PMI and four of whom died as a result of being shot.

Kesic Thomas and Ogloff (2010) studied 48 fatal police shootings in Victoria, Australia between 1982 and 2007 and found a high prevalence of Axis 1 disorders among the victims.[8] Also, the vast majority of victims had contact with both mental health and criminal justice services prior to their shooting. They maintain the problem, then, is how to provide police with more relevant information about PMI they encounter and providing police with de-escalation and crisis intervention skills. They recommend the creation of a database shared by mental health and police practitioners that contains information about these "high risk" individuals.

Just as PMI may be the victims of the lethal use of force by police, so too are police sometimes the victims of lethal use of force by PMI. For example, 3% of the 133 Canadian police officers murdered in the line of duty between 1961 and 2000 occurred while the police officer was apprehending a psychiatric patient (Statistics Canada, 2010).[9] Similarly, 2% of American police killed in the line of duty between 1978 and 1998 were killed by "mentally deranged" persons (Brown & Langan, 2001).

The risk that a police–PMI encounter will result in the use of deadly force by one of the participants' points out the need for a clear understanding of the circumstances that give rise to these encounters. The following section considers the role played by uniformed patrol officers (UPO) in encounters with PMI.

Uniformed Patrol Officers and PMI

The most likely outcome when police encounter PMI is that it will involve one or more uniformed patrol officer. This is because UPO compose, by far, the single largest group in police organizations and because their primary function is to respond calls for service from the public. Given the ubiquity of UPO–PMI encounters one would assume that UPO receive extensive training and orientation to the needs of PMI. Unfortunately, this is not the case.

UPO do not routinely receive significant specialized training in dealing with PMI. For example, Hails and Borum (2003) found in their study of 84 American police services that basic recruits received a median of just 6.5 hours of mental health related instruction. At the opposite extreme, Parent (2011) reports that police in the Vancouver area receive 30 hours of in-service crisis intervention training.[10] However, overall, most UPO are not receiving the specialized training they require to effectively manage their encounters with PMI.

UPO are forced to rely on their interpersonal skills and use of force training when they encounter PMI due to their relative lack of specialized training dealing with these individuals. As we saw above, police use of force training emphasizes the use of violent conflict resolution. When this emphasis on the use of force is coupled with the sense of urgency UPO feel to clear the current call, it creates a situation in which UPO are prone to engage and consequently escalate violent situations rather than de-escalating them (Panzarella & Alicea, 1997, p. 336). Several Canadian studies have found that a large number of fatal police shootings occurred while police were confronting the victim (Abraham et al., 1981; Chappell & Graham, 1985; Stansfield, 1993).

The tendency of UPO to quickly engage can be clearly seen in the Edmund Yu incident. Yu was contained within an empty bus at the time and responded to police entering the bus by producing a hammer from his pocket and brandishing it at the police. Constable Pasquino followed his UOFM training and met Yu's force – a hammer – and exceeded it by deploying his gun. When Yu ignored Pasquino's command to drop the hammer and continued to approach, Pasquino fatally shot Yu three times.

In retrospect, we can see the UPO escalated the conflict by entering the bus rather than closing the bus door and trapping Yu inside. Presumably, police followed this course of action (i.e., engagement/confrontation) because they were feeling the pressure to engage Yu and resolve the situation in a timely manner. For his part, Yu responded to the police escalation and upped the ante by producing a hammer and using it to threaten the police. The police then re-escalated by deploying their firearms and shooting Yu when he failed to withdraw. The police actions in this shooting were quite rational and, as previously mentioned, conformed to the UOFM; however, what the police did not consider was that Yu, suffering from schizophrenia, would respond in an irrational fashion (i.e., pitting a hammer against a gun). Could the tragic outcome of this incident have been prevented? It is possible a change in police strategy (e.g., containment rather than engagement) may have resulted in a different and less violent outcome.

Research suggests that females, non-whites, and more experienced officers have more positive attitudes toward PMI, although greater exposure to PMI during the most recent month was associated with more negative attitudes (Clayfield, Fletcher, & Grudzinskas, 2011). Also, there is evidence to suggest that educational programs for law enforcement officers may reduce stigmatizing attitudes toward persons with schizophrenia (Compton et al., 2006). Johnson (2011), in his study of police use of force with PMI, utilized a dataset from Oregon that involved police interactions with 619 criminal suspects and found "no evidence to suggest that mentally disordered individuals receive harsher treatment at the hands of officers than do non-disordered persons." However, he also found that "suspects who physically resisted officers, possessed a weapon, and displayed a hostile demeanor were significantly more likely to receive force compared to suspects who did not behave in this manner" (p. 141). This finding is important because PMI may engage in these aggressive behaviours because of their disorder and consequently be subjected to greater use of force than others.

Studies have found that strategies such as "manipulating time and involuntariness," making "highly volatile encounters more private" (Fyfe, 1989, pp. 493-508), "maintaining communication" (Panzarella & Alicia, 1997, p. 332), and making "meaningful contact with the involved party, obtaining and employing intelligence appropriately, and understanding the mind-set and interests of the subject" (Greenstone, 2007, pp. 110-115) increase the likelihood that police–PMI encounters will be resolved non-violently.

Parent (2011) has argued that the manner in which police are dispatched to an encounter plays an important role in the outcome. For example, he notes,

> Call-takers and dispatch personnel within police agencies should be aware of the precarious dynamics associated with mental health-related calls for assistance. It is crucial that call-takers and dispatch personnel solicit pertinent information from members of the public who summon the police. Police dispatchers must relay this information to the police units to allow for a planned and safe response. (pp. 69-70)

This underscores the importance of a "systematic approach" to police encounters with PMI (Coleman & Cotton, 2010). That is, police organizations need to rethink every stage of their interactions with PMI to plan and design processes that take the special needs of PMI into consideration.

The tendency for UPO–PMI encounters to end with either a police officer or a PMI seriously injured or dead has led to a call for more specialized mental health training for police and the creation of specialized mental health teams to help manage these incidents. In the section that follows, we will consider some of these efforts.

Crisis Intervention Teams and PMI

Crisis intervention teams (CIT) were first developed in 1988 in the United States following the fatal shooting of a PMI by members of the Memphis Police (Dupont & Cochran, 2000; Compton et al., 2008). Since then the CIT model has been widely adopted in many countries including Canada. Despite the widespread adoption of CIT, there is no conclusive evidence of their effectiveness, which has prompted calls for further research (Fisher & Grudzinskas, 2010).

Despite the lack of conclusive evidence of their effectiveness, there have been numerous anecdotal reports that CIT are effective. For example, Canada, Angell, and Watson (2010) note "a growing body of research suggests that CIT helps police personnel better manage mental health calls" (p. 98). Similarly, Hanafi et al. (2008) reported that a 40-hour CIT training session with police in Atlanta produced an "increased knowledge and awareness of mental illnesses" and provided participants with better understanding of the "skills required to effectively de-escalate crisis situations" (p.431). Watson et al. (2010), examined CIT programs in Chicago and found the program was having the greatest impact on the decisions of officers who had personal familiarity with mental illness (e.g., a family member) and positive perceptions of the mental health services in their area. Also, Franz and Borum's (2011) analysis of CIT encounters with PMI in Central Florida between 2001 and 2005, found evidence that CIT are useful in reducing discretionary arrests among PMI. Morabito et al. (2012), in their study of CIT programs in Chicago between 2002 and 2005, found that CIT officers were likely to respond with less force than UPO in their encounters with PMI. Van den Brink et al. (2012), studied police encounters with PMI in the Netherlands and found police play an important role in referring PMI to mental health services.

In contrast to the studies that have found positive effects of CIT, Compton et al. (2009) found no correlation between the deployment of CIT and a reduction in the number of calls for service for emergency response teams. Similarly, Strauss et al. (2005), studied CIT officers in Louisville and found no difference in the rates CIT and UPO officers referred PMI except for individuals suffering from schizophrenia, who were twice as likely to be referred by a CIT officer as a UPO. Kerr, Morabito, and Watson (2010), analysed 865 encounters in which police or PMI suffered injuries in Chicago in 2008 and found that injuries are rare in police encounters with PMI and when injuries do occur they are similar to those experienced by the general population. They also found that CIT training had no effect on injuries in police encounters with PMI. As well, there is no evidence to suggest that police who volunteer for CIT training are more empathetic to PMI (Compton, 2011).

Canada, Angell, and Watson (2012) have identified six areas in which CIT police differ from their UPO colleagues when responding to PMI: assessments, listening, talking, response tactics, time management, and dispositions. In particular, they note CIT reported "a more comprehensive assessment of danger" (p. 750) in their encounters with PMI and a more varied understanding of PMI behavior. Also, CIT reported using "response tactics" such as talking to de-escalate situations, making an extra effort to listen to PMI, and allowing themselves extra time to non-violently resolve encounters. Lastly, CIT were able to identify more options such as making referrals, providing relevant information, and offering transportation to medical practitioners, rather than merely hospitalizing or arresting PMI. Similarly, Steadman et al. (2001) identified several key components to an effective CIT program. These include 24-hour police-friendly specialized response sites, crisis services that provide on-site treatment, and appropriate referrals for PMI who are stabilized.

Lord et al. (2011) conducted one of the more interesting studies when they interviewed 3,532 "consumers" of CIT services in a mixed urban/rural county of a southern US state. They found that most incidents with consumers were resolved by a voluntary commitment or an informal resolution at the scene. They also noted the important role played by hospital admission policies on the behavior of CIT officers. Specifically, CIT officers were more likely to arrest

PMI, especially in smaller rural communities, if they were required to remain with the PMI until he or she was either admitted or discharged. In their study of 2,174 CIT officer's reports of encounters with individuals in Ohio from 2000 and 2005, Ritter et al. (2011) found that CIT officer decisions about whether to transport individuals to hospital were based on their own assessments and not how the calls for service were dispatched to them.

The relative success of CIT over the past two decades has catalyzed thinking about additional ways police organizations can effectively respond to the special needs of PMI. At their simplest, these innovative approaches, like CIT, involve some element of increasing cooperation between police and mental health practitioners.

Recent Innovations

There have been several recent innovations since the first CIT was developed in Memphis in 1988. Specifically, Douglas and Lurigo (2010) note the introduction of youth CIT, which was developed to replicate the advantages of adult CIT such as reducing arrests, increasing referrals, and decreasing the risk for both police and youth during police–PMI encounters. Also, McGriff et al. (2010) describe the implementation of a CIT program in an airport setting. They found the "scrutiny facilitated by video monitoring and hundreds of onlookers heightens the tension and necessity to successfully de-escalate mental health crises in an effective way" (p. 163).[11] This study suggests police organizations possess the skills to non-violently resolve many encounters with PMI through de-escalation tactics but require the motivation to utilize these skills.

Another recent development in the area of police–PMI encounters has been the creation of integrated mobile response teams (IMRT). These teams consist of a combination of police and mental health practitioners that patrol in police vehicles ready to respond to calls for service involving PMI. Since the development of IMRT there have been several studies that have evaluated their effectiveness.

Kisley et al. (2010) evaluated an integrated mobile crisis team in Nova Scotia and concluded the "introduction of an integrated mobile crisis service involving clinicians and police officers was associated with improved response times in spite of an increased use by patients, families, and service partners" (p. 662). Similarly, Steadman et al. (2000), in their study of three mobile crisis intervention teams, found that the existence of a psychiatric triage or drop-off centre where police could transport PMI and then leave them to return to regular patrol was a key factor in the program's success. Another key factor was the centrality of community partnerships such that each program was part of a community policing strategy. Finally, Coleman and Cotton (2010), using as "systems approach," have proposed twelve principles to guide police interactions with PMI.

More recently, Coleman and Cotton (2014) have proposed fundamental changes for police education and training. These changes can be summarized as:

► anti-stigma education to challenge the attitudinal barriers that lead to discriminatory actions,

► the de-escalating/defusing interactions with people with mental illness (PMI) by means of effective verbal and non-verbal communications, and

► ethical decision making, human rights protection and social responsibility. (p.7)

Specifically, they suggest that police use of force training "ensure[s] that ample time is dedicated to understanding, learning and practicing how to resolve situations without the use of force" (p.7). Clearly, police require more education training in non-violent conflict resolution among other areas.

Recommendations

The studies reviewed for this chapter make it clear that police need more training in how to respond to the special needs of PMI. Specialized, crisis intervention training that orients police to the needs of PMI and teaches them how to de-escalate conflicts is needed for all police – not just those assigned to CIT. De-escalation strategies should emphasize the importance of time management and the desirability of containment and withdrawal strategies where appropriate.

Highly trained, specialized police dealing with PMI is pointless if police are not properly prepared when they encounter PMI. This points to the importance of police dispatchers providing police with the most detailed and accurate information available before they arrive at the scene. As we have seen in several of the studies reviewed in this chapter, when a police officer arrives at the scene and is surprised by a PMI armed with a weapon, the likelihood the PMI or the police officer will be killed is extremely high, regardless of the training the police officer has received.

A wider range of intermediate use of force options is needed. Several studies have reported that ECD may not be effective in neutralizing a PMI in crisis. If police cannot rely on ECD in this situation, then their only option is to escalate to a firearm when confronted by a PMI armed with a weapon. When a police firearm is deployed the risk of someone – police or PMI – dying increases dramatically.[12]

Also, a consensus is emerging that CIT programs are the most effective way to safely and efficiently manage police encounters with PMI; however, additional research is needed to validate this belief. Nevertheless, it is important mental health facilities accept PMI delivered to them by police and allow police to leave in a timely fashion. Otherwise, police are reluctant to use these medical services and resort to arrest as an alternative. In short, a high level of cooperation between police and mental health practitioners is necessary for these programs to succeed.

The implementation of these recommendations, along with others we have discussed in this chapter, could go a long way to saving lives – PMI and police. The only thing stopping the implementation of these policies are the resources (e.g., training) and will (e.g., police and politicians) to implement them. As we ponder these issues it behooves us to remember that a society is judged by how well it treats its least advantaged members. Clearly, PMI are among the least advantage members of our society; if we fail to take the steps necessary to save their lives and the lives of the first responders who try to help them, then we will have failed them and ourselves too.

Conclusions

Canadian police are authorized by law to use force, including lethal force, to resolve conflict. With the development of anti-psychotic drugs and the deinstitutionalization of many PMI, police have become the first responders to PMI in crisis. While most of these encounters are resolved non-violently, a significant number are not, and, as a result, too often police and PMI are seriously injured and even killed. The risk to police and PMI can be reduced by teaching police and particularly UPO more effective strategies, such as better time management and negotiating skills, to manage these encounters. Also, the utilization of more CIT would help to reduce the risk to both police and PMI when the two groups come into conflict.

Case Study 1 – What should be done?

In late July 2013, Torontonians awoke to the news of a deadly shooting. Eighteen-year-old Sammy Adib Yatim had been shot by a police officer in a streetcar in the downtown area. Police were called to the incident shortly after midnight after the driver reported that the other streetcar passengers had exited the vehicle due to Yatim's behaviour. The young man was holding a knife. Witnesses to the events leading up to the evacuation of the streetcar indicated that Yatim had exposed himself, behaved in an aggressive manner, and brandished a knife. The police entered the Toronto Transit Commission vehicle and some form of interaction between Yatim and the police occurred. Yatim was shot several times by a police officer, and then Tasered. He died shortly thereafter in hospital.

Questions arose about the necessity for the use of lethal force in the wake of the death of Sammy Yatin. Public demonstrations followed in the downtown core of the city led by Yatin's mother and friends. Less than a month later, Toronto Police Constable James Furcillo was charged with second-degree murder in the case. The charges were brought by the Special Investigations Unit (SIU) who stated that "the Director of the Special Investigations Unit, Ian Scott, has reasonable grounds to believe that a Toronto Police Service officer committed a criminal offence in relation to the shooting."

What distinguishes the Yatim case is that an individual captured some of the images involved in the interaction on the streetcar on video. Readers can easily access this video online at https://www.youtube.com/watch?v=lG6OTyjzAgg&list=PLx6HYhbH1bCxGeFSjwgLKMV5e-vfn-FW9

Consider the following factors:

1. Twenty police officers were on the scene when Yatim was fatally shot. As the Yatim family related in their response to charges being laid in their son's death, "no one stepped forward to stop the gun shots or offer any mediation." The Yatim family wants the SIU to look into the lack of response from supervisory officers on the scene.
2. Yatim had no history of mental illness or violence, according to his family.
3. The police fired nine shots; first three shoots and then an additional six.
4. Yatim was Tasered when he was lying on the floor of the streetcar having been shot multiple times.
5. Tasers were not deployed until after he was shot.

Case Study 1 – *continued*

Watch the video and discuss these questions:

1. Did police act within the law in the Yatim incident?
2. Would the officer's actions be viewed differently if Yatim has a history of mental illness?
3. How much and what training should police receive in dealing with potentially deadly situations?
4. Should all police officers been trained in the use of, and carry Tasers?

Sources: Visser, J. (2013, August 19). Toronto police officer charged with second degree murder in streetcar death of Sammy Yatim. *Toronto Star,* Fatima, S. (2013, July 27). Man dead after police shooting on Dundas streetcar. *Toronto Star*.

Case Study 2 – The Coroner's Inquest

Coroner's inquests are normally heard to address issues with the administration of justice and the untimely death of individuals where law enforcement officials are concerned. They also hold inquests into deaths in custody and other cases where there are issues that are unresolved to the satisfaction of the coroner or the family of the deceased. Inquests make recommendations on changes to policy or practices that might, for example, prevent an unnecessary loss of life in the future. On October 15, 2013, an inquest began into the deaths of three mentally ill persons who had been killed by Toronto police. The inquest is considering three cases:

1. Michael Eligon, 29, was shot by police on February 3, 2012. He had escaped from hospital dressed in a hospital gown. When confronted on Milverton Avenue, a few blocks from East General Hospital, he had a pair of scissors in each of his hands. He was surrounded by 12 officers. Three rounds were fired and he subsequently died.
2. Jardine-Douglas, 25, was killed on August 29, 2010. His family had contacted police asking for their son to be taken to hospital. He was discovered by police on a bus on Victoria Park Avenue in Toronto. He came towards a police officer with a knife. Of the four shots fired, two hit Douglas. He died shortly thereafter.
3. Sylvia Klibingaitis, 52 was shot and killed after police were summoned to her home in North York, a Toronto suburb. She had indicated she had a knife and was planning on committing a crime. Klibingaitis was known to suffer from bipolar disorder and psychotic episodes. A Toronto police officer fired three rounds at her, with one hitting her in the chest.

Case Study 2 – *continued*

Questions to consider

1. An inquest into the police shooting of Edmond Yu in 1997 yielded a number of recommendations regarding police training in dealing with the mentally ill. Yu was shot by police on an empty Toronto bus wielding a knife. Why do you think police training and/or education about dealing with the mentally ill might not be adequate given the three cases cited above?
2. Police officers receive two days of use of force training annually, including dealing with the mentally ill. What recommendations on training would you make in light of the above deaths if you were a member of a coroner's jury.
3. A coroner's inquest is mandatory when more than two deaths occur because of a "common cause." Consider the following fact; more than nine mentally ill persons have died as the result of police use of deadly force from the 1980s to the present.
4. Does the mental state of the victim justify police use of deadly force in your opinion?
5. How do officers balance the need to protect others with the right to not be gravely injured or killed on the job?

Sources: Pagliaro, J. (2013, August 8). Inquest into three police shootings set for Oct. 15. *Toronto Star*; Rush, C. (2013, July 24). Sammy Yatim latest in a long list of Toronto police shooting deaths. *Toronto Star*.

Glossary of Key Terms

Anti-psychotic medications – powerful drugs used to treat mental illnesses such as schizophrenia. These drugs often have unpleasant side effects.

CID – crisis intervention and de-escalation training for police.

CIT – a crisis intervention team consisting of police officers with specialized training in dealing with persons with mental illness.

Deinstitutionalization – the process by which most people with mental illness were no longer held in psychiatric institutions following the development of anti-psychotic medications in the 1970s.

ERT – an emergency response team consisting of police trained in the use of specialized weapons and non-violent conflict resolution skills.

IMRT – An integrated mobile response team consisting of a combination of police and mental health practitioners.

PMI – a person with a mental illness. The term "is used to denote anyone whose behavior at the time in question appears to be influenced by the presence of significant mental distress or illness. It may be that the person is experiencing a persistent and severe illness such as schizophrenia, or it may be that they are experiencing a transitory period of distress and are temporarily experiencing symptoms that may be expected to abate, as in the case of an acute anxiety problem" (Coleman & Cotton, 2010, p54).

ECD – An electronically controlled device such as a Taser used by police as a use of force response option. Considered to be more forceful than a baton and less forceful than a firearm.

UPO – a uniformed patrol officer. These individuals constitute the overwhelming majority of all police and are the least trained. Due to their large numbers, they are most likely to respond to persons with mental illness, and due to their relative lack of training, they are the most at risk to be seriously injured or to seriously injure a person with mental illness.

Appendix

Figure 1 – The Incident Management Intervention Model

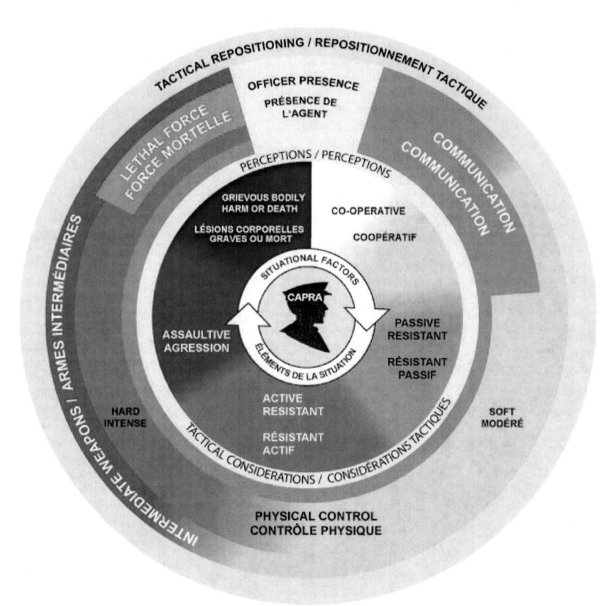

Source: RCMP (2015). Incident management/intervention model. Retrieved from http://www. rcmp-grc.gc.ca/ccaps-spcca/cew-ai/imim-migi-eng.htm#imim

Table 1 – Use of Force Response Options

Level	Citizen Behaviour	Explanation	Police Response	Explanation
1	Cooperative	The subject responds appropriately to the officer's presence, communication and control.	Officer Presence	While not strictly an intervention option, the simple presence of an officer can affect both the subject and the situation. Visible signs of authority such as uniforms and marked police cars can change a subject's behaviour.
2	Passive Resistant	The subject refuses, with little or no physical action, to cooperate with the officer's lawful direction. This can assume the form of a verbal refusal or consciously contrived physical inactivity. For example, some subjects will go limp and become dead weight.	Communication	An officer can use verbal and non-verbal communication to control and/or resolve the situation.
3	Active Resistant	The subject uses non-assaultive physical action to resist, or while resisting an officer's lawful direction. Examples would include pulling away to prevent or escape control, or overt movements such as walking away from an officer. Running away is another example of active resistance.	Physical Control	The model identifies two levels of physical control: soft and hard. In general, physical control means any physical technique used to control the subject that does not involve the use of a weapon. *Soft* techniques may be utilized to cause distraction in order to facilitate the application of a control technique. Distraction techniques include but are not limited to open hand strikes and pressure points. Control techniques include escorting and/or restraining techniques, joint locks and non-resistant handcuffing which have a lower probability of causing injury. *Hard* techniques are intended to stop a subject's behaviour or to allow application of a control technique and have a higher probability of causing injury. They may include empty hand strikes

Table 1 – *continued*

Level	Citizen Behaviour	Explanation	Police Response	Explanation
				such as punches and kicks. Vascular Neck Restraint (Carotid Control) is also a hard technique.
4.	**Assaultive**	The subject attempts to apply, or applies force to any person; attempts or threatens by an act or gesture, to apply force to another person, if he/she has, or causes that other person to believe upon reasonable grounds that he/she has the present ability to effect his/her purpose. Examples include kicking and punching, but may also include aggressive body language that signals the intent to assault.	**Intermediate Weapons**	This intervention option involves the use of a less-lethal weapon. Less-lethal weapons are those whose primary use is not intended to cause serious injury or death. Kinetic energy weapons, aerosols and conducted energy weapons fall within this heading.
5.	**Grievous Bodily Harm or Death**	The subject exhibits actions that the officer reasonably believes are intended to, or likely to cause grievous bodily harm or death to any person. Examples include assaults with a knife, stick or firearm, or actions that would result in serious injury to an officer or member of the public.	**Lethal Force**	This intervention option primarily involves the use of conventional police firearms (duty pistol, shotgun, rifle, patrol rifle etc). The use of these firearms are intended to, or are reasonably likely to cause serious bodily injury or death through ballistic force, i.e., a lead projectile, when facing subject behaviour(s) that may result in Grievous Bodily Harm or Death.

Source: RCMP (2014). Retrieved from http://www.rcmp-grc.gc.ca/ccaps-spcca/cew-ai/imim-migi-eng.htm#decision

Notes

[1] Johnson (2011) found that "mentally unstable suspects were significantly more likely to physically resist, assault officers and possess a weapon than suspects not labeled mentally unstable" (p. 140).

[2] 25.(1) Everyone who is required or authorized by law to do anything in the administration or enforcement of the law

    (a) as a private person,

    (b) as a peace officer or public officer,

    (c) in aid of a peace officer or public officer, or

    (d) by virtue of his office,

is, if he acts on reasonable grounds, justified in doing what he is required or authorized to do and in using as much force as is necessary for that purpose.

(3) Subject to subsection (4), a person is not justified for the purposes of subsection (1) in using force that is intended to or is likely to cause death or grievous bodily harm unless he believes on reasonable grounds that it is necessary for the purpose of preserving himself or anyone under his protection from death or grievous bodily harm.

(4) A peace officer who is proceeding lawfully to arrest, with or without warrant, any person for an offence for which that person may be arrested without warrant, and everyone lawfully assisting the peace officer, is justified, if the person to be arrested takes flight to avoid arrest, in using as much force as is necessary to prevent the escape by flight, unless the escape can be prevented by reasonable means in a less violent manner. R.S., c. C-34, s.25.

[3] Alpert, Dunham, and MacDonald, (2004) found that "police use-of-force interactions with civilians are more likely to involve greater use of force by the police relative to the suspect when a suspect appears to have less authority relative to the police officer" (p. 484).

[4] The ECD failed to have effect in all three incidents (Parent, 2011).

[5] They were apparent because there was not a clinical diagnosis in every case.

[6] The decedents all used edged weapons, not firearms.

[7] The comparable number of police deaths during the same period was 15 (Statistics Canada, 2010).

[8] Axis 1 disorders include bi-polar, schizophrenia, anxiety and depressive disorders, psychosis.

[9] This underestimates the actual number of incidents in which a PMI was implicated in the death of a police officer since Statistics Canada only reports deaths that occurred while the police victim was attempting to apprehend a psychiatric patient.

[10] The calendar describing the Basic Constable Training Course (2012) at the Ontario Police College does not specifically identify mental health/illness as one of the topics covered in the program of study. Similarly, the Cadet Training Program (2012) published by the RCMP makes no mention of mental health/illness.

[11] This finding stands in sharp contrast to the Robert Dziekanski incident which occurred in the Vancouver Airport on October 14, 2007. In this incident, Dziekanski was Tasered by police while being arrested and subsequently died. Importantly, the distraught Mr. Dziekan-

ski was apprehended by UPO who precipitously engaged him with little or no effort to communicate first.

[12] The common assumption is that PMI will be shot and killed, which is a frequent result. However, it is also the case the police officer may be disarmed and shot with his or her own weapon in this situation. Eleven percent of Canadian police who were killed in the line of duty between 1960 and 1991 were disarmed and shot with either their own or a colleague's firearm (Canadian Centre for Justice Statistics, 1992).

Suggested Readings

Coleman, T. G., & Cotton, D. H. (2010). Reducing risk and improving outcomes of police interactions with people with mental illness. *Journal of Police Crisis Negotiations, 10,* 39-57.

Hock, J. S., Hartford, K., Heslop, L., & Stitt, L. (2009). Mental illness and police interactions in a mid-sized Canadian city: What the data do and do not say. *Canadian Journal of Community Mental Health, 28*(1), 49-66.

Kesic, D., Thomas, S. D. M., & Ogloff, J .R. P. (2012). Analysis of fatal police shootings: Time, space and suicide by police. *Criminal Justice and Behavior 39*(8), 1107-1125.

Parent, R. (2011). The police use of deadly force In British Columbia: Mental illness and crisis intervention. *Journal of Police Crisis Negotiations, 11,* 57-71.

References

Abraham, J. D., Field, J. C., Harding R. W., & Skurka, S. (1981). Police use of lethal force: A Toronto perspective. *Osgoode Hall Law Journal, 19,* 199-236.

Alpert, G., Dunham, R., & MacDonald, J. (2004). Interactive Police–citizen encounters that result in force. *Police Quarterly, 7,* 475-488.

Brown, J. M., & Langan, P. A. (2001). *Policing and Homicide, 1976-1998: Justifiable homicide by police, police officers murdered by felons.* U.S. Department of Justice, Bureau of Justice Statistics.

Canada, K. E., Angell, B., & Watson, A. C. (2010). Crisis intervention teams in Chicago: Success on the ground. *Journal of Police Crisis Negotiations, 10,* 86-100.

Canada, K. E., Angell, B., & Watson, A. C. (2012). Intervening at the entry point: Differences in how CIT trained and non-CIT trained officers describe responding to mental health-related calls. *Community Mental Health Journal, 48,* 746-755.

Canadian Centre for Justice Statistics. (1992, March). *Homicide project: Police officers murdered while on duty, 1961-1990.* Unpublished Report. Ottawa.

Chappell, D., & Graham, L. P. (1985). *Police use of deadly force: Canadian perspectives.* Toronto, Centre of Criminology, University of Toronto.

Charette, Y., Crocker, A.G., & Billette, I. (2011). The judicious judicial juggle: Characteristics of police interventions involving people with a mental illness. *Canadian Journal of Psychiatry, 56*(11), 677-685.

Clayfield, J. C., Fletcher, K. E., & Grudzinskas Jr., A. J. (2011). Development and validation of the mental health attitude survey for police. *Community Mental Health Journal, 47,* 742-751.

Coleman, T. G., & Cotton, D. H. (2005, July). *A Study of fatal interactions between Canadian police and mentally ill persons 1992-2002, phase 1.* Paper presented at International Conference of Law and Mental Health, Paris.

Coleman, T. G., & Cotton, D. H. (2010). Reducing risk and improving outcomes of police interactions with people with mental illness. *Journal of Police Crisis Negotiations, 10*, 39-57.

Coleman, T.G., & Cotton, D.H. (2014). *TEMPO: Police interactions – A report toward improving interactions between police and people living with mental illness.* Ottawa: Mental Health Commission of Canada.

Compton, M. T., Bahora, M., Watson, A. M., & Oliva, J. R. (2008). A comprehensive review of extant research on crisis intervention team (CIT) programs. *Journal of American Academy of Psychiatry Law, 60*, 831-833.

Compton, M. T., Broussard, B., Hankerson-Dyson, D., & Stewart-Hutto, T. (2011). Do empathy and psychological mindedness affect police officers' decision to enter crisis intervention training? *Psychiatric Services, 62*, 632-638.

Compton, M. T., Demir, B., Oliva, J. R., & Boyce, T. (2009). Crisis intervention team training and special weapons and tactics call outs in an urban police department. *Psychiatric Services, 60*, 831-833.

Compton, M. T., Esterberg, M. L., McGee, R., & Kotwicki, R. J. (2006). Crisis intervention team training: Changes in knowledge, attitudes and stigma related to schizophrenia. *Psychiatric Services, 57*(8), 1199-1202.

Crocker, A. G., Harford, K., & Heslop, L. (2009). Gender difference in police encounters among persons with and without serious mental illness. *Psychiatric Services, 60*, 86-93.

Douglas, A. V., & Lurigo, A .J. (2010). Youth crisis intervention teams (CITS): A response to the fragmentation of the educational, mental health and juvenile justice systems. *Journal of Police Crisis Negotiations, 10*, 241-263.

Dupont, R., & Cochran, S. (2000). Police response to mental health emergencies — Barriers to change. *Journal of the American Academy of Psychiatry and the Law, 28*, 338-344.

Fisher, W. H., & Grudzinskas Jr., A .J. (2010). Crisis Intervention teams as the solution to managing crisis involving persons with serious psychiatric illnesses: Does one size fit all? *Journal of Police Crisis Negotiations, 10*, 58-71.

Franz, S., & Borum, R. (2011). Crisis intervention teams may prevent arrests of people with mental illnesses. *Police Practice and Research, 12*(3), 265-272.

Fyfe, J. (1989). The split second syndrome and other determinants of police violence. In R. Dunham & R. Alpert (Eds.), *Critical issues in policing: Contemporary readings* (2nd ed.) (pp. 493-508). Prospect Heights, IL: Waveland Press.

Gill, J. R., & Pasquale-Styles, M. (2009). Firearm deaths by law enforcement. *Journal of Forensic Science, 54*(1), 185-188.

Greenstone, J. L. (2007). The twenty-five most serious errors made by police hostage and crisis negotiators. *Journal of Police Crisis Negotiations, 7*, 107-116.

Hails, J., & Borum, R. (2003). Police training and specialized approaches to respond to people with mental illness. *Crime and Delinquency, 49*(1), 52-61.

Hanafi, S., Bahora, M., Demir, B. N., & Compton, M. T. (2008). Incorporating crisis intervention team (CIT) knowledge and skills into the daily work of police officers: A focus group study. *Community Mental Health Journal, 44*, 427-432.

Hock, J. S., Hartford, K., Heslop, L., & Stitt, L., (2009). Mental illness and police interactions in a mid-sized Canadian City: What the data do and do not say. *Canadian Journal of Community Mental Health, 28*(1), 49-66.

Hon, A. (2012). Factors influencing the adherence to antipsychotic medication (Aripiprazole) in first episode psychosis: Findings from a grounded theory study. *Journal of Psychiatric and Mental Health Nursing, 19,* 354-361.

Johnson, R. R. (2011). Suspect mental disorder and police use of force. *Criminal Justice and Behavior, 38*(2), 127-145.

Kaminski, R. J., DiGiovanni, C., & Downs, R. (2004). The use of force between the police and persons with impaired judgment. *Police Quarterly, 7,* 311-338.

Kerr, A. M., Morabito, M., & Watson, A. C. (2010). Police encounters, mental illness, and injury: An exploratory investigation. *Journal of Police Crisis Negotiations, 10,* 116-132.

Kesic, D., Thomas, S .D. M., & Ogloff, J. R. P. (2010). Mental illness among police fatalities in Victoria 1982-2007: A case linkage study. *Australian and New Zealand Journal of Psychiatry, 44*(5), 463-468.

Kesic, D., Thomas, S. D. M., & Ogloff, J. R. P. (2013). Use of nonfatal force on and by persons with apparent mental disorder in encounters with police. *Criminal Justice and Behavior, 4*(3), 321-337.

Kisley, S., Campbell, L. A., Peddle, S., Hare, S. Psyche, M., Spicer, D., & Moore, B. (2010). A controlled before-and-after evaluation of a mobile crisis partnership between mental health and police services in Nova Scotia. *Canadian Journal of Psychiatry, 55*(10), 662-668.

Lawton, B. A. (2007). Levels of nonlethal force: An examination of individual, situational and contextual factors. *Journal of Research in Crime and Delinquency, 44,* 163-184.

Lord, V. B., Bjerregaard, B., Blevins, K .R., & Whisman, H. (2011). Factors influencing the responses of crisis intervention team-certified law enforcement officers. *Police Quarterly, 14*(4), 388-406.

Martinez, L. E. (2010). Police Department's response in dealing with persons with mental illness. *Journal of Police Crisis Negotiations, 10,* 166-174.

McGriff, J. A., Broussard, B., Demir Neubert, B. N., Thompson, N. J., & Compton, N. T. (2010). Implementing a crisis intervention team (CIT) police presence in a large international airport setting. *Journal of Police Crisis Negotiations, 10,* 153-165.

Mills, M. J,. & Cummins, B. D. (1982). Deinstitutionalization reconsidered. *International Journal of Law and Psychiatry, 5,* 271-284.

Morabito, M. S., Kerr, A. N., Watson, A., Draine, J., Ottati, V., & Angell, B. (2012). Crisis intervention teams and people with mental illness: Exploring the factors that influence use of force. *Crime and Delinquency, 58*(1), 55-77.

O'Brien, A. J., McKenna, B. G., Thom, K., Diesfeld, K., & Simpson, A. I. F. (2011). Use of Tasers on people with mental illness: A New Zealand database study. *International Journal of Law and Psychiatry, 34,* 39-43.

Ontario Police Commission. (1989). *Review of police tactical units.* Toronto: Ministry of the Solicitor General.

Ontario Police College. (2012). *2012 course calendar.* Retrieved from www.opconline.ca

Panzarella, R., & Alicia, J. O. (1997). Police tactics in incidents with mentally disturbed persons. *Policing, 20*(2), 326-338. doi: 10.1108/13639519710169162.

Parent, R. (2011). The police use of deadly force in British Columbia: Mental illness and crisis intervention. *Journal of Police Crisis Negotiations, 11,* 57-71.

Parent, R. B., & Verdun-Jones, S. (1998). Victim precipitated homicide: Police use of deadly force in British Columbia. *Policing: An International Journal of Police Strategies and*

Management, 21(3), 432-448.

RCMP. (2012). *Cadet training brief overview.* Retrieved from http://www.rcmp-grc.gc.ca/depot/ctp-pfc/index-eng.htm#aps-spa

Ritter, C., Teller, J. L. S., Marcussen, K., Munetz, M. R., & Teasdale, B. (2011). Crisis intervention team officer dispatch, assessment and disposition: Interactions with individuals with severe mental illness. *International Journal of Law and Psychiatry, 34*, 30-38.

Scull, A. (1985). Deinstitutionalization and Public Policy. *Social Science and Medicine, 20*(5), 545-552.

Stansfield, R. T. (1993). *The evolution of police forms and structure: A transpersonal perspective.* (Unpublished doctoral dissertation). York University, North York, ON.

Statistics Canada. (2010). *Police officers murdered in the line of duty, 1961-2009.* (Cat. No. 85-002-X). *Juristat, 30*(3).

Steadman, H. J., Deane, H. W., Borum, R., & Morrissey, J. P. (2000). Comparing outcomes of major models of police responses to mental health emergencies. *Psychiatric Services, 51*(5), 645-649.

Steadman, H. J., Stainbrook, H. K., Griffin, P., Draine, J., Dupont, R., & Horey, C. (2001). A specialized crisis response site as a core element of police based diversion programs. *Psychiatric Services, 52*(2), 219-222.

Strauss, G., Glenn, M., Reddi, P., Afaq, I., Podolskaya, A., Rybakova, T., Saeed, O., Shah, V., Singh, B., Skinner, A., & El-Mallakh, R. (2005). Psychiatric disposition of patients brought in by crisis intervention team police officers. *Community Mental Health Journal, 41*(2), 223-228.

Teplin, L. A., & Pruett, N. S. (1992). Police as street-corner psychiatrist: Managing the mentally ill. *International Journal of Law and Psychiatry, 15*, 139-156.

Terrill, W. (2005). Police use of force: A transactional approach. *Justice Quarterly, 22*, 107-138.

Toronto Police Service. (1998). *Use of Force Committee: Final report.* Retrieved from http://www.torontopolice.on.ca/publications/files/reports/1998useofforce.pdf

Watson, A. (2010). Research in the real world: Studying Chicago Police Department's Crisis Intervention Team Program. *Research on Social Work Practice, 20*(5), 536-543.

Watson, A. C., Corrigan, P. W., & Ottati, V. (2004). Police officer's attitudes towards and decisions about persons with mental illness. *Psychiatric Services, 55*(1), 49-53.

Watson, A., Ottati, V., Morabito, M., Draine, J., Kerr, A. N., & Angell, B. (2010). Outcomes of police contacts with person with mental illness: The impact of CIT. *Administration and Policy in Mental Health, 37*, 302-317.

van den Brink, R. S. H., Broer, J., Tholen, A. J., Winthorst, W. H., Visser, E., & Wiersma, D. (2012). Role of the police in linking individuals experiencing mental health crises with mental health services Title of article. *BMC Psychiatry, 12*, 171-178.

Forging the Disciplined Global Body: Police Deviance, Lawlessness, and the Toronto G20

Chapter 17

Patricia O'Reilly and Thomas Fleming

Learning Objectives

In this chapter you will...

▶ gain an understanding of to legislation historically used to protect public works and its contemporary, problematic uses in the context of protest

▶ learn about the misuse of force by police as a form of violence

▶ consider how jailing those arrested during the G20 is a form of violence and intimidation

▶ examine the aftermath of the arrests in terms of pubic and legal response, including accountability for police acts of deviance and violence

▶ explore the question of police powers and how they can be controlled

---

> This isn't Canada right now … [and] … there is no civil rights here in Ontario.
> — Police officer to a citizen who questions being asked to have her purse searched at G20 (qtd. in Marin, 2010, p. 108).

Introduction: Rights, Control, and Policing

States exercise power through bureaucracies and institutions manifest in the criminal justice system and interwoven points of control situated throughout society. The imagination and implementation of disciplinary regimes on citizens is intended to produce what Foucault (1973) termed "docile subjects." The power of the state creates the environment through which the jurisprudential and penal systems are able to forge a "law and order" regime (Ratner & McMullan, 1985) that moulds the docile citizen into a specific order codified and absorbed by citizens through social regulations and forms of social control. In Canada, the passage of the *Canadian Charter of Rights and Freedoms* (1982) enshrined a significant number of fundamental freedoms that represent not only rights enjoyed by all citizens, but also a well understood and expected set of freedoms that have been held to be unassailable within reasonable limits established through legal precedent. All rights and freedoms that flow from the *Charter* are supposedly "guaranteed," and one might argue that until the events surrounding the G20 this would have been the universal understanding of the *Charter*. Such social contracts are singularly important in maintaining the cooperation of the populace. As Colaguori (2012) asserts, the state maintains legitimacy "by codifying the parameters of socially and legally acceptable behaviour" (p. 99) to produce consensus and social stability. Among the four "fundamental freedoms" enshrined in the document are: "(a) freedom of thought, belief, opinion and expression, including freedom of the press and other media of communication; (b) freedom of peaceful assembly; and (c) freedom of assembly." Among the legal rights enumerated are: "the right to life, liberty and security of the person and the right not to be deprived thereof except in accordance with the principles of fundamental justice; the right to be secure against unreasonable search or seizure; and the right not to be arbitrarily detained or imprisoned" (*Constitution Act*, 1982, c. 11(U.K.), Schedule B, Part 1, Sections 1-12). Additionally, citizens have the right upon arrest to be informed promptly of the reasons for their arrest, to retain and instruct counsel without delay, and not to be subjected to cruel and unusual treatment or punishment. All of the above enumerated rights form a cornerstone of civil society within Canada. They represent a codification of the parameters that constrain police and the judicial system in regard to democratic rights. Central to the analysis that follows is the inherent right to traverse public spaces in Canada without being required to produce identification or permit a search of one's person or belongings unless one is placed under arrest. This was the understanding of the rights held by Canadians prior to the commencement of the G20 meetings. It provided a framework for planning by protest organizers who were liaising with police in the lead up to the G20, and this is central to understanding why police reverted to force rather than cooperation as the model of interaction in the streets. Given the infiltration of protest groups by police agencies, police commanders and intelligence officers would have been well aware of the lack of knowledge possessed by protesters as to the new law's enactment.

As numerous studies of the policing of public protest in Canada and beyond have understood there are two distinct approaches: promoting police recognition of rights versus confrontation tend to have very dramatically different outcomes (Brodeur, 1983). The alternative involves police engaging in clandestine infiltration of protest groups in order to effect coercive control (Hall & DeLint, 2009; King & Brearly, 1996; King & Waddington, 2005; Sheptycki, 2005). In the latter case, the potential for public mistrust and denunciation of police actions is, in our opinion, accentuated. Within Western democratic countries, police deviance, misuse of power, and violence can invoke public fears concerning the rise of "para-militarism" and a decline down the slippery slope of the diminishing or unjustified temporary suspension of legal rights in order to chill protests (Marin, 2010; Waddington, 1987). In North America, the deregulation of financial rules that led to the 2008 economic collapse has created an atmosphere of mistrust of the ability of governments to control (Klein, 2007) institutions and perhaps policing authorities with any degree of effectiveness. The G20 protests represent an opportunity for those disenfranchised to question decision making that is not consultative and that, arguably, has been ineffective given the continuing global financial crisis, rising youth unemployment, and the creation of what appears to be a permanent underclass. Police agencies have generally fared well in the shadow of fear created by 9/11. While economic cutbacks and wage freezes reign in the public and private service sector of Ontario, police officers have still received significant wage increases. Police budgets continue to balloon despite declining crime rates. In Toronto, for example, the police budget hovered near the billion-dollar mark in

2010 while essential social programs suffer continuing cuts and public pensions are under attack. The preceding enumeration of the fundamental rights of Canadian citizens was essential to establishing a base for understanding the illegality of police actions during the G20 and the threat that attempted erosions in fundamental rights and freedoms have signaled to citizens. The impact of these actions on producing fear and insecurity and thus quelling public protest is a serious concern for analysts of public order policing in Canada and beyond (Brodeur, 1983, 2010; King & Brearly, 1996; Sheptycki, 2005).

The Public Works Protection Act: "Secret Legislation" and the *Charter* Gap

There is a real and insidious danger associated with using subordinate legislation, passed behind closed doors, to increase police authority, and I believe that this practice should be sedulously avoided.
– Andre Marin, Ombudsman of Ontario (2010, p. 101)

In the period immediately preceding the G20 summit, the chief of police of the Toronto Police Service requested the Province of Ontario to grant a designation under the virtually unknown *Public Works Protection Act* (PWPA) to

support the establishment and control of the security *perimeter* for the G20 summit ... [to] ... offer legal support for the extraordinary security measures being undertaken for this unusual event ... to control the security *perimeter*. Those powers include requiring persons entering the public works to identify themselves and state their purpose for entering and authority to search people and vehicles attempting to enter. (Marin, 2010, pp. 52-53, emphasis added)

We note that the chief repeatedly refers to the "security perimeter." Reasonably, one might presume he was referring to the 15-foot-high chain link fence built in the downtown core of the city and the several block radius it encompassed. However, as events unfolded, it became clear that the officers on the street and their commanders expanded the "perimeter" for three or four kilometres from the fence edge into the heart of the downtown of Toronto. As Marin (2010) points out, there was a clear understanding on the part of government officials that the public works included in the PWPA were contained strictly at the perimeter and within the security fence, referred to by police as "the interdiction zone" (p. 60). It is also important to consider that more than ample means exist under federal criminal law and municipal bylaws to effect arrests for trespass, public disorder, and involvement in criminal activities. Further, as Canada is a signatory to United Nations protocols on the security required for visiting leaders, it would appear that the Royal Canadian Mounted Police, Ontario Provincial Police, Toronto Police Service, and the other police services on duty had more than ample means at their disposal to handle the protests, particularly since the events that transpired did so far from the secured area where the meetings were held.

Prior to the commencement of the G20 meetings the provincial government decided to invoke the *Public Works Protection Act* through Regulation 233/10. Normally when the province is either introducing, modifying, or reactivating a piece of legislation, it will publish notice of this in newspapers, may make announcements on radio and television, and publish their intent in law journals and other suitable venues. In other words, the province will ensure that the public is fully aware of the law. The amendments to the *Act* were announced in a little-read e-journal, and so no opportunity for public opposition to its implementation was possible. As the Canadian Civil Liberties Association (CCLA) noted in their condemnation of the lack of transparency and public notice in the way in which the legislation was introduced: "Secretive processes only serve to diminish the public trust in government" (CCLA, 2010a, p. 9). Indeed, the ombudsman called the PWPA "one of the best kept secrets in Ontario's legislative history" (Marin, 2010, p. 95). Beyond this, if there is intent to use the law for a specific purpose, indeed, if the law could be successfully challenged as to its illegality or contravention of the *Charter*, it would be normal practice to consult widely on its appropriateness. It is self-evident that the law was in contravention of the rights enumerated in the *Charter* and would not withstand a court challenge. In fact, Marin (2010) went even further in concluding that the province "was promoting legislation that substantially limited the rights and freedoms" (p. 97) of those in Toronto. Even more disconcerting is that, in the intelligence gathering that preceded the summit, the ministry and police agencies would have been well aware through their monitoring of internet sites that "demonstrators were being given rights advice, which, if followed after Regulation 233/10's enactment, could land unsuspecting protestors in jail (Marin, 2010, p. 97). The Toronto Police Service (TPS) knew that protestors and, indeed, any citizen on the street, would not know of the existence of this law and its sweeping powers, which left the TPS "holding the deck of 'go directly to jail' cards" (Marin, 2010, p. 97).

The PWPA cancelled many of the core civil rights on Canadians:

> A statute containing unusual, even extravagant police powers that could be – and in fact were – used to intimidate and arrest people who had done no harm … A new landscape was created in which people were compelled to identify themselves and explain why they wanted to enter, sometimes even in writing, and they were required to submit to warrantless searches. And even if they were refused entry, changed their mind and wished to walk away, they were still required to identify themselves, answer questions and submit to a search. Those who decline could be arrested. Those who decline could even be prosecuted and jailed. (Marin, 2010, p.98)

However, it appears evident that the province and policing agencies knew full well that the G20 arrests would occur and that the court challenges would either disappear because of the costs associated with such a legal challenge and/or would take years to come before the courts. Thus, the goal of their implementation of the *Act* would be realized without the possibility of a challenge preempting its use. In contrast, information regarding which highways, expressways, streets, and downtown core areas would be closed were heavily circulated in the media in the weeks leading up to the summit. The City of Toronto also mailed out brochures to over 100,000 houses in the downtown core advising citizens of "what to expect." Thus, it was considered extremely important to ensure citizens knew which roads not to use, but not that that their constitutionally guaranteed rights were going to be suspended. However, as we have noted, no mention was made in any press release or any other information channel concerning the revocation of fundamental rights and freedoms via the PWPA. It is useful to note that a number of police services were involved in the G20 operations in Toronto. The RCMP was responsible for the summit meetings assigning 5,000 officers. Toronto Police Service, York Regional Police, and Peel Police (two large forces policing in regions on the outskirts of Toronto) were involved, and other police officers were recruited from various Canadian services. Finally, both the Canadian Intelligence Services and the Canadian Army had persons involved in security for the summit (McNeilly, 2012; Morden, 2012). In total, some 19,000 officers were deployed to protect the G20 leaders and staff. The total cost of security for the summit reached one billion dollars.

Before the G20 meetings, the overwhelming majority of Ontarians had no idea of the existence of the PWPA. There are several examples of laws that are enacted for a specific purpose at one point in history and fall into general disuse but have been revivified to address an issue not contemplated by the original drafters of the law (Fleming, 1993). The PWPA was brought into force in 1939. This should give you some clue as to the nature of the *Act*. World War II prompted the passage of this *Act*, which was intended to give police agencies sweeping powers in or around hydro dams, military bases, weapons installations, electrical works, and munitions factories to prevent the enemy from sabotaging any of these facilities. It was intended as a temporary *Act* to address a specific issue within a limited time frame. Its use from the end of the war until today had been confined to regulating searches for individuals entering court premises and the security surrounding nuclear generation facilities. What did the *Act* allow police to do? Under the *Act*, police believed they had the authority to demand identification from anyone in or near the vicinity of the secure zone for the G20 or within miles of the summit fence and arrest them if they failed to produce identification. Furthermore, they believed they had other sweeping powers to arrest anyone under suspicion they were engaged in any activity designed to disrupt the "public works" – namely, the G20 meetings. In effect, through a process of illegal "ballooning," the PWPA was blown up and extended throughout the entire downtown area of Toronto. Thus, the designated "public works" encompassed the entire downtown rather than the specific limits of the *Act* to protect the summit site.

"Unusual and Extravagant Powers"

The ombudsman of Ontario, Mr. Marin (2010), and his staff undertook an investigation into the police actions during the G20 in the wake of 350 citizen complaints to police regarding their arrest and treatment. The report has the interesting title, "Caught in the Act," which reflects not only the video footage and photographs taken during the G20 protests but the fact that police actions took place in a very public forum. Social media, video, and photographs, along with the observations of independent monitors from the CCLA, have provided us with a very rich record of police misuse of power. Sir Hugh Orde, cited in Hoggett and Stott (2012) in his role as president of the Association of Police Officers, warned of the negative impacts of police use of excessive force in the context of British riots. He has stated that this will have dire consequences for the future of the police service. When citizens come to believe that the police are misusing or exceeding their powers, and on innocent persons in some cases (as was the case in the Toronto G20 arrests), an essential societal bond is fractured. A balanced approach to policing social protest and professional conduct by police with regard to rights and freedoms is viewed by many as essential for maintaining the rule of law. The "escalated force" model employed in the policing of the Toronto G20 commencing in the evening of the first day of the summit resulted, in our opinion, from the failure of police to engage the small group of protestors on the first day of the conference who rioted on Toronto's Yonge Street, smashing store windows over a three-block radius and setting fire to police vehicles. Toronto police were not available to deal with the offshoot group of 100 to 150 protestors who left the main peaceful group of approximately 25,000 to engage in extensive property damage. To put it bluntly, they were engrossed in ensuring that no one came close to the security fence surrounding the summit (Church, 2012). While Toronto police requested assistance from other agencies, that assistance did not materialize for twelve hours following the rampage on Yonge Street. Moreover, while we are addressing police deviance during the G20, we believe it is important to note that in the week preceding the summit, a huge police presence was evident in the downtown core of Toronto, enacting "systematic and widespread searches" (CCLA, 2010a, p. 11) outside subway stations, at the entrance to public parks, and in other locations. The CCLA monitors noted that "the police stated no basis for conducting the search" (CCLA, 2010a, p.11). Given this mass police presence in the downtown core, it is important to acknowledge that there was a significant and sustained media campaign to paint protestors as violent anarchists and terrorists bent on causing property damage and hurting innocent citizens. By contrast, the police were presented as working to prevent a catastrophe. This juxtaposing is a common media strategy engaged in by governments and policing authorities, bolstered particularly by conservative news agencies (Fleming, 1993). This has become more accentuated in the post 9/11 era as the usurping of civil rights is presented as necessary for ensuring the security of all (Colaguori, 2012; Dowler, Fleming, & Muzzatti, 2006; Fleming et al., 2008; Murphy, 2007). The large, visible presence of police engaged in unlawful searches created public perception from some that police were being proactive in protecting citizens from some form of terrorist attack. On the other hand, those who understood it directly infringed their *Charter* rights were greatly disturbed. The specter of 9/11 and the London bombings have contributed to a public consensus about the need for security, and, in the context of protecting world leaders, it can be viewed as necessary and responsible to take extra precautions in terms of potential terrorist activities. Again, the question remains, to what degree are we prepared to grant the police powers that suspend core civil liberties? Perhaps more centrally is the issue of whether the measures taken at the G20 by policing agencies is reasonable, effective, and warranted.

When Toronto police did not effectively respond to the riot on Yonge Street, the reaction of the news media, including coverage by CNN, portrayed the Toronto Police Service as inept and unprepared, preferring to literally stand idly by while a small group of individuals engaged the destruction of private property. This was in direct contrast to the massive police presence that had been observed in the downtown core in the days leading up to the summit. Police spokespersons, who argued that the police inaction was appropriate to "prevent injury" had, by the evening of the first day of the summit, decided to engage in what may be described as a prolonged, expansive, and unnecessary show of force throughout Toronto's downtown core.

According to a variety of reports and direct observations, constitutional protections regarding unwarranted searches and arbitrary detention were not in force after 5 p.m. of the first day of the summit (CCLA, 2010a, p. 11). Citizens walking on public sidewalks or through public parks were arbitrarily stopped by police and subject to interrogation and search. In the lead up to the G20, the police indicated that they would be employing newly purchased and expensive sound cannons (also known as LRADS – long range acoustic devices) in an effort to control crowds. This might have signaled the intention of the police to resort to new and untried methods to address what the Chief Bill Blair termed "the extraordinary security... for this unusual event" (qtd. in Marin, 2010, p. 52). While we can appreciate that security is necessary (King & Brearly, 1996; Sheptycki, 2005) in the context of public protest, the intended use of the cannons at a decibel level that would deafen peaceful protestors with the potential for lasting damage to hearing prompted a successful legal challenge by the CCLA.

"A Real and Insidious Danger"

The employing of "extraordinary" measures with regard to peaceful protest is problematic at best and open to significant criticism given the element of violence that characterizes police control efforts, including the violent apprehension of persons resting in a public park following a protest march, the tackling and forceful arrest of those awaiting arrested individuals at jail facilities to be released, or the ridiculous arrest of a young woman blowing bubbles at a police officer (Dicks & Davies, 2011). During the weekend of the summit, police began to appear throughout the downtown core in large groups wearing riot gear. They were seen, and can be viewed in social media, sporting guns used to pepper spray crowds, tasers, tear gas guns, and a weapon that shoots projectiles (CCLA, 2010a, p. 13). A series of police attacks on peaceful assemblies continued throughout the weekend. The area of Queen's Park, which houses the Ontario Houses of Parliament, was designated by the chief of police as a "free speech zone." In other words, this area was publicly declared to be a safe area for protestors to gather and meet. However, it soon became clear that police commanders on the ground either ignored or were ordered to disregard the free speech gathering zone, charging individuals who failed to respond to a command to disperse issued on a loud speaker that was not loud enough to be heard, and in setting where all dispersal routes were blocked, leading to violent, mass arrests, and the use of tear gas and rubber bullets.

Essentially, police designated any space within the downtown area at random as a "public work." Therefore, the powers granted under the *Act* were presumed by the police to be in effect. But did police administrators believe this to be the case? One of the reasons we announce changes to law widely is to permit public debate and dissent. We also encourage court challenges as noted above. The very serious problem with police use of this *Act* was that, by the time it had been used, and persons held, jailed, and, for the most part, released, no reasonable challenge to the authority of the *Act* and its legality could be mounted. As Marin (2010, pp. 98-101) commented, this constituted a "real and insidious danger," despite the premier's assurances that the law would not be used further and the Toronto Chief of Police's defense of the use of the powers under the *Act*. As Marin (2010, p.98) points out: "Apart from insiders in the government of Ontario, only members of the Toronto Police Service knew the rules of the game had changed, and they were the ones holding the deck of "go directly to jail cards." The police began preparing for the protests by requisitioning a piece of land on Eastern Avenue in the city's east end and constructing a large scale temporary jail that had reinforced fences and security around the perimeter. Did the government make a massive investment in this facility because they anticipated arresting protestors and non-protestors alike under the *Public Works Protection Act*? What would that investment have looked like to taxpayers if protests were peaceful and few arrests were made?

The essential problems of the use of the *Act* were reflected in the abuses of authority exercised by the police and the misuse of the *Act* to police security during an event rather than to protect publicly owned structures. Marin (2010, p.98) reflects that the *Act* was probably "invalid for having exceed the authority of the enactment under which it was passed." He noted that the government should have communicated with the public concerning the *Act* since it conferred "exceptional powers" and the result is that "police officers can adopt illegal strategies to limit protest because by the time legal action can be taken those strategies will have played themselves out" (Marin, 2010, p.99). Given that civil liberties cases are both expensive to mount, thus placing in many cases beyond the financial means of the individual protestor, and difficult to win, there was an onus on the government, as should be the case with the introduction of any law with wide sweeping powers, to test the law through broad consultation before its implementation. Moreover, it was apparent that, before these powers were conferred on police, there should have been a great deal of discussion with legal experts on the advisability of granting these draconain powers to the police. The misuse of laws from other eras to achieve a purpose for which it was not intended is not confined to this case. In examining the Toronto bathhouse raids, Fleming (1993) argued that the use of bawdy house laws to arrest gay men in a privatized setting was an abrogation of the intent of the purpose for which the original law was drawn. It was basically a law intended for police to arrest patrons of houses of ill repute (prostitute domiciles) during a much earlier era in Canadian history. It is instructive that the misuse of that law resulted in what was to be, until recently, the largest single arrest in Canadian history with over 400 people incarcerated. Eventually, only a few people were actually convicted of the charges leveled by police in the bathhouse raids, which cost taxpayers in excess of one million dollars. The raids actually had the opposite effect of that intended, serving to undermine the public's confidence in the police rather than bolstering support as they had supposed it would do.

The G20 arrests were to supplant those of the bathhouse raids (Fleming, 1993) as the largest single arrest sequence in Canadian history with over 1,000 individuals being apprehended by police. Given that the public and protestors were not informed of what has been referred to as the "five meter rule" – that anyone within a specific range of the "no go" zone in the heart of downtown would be subject to arrest – the effect was to be a chilling one on protestors. Premier McGuinty in the aftermath of the mass arrests, kettling, and illegal confinement, conceding that the government could have "acted on that sooner to make it clear," commented:

> What we did say is " if you want to come on the other side of this fence, if you want to come nearer to the G20 leaders … then we're going to have a new rule in place that we think is very important and in keeping with the standards and values of Ontarians." (CBC, 2010)

However, as we have already learned, this appropriation of the *Act* was not well publicized or publicly debated by Ontarians or their leaders before its use. Do Ontarians support the suppression of free public dissent? Is the suspension of their *Charter* rights something that reflects their standards and values? More intriguing perhaps is the issue that the majority of the arrests were made far from the security zone and, in most cases, were of persons who had no interest in getting beyond the fence. In fact, with the height of the fence, the massing of thousands of police around the zone, concrete abutments, CCTV cameras, and other security measures, one can argue that it was a virtual impossibility for persons to actually enter the security zone. Thus, we are left with the policing of neutral zones, free public places in the heart of Toronto where the arrests took place.

Police Deviance and Violence Made Visible: Isolation, Confrontation, Assault, and Arrest

A detailed cataloguing of police activities, including deviant and unlawful behaviours, has been collected by the Marin (2010), McNeilly (2012), and Morden (2012) inquiries. Additionally, video, photographs, newspaper reports, and monitor reports have provided analysts with a tremendous depth and breadth of information about police deviance at the Toronto G20. We refer readers to these reports for almost minute-to-minute accounts of the major events of police lawlessness. In this section of the chapter, we will examine key issues surrounding several of the events and their implications for policing public order. First, in the wake of the rioting on Yonge Street, we have established that police felt they had the authority to use the power of the PWPA and extended it far beyond the security fence perimeter where it was intended to be used. On Saturday June 26, 2010, police confronted a crowd of individuals gathered in the free speech zone at Queen's Park. The crowd was described as peacefully sitting in the park either having come from earlier protests or were interested passersby who were not engaged in protest. Police ordered the crowd to disperse. A majority of individuals in the park did not hear the police command. Rather than giving the crowd time to disperse, riot police descended on the park and fired rubber bullets and tear gas. This was the first time that tear gas was deployed in the history of Toronto, and it was against individuals who were *not* engaged in any form of protest. There is clear evidence of excessive use of force by police in video footage and accounts provided by those in the free speech zone (CCLA, 2010b, pp. 2-3). We also note that there is clear evidence of police on this occasion, and several others, failing to provide an exit for persons who wished to leave a location when so ordered (and when they could hear the command). Essentially, protestors and innocent bystandards were "boxed in" by riot police, and their right of peaceful protest was taken from them contrary to the *Charter*. There was, and is, no excuse for violating the fundamental rights of peaceful protestors who have committed no crime. This is contrary to international standards of police practice and indicative of the state of mind of police commanders and their officers during the weekend. One incident, in particular, received considerable media attention. According to his account, John Pruyn, a 57-year-old man was tackled to the ground by police. Once on the ground one officer "yanked" his artificial leg off and commanded him to "hop" to a waiting police van (while handcuffed). Police dragged him to the van and confiscated his leg as a "weapon" (*MacLeans*, 2010). He was released the next day without charge, and his "weapon" was returned to him. Like Pruyn, hundreds of individuals were arrested at various locations on Saturday and Sunday.

Throughout Saturday evening there were various encounters between police and peaceful protestors in the downtown core. Police were usurping the rights of over 1,000 persons in a search for a small group of what police described variously as "terrorists" or "protestor/terrorists" (CCLA, 2010b). The use of riot police and the cordoning off of intersections more than several miles from the security zone added to an atmosphere intended to convince citizens with no direct experience of the unfolding events of the threat to the city and its citizens. Arrests continued outside of the Esplanade, a small upscale shopping mall located on the edge of Toronto's trendy Yorkville district, on Saturday evening. As the specter of "marauding terrorists" (Marin, 2010, p. 60) running amok in Toronto was fed to media outlets, police who had received two and half hours training for this event (delivered online and face-to-face) were found by the independent inquiries to have been the overwhelming source of violence being committed. Police commanders believed that they were going to be confronted with "dangerous" and violent individuals in the streets, when, in fact, peaceful protestors and citizens going about their daily business were, overwhelmingly, all they were to encounter.

It is arguably the events of the evening of Sunday, June 27 that have prompted the harshest criticism of police tactics. At six o'clock, gear-clad police "boxed in" a group of protestors, bystanders, and news reporters at the juncture of Queen and Spadina, in the downtown core of the city, moving in from the north shouting "move" until they had trapped persons on all four sides. This is an area near but not directly beside the security perimeter. According to accounts provided by dozens of individuals and live news reports, hundreds of people were "kettled" – that is, surrounded by riot police with no point provided to leave the area. There was no order issued for persons to leave the area, and anyone attempting to leave was immediately placed under arrest. Weather conditions worsened; as night came on, temperatures began to drop and the rain was torrential. Police had trapped this group of persons – some kettled after leaving local restaurants, some innocent bystanders, and most dressed for early summer weather, unprepared to be out in a very heavy downpour – for hours. The entire episode was captured live on television. As viewers wondered why police were holding such a large number of persons, who were obviously not protesting, the deafening sound of the silence from the crowd and from the police officers who would not respond to their questions as to why they were being held, began to raise serious questions about the police tactics. For the CCLA (2010b, p. 4), the response from police was disproportionate to the risk involved (Ericson, 2006; Ericson & Haggerty, 1997). What threat could teenaged girls in tank tops and middle-aged couples pose that would permit police to mistreat them in public? The spectacle of riot police holding citizens in the heart of Toronto, disregarding their constitutional rights, was symbolic of a lack of leadership in policing. The chief was at a meeting when the kettling began; he claims to have ordered the commander in charge of this operation to let people go. That did not happen for over three hours. By this point, individuals were being removed for medical reasons, including hypothermia. It was not until 9:43 p.m. that the chief ordered all those arrested released without paperwork since the "breach of the peace" was over (Morden, 2012, pp. 178-183).

While space does not permit an extensive examination of the incarceration of protestors, we note that individuals were taken to a converted movie studio on the far east side of the city in an industrial area. Through video imagery and arrestee accounts, we are able to form a picture of further denial of fundamental rights to those confined. Cells were constructed like animal cages of wire with an open toilet. Prisoners had their hands bound with plastic ties throughout their confinement. Contrary to the *Charter*, many were denied access to a telephone or legal counsel. There was inadequate food for the arrested, and insufficient water was provided to them over the 18 to 24 hours they were confined (see Marin, 2010; CCLA, 2011; McNeilly, 2012; Morden, 2012).

We also note that many were given bail on expanded grounds that far exceed the reasonable grasp of the law. Individuals were forced to agree to bail conditions, including not engaging in any protest in Toronto (even against the rights violations of the G20 effected by police), not speaking to reporters, and not holding fundraisers to assist in their legal costs. These overly broad and restrictive conditions infringed their rights further by their non-conformance to regular legal practice. These arbitrary detentions have more in common with paramilitary operations than the exercise of justice in a free society (Waddington, 1987).

The swamping of protest grounds in the urban interstices by police and the use of riot police in the face of peaceful protest has been a subject of some criticism in the Canadian context and beyond. The APEC Inquiry Commission addressed the use of heavy police force during the Asia-Pacific Economic summit in Vancouver (Hughes, 2001). Hughes argued that at events requiring crowd control, police should ensure that protestors could not only be seen by those they were protesting against, but also that they should be able to view the subjects of their protest efforts. In citing the unprofessional and substandard conduct of the RCMP in policing protestors, he concluded that the intent of police was clearly to cut short demonstration and to achieve the illusion that there was no dissent concerning the subject matter of the meetings. He warned, as we have indicated in our argument, that police must be accountable and not engage in actions that violate *Charter* rights. To argue that police merely follow orders denies their responsibility to question and not carry out orders that violate fundamental legal rights. Similarly, the UK Joint Committee Report on the 2009 London G20 questioned the negative potential of a Draconian police presence. They argued that "the deployment of riot police can unnecessarily raise the temperature at protests. The PSNI had shown how fewer police can be deployed at protests, in normal uniform, apparently with success" (Secretary of State, 2009, p. 14). Further, in addressing the issues of the use of extraordinary police measures and the need to strike a balance between security and the right to protest, the committee members commented: "We were struck by the accounts of the use of a wide range of police powers against protestors and others. These factors could serve to diminish, rather than facilitate, protest and also risk encouraging conflict rather than co-operation between protestors and the police" (Secretary of State, 2009, p. 3).

Constructing Public Order Policing in Canada: The Future

The day that the 20 most powerful leaders in the world come to town, and that no one cares enough to present their cause or the cause of others, is the day that democratic life is finished. We should worry about that the next time we accept that peaceful protestors are punished because they wanted to be heard. (CCLA, 2010b, p. 4)

The aftermath of the G20 meetings in Toronto generated a series of large-scale inquiries into the conduct of the police and the issue of the public order policing (CCLA, 2010a, 2011; Marin, 2010; McNeilly, 2012; Morden, 2012). The cost of post-G20 reflections on police misconduct have cost millions of additional public funds but generated little in the way of apology, justice, or change. The PWPA legislation that has generated such negative public criticism and which generated four class-action law suits against various actors involved in its use was further examined by former chief justice and legal scholar Roy McMurtry (2011). He concluded that the PWPA should be repealed because "the vagueness of the PWPA permits it to be use in situations where it is arguably not necessary and potentially abusive" (p. 54). For McMurtry, the PWPA does not strike the balance required for the police to provide adequate protection in society and the rights and freedoms of the individual. As he astutely points out, the declaration of an "emergency" may be invoked by governments as they see fit. While he asserts that oversight by public boards, commissions, and inquiries provides a balance to police abuse of power, we would suggest that the slow process with which such bodies report, with little or no power to directly address damages to victims of police brutality or abuse, provide little in practical remedy. Moreover, the lasting damage to public perceptions of the guarantee of rights and freedoms, and more importantly, the seeming ease with which they can be temporarily, and perhaps permanently, erased is more of a cause for concern.

A number of obvious prescriptions for more publically palatable and legally valid policing of protests emerge out of the failures associated with the use of the PWPA and police deviance during the G20. First, as Hoggett and Stott (2012) have suggested, there is a need for evidence-based policing that adopts a scientific approach to policing protest rather than ad hoc, in the moment, or approaches that are not cognizant of historical lessons learned from other episodes. In this way, they suggest, "decision making can move away from personal preference and unsystematic experience towards those based on the best available scientific evidence" (p. 180). There is a pronounced need, if perhaps not the will, for police training so that the mistakes of the Toronto G20 are not repeated. This is of central importance given two factors: the view of police that their powers have been contracting since the *Charter* became part of Canadian law (Murphy, 2007); and a widely held conservative belief that police are handicapped in the post-9/11 world and need even more powers returned or granted to them. The trend of legislation has been towards the granting of police wide powers regarding search warrants, surveillance, the compelling of testimony, and expanded powers of arrest.

Second, emerging out of the public investigations, inquiries, and scholarship has been the call for a legislative framework to govern police conduct at public protests and guidelines as to the construction of security zones (Pue & Diab, 2010). Research on the policing of serial homicide in Canada has amply demonstrated that the historical lessons of investigations are lost on new generations of police officers, even when there have been widely publicized inquiries into recurring police investigative flaws (Fleming & O'Reilly, 2010, 2011). Given the findings of the APEC committee and the saturated media attention it generated, it seems evident that police management should have been well aware of the dangers instituting the PWPA could create. The "make it up as we go along" approach, which seems to best characterize the approach taken in Toronto, cannot be repeated without serious damage to the rights of Canadians. The police relied on the argument that they had inadequate time to prepare for the G20. Apparently four months was an insufficient period to institute proper security measures. Apprehension regarding their ability to prevent mass violence without recourse to extraordinary powers may, to some extent, explain their request for the powers of the PWPA. But given the resources of Canada's largest city, and both the provincial and federal governments, this argument is weak. Further, the Toronto Public Order Unit had offered training to police services around the country in 2009, well in advance of the G20, and called upon volunteer officers from these services to participate in the G20 (International Association of Women Police, 2010).

Two years after the events of June 2010, 45 police officers from the Toronto Police Service were charged with disciplinary offenses related to the G20. These are internal rather than criminal charges (Dubinsky & Seglins, 2012). The incident commander at the Spadina kettling has been charged with discreditable conduct and unlawful use of authority. However, we note that he was told by the deputy chief to "take back the streets" after the riot on Yonge Street. A number of officers were docked one day's wages for removing their identity badges, which was intended to prevent individuals from lodging complaints, criminal charges, or lawsuits. One office was found guilty of an assault on a single protestor in the fall of 2013, while the backlog of charges against other officers has not seen a court. In fact, there have been calls to dismiss the charges since the time between the laying of the charges and the opportunity to answer the charges will have stretched to approximately four years at the time of writing this chapter.

We began our chapter with an assertion that the legitimacy of the state rests upon certain agreed upon laws that both set out the boundaries of behaviour and establish rights and freedoms such as those contained in the *Charter*. Justice for those innocent passersby and protestors who were physically abused, terrorized, jailed, denied access to legal assistance, and treated cruelly and inhumanely has still not come after numerous inquiries. The only apology emanating from any recognized authority was offered by the chair of the Toronto Police Service Board, a civilian who offered merely his own "personal" apology (Mills, 2012), conceding that "[i]nnocent people had their rights abridged, their liberty interfered with and their physical safety jeopardized," in the wake of calls for both his resignation and that of the chief of police. In the production of docile bodies, no weapon is as effective as creating insecurity concerning the irrevocable nature of fundamental rights and freedoms. As Cogalauri (2012) points out, the use of fear and insecurity through media manipulation were used at the G20 and are used generally to force insecure subjects to align themselves with repressive authority to create "a necessary barrier of defence, protection and self-preservation" (p. 204) against a perceived threat. In concert with media preceding the G20, the justification for a $1 billion security budget was cloaked in a vision of violent terrorists, anarchists, and hoodlums bent on tearing down the city (CCLA, 2010b).

The use of violent and unprovoked attacks on protestors by police, the use of agent provocateurs by the police (officers posing as protestors), the intimidation of citizens in the weeks leading up to the G20, kettling practices, as well as the use of tear gas, rubber bullets, and violent take downs of protestors is a frightening legacy of the G20. The violence of police actions resides not only in the physical arrests of protestors and innocent citizens but also in their confinement without legal counsel in violation of every Canadian's *Charter* rights. Violence manifests itself also in the psychological trauma experience of unwarranted arrests, which creates an atmosphere of fear in law-abiding citizens. The violence of a police force freed of their legal obligation to uphold and respect fundamental human rights in Canada's largest city has had a profound chilling effect upon possible future protests. As of June 2014, the PWPA is still in force, despite Justice McMurty`s conclusion that is should be scrapped. It stands ready for use by the police to control Ontario's citizens, engage in illegal acts, and remove their *Charter* rights whenever it is deemed necessary.

What the G20 forged, perhaps, was a broader public recognition of just how fragile freedoms are in Canada, and how easily, behind closed doors, they can be taken away with one swipe of a pen. What is more disconcerting is the fact that the police were able to ignore enshrined human rights, unlawfully arrest people, and further deny their rights while under conditions that were inhumane and unacceptable in a free society. We cannot speculate in the context of the complexity of the G20 protest, with its emphasis on the absolute power of a small group of world leaders to make decisions that will impact our future without meaningful input by critics and social protestors, whether this signals a new willingness of Canadian police to violate protestors rights in the future, but it is clear that it takes little in the way of public violence by a small group to provoke a Draconian police response. It is troubling that the consequences for those charged with leadership of the government, police agencies and police boards are non-existent for such a serious breach of Canadian legal principles. While all of the inquiries have documented the events of those violent days in June 2010, it is clear that the potential for a repeat of police deviance in maintaining public order remains, given that the consequences for government officials and police are almost non-existent. This state of affairs might best be summarized by a police officer who, upon detaining an individual as he entered a public park, commented that if he were unhappy with his rights being violated, he could always go to court.

In other words, we will deny your rights, the harm has been done, and now you can spend your time and money trying to prove that we did this. The point is, the police should never act in a way that is contrary to our unassailable rights. Whether the events of the G20 detailed in this chapter have the potential to create more docile citizens or greater political unrest will have to be seen. Perhaps it will be a call to the citizens of Toronto to "take back the city" from the lawless pursuit of power.

Keywords

Police deviance, rights, protest, violence

Review Questions

1. In what ways did the use of the PWPA violate the *Charter* rights of Canadians?
2. Violence is often manifested in various forms, from the physical to the psychological. How might police actions, including kettling protestors and passersby, have affected individuals?
3. If you were appointed chief of police, what policies and practices would you initiate to control protestors in a manner consistent with their legal rights to protest?
4. Should individual police officers or police management be held accountable for acts of violence and/or violation of *Charter* rights?
5. What, in your opinion, can individual citizens do to combat the passing and use of laws which take away our *Charter* rights?

References

Brodeur, J.-P. (1983) High policing and low policing: Remarks about the policing of political activists. *Social Problems, 30*(5), 507-520.

Brodeur, J.-P. (2010). *The policing web*. Oxford: Oxford University Press.

Canadian Civil Liberties Association (CCLA). (2010a, June 29). *A breach of the peace: A preliminary report of observations during the 2010 G20 Summit*. Retrieved from http://ccla.org/2010/06/29/ccla-releases-a-preliminary-report-of-observations-during-the-g20-summit/

Canadian Civil Liberties Association (CCLA). (2010b). *Looking back, moving forward: Two months after the G20*. Retrieved from http://ccla.org/.org/our-work/focus-areas/g8andg20-/twomonths-after-the-g20/.

Canadian Civil Liberties Association (CCLA). (2011, February). *Breach of the peace: G20 summit: Accountability in policing and governance. Public hearings, November 10 to 12,*

2010, Toronto and Montreal. Ottawa: National Union of Public and General Employees and Canadian Civil Liberties Association.

Church, E. (2012, June 28). Police protected G20 security fence instead of stopping riot, report finds. *Globe and Mail* (Toronto), p. 1

Colaguori, C. (2012). *Agon culture: Competition, conflict and the problem of domination.* Whitby, ON: de Sitter Publications.

The Constitution Act, 1982, c. 11 (U.K.), Schedule B. Retrieved from http://laws-lois.justice.gc.ca/eng/Const/page-15.html

De Lint, W. B., & Hall, A., (2009) *Intelligent control: Developments in public order policing in Canada.* Toronto: University of Toronto Press.

Dicks, D., & Davies, S. *Into the fire.* Independent video: Press for truth. Retrieved from www.youtube.com/watch?v=zejDOUkMGGY.

T. Fleming, Dowler, K. & Ramcharan, S. (2008). *The Canadian criminal justice system.* Toronto: Prentice Hall.

Dowler, K., Fleming, T., & Muzzatti, S. (2006). Constructing crime: Media, crime and popular culture. *Canadian Journal of Criminology and Criminal Justice, 48*(6), 37-851.

Dubinsky, Z., & Seglins, D. (2012, May 18). G20 "kettling" commander among 45 to be charged. CBC News. Retrieved from http://www.cbc.ca/news/canada/toronto/g20-kettling-commander-among-45-officers-to-be-charged-1.1202465

Ericson, R. V. (2006). Ten uncertainties of risk management. *Canadian Journal of Criminology and Criminal Justice, 48*(3), 345-357.

Ericson, R., & Haggerty, K. (1997). *Policing the risk society.* Toronto: University of Toronto Press.

Fleming, T. (1993). The bawdy house 'boys': Some notes on media, sporadic moral crusades, and selective law enforcement. In A. Jennie & E. Sheehy (Eds.), *Criminal law and procedure: Cases, context and critique* (pp. 76-82). Toronto: Captus Press.

Fleming, T., & O'Reilly, P. (2010, February 5). History repeats itself: Recurring errors in Canadian serial murder investigation. Paper presented at the Western Society of Criminology, Honolulu.

Fleming, T., & O'Reilly, P. (2011, March 5). Police investigative failures in the Pickton investigation. Paper presented at the Academy of Criminal Justice Sciences, Sheraton Hotel, Toronto.

Fleming, T., Ramcharan, S., Dowler, K., & DeLint, W. (2008). *The Canadian criminal justice system.* Toronto: Pearson.

Foucault, M. (1973). *Discipline and punish: The birth of the prison.* New York: Pantheon.

Hall, A., & DeLint, W. (2003). Policing labour in Canada. *Policing and Society, 13,* 219-234.

Hoggett, J., & Stott, C. (2012). Post G20: The challenge of change, implementing evidence-based public order policing. *Journal of Investigative Psychology and Offender Profiling, 9,* 174-183.

Hughes, T. (2001). *APEC – Interim commission report.* Vancouver: Commission for Public Complaints against the RCMP.

International Association of Women Police. (2010, September–November). G20 Summit. *Women Police.* Retrieved from www.iawp.org./news/archives/2010_archives.htm

Klein, N. (2007). *The shock doctrine: The rise of disaster capitalism.* Toronto: Knopf Canada.

King, M., & Brearly, M. (1996) *Public order policing: Contemporary perspectives on strategy and tactics.* Leicester: Perpetuity Press.

King, M., & Waddington, D. (2005). Flashpoints revisited: A critical application to the policing of anti-globalization protest. *Policing and Society, 15*(3), 255-282.

MacLeans.ca. (2010, July 7). G20 police seized man's prosthetic leg, called it a weapon. Retrieved from http://www2.macleans.ca/2010/07/07/g20-police-seized-mans-prosthetic-leg-called-it-a-weapon/

Marin, A. (2010). *Caught in the act: Investigation into the Ministry of Community and Safety and Correctional Services' conduct in relation to Ontario Regulation 233/10 under the Public Works Protection Act*. Toronto: Office of the Ombudsman Ontario.

McMurtry, R. R. (2011, April). *Report of the Review of the Public Works Protection Act*. Toronto: Government of Ontario, Ministry of Community Safety and Correctional Services.

McNeilly, G. (2012). *Policing the right to protest – G20 systemic review*. Office of the Independent Police Review Director. Retrieved from https://www,oiprd.on.ca/CMS/getattachment/publications/Reports/G20_Report_Eng.pdg.aspx

Mills, C. S. (2012, July 19). Police board chair apologizes to lawful G20 protestors. *Globe and Mail* (Toronto), p. 1.

Morden. Hon. J. W. (2012, June). *Independent civilian review into matters relating to the G20 summit*. Toronto: Toronto Police Service Board.

Murphy, C. (2007). Securitizing Canadian policing: A new policing paradigm for the post 9/11 security state. *Canadian Journal of Sociology, 32*(4), 449-475.

Province of Ontario. Ontario Regulation 233/10 made under the Public Works Protection Act, Made: June 2, 2010; Filed: June 14, 2010; Published on e-Laws; June 16, 2010; Printed in *The Ontario Gazette*, July 3, 2010.

Pue, W., & Diab, R. (2010). The gap in Canadian police powers: Canada needs "public order policing" legislation. *Windsor Review of Legal and Social Issues, 28*(1), 87-107.

Ratner, R., & McMullan, J. (1985). Social control and the use of the 'exceptional state' in Britain, the United States and Canada. In T. Fleming (Ed.), *The new criminologies in Canada: State, crime and control* (p. 185-205). Toronto: Oxford University Press.

Secretary of State for the Home Department. (2009, May). *Demonstrating respect for rights? A human rights approach to policing protest*. (The government reply to the seventh report from the Joint Committee On Human Rights session 2008-09). (HL paper 47, HC 320).

Sheptycki, J. (2005). Policing political protest when politics go global: Comparing public order policing in Canada and Bolivia. *Policing and Society, 15*, 327-352.

Waddington, P. A. (1987). Towards paramilitarism? Dilemmas in the policing of public order. *British Journal of Criminology, 27*(1), 37-46.

Waddington, P.A. (2007). *Policing public disorder: Theory and practice*. Cullompton, UK: Willan Publishing.

Waddington, D., Jones, K., & Critcher, C. (1989). *Flashpoints: Studies in public disorder*. London: Routledge.

C

Caetano, R., 27, 38
Caffaro, J., 132, 135
Calboli, F., 160, 166
Campbell, A., 111, 147, 150, 200, 265
Canada, K., 263
Canadian Centre for Elder Law, 129, 130, 135
Canadian Centre for Justice Statistics, 122, 263
Canadian Centre for Justice Studies, 134, 136
Canadian Centre for Occupational Health and Safety, 59, 69
Canadian Civil Liberties Association, 270, 280, 281
Canadian Coalition for Farm Animals, 157, 166
Cantin, J., 62, 69, 72
Card, D., 181, 186
Carlson, K., 134, 136
Carmody, D., 76, 85
Carr, J., 61, 69
Carroll, P., 180, 186
Casas, M., 81, 85
CBC News, 150, 163, 166, 232, 241, 245, 246, 281
Chalk, F., 221, 232
Chan, J., 2, 5, 18, 60, 69, 102
Chandler, S., 180, 186
Chang, J., 237, 245
Chansonneuve, D., 109, 110, 111, 119
Chappell, D., 58, 69, 73, 251, 263
Charette, Y., 248, 263
Charleton, J., 58, 69
Chartier, M., 29, 35
Chartrand, P., 140, 146, 148, 150
Chaulk, K., 28, 35
Chermak, S., 92, 93, 94, 101
Chevalier, L., 23, 36
Chiricos, T., 28, 36, 77, 81, 84, 85, 96, 97, 98, 101, 102
Chomsky, N., 76, 83, 86
Chouinard, V., 60, 69
Chrisjohn, R., 109, 110, 111, 119, 224, 225, 232

Christensen, J., 195, 205
Christopher, F., 27, 36
Chunn, D., 199, 202
Church, A., 120, 156, 169, 272, 281
Clark, L., 14, 17, 27, 38, 75, 85
Clarke, J., 85, 176
Clayfield, J., 252, 263
Coakley, J., 180, 186, 187
Cochran, S., 252, 264
Coderre, C., 192, 204
Cogan, J., 51, 55
Cohen, S., 14, 17, 77, 78, 85, 99, 101, 109, 111, 119, 122, 141, 150, 204
Colaguori, C., 15, 18, 268, 272, 281
Colburn, K., Jr. 31, 36
Coleman, C., 250, 252, 254, 258, 263, 264
Collins, B., 130, 136, 184, 187
Comack, E., 111, 119, 139, 150, 198, 202
Comer, D., 62, 73
Compassion in World Farming, 157, 166
Compton, M., 252, 253, 264, 265
Comstock, R., 184, 187
Conn-Caffaro, A., 132, 135
Cook, K., 102, 193, 203, 214
Cormack, P., 176, 186
Cornell, S., 52, 55
Corrado, R., 109, 111, 119, 122, 141, 150
Corrigan, P., 249, 266
Corsilles, A., 195, 202
Cosgrave, J., 176, 186
Côté, A., 197, 202
Cote, H., 109, 111, 118, 119
Cotton, A., 196, 202, 250, 252, 254, 258, 263, 264
Coughlan, S., 130, 136
Couture, J., 113, 119
Cowling, M., 10, 18
Crasnow, R., 68, 69
Cretney, A., 196, 202
Critcher, C., 85, 282
Crocker, D., 32, 36, 248, 250, 263, 264
Crosby, C., 3, 193, 204

Crosset, T., 179, 180, 186
CTV News, 167
Cudworth, E., 163, 167
Cummings, J., 26, 36
Cummins, B., 248, 265
Cunneen, C., 54, 55
Currie, R., 222, 223, 232
Curry, T., 179, 186

D

D'Entremont, D., 145, 150
Dahl, G., 181, 186
Dahlberg, L., 154, 168
Dahrendorf, R., 10, 18
Dale, A., 29, 36, 133, 136
Daly, M., 15, 18, 89, 101
David, P., 68, 183, 186
Davies, S., 273, 281
Davis, L., 61, 69, 85, 101, 143, 150, 154, 157, 167, 183, 186, 196, 202
Dawson, T., 194, 195, 202
Day, K., 90, 120, 185, 187, 271, 277
De Luca, R., 33, 38
de Roten, Y., 25, 36
Deane, L., 119, 266
DeKeseredy, W., 79, 85, 155, 168, 192, 199, 202
DeLint, W., 268, 281
Demczuk, I., 197, 204
Demir, B., 264, 265
Department of Justice Canada, 55, 127, 132, 133, 134, 136
Desroches, F., 13, 18
Devine, C., 58, 70
Devlin, R., 71, 72
Di Martino, V., 58, 69
Diab, R., 278, 282
Dickason, O., 109, 119, 121, 152
Dicks, D., 273, 281
Dietz, M., 13, 18
DiGiovanni, C., 248, 265
Dinovitzer, R., 195, 202
Ditton, J., 93, 96, 101
Dixon, T., 81, 85, 174, 186
Dobash, R., 193, 197, 202
Doctors and Lawyers for Responsible Medicine, 158, 167

multistage probability sampling, 41

N

Native Women's Association of Canada's Sisters in Spirit, 106

news and entertainment, 76, 78, 79, 84

9/11, 54, 209, 216, 219, 237, 272, 282

non-probability sampling, 27, 31, 40, 42, 43

nonhuman animals, 3, 153, 155-165

O

official crime statistics, 79, 93

online obsessive relational intrusion, 28, 29, 35, 42

online survey, 28, 42

Ontarians with Disabilities Act, 59, 65, 68

Ontario Health and Safety Amendment Act, 65

operational definition, 42

oppression, 52, 55, 69, 70, 72, 83, 153, 154, 155, 162, 163, 165, 166, 171, 173, 196

P

panel design, 42

participant, 22, 25, 26, 31-35, 42, 43

participant observation, 31, 32, 34, 35, 42

participatory action research, 31, 42

Patriot Act, 215, 237

persons with mental illness (PMI), 247-256, 258, 259, 262, 263, 266

pet-keeping, 160, 165

phenomenological-hermeneutic method, 32, 42

phenomenology, 32, 42

police deviance, 4, 267, 268, 272, 275, 278, 280

police investigative failures, 149, 151, 281

police use of force, 4, 247, 248, 251, 252, 255, 265, 266

policing, 4, 9, 55, 85, 86, 114, 118, 120, 139, 143, 145-149, 151, 218, 235-237, 241, 242, 244, 245, 254, 263-272, 274-278, 280-282

political culture, 209, 211, 212, 217

political violence, 244, 245

positive relationship, 26, 42

poverty, 9, 12, 15, 28, 61, 82, 83, 92, 111, 114, 116, 130, 131, 156, 237, 238, 246

privacy, 4, 24, 34, 39, 42, 215-218

Privacy Act, 24

probability sampling, 27, 31, 40-43

protest, 4, 5, 163, 218, 235-239, 244, 245, 249, 267-269, 271, 273-282

Public Safety Act, 236

Public Works Protection Act, 5, 86, 241, 242, 269, 273, 282

Q

qualitative approach, 24, 34, 42

qualitative research, 24, 30, 32, 35, 40

quantitative approach, 42

quantitative research, 24, 28, 32

questionnaire, 25, 28, 42

R

racism, 2, 47, 48, 53, 54, 82, 119, 140, 147-149, 163, 165, 246

randomly assigned, 26, 42

rational choice theory, 12

RCMP, 141, 142, 145, 147-149, 152, 214, 240, 259, 261, 262, 266, 270, 277, 281

reliability, 24, 25, 36, 37, 41-43

repression, 10, 244, 246

research method, 23

researching violence, 21, 34, 37, 40, 203

residential schools, 105, 108, 109, 110, 111, 115, 118, 120-122, 224-233

resistance, 55, 154, 170, 202, 244, 246, 260

riots, 182, 185, 188, 212, 271

routine activities theory, 14, 15, 17

S

sampling, 27, 31, 36, 37, 40-43

scenario-based self-report questionnaire, 25, 42

secondary analysis, 22, 29, 36

secondary data analysis, 22, 42

seductions of crime, 13, 18

self-report, 25, 28, 33, 37, 42, 43

semi-structured interviews, 25, 28, 30, 32, 43

sensationalism, 94

serial murderers, 141, 143-145, 147-152, 171, 281

sex trade workers, 15, 17, 140, 145-149

sexual violence, 122, 184, 185, 193, 201-203, 205

sibling abuse, 132, 135

snowball sampling, 31, 43

social control, 1, 9, 186, 245, 267, 282

social determinants of health, 68, 71

social justice, 62, 66, 68, 154, 155, 169

social model of disability, 60, 68

social movements, 235, 244

sport riots, 182, 188

sports, 1, 3, 4, 17, 34, 173, 174, 176, 177, 179-188

state violence, 4, 9, 10, 16, 235, 237, 245

stereotypes, 53, 60, 66, 80, 81, 84, 94, 147

stimulus, 15, 26, 40, 41, 43

Stolen Sisters, 5, 119, 139, 145, 149, 150

structural violence, 153, 156, 163-167

structured interview, 31, 43

subcultural theory, 11

subcultures of violence, 11, 12

Supreme Court of Canada, 71, 149

Krista Banasiak earned an MA from the University of Toronto and is currently a PhD candidate studying sociology at York University. Her dissertation research examines the relationship between social structure and lived experience through an analysis of women's stories of belly dancing, exploring themes of Orientalism, male and colonial gazes, and embodiment. Her work has been published in the *Journal of Critical Race and Whiteness Studies* and she has presented at numerous conferences in Canada and the US. Her other research interests include qualitative research methods, globalization, and the media.

Susan Barak, BA (Hons), MEd, is pursuing a PhD in Critical Disability Studies (Human Rights and Social Justice) at York University, Toronto. Her experience and observations as a career and employment counsellor impelled her to investigate the phenomenon of disability discrimination and harassment in the workplace. Mother of four, writer, and certified yoga teacher, she also teaches the violin and viola and regularly performs in a variety of orchestras and chamber groups.

Howard A. Doughty holds a BA in Political Science from Glendon College and graduate degrees in Political Science from the University of Hawai'i and York University, as well as in History and Philosophy of Education from the University of Toronto. He has taught at Seneca College in Ontario since 1969 and has been Visiting Professor in the College of International Studies and the MA program in Diplomacy and Military Studies at Hawai'i Pacific University in Honolulu. The founding editor of *The College Quarterly* (www.collegequarterly.ca) and Book Review Editor of *The Innovation Journal* (www.innovation.cc), he has published 400 articles in peer-reviewed journals and presented over 80 papers at professional conferences. His recent books include *Culture and Difference* (Toronto: Guernica Editions, 2011) and *Discourse and Community* (Guernica Editions, 2007), both edited with Marino Tuzi.

Kenneth Dowler is an associate professor and chair of Department of Criminology at Laurier Brantford. His work has been published in several journals, including the *Journal of Criminal Justice, American Journal of Criminal Justice, Journal of Criminal Justice and Popular Culture, Journal of Crime and Justice, Canadian Journal of Criminology, Policing Society, Police Quarterly, International Journal of Police Science and Management, Police Practice and Research,* and *Contemporary Justice Review*. He has also served as guest editor for two journals and has published one text book on *Criminal Justice in Canada*. Currently, his research interests include: wrongful convictions, the portrayal of homicide in the media, and the criminology of sport.

Thomas Fleming is professor of criminology at Wilfrid Laurier University where he developed the criminology program and served as the first Director of the M.A. Criminology program. He has taught at The University of Windsor, York University, The University of Toronto, The University of Alberta and Trent University. Dr. Fleming has published 10 books in the field of criminology as well as numerous chapters and articles. He is the recipient of a Leadership in Faculty Teaching Award (LIFT) from the Province of Ontario for his contributions to teaching and the profession and a member of the Laurier Teaching Hall of Fame. He co-founded and was the President of the Canadian Society of Criminology from 2002-2010. Dr. Fleming a Fellow of McLaughlin College, York University.

Jennifer Fraser received her PhD in criminology from the University of Ottawa and is an assistant professor in criminal justice and criminology at Ryerson University. Her research interests include women's activism and sociopolitical responses to violence against women.

Nicholas (Nick) A. Jones is an associate professor and coordinator of the Police Studies program in the Department of Justice Studies at the University of Regina. He earned a Master of Science in Criminal Justice Administration from San Jose State University in 1997. Prior to his furthering his academic career he worked with federal parolees and in a youth custody facility. He returned to the University of Calgary and completed his Doctorate in Sociology in 2006 for his work focussing on the judicial response to the Rwandan Genocide. He joined the Faculty of Arts at the University of Regina in 2006. He published *The Courts of Genocide: Politics and the Rule of Law in Rwanda and Arusha* with Routledge – Cavendish U.K., nominated for the Academy of Criminal Justice Sciences book of the year award in that same year. His research interests include genocide, restorative justice (theory, practice, and evaluation), transitional justice, Aboriginal justice issues, policing, and criminological theory.

Atsuko Matsuoka is an associate professor at the School of Social Work at York University. In 2013 she co-authored, with John Sorenson, the article "Human consequences of animal exploitation: Needs for redefining social welfare," which appears in *Journal of Sociology and Social Welfare*. In 2014, she co-edited *Defining Critical Animal Studies: An Intersectional Social Justice Approach to Liberation* (Peter Lang Publishing) with Anthony Nocella II, John Sorenson and Kim Socha.

Lisa Monchalin is of Algonquin, Métis, Huron, and Scottish ancestry. As a proud Aboriginal woman she is determined to reduce the amount of crime that affects Aboriginal people through her teaching and writing. She has published on topics relating to Aboriginal justice; evidence-based crime prevention; and Aboriginal social movements and collective action. She has her Bachelor's and her Master's degrees in Criminology from Eastern Michigan University, and a Ph.D. in Criminology from the University of Ottawa. Lisa currently lives in Surrey, British Columbia where she teaches in the department of Criminology at Kwantlen Polytechnic University.

Patricia O'Reilly was a labour lawyer working on behalf of injured workers for eight years before commencing her teaching career. She has also taught at Grant MacEwan College, and has taught life skills to federal inmates. Patricia has also worked as a researcher for the Office of the Native Childrens' Guardian in Alberta, as a community education teacher and organizer in South London, U.K., and is an activist for womens' rights, and on behalf of the homeless. Patricia is one of the co-editors of *Youth Injustice* (2002) and has recently co-authored contributions to *The Sage Encyclopedia of Criminal Justice Ethics*. She has presented at numerous international conferences over the past seven years including The Western Society of Criminology, The Academy of Criminal Justice Sciences, The Critical Criminology Conference, and The Law and Society Association Conference.

Monica Pauls is part-time faculty with the Department of Child and Youth Studies at Mount Royal University and also works as an independent research consultant. Prior to this, she worked for several years with high-risk youth in children's institutions and community residential facilities. Monica has extensive experience conducting research and policy analysis, developing and directing projects on various justice-related issues and topics.

Barbara Perry has written extensively in the area of hate crime. She has written several books, including *In the Name of Hate: Understanding Hate Crimes*, *Hate and Bias Crime: A Reader*, and *The Silent Victims: Hate Crimes Against Native Americans.* She is also General Editor of a five-volume set on hate crime (Praeger), and Editor of Volume 3: *The Victims of Hate Crime*, which is part of that set. Dr. Perry has also written on policing diverse communities, including work on social control in Native American communities. She has made substantial contributions to the limited scholarship on hate crime in Canada. Most recently, she has contributed to a scholarly understanding of anti-Muslim violence, hate crime against LGBTQ communities, and the community impacts of hate crime.

Jeff Shantz (PhD York University, Toronto) is a full-time faculty member in the Department of Criminology at Kwantlen Polytechnic University in Metro Vancouver. He currently teaches community advocacy, human rights, elite deviance, contemporary sociological approaches, and critical theory. Shantz is the author of *Commonist Tendencies: Mutual Aid Beyond Communism* (Punctum, 2013). He is the editor of *Racism and Borders: Representation, Repression, Resistance* (Algora, 2010). Shantz is the founder of the Critical Criminology Working Group (http://www.radicalcriminology.org/) and the founding editor of the journal *Radical Criminology* (http://journal.radicalcriminology.org/index.php/rc). He is the founding editor of a new book imprint in radical criminology, *Thought | Crimes*. Scholarly interests include critical theories, migration, critical surveillance studies, corporate crime, transnational crime, and social movements.

John Sorenson is a professor in the Department of Sociology at Brock University, where he teaches on corporate globalization, and critical animal studies. Recent publications include the edited book *Critical Animal Studies: Thinking the Unthinkable.* (Canadian Scholars Press); *Defining Critical Animal Studies: An Intersectional Social Justice Approach to Liberation* (Peter Lang Publishing) co-edited with Anthony Nocella II, Kim Socha, and Atsuko Matsuoka; *Animal Rights – About Canada* (Fernwood); and *Ape* (Reaktion).

Ron Stansfield is an associate professor in the Department of Sociology and Anthropology at the University of Guelph. Prior to becoming an academic he was employed as a police officer.

Alicia C. Tomaszczyk is a PhD candidate at York University. She completed her Master of Arts in Sociology with a specialization in Survey Methodology at the University of Waterloo. Alicia earned her Bachelor of Science (Hons) from the University of Toronto. Her major research interests are sociological research methods and political sociology. She is currently conducting mixed methods research on the Census of Population in Canada.

John Winterdyk is the former director of the Centre for Criminology and Justice Research at Mount Royal University. He has published in excess of 25 books and numerous articles covering a wide spectrum of subject areas. His current areas of academic focus are human trafficking, fear of crime, youth justice, and crime prevention.

CPSIA information can be obtained at www.ICGtesting.com
Printed in the USA
LVOW09s2235080615

441664LV00010B/67/P

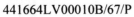